Lecture Notes in Business Information Processing   **361**

Series Editors

Wil van der Aalst
RWTH Aachen University, Aachen, Germany
John Mylopoulos
University of Trento, Trento, Italy
Michael Rosemann
Queensland University of Technology, Brisbane, QLD, Australia
Michael J. Shaw
University of Illinois, Urbana-Champaign, IL, USA
Clemens Szyperski
Microsoft Research, Redmond, WA, USA

More information about this series at http://www.springer.com/series/7911

Claudio Di Ciccio · Renata Gabryelczyk ·
Luciano García-Bañuelos ·
Tomislav Hernaus · Rick Hull ·
Mojca Indihar Štemberger ·
Andrea Kő · Mark Staples (Eds.)

Business Process Management

Blockchain and Central and Eastern Europe Forum

BPM 2019 Blockchain and CEE Forum
Vienna, Austria, September 1–6, 2019
Proceedings

 Springer

Editors
Claudio Di Ciccio ⓘ
Vienna University of Economics
and Business
Vienna, Austria

Luciano García-Bañuelos ⓘ
Tecnológico de Monterrey
Monterrey, Mexico

Rick Hull
IBM T. J. Watson Research Center
Yorktown Heights, NY, USA

Andrea Kő ⓘ
Corvinus University of Budapest
Budapest, Hungary

Renata Gabryelczyk ⓘ
University of Warsaw
Warsaw, Poland

Tomislav Hernaus ⓘ
University of Zagreb
Zagreb, Croatia

Mojca Indihar Štemberger ⓘ
University of Ljubljana
Ljubljana, Slovenia

Mark Staples
Data61 (CSIRO) and UNSW
Eveleigh, NSW, Australia

ISSN 1865-1348   ISSN 1865-1356   (electronic)
Lecture Notes in Business Information Processing
ISBN 978-3-030-30428-7   ISBN 978-3-030-30429-4   (eBook)
https://doi.org/10.1007/978-3-030-30429-4

This Springer imprint is published by the registered company Springer Nature Switzerland AG
The registered company address is: Gewerbestrasse 11, 6330 Cham, Switzerland

Preface

This volume contains the papers presented at the Blockchain Forum and at the Central and Eastern Europe Forum (CEE Forum) of the 17th International Conference on Business Process Management (BPM 2019). The conference provided forums for researchers and practitioners in the broad and diverse field of BPM. The conference was held in Vienna, Austria, during September 1–6, 2019. The forums took place during September 3–5, 2019.

The Blockchain Forum aims at providing a platform for the discussion of ongoing research and success stories on the use of blockchain for collaborative information systems. Conceptual, technical, and application-oriented contributions were pursued within the scope of this theme. The papers selected for the Blockchain Forum showcased fresh ideas from exciting and emerging topics in the area of blockchain technologies with a special focus on, yet not limited to, business process management. Moreover, we had two keynotes. Ingo Weber from TU Berlin illustrated the last four years of research integrating blockchains and business process management, also covering related use cases and applications. The keynote of Stefan Schulte from TU Wien revolved around blockchain interoperability, with a special focus on cross-blockchain token transfers and cross-blockchain smart contract invocation and interaction.

The objective of the CEE Forum was to foster discussion for BPM academics from Central and Eastern Europe to disseminate their research, compare results, and share experiences. This first-time proposed CEE Forum was an opportunity for both novice and established BPM researchers who have not yet had the chance to attend the international BPM conference to get to know each other, initiate research projects, and join the international BPM community. The papers selected for the CEE Forum illustrate novel and applied methods for the development of both the theory and practice of business process management in the process of BPM adoption within the Central and Eastern European area.

Each submission was reviewed by at least three Program Committee (PC) members. The Blockchain Forum received a total of 31 submissions, out of which the top 10 papers were accepted. The CEE Forum received a total of 16 submissions, out of which 6 papers were accepted as full papers and 6 papers were accepted as poster papers. In addition, we included in our proceedings three papers from the main conference, out of which two were presented in the CEE Forum and one in the Blockchain Forum.

We thank the colleagues involved in the organization of the conference, especially the members of the PCs and the Organizing Committee. We also thank the Platinum sponsor Signavio; the Gold sponsors Austrian Center for Digital Production, Bizagi, Camunda, Celonis, FireStart, and Process4.biz; the Silver sponsors Heflo, JIT, Minit, Papyrus Software, and Phactum; the Bronze sponsors Con-Sense, DCR, and TIM Solutions; Springer and Gesellschaft für Prozessmanagement for their support. We would also like to thank WU Vienna and the University of Vienna for their enormous and high-quality support. Finally, we thank the Organizing Committee and the local Organization Committee, namely Martin Beno, Katharina Distelbacher-Kollmann, Ilse Dietlinde Kondert, Roman Franz, Alexandra Hager, Prabh Jit, and Doris Wyk.

September 2019

Claudio Di Ciccio
Renata Gabryelczyk
Luciano García-Bañuelos
Tomislav Hernaus
Rick Hull
Mojca Indihar Štemberger
Andrea Kő
Mark Staples

Organization

The 17th International Conference on Business Process Management (BPM 2019) was organized by the Vienna University of Economics and Business (WU Vienna) and the University of Vienna, and took place in Vienna, Austria. The Blockchain Forum and the Central and Eastern Europe Forum were co-located with the main conference, which took place during September 1–6, 2019.

Executive Committee

BPM General Chairs

Jan Mendling	WU Vienna, Austria
Stefanie Rinderle-Ma	University of Vienna, Austria

Blockchain Forum

Program Committee Chairs

Claudio Di Ciccio	WU Vienna, Austria
Luciano García-Bañuelos	Tecnológico de Monterrey, Mexico
Richard Hull	IBM Research, USA
Mark Staples	Data61, CSIRO, Australia

Program Committee

Mayutan Arumaithurai	University of Göttingen, Germany
Clemens H. Cap	University of Rostock, Germany
Riccardo De Masellis	Stockholm University, Sweden
Alevtina Dubovitskaya	Lucerne University of Applied Sciences and Arts, Switzerland
Gilbert Fridgen	Fraunhofer FIT, Germany
Marko Hölbl	University of Maribor, Slovenia
Sabrina Kirrane	WU Vienna, Austria
Qingua Lu	Data61, CSIRO, Australia
Raimundas Matulevicius	University of Tartu, Estonia
Giovanni Meroni	Politecnico di Milano, Italy
Alexander Norta	Tallinn University of Technology, Estonia
Petr Novotny	IBM, USA
Sooyong Park	Sogang University, South Korea
Stefanie Rinderle-Ma	University of Vienna, Austria
Matti Rossi	Aalto University, Finland
Stefan Schulte	TU Wien, Austria
Volker Skwarek	Hamburg University of Applied Sciences, Germany
Stefan Tai	Technical University of Berlin, Germany

Nils Urbach   University of Bayreuth, Germany
Shermin Voshmgir   WU Vienna, Austria
Edgar Weippl   SBA Research, Austria
Kaiwen Zhang   École de technologie supérieure ÉTS, Canada

Central and Eastern Europe Forum

Program Committee Chairs

Renata Gabryelczyk   University of Warsaw, Poland
Tomislav Hernaus   University of Zagreb, Croatia
Mojca Indihar Štemberger   University of Ljubljana, Slovenia
Andrea Kö   Corvinus University of Budapest, Hungary

Program Committee

Agnieszka Bitkowska   Warsaw University of Technology, Poland
Vesna Bosilj-Vukšić   University of Zagreb, Croatia
Maja Cukusic   University of Split, Croatia
György Drótos   Corvinus University of Budapest, Hungary
Jure Erjavec   University of Ljubljana, Slovenia
Andras Gabor   Corvinus University of Budapest, Hungary
Constantin Houy   University of Saarland, Germany
Tomaz Kern   University of Maribor, Slovenia
Marite Kirikova   Riga Technical University, Latvia
Krzysztof Kluza   AGH University of Science and Technology, Poland
Michal Krčál   Masaryk University, Czech Republic
Anton Manfreda   University of Ljubljana, Slovenia
Ivan Matic   University of Split, Croatia
Jan Mendling   WU Vienna, Austria
Andrzej Niesler   Wrocław University of Economics, Poland
Igor Pihir   University of Zagreb, Croatia
Amila Pilav-Velic   University of Sarajevo, Bosnia and Herzegovina
Gregor Polančič   University of Maribor, Slovenia
Natalia Potoczek   Polish Academy of Sciences, Poland
Dragana Stojanović   University of Belgrade, Serbia
Peter Trkman   University of Ljubljana, Slovenia

Additional Reviewers

Kristof Böhmer   Jakob Hackel   Vincent Schlatt
Anselm Busse   Mubashar Iqbal   Yahya Shahsavari
Syed Muhammad Danish   Aleksandr Kormiltsyn   Nicholas Stifter
Vipin Deval   Eva Krhač   Lars Wederhake
Benedict Drasch   Jannik Lockl   Karolin Winter
Vimal Dwivedi   Markus Sabadello
Walid Fdhila   Philipp Schindler

Blockchain and BPM - Reflections on Four Years of Research and Applications (Abstract of Keynote Talk)

Ingo Weber(iD)

Technische Universitaet Berlin, Germany
ingo.weber@tu-berlin.de

Abstract. With the introduction of smart contracts, blockchain technology has become a general-purpose execution framework that offers highly interesting properties, like immutability and censorship resistance. This has sparked investigations across almost all industry sectors on possible uses of the technology, and resulted in a number of productive deployments to date. In many of these cases, cross-organizational business processes are moved onto the blockchain to enable better collaboration.

In this keynote, I will summarize and reflect on research on BPM and blockchain over the last four years, including model-driven engineering, process execution, and analysis and process mining. I will also cover selected use cases and applications, as well as recent insights on adoption. The keynote will close with a discussion of open research questions.

Keywords: Blockchain • Business Process Management • Model-driven engineering • Process mining

Contents

Blockchain Forum Keynote

Towards Blockchain Interoperability 3
  Stefan Schulte, Marten Sigwart, Philipp Frauenthaler,
  and Michael Borkowski

Blockchain Forum

Comparison of Blockchain-Based Solutions to Mitigate Data Tampering
Security Risk 13
  Mubashar Iqbal and Raimundas Matulevičius

License Chain - An Identity-Protecting Intellectual Property License
Trading Platform. 29
  Julian Kakarott, Katharina Zeuch, and Volker Skwarek

Defining and Delimitating Distributed Ledger Technology:
Results of a Structured Literature Analysis 43
  Maik Lange, Steven Chris Leiter, and Rainer Alt

Trusted Artifact-Driven Process Monitoring of Multi-party Business
Processes with Blockchain 55
  Giovanni Meroni, Pierluigi Plebani, and Francesco Vona

Mining Blockchain Processes: Extracting Process Mining Data
from Blockchain Applications. 71
  Christopher Klinkmüller, Alexander Ponomarev, An Binh Tran,
  Ingo Weber, and Wil van der Aalst

Balancing Privity and Enforceability of BPM-Based Smart Contracts
on Blockchains. 87
  Julius Köpke, Marco Franceschetti, and Johann Eder

Performance and Scalability of Private Ethereum Blockchains 103
  Markus Schäffer, Monika di Angelo, and Gernot Salzer

Executing Collaborative Decisions Confidentially on Blockchains 119
  Stephan Haarmann, Kimon Batoulis, Adriatik Nikaj, and Mathias Weske

Permissioned Distributed Ledgers for Land Transactions; A Case Study. 136
  Duneesha Fernando and Nalin Ranasinghe

Towards a Multi-party, Blockchain-Based Identity Verification Solution
to Implement Clear Name Laws for Online Media Platforms   151
Karl Pinter, Dominik Schmelz, René Lamber, Stefan Strobl,
and Thomas Grechenig

Data Quality Control in Blockchain Applications   166
Cinzia Cappiello, Marco Comuzzi, Florian Daniel,
and Giovanni Meroni

Central and Eastern Europe Forum

Process Maturity of Organizations Using Artificial Intelligence
Technology – Preliminary Research............................   185
Piotr Sliż

A Generic DEMO Model for Co-creation and Co-production as a Basis
for a Truthful and Appropriate REA Model Representation   203
Frantisek Hunka and Steven van Kervel

Integration of Blockchain Technology into a Land Registration System
for Immutable Traceability: A Casestudy of Georgia   219
Nino Lazuashvili, Alex Norta, and Dirk Draheim

A Conceptual Blueprint for Enterprise Architecture Model-Driven Business
Process Optimization..   234
Dóra Őri and Zoltán Szabó

Individual Process Orientation as a Two-Dimensional Construct:
Conceptualization and Measurement Scale Development   249
Monika Klun and Michael Leyer

Performance Effects of Dynamic Capabilities: The Interaction Effect
of Process Management Capabilities   264
Jasna Prester, Tomislav Hernaus, Ana Aleksić, and Peter Trkman

Robotic Process Automation: Systematic Literature Review   280
Lucija Ivančić, Dalia Suša Vugec, and Vesna Bosilj Vukšić

An Empirical Investigation of the Cultural Impacts on the Business Process
Concepts' Representations   296
Gregor Polančič, Pavlo Brin, Saša Kuhar, Gregor Jošt,
and Jernej Huber

Central and Eastern Europe Forum Posters

Using Enterprise Models for Change Analysis in Inter-organizational
Business Processes 315
  Martin Henkel, Georgios Koutsopoulos, Ilia Bider, and Erik Perjons

Business Process Management vs Modeling of the Process of Knowledge
Management in Contemporary Enterprises 319
  Agnieszka Bitkowska

BPM Adoption in Serbian Companies 324
  Dragana Stojanović, Ivona Jovanović, Dragoslav Slović,
  Ivan Tomašević, and Barbara Simeunović

Conceptualizing the Convergence Model of Business Process Management
and Customer Experience Management 328
  Dino Pavlić and Maja Ćukušić

The Value of Customer Journey Mapping and Analysis in Design
Thinking Projects 333
  Péter Fehér and Krisztián Varga

The Presence of Order-Effect Bias in Moscow Administration 337
  Dmitry Romanov, Nikolai Kazantsev, and Elina Edgeeva

Author Index 343

Blockchain Forum Keynote

Towards Blockchain Interoperability

Stefan Schulte[1]([✉]), Marten Sigwart[1], Philipp Frauenthaler[1],
and Michael Borkowski[2]

[1] Distributed Systems Group, TU Wien, Vienna, Austria
{s.schulte,m.sigwart,p.frauenthaler}@infosys.tuwien.ac.at
https://www.dsg.tuwien.ac.at
[2] Institute of Flight Guidance, German Aerospace Center (DLR),
Brunswick, Germany
michael.borkowski@dlr.de
https://www.dlr.de

Abstract. In recent years, distributed ledger technologies like blockchains have gained much popularity both within industry and research. Today, blockchains do not only act as the underlying technology for cryptocurrencies like Bitcoin, but have also been identified as a potentially disruptive technology in many different fields, e.g., supply chain tracking and healthcare. The widespread attention for blockchains has led to manifold research and development activities. As a result, today's blockchain landscape is heavily fragmented, with different, incompatible technologies being available to potential users. Since interoperability between different blockchains is usually not foreseen in existing protocols and standards, functionalities like sending tokens from one participant to another, or invoking and executing smart contracts can only be carried out within a single blockchain.

In this paper, we discuss the need for blockchain interoperability and how it could help to stimulate a paradigm shift from today's closed blockchains to an open system where devices and users can interact with each other across the boundaries of blockchains. For this, we consider the areas of cross-blockchain token transfers, as well as cross-blockchain smart contract invocation and interaction.

Keywords: Blockchain · Interoperability · Distributed ledger

1 Introduction

Originally, blockchains have been primarily perceived as the underlying technological means to realize monetary transactions in a fully decentralized way, thus enabling cryptocurrencies. While blockchains of the first generation like the one established by Bitcoin [1] provide the means to store data and to enact transactions in a distributed ledger, second-generation blockchains like Ethereum [2] enable the execution of almost arbitrary software functionalities within the blockchain, using so-called *smart contracts* [3]. For this, second-generation blockchains

© Springer Nature Switzerland AG 2019
C. Di Ciccio et al. (Eds.): BPM 2019 Blockchain and CEE Forum, LNBIP 361, pp. 3–10, 2019.
https://doi.org/10.1007/978-3-030-30429-4_1

provide quasi Turing-complete scripting languages like *Solidity*, and an according execution environment like the *Ethereum Virtual Machine* (EVM) [4].

Because of their capabilities, blockchains have the potential for wide-spread application in many different areas. These areas range from generic industrial applications to more specific use cases in Business Process Management (BPM) [5,6], anti-counterfeiting [7], or healthcare [8]. In brief, blockchains might be applied in any scenario where it is useful to execute transactions and store data in a tamper-proof and fully decentralized manner without being dependent on a centralized third party.

Naturally, different use cases have different requirements and thus demand different capabilities of blockchains. As a result, research and development in the blockchain field often focus on the creation of entirely new blockchains and cryptocurrencies, or on altering major blockchains like Bitcoin to satisfy additional requirements [9]. This leads to incompatible novel technologies.

The constant increase in the number of independent, unconnected blockchain technologies causes significant fragmentation of the research and development field since (industrial) users and developers have to choose which cryptocurrency and which blockchain to use for each use case scenario. Choosing novel, innovative blockchains enables users and developers to utilize new features and to take advantage of state of the art technology. However, the risk of security breaches potentially leading to a total loss of funds in novel blockchain networks is substantially higher than in established ones, due to a higher likelihood of bugs and the smaller user base in the beginning [10]. On the other hand, choosing mature, well-known blockchains reduces the risk of losses, since these blockchains are more likely to have been analyzed in-depth [11], but novel features remain unavailable.

Therefore, providing means to bridge the gaps between different blockchain technologies would evidently have a large impact since users could select and combine blockchains based on their current demands while not being locked-in to one particular technology. However, the ways in which different blockchains could potentially interact with each other remain mostly unexplored. Most importantly, today, the following functionalities can only be carried out within a single blockchain:

- Sending tokens from one participant to another
- Executing smart contracts saved in a blockchain
- Guaranteeing validity of data stored in a blockchain

In this paper, we further discuss the need for blockchain interoperability, and potential solution approaches. We consider blockchain interoperability on different levels, namely cross-blockchain token transfers (Sect. 2) and cross-blockchain smart contract invocation and interaction (Sect. 3).

2   Cross-Blockchain Token Transfers

2.1   State of the Art

Following their original purpose to serve as the underlying technology for cryptocurrencies, the most obvious research question in the field of blockchain interoperability is surely "How can we transfer tokens between different blockchains?". Today, tokens like cryptocurrency coins can only be used in one particular blockchain. Therefore, one promising research direction is to establish approaches for transferring tokens between different blockchains, i.e., from a source blockchain to a target blockchain. To achieve this, according token transactions need to be autonomously synchronized between the involved blockchains in a decentralized manner. The solution needs to prevent double spending and the faking of transactions in order to avoid tokens being created on the target blockchain without first being destroyed on the source blockchain. Since it is difficult to fully replicate the state of one blockchain within another blockchain [12], efficient mechanisms are necessary that allow the verification of events taking place on one blockchain from within another blockchain without relying on a third party.

One of the earliest contributions in the field of blockchain interoperability is the idea of a trustless cryptocurrency exchange realized in the form of atomic cross-chain swaps (also simply labeled as "atomic swaps"). Atomic swaps enable users of different cryptocurrencies to swap their assets in an atomic and trustless manner, e.g., Alice sends one Bitcoin to Bob on the Bitcoin blockchain and Bob sends 50 Ether to Alice on the Ethereum blockchain. In recent years, atomic swaps have received attention from industry and academia likewise. For instance, the approach is being adapted by platforms like Komodo's BarterDex [13] to enable the decentralized exchange of cryptocurrencies. In academia, work has focused on approaches to extend the protocol to more than two users and on the best ways to match users seeking to perform atomic swaps [14]. However, atomic swaps do not enable the transfer of a token from one blockchain to another in a sense that a certain amount of assets is destroyed on the source blockchain and the same amount is (re-)created on the destination blockchain, e.g., transfer a token T from Bitcoin to Ethereum such that T can be used on Ethereum after the successful completion of the transfer. As the name implies, atomic swaps provide not transfers, but exchanges of tokens across the boundaries of blockchains. Therefore, atomic swaps always need a counterparty willing to exchange tokens. An indirect way to exchange tokens is offered by online marketplaces. So far, however, this requires the existence of a trusted, centralized entity, which counteracts the decentralized nature of blockchains, and can therefore only be seen as an intermediate step towards full decentralization.

2.2   Research Directions

Despite the existing first attempts to decentralized solutions using atomic swaps, research in the field of cross-blockchain token transfers is still limited. In particular, so far, no practical solution exists that enables the transfer of a single token between different blockchains.

Ideally, a cross-blockchain token enables users to freely choose on which blockchain they want to hold their assets. Users should not be tied to particular blockchains and should be able to hold different denominations of a token on multiple blockchains at the same time. If a new blockchain technology emerges and offers novel features, users should be able to transfer their tokens to this new blockchain taking advantage of the novel capabilities. Finally, the distribution of assets across the participating blockchains could give an indication about the significance of a particular blockchain.

In general, when transferring tokens between blockchains, it needs to be ensured that the total amount of tokens remains the same, i.e., it must not be possible to create tokens out of nothing, since this would effectively lead to uncontrolled inflation. In [15], we present a first prototype that uses reward-incentivized third-party witnesses to propagate token transfers across an ecosystem of blockchains hence enabling a first kind of cross-blockchain token. This prototype synchronizes balances of the cross-chain token across all participating blockchains. However, this first prototype poses a couple of limitations. First, the synchronization of any balance change across all blockchains leads to excessive synchronization cost. The more blockchains are supported by the protocol, the higher the synchronization cost become. Second, the devised approach provides no means of adding a new blockchain later on. Since every blockchain stores the current balance of each wallet, these balances must also be synchronized with a new blockchain. This leads inevitably to the open question how all existing balances can be transferred to a new blockchain without relying on a trusted third party. Third, in order to verify digital signatures, all blockchains must support the same implementations of the required cryptographic primitives. Fourth, the proposed approach does not allow to determine the significance of individual blockchains (e.g., how much assets are stored on each blockchain), since each blockchain stores the same wallet balances.

Since it is not possible to fully replicate one blockchain within another blockchain [12], solutions are necessary to provide enough information to the target blockchain so that it can prove or be otherwise certain that the transferred amount of tokens has actually been destroyed on the source blockchain and can thus securely be created on the target blockchain. Since this information has to come from an external source, two strategies are promising. Either, (a) the provided information acts as a cryptographic proof that can be verified by the target blockchain to prove that the tokens were actually destroyed on the source blockchain, or (b) the target blockchain relies on information provided by oracles [16], to attest whether or not the tokens have actually been destroyed.

For (a), several limitations have to be tackled to make such a proof-based strategy work in praxis. In particular, proof construction and validation have to be efficient for the benefits of a cross-blockchain token transfer to outweigh the associated cost. For (b), since this approach relies on third parties or oracles to provide valid information, the challenges lie in aligning incentives in such a way that the third parties are always inclined to behave honestly, and designing the system so that it is difficult or near impossible for malicious actors to perform manipulations. Note that these challenges are not specific to strategy (b), but rather are inherent challenges of blockchain technologies. For instance, 51% attacks are theoretically possible, but with the right incentive structure and consensus algorithm very difficult to do in practice for most of today's major blockchains.

In addition, different blockchains employ different consensus mechanisms, block sizes, confirmation times, hashing algorithms, and network models. Further, not all blockchains provide the same level of scripting capabilities, e.g., Ethereum's scripting language is quasi Turing-complete, whereas other languages like Script, which is employed by Bitcoin, are more limited. Hence, a major research challenge is to develop a solution for secure cross-blockchain token transfers that accounts for this diversity. Finally, special cases like potential blockchain forks need to be addressed by a solution, since blocks in forks are usually valid, but are not (or not yet) confirmed by the majority of participants.

3   Cross-Blockchain Smart Contract Interaction

3.1   State of the Art

With smart contracts being in the focus of most currently discussed application areas of blockchain technologies, the second quite obvious dimension of blockchain interoperability leads to the research question "Which possibilities exist to enable invocations of smart contracts across blockchains and therefore to realize cross-blockchain applications?".

Multiple projects aim to tackle the problem of general blockchain interoperability in contrast to the more specific use case of cross-blockchain token transfers discussed above. General interoperability is largely concerned with generic communication between blockchains, i.e., the passing of arbitrary information from one blockchain to another in a decentralized and trustless way. The ability to establish generic communication between blockchains would in turn enable cross-blockchain smart contract interaction or even cross-blockchain smart contracts. The latter describe smart contracts which do not only interact with each other, but which run on different blockchains, and could be transferred from one blockchain to another.

In [17], Jin et al. elaborate on different blockchain interoperation schemes such as an active mode and a passive mode. In terms of the passive mode, a blockchain monitors transactions or events occurring on another blockchain, whereas a blockchain in active mode first sends information to another blockchain, and then waits for the feedback from this blockchain. Furthermore, different challenges in realizing interoperability are discussed, e.g., guaranteeing atomicity, efficiency, and maintenance of security. Jin et al. further discuss possible concepts for establishing interoperability on different layers. More precisely, they discuss ideas and challenges in the terms of unifying data structures, network communication, consensus mechanisms, cross-chain contracts, and blockchain applications.

A more generic multi-blockchain framework is proposed by PolkaDot [18]. PolkaDot aims to provide a platform for blockchain interoperability managed by a central relay blockchain which validates transactions taking place on so-called parachains. Parachains are blockchains which can be more or less specialized for specific applications and purposes. The aim of the relay blockchain is to enable interchain communication of parachains by a message-passing protocol and to let parachains pool their security, thus lowering the entry barriers for new blockchain projects. While the initial PolkaDot whitepaper mentions basic ideas about how the interaction of parachains with the relay blockchain might take place, no details are given about the actual validation process taking place on the relay blockchain. Further, the project seems to be in an early stage of development, and only individual parts have been prototyped so far. Also, the planned parachains have to comply to specific interfaces in order to interact with the relay blockchain. Existing blockchains like Ethereum will have to be integrated via so-called bridge blockchains.

Cosmos [19] is another project aiming to bring generic interoperability capabilities for blockchains to the industry. Similarly to PolkaDot, interoperability in Cosmos takes place between multiple blockchains called zones. Cosmos zones all run on the Proof-of-Stake consensus mechanism Tendermint. One zone, called the Cosmos hub, acts as a central communication blockchain between the other zones. The Cosmos hub keeps track of all committed block headers occurring in the other zones and likewise the zones keep track of the blocks of the hub. Via Merkle proofs, zones can prove to each other the existence of messages on their respective blockchains, this way enabling interchain communication. Similar to PolkaDot, one drawback of Cosmos is that it does not enable interoperability between existing blockchains out of the box. Instead, all zones have to implement the same consensus mechanism. While it is planned to also integrate existing blockchains like Ethereum via specific adapter zones, no details how this could be achieved are provided so far.

3.2   Research Directions

As it can be seen from the discussion above, generic blockchain interoperability is a highly active research field, however, so far, tangible progress is slow. Hence, cross-blockchain smart contract interaction is currently not possible in an efficient and trustless manner.

The basic prerequisite to establish cross-blockchain smart contract interaction is to establish an inter-blockchain communication protocol which can be used to exchange arbitrary data between blockchains in a decentralized and trustless way. Cross-blockchain token transfers as discussed above constitute a specific use case of inter-blockchain communication, since the existence of a particular piece of information (i.e., the transaction destroying tokens) on the source blockchain needs to be proven on the target blockchain. Hence, the same challenges and constraints that apply to cross-blockchain token transfers also apply to generic inter-blockchain communication and therefore cross-blockchain smart contract interaction.

Therefore, a major research challenge is to generalize research results and solutions developed for cross-chain token transfers in order to allow the reliable verification of arbitrary data from one blockchain on another. Ideally, a protocol is developed, where generic information can be passed between multiple blockchains, comparable to the transport layer of the Internet. Once such a protocol exists, further research will be required to determine the efficient usage of this protocol, e.g., whether communication happens synchronously or asynchronously, via request and reply patterns, etc. Similar to cross-blockchain token transfers, in order to develop a solution capable of running on multiple different blockchains, a wide diversity of different systems needs to be taken into account, i.e., different consensus mechanisms, confirmation times, block sizes, header sizes, network models, the frequency of forks, scripting languages, etc.

4 Conclusions

The peculiar properties of blockchain technologies have lead to activities aiming at the application of blockchains in many different areas. To account for the diverse requirements of these application areas, existing blockchain protocols are adapted or completely new protocols are presented for new use cases. This has lead to today's widely fragmented blockchain landscape. Hence, solutions for blockchain interoperability are needed, e.g., the possibility to transfer tokens from one blockchain to another, or to achieve interoperability between smart contracts on different blockchains.

Within this paper, we have discussed the current state of the art in these areas and have given some thoughts about possible research directions. Our own concrete research in this area is currently aiming at cross-blockchain token transfers, which we see as a first step into the direction of more generic inter-blockchain communication. This, in turn, would enable more complex scenarios, such as cross-blockchain smart contracts.

Acknowledgments. The work presented in this paper has received funding from Pantos GmbH[1] within the TAST research project.

References

1. Nakamoto, S.: Bitcoin: A Peer-to-Peer Electronic Cash System. Whitepaper (2008)
2. Buterin, V.: A Next Generation Smart Contract & Decentralized Application Platform (2013) Whitepaper, Ethereum Foundation
3. Tschorsch, F., Scheuermann, B.: Bitcoin and beyond: a technical survey on decentralized digital currencies. IEEE Commun. Surv. Tutor. **18**(3), 2084–2123 (2016)
4. Dannen, C.: Introducing Ethereum and Solidity. Apress (2017)

---

[1] https://pantos.io/.

5. Prybila, C., Schulte, S., Hochreiner, C., Weber, I.: Runtime Verification for Business Processes Utilizing the Bitcoin Blockchain. Futur. Gener. Comput. Syst. (2019, in press)
6. Mendling, J., et al.: Blockchains for business process management - challenges and opportunities. ACM Trans. Manag. Inf. Syst. **9**(1), 4 (2018)
7. Lu, D., et al.: Reducing automotive counterfeiting using blockchain: benefits and challenges. In: 2019 IEEE International Conference on Decentralized Applications and Infrastructures, pp. 39–48 (2019)
8. Li, M., Xia, L., Seneviratne, O.: Leveraging standards based ontological concepts in distributed ledgers: a healthcare smart contract example. In: 2019 IEEE International Conference on Decentralized Applications and Infrastructures, pp. 152–157 (2019)
9. Yli-Huumo, J., Ko, D., Choi, S., Park, S., Smolander, K.: Where is current research on blockchain technology?-A systematic review. PLOS ONE **11**(10), e0163477 (2016)
10. Nofer, M., Gomber, P., Hinz, O., Schiereck, D.: Blockchain. Bus. Inf. Syst. Eng. **59**(3), 183–187 (2017)
11. Li, X., Jiang, P., Chen, T., Luo, X., Wen, Q.: A survey on the security of blockchain systems. Future Gener. Comput. Syst. (2017, in press)
12. Borkowski, M., Ritzer, C., McDonald, D., Schulte, S.: Caught in chains: claim-first transactions for cross-blockchain asset transfers. Technische Universität Wien, Whitepaper (2018)
13. Komodo Platform: Blockchain Interoperability: Cross-Chain Smart Contracts (2018). https://komodoplatform.com/interoperability-cross-chain-smart-contracts/. Accessed 26 Apr 2019
14. Herlihy, M.: Atomic cross-chain swaps. In: 2018 ACM Symposium on Principles of Distributed Systems. ACM, pp. 245–254 (2018)
15. Borkowski, M., Sigwart, M., Frauenthaler, P., Hukkinen, T., Schulte, S.: DeXTT: decentralized cross-chain token transfers. arXiv:1905.06204 (2019)
16. Gatteschi, V., Lamberti, F., Demartini, C., Pranteda, C., Santamaria, V.: Blockchain and smart contracts for insurance: is the technology mature enough? Future Internet **10**(2), 20 (2018)
17. Jin, H., Dai, X., Xiao, J.: Towards a novel architecture for enabling interoperability amongst multiple blockchains. In: 38th International Conference on Distributed Computing Systems, pp. 1203–1211 (2018)
18. Wood, G.: Polkadot Whitepaper (2019). https://polkadot.network/PolkaDotPaper.pdf. Accessed 26 Apr 2019
19. Kwon, J., Buchman, E.: Cosmos Whitepaper (2019). https://github.com/cosmos/cosmos/blob/master/WHITEPAPER.md. Accessed 26 Apr 2019

Blockchain Forum

Comparison of Blockchain-Based Solutions to Mitigate Data Tampering Security Risk

Mubashar Iqbal$^{(\boxtimes)}$ (iD) and Raimundas Matulevičius (iD)

Institute of Computer Science, University of Tartu, Tartu, Estonia
{mubashar.iqbal,raimundas.matulevicius}@ut.ee

Abstract. Blockchain-based applications are arising because they ensure integrity, anti-tampering, and traceability. The data tampering risk is one of the main security concerns of data-centric applications. By the nature of the blockchain technology, it is befitting a revolutionary solution to mitigate the tampering risk. But there exists no proper guidance to explain how blockchain-based application could mitigate this risk. In this paper, we consider tampering risk management and discuss how blockchain-based applications could mitigate it. The study includes a comparison of different solutions.

Keywords: Blockchain · Security risks ·
Data tampering security risk · Security risk management ·
Security modelling

1 Introduction

Blockchain is a decentralised distributed and immutable ledger technology [1]. The use of blockchain technology ensures integrity, anti-tampering, and traceability [2]. The blockchain performs a consensus mechanism and data validation before saving on the immutable ledger. The blockchain-based application detects and discards all the unauthorised data changes during the consensus and data validation if the majority of the network is honest (i.e., not controlled by an adversary). This process establishes a tamper-proof environment [3].

Blockchain technology is emerging in different application domains to overcome various security challenges. Data tampering is the main security concern, which developers attempt to mitigate by blockchain-based solutions [4]. Data tampering involves the malicious modification of data by an unauthorised user [5]. Data exists in two states; either in transit or stored. In both cases, data could be intercepted and tampered [6]. Damage to the critical data could cause disruption to revenue-generating business operations. In the worst case scenario, it could put people life at risk, e.g., the tampering in the healthcare data [7].

Data becomes one of the most valuable assets in an organization. In order to help an organization to build secure software, various programs (e.g., OWASP

© Springer Nature Switzerland AG 2019
C. Di Ciccio et al. (Eds.): BPM 2019 Blockchain and CEE Forum, LNBIP 361, pp. 13–28, 2019.
https://doi.org/10.1007/978-3-030-30429-4_2

[8]) and threat modelling (e.g., STRIDE [9]) are working to communicate and reduce the tampering risk. Recently, the blockchain-based solutions are appearing to mitigate the data tampering risks [10,11]. In this paper, we follow the ISSRM domain model [12,13] and perform the data tampering risk management. The main objective is to compare the architectures for the blockchain-based solutions in order to explain how tampering risk could be mitigated. Hence, we consider (i) the assets to secure from the tampering risk, (ii) vulnerabilities, which cause the tampering risk, (iii) security requirements for risk treatment, and (iv) the potential countermeasures to mitigate the tampering risk. The main contributions of our work are: (1) data tampering risk analysis to identify what resources should be secured, (2) traditional technique-based countermeasure architecture to mitigate tampering risk, (3) Ethereum-based countermeasure architecture, (4) Hyperledger fabric-based countermeasure architecture to mitigate tampering risk, and (5) the comparison of countermeasure for the tampering risk.

The rest of the paper is structured as follows: Sect. 2 bestows a background and literature review. Section 3 presents the context and assets identification. Section 4 presents the mitigation of tampering security risk. Section 5 yields a comparison of tampering risk countermeasures. Section 6 provides the discussion and Sect. 7 concludes the paper.

2   Background

Blockchain is a peer-to-peer (P2P) network-based distributed ledger technology. It forms a chain by a sequence of blocks where each block is attached to the previous block by a cryptographic hash. Blockchain is classified as a permissionless or permissioned [14]. Permissionless blockchain allows anyone to join or leave the network and transactions are publicly visible. In permissioned blockchain, only predefined verified nodes can join the network and transactions visibility is restricted [14,15].

Ethereum platform is an example of permissionless blockchain. It uses the Ether cryptocurrency for the administration fee and proof of work (POW) consensus mechanism. Hyperledger fabric (HLF) is an example of permissioned blockchain and it follows the practical Byzantine fault tolerance (PBFT) based consensus mechanism. HLF uses permissioned settings to allow different participants to access a different set of data.

A system is secure whenever there is no possible way to attack it and it is less likely to be possible even with the blockchain technology. Blockchain helps one to overcome various security risks [4] and is acknowledged to be less vulnerable because of the decentralised consensus paradigm to validate the transactional information. The software security modelling can help to identify/visualize the security issues, and to uncover the hidden security needs. In this paper, we present the management of data tampering risk to explicate how the blockchain-based solutions are supporting the mitigation of this risk.

2.1   ISSRM Domain Model

In this paper, we follow an information systems security risk management (ISSRM) domain model [12,13]. ISSRM comprises three main concepts groups: (*i*) asset-related concepts, (*ii*) risk-related concepts, and (*iii*) risk treatment-related concepts. The asset could be classified as an IS system asset or business asset. The business asset has value and system asset (or IS asset) supports it. Security criteria (confidentiality, integrity and availability) distinguish the security needs. In risk-related concepts, the risk is a combination of risk event and impact. The risk event constitutes the threat and one or more vulnerabilities. The threat targets the IS asset and it is triggered by the threat agent, who uses an attack method and exploits the vulnerability. Impact harms the asset and negates the security criteria. The risk treatment presents a decision to treat the security risk and to define the security requirements. Security requirements are implemented as the controls (security countermeasures) to improve the security of the system.

2.2   Literature Review

In [4], we report on a literature review where security risks to blockchain-based applications are presented. The study explains what security risks of centralised application are mitigated and what security risks appear after introducing the blockchain technology. It also aggregates a list of possible countermeasures. The study categorises the findings by permissionless (i.e., Bitcoin, Ethereum & Customised permissionless), permissioned (i.e., Hyperledger fabric & Customised permissioned) and generic blockchain platforms. The results show that data tampering risk is one of the main security risks. In this study, we consider only the data tampering risk. Currently, Ethereum and HLF platforms provide the complete blockchain solution to build decentralised applications (dApps). Other blockchain platforms are also suitable to build dApps (e.g. EOS & R3 Corda etc.), but these are not yet widely adopted. Hence, we include only those literature studies where the Ethereum and HLF applications are considered to mitigate the data tampering risk.

Ethereum Solutions. In [16], authors illustrate how to protect the user preferences and privacy policies in the IoT systems. The authors of [17] present the blockchain solution in healthcare domain to protect the patient and medical data. In [18], secure mutual authentication scheme is discussed to protect the authentication credentials and response messages from the tampering risk. In the resource monitoring domain [19], the authors incorporate the blockchain-based authorisation system to secure the resource consumption data. Hjalmarsson *et al.* [20] utilize the blockchain to maintain the integrity of voting data and voting results by mitigating the tampering risk. Pop *et al.* [21] employ the blockchain solution as a security layer to protect the bidding and big-offer data.

Hyperledger Fabric Solutions. The authors [10,19] present a blockchain solution to protect the patient and medical data from being tampered. Yu *et al.* [22]

incorporate the blockchain solution as a security layer to protect the voting data from tampering risk. The study [11] builds the blockchain-based IoT video surveillance system to protect the videos recordings and settings from being tampered. In order to mitigate the drug counterfeit [23], the authors implement the blockchain-based solution.

In this paper, we will base our discussion on these studies (see Sect. 2.2). We will show the tampering risk context, its components and potential mitigation countermeasures.

3   Context and Assets Identification

In this section, we define the context and assets, which relate to the data tampering risk. Next, we analyse how tampering could harm the protected assets.

Table 1 shows assets secured from the tampering risk. It also presents the relationship between business assets, security criteria and system assets. For

Table 1. Assets and their security criteria

Paper	Business asset	System asset
HLF-based applications assets and security criteria		
[24]	Patient data (C, I), Healthcare data (I)	*Storage* (Healthcare data), *Service* (Store data), *Service* (Request data)
[22]	Voting data (I)	*Storage* (Voters data), *Storage* (Voting data), *Service* (Store data)
[10]	Patient data (C), Medical records (I)	*Storage* (Patient data), *Storage* (Medical records), *Service* (Store data)
[11]	Video recordings (I), Monitoring (A), CCTV settings (I)	*Storage* (Video recordings), *Storage* (CCTV settings), *Service* (Store data)
[23]	Drug certificate (I)	*Storage* (Drugs data), *Storage* (Supply chain data), *Service* (Store data)
Ethereum-based applications assets and security criteria		
[16]	User preferences (I), Privacy policies (I)	*Storage* (User preferences data), *Service* (Store data)
[17]	Patient data (I), Medical data (I)	*Storage* (Patient data), *Storage* (Medical data), *Service* (Store data)
[18]	Authentication (A), Response message (I)	*Storage* (Response message), *Service* (Manage access rights), *Service* (Store data)
[19]	Resource consumption data (I)	*Storage* (Resource consumption), *Service* (Store data)
[20]	Voting data (I), Voters data (C, I), Voting result (I)	*Storage* (Voting data), *Storage* (Voters data), *Storage* (Voting result), *Service* (Store data)
[21]	Bidding data (I), Bid-offer data (I)	*Storage* (Bidding data), *Storage* (Bid-offer data), *Service* (Store data)

example, the business assets (i.e., patient and healthcare data) are supported by the system assets (i.e., storage of healthcare data, service of store and request data). Security criteria (C - Confidentiality, I - Integrity, A - Availability) are constraints of the business assets.

The architecture, presented in Fig. 1, is an abstraction of the system assets defined from the literature study in Table 1. It characterises the system components at four layers. The *User Layer* exposes the users who interact with the application. The *Interface Layer* presents the various interfaces of the application. The user interacts with the services, which are present in a *Service Layer*. The *Data Storage Layer* shows the database.

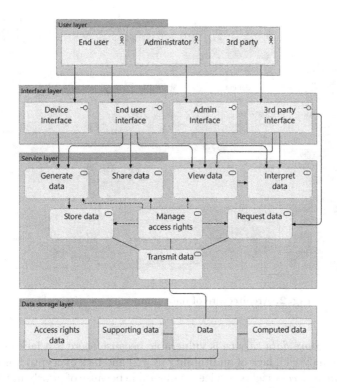

Fig. 1. Architecture of traditional system assets

In Fig. 2, an abstraction of the data tampering risk is presented. The details are collected from the literature studies. Figure 2 demonstrates the security risks, vulnerabilities and the main components of a traditional application. It helps to visualize the vulnerable system assets. The *Threat Agent (Attacker)* commands the *Data Tampering Threat* and leads to the *Data Tampering Risk*. *Risk* is a combination of *Threat* and *Vulnerabilities* that provokes a negative *Impact* and negates the *Security Criteria*. The vulnerabilities are connected to the system assets and depict their weaknesses. It allows an attacker to harm vulnerable system assets. The following vulnerabilities are obtained:

V#1: Lack of information validation
V#2: Lack of auditability
V#3: Lack of crypto functionality
V#4: Poorly implemented access control
V#5: Weak transmission channel

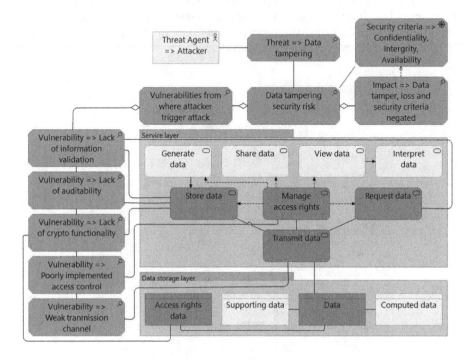

Fig. 2. Architecture of data tampering security risk

For example, *Store data* service is vulnerable because there is a lack of information validation (V#1), lack of auditability (V#2) and lack of crypto functionality (V#3). *Manage access rights* service is vulnerable because of poorly implemented access control (V#4). Similarly, the *Request data* service is vulnerable due to a lack of information validation (V#1) and *Data storage* – due to a lack of crypto functionality (V#3) and weak transmission channel (V#5).

Based on the mentioned literature sources (see Sect. 2.2), the following security requirements (SR) are set to mitigate the tampering risk:

SR#1: The system should perform data validation
SR#2: The system should provide the data auditability
SR#3: The system should incorporate the crypto functionality
SR#4: The system should provide access control
SR#5: The system should provide a secure transmission channel

In the next section, we will discuss how these requirements are implemented to mitigate tampering risk using traditional countermeasures, and using the blockchain-based applications.

4 Mitigation of Tampering Security Risk

In order to address the mitigation of tampering risk, we present the three countermeasure architectures: (*i*) the traditional techniques-based countermeasure architecture, (*ii*) the permissionless blockchain-based countermeasure architecture following the *Ethereum* platform, and (*iii*) the permissioned blockchain-based countermeasure architecture following the *Hyperledger fabric* platform.

4.1 Traditional Countermeasure Architecture

Figure 3 shows how the identified vulnerabilities are mitigated by the traditional countermeasure techniques. The data tampering threat is represent in the STRIDE threat model [9], which has the corresponding set of security countermeasures (SC) to reduce tampering threat:

SC#1: Validate and filter input data
SC#2: Create secure audit trails
SC#3: Incorporate the crypto functionality and use digital signatures
SC#4: Use strong authorisation and access control
SC#5: Secure communication with protocols

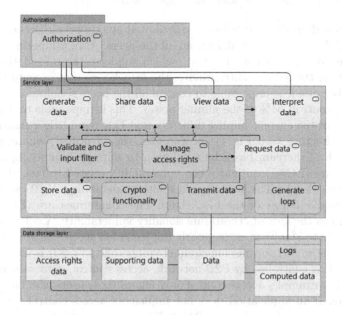

Fig. 3. Traditional techniques-based countermeasure architecture

Based on these countermeasures the architecture (see Fig. 3) is build to exhibit the countermeasures components which are applied to reduce tampering risk. For example, the security countermeasure (SC#1) employs on the Store data and Request data to mitigate the vulnerability related to lack of information validation (V#1). The countermeasure (SC#2) regarding the secure audit trails helps to mitigate the lack of auditability vulnerability(V#2) of Store data. The countermeasure (SC#3) of crypto functionality and the use of digital signatures approach mitigates the lack of crypto functionality vulnerability (V#3) of Database and Store data. The countermeasure (SC#4) mitigates the poorly implemented access control vulnerability (V#4). The countermeasure (SC#5) helps to mitigate the weak transmission channel vulnerability (V#5).

4.2   Ethereum-Based Countermeasure Architecture

Ethereum platform provides immutable decentralised distributed ledger, which ensures tamper-proof recording of transactions [17]. Along with the blockchain solution, Ethereum-based decentralised applications introduce several other techniques, which we consider as countermeasures. These Ethereum-based countermeasures (EC) are collected from the literature studies (see Table 1), which are utilized to secure an application. These countermeasures also help to clarify the security needs of Ethereum application:

> EC#1: Transaction data validation [18]
> EC#2: Store an encrypted data on the immutable ledger [16,17,20,23]
> EC#3: Blockchain-based access control [16,21]
> EC#4: Split the data and store in random locations [17]

Ethereum-based application ledger is distributed among peers. Because of this, it is impossible to remove the data from all the peers. Also, tampering is impossible because of the blockchain nature, which validates the information before recording it on the ledger. Furthermore, the attacker cannot execute the malicious code because it is impossible to control all the peers simultaneously unless the attacker controls 51% of the mining power. This is impossible to achieve for him because of the current mining difficulty and Ethereum ledger maturity.

The architecture (see Fig. 4) incorporates the identified countermeasures along with the Ethereum blockchain solution to mitigate tampering risk. The countermeasure (EC#1) mitigates the vulnerability related to lack of information validation (V#1). The lack of auditability vulnerability (V#2) is mitigated by an immutable ledger of the blockchain. The countermeasure (EC#2) approach mitigates the lack of crypto functionality vulnerability (V#3). The countermeasure (EC#3) mitigates the poorly implemented access control vulnerability (V#4). The weak transmission channel vulnerability (V#5) is not mitigated directly but it is controlled by P2P network, access control, data validation and consensus. For example, access control only allows those users who have specific access rights. If an application does not implement access control then invalid transmitted data is discarded on data validation and consensus stages. Data

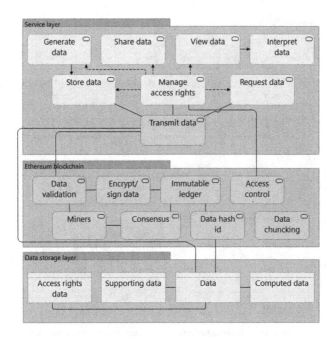

Fig. 4. Ethereum-based countermeasure architecture

chunking (EC#4) is used to deals with limitation of large file storage on the ledger but it also provides tampering resistance. The data file chunks are stored on several random locations along with unique hash id and indexes. If an adversary tampers the chunk then it invalidates the hash and that particular data chunk becomes invalid.

4.3 Hyperledger Fabric-Based Countermeasure Architecture

As compare to Ethereum-based solutions, HLF solves performance, scalability, and privacy issues by permissioned mode of operation and fine-grained access control. Likewise, HLF-based decentralised applications introduce several other techniques to mitigate tampering risk, that we consider as countermeasures. These HLF-based countermeasures (HC) are collected from the literature studies (see Table 1). These countermeasures also help to clarify the security needs of HLF application:

HC#1: Transaction data validation [23,24]
HC#2: Traceability of ledger transactions [10]
HC#3: Store an encrypted data on the immutable ledger [11,22,23]
HC#4: Blockchain-based access control [24]

In Fig. 5 the suggested countermeasures are illustrated. HLF introduces a PBFT based consensus mechanism. It performs the data validation and writes the records on the immutable distributed ledger.

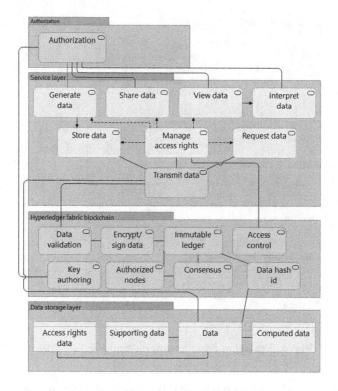

Fig. 5. HLF-based countermeasure architecture

The architecture (Fig. 5) incorporates the identified countermeasures along with the HLF blockchain solution to mitigate tampering risk. The countermeasure (HC#1) mitigates the vulnerability related to a lack of information validation (V#1). The lack of auditability vulnerability(V#2) is mitigated by an immutable ledger of the blockchain and traceability of ledger transactions (HC#2). The countermeasure (HC#3) mitigates a lack of crypto functionality vulnerability (V#3). The countermeasure (HC#4) mitigates the poorly implemented access control vulnerability (V#4). Similarly to Ethereum case, the weak transmission channel vulnerability (V#5) is not mitigated directly but it is controlled by P2P network, access control, data validation and consensus.

5   Comparison

In this section, we compare the above-mentioned approaches by their potential vulnerabilities and respective countermeasure techniques.

Table 2 lists the vulnerabilities and their respective countermeasures used in different solutions. For example, to mitigate V#1, traditional application implements centralised data validation and input filtering before recording in the database. The Ethereum-based application performs distributed data validation

Table 2. Comparison of different solutions which mitigate data tampering risk

	Traditional	Ethereum	HLF
V#1	Centralised validation and filter input data	Distributed data validation by unverified nodes [18]	Distributed data validation by verified nodes [23, 24]
V#2	Audit trails	Tamper-proof immutable distributed ledger [16, 17, 20, 23]	Tamper-proof immutable distributed ledger, and traceability of ledger transactions [10]
V#3	Crypto functionality and digital signatures	Blockchain-based crypto functionality, hashing and digital signatures [16, 17, 20, 23]	Blockchain-based crypto functionality, hashing and digital signatures [11, 22, 23]
V#4	Authorisation and access control	Blockchain-based access control [16, 21]	Predefined verified nodes, Blockchain-based access control [24]
V#5	Secure communication with protocols	Split the data and store in random locations [17], and encrypted data communication [17, 23, 25]	Encrypted data communication [24–26]

by unverified nodes called miners. Miners validate the data and only record in tamper-proof immutable ledger if valid. Similarly, HLF performs distributed data validation by verified nodes. As mentioned above HLF is a permissioned blockchain and the participant nodes are verified. These mitigation techniques have benefits and limitations against one another. For instance, the traditional application performs faster data validation but it lacks the full control [27]. As the data validation and filtering rule are centralised and written by developers, they could be error prone [27,28]. Ethereum performs data validation through validator nodes [29] by checking the data against the defined validation rules, including historical data in the ledger. Ethereum provides a transparent platform to define data validation rules which agreed upon by other nodes. Then, all the nodes follow those rules to validate the incoming data. Also, blockchain is an append-only structure and user can only add data but can not modify or delete them [28]. Hence, this process reduces human error. But POW is an energy-waste consensus mechanism. It takes time to validate and also pays an administration fee to the miners for performing this activity. These limitations are overcome by HLF which does not require POW or administration fee. It uses the PBFT consensus for data validation. By the nature of HLF, it leverages the benefits of permissionless blockchain (e.g., Ethereum) as well as it provides faster, inexpensive, efficient and privacy-oriented data validation [24].

In order to mitigate V#2, traditional application separately implements functionality for keeping audit trails (aka logs). Audit trails provide transparency and proof for records integrity and accuracy. It also protects sensitive data from an intentional misuse or harm from involving parties in the business process. The audit trails in the traditional application are weak, vulnerable and subject to attacks [30]. The control remains to a designated authority in a traditional centralised approach. It does not provide transparent traceability and trust-able proof of audit trails integrity. In contrast, blockchain-based decentralised application manage records in an immutable ledger, which provides tamper-proof transparent audit trails with backward traceability [27]. In Ethereum, whenever a new transaction occurs it appends on the ledger and replicates among nodes over P2P network. Similarly, HLF provides the immutable ledger and rich traceability of ledger transactions [10].

The third vulnerability (V#3) is mitigated by incorporating the crypto functionality and digital signatures. The traditional application integrates crypto functionality to save data securely. Again, it lacks control over data. Since the centralised authority is responsible for an administration of the database and if the security is compromised then the attacker can steal, modify or remove the data. It does not matter if the data is stored is an encrypted format or not. These attacks are common in centralised traditional application [31]. Ethereum and HLF allow to save encrypted data on the ledger, so it becomes possible for a client node to encrypt the data before submitting a transaction. The records are difficult to modify or delete because of the consensus mechanism and ledger redundancy among nodes over P2P network and also because of an append-only structure of the blockchain. As Ethereum is a permissionless blockchain and anyone can read the data from the ledger, it is possible for an attacker to trigger deanonymization (linking) attack. In contrast, HLF overcomes this limitation by verified nodes and permissioned settings of the ledger.

The fourth vulnerability (V#4) is mitigated by implementing authorisation and access control. It is a security control [32] to check who can access the system and data. In a traditional application, authorisation and access control settings could be tampered because of centralised storage and weak auditing. Ethereum-based access control settings are hard to tamper because those are validated by the nodes. Also, the settings are distributed among nodes which makes impossible for an attacker to change on all the nodes. In Ethereum, it requires an extra effort/work to implement access control. In HLF, only verified nodes are allowed to participate in the network. It also provides fine-grained access control to share specific access rights among various nodes.

The last vulnerability (V#5) is related to the weak transmission channel. In the traditional application, it mitigated by providing secure communication with protocols that ensures the integrity of transit data. The weak implementation of communication protocols could be broken [33]. In this case, an attacker can intercept data transmission and modify the data. Ethereum overcomes this issue by splitting the data and storing them in random locations with their respective indexes. It also provides encrypted data communication. In the Ethereum-based P2P system, nodes can send and receive data directly from each other, also behave both as a server and as a client [34]. In Ethereum, the valid transaction is usually signed before submitting but the associated data is not encrypted by default [35]. In this case, the client node encrypts the transaction data and then submits it to the network [25]. The acting server node knows that the transacting data is correct and valid because of validation and consensus process [27]. Let's suppose, if an attacker tampers the data then it would not be validated during the validation and consensus process. Similarly, HLF provides encrypted data communication and validates the transit data.

6   Discussion

Even though implementing the STRIDE countermeasures to protect from tampering risk, the traditional approaches lack full control over data security. For example, the attacker could get access to the database, could tamper or delete it. The attacker could trigger a ransomware attack and encrypt the database. The attacker could send the malicious code and tamper the record. He leaves no traces because of the weak audit trails. The application has a weak authorisation and access control. Crypto functionality is not properly implemented. These are only a few limitations which counter by the traditional application.

Here it comes the blockchain solutions, which record each transaction in a tamper-proof immutable ledger. Blockchain supports an append-only ledger and saves every transaction with a unique cryptography hash. The consensus mechanism and validator nodes validates incoming data. The immutable ledger provides rich transparency, audibility and traceability. It ensures that the records on the ledger are accurate and unaltered. Ethereum is a permissionless blockchain platform for building a decentralised application. In some cases, Ethereum-based application is also not feasible; for example, a bank/financial or healthcare application where data visibility and privacy is critical. Ethereum platform is based on the permissionless blockchain so the ledger is publicly accessible. It is also expensive because of the administration fee and energy-waste POW consensus mechanism. In this case, permissioned blockchain-based solution is a feasible choice, for example, the application of the permissioned HLF platform.

Our current study has a few limitations. For example, the current approach has a limited number of literature sources which address mitigation of data tampering risk as comparing it to the existing ones. In this work, we performed a subjective literature based comparison. In general, the blockchain technology looks promising in the perspective of organisation security, but it is still in its infancy. There are not many blockchain applications in production to assess the security and their countermeasures on a larger scope. By overcoming these limitations could bring richer insights and enhancement in this paper results.

7   Concluding Remarks

In this work, we present a comparison of different solutions to mitigate the data tampering risk. More specifically we considered: (*i*) traditional techniques-based solutions, (*ii*) permissionless Ethereum-based solutions and (*iii*) permissioned

HLF-based solutions. Results of the study could be considered when evaluating the software design in the perspective of tampering risk to produce secure software.

Apart from the tampering risk, blockchain-based applications could help mitigating other security risks [4], like DoS/DDoS attack, MitM attack, side-channel attack and etc. However, the blockchain-based applications are not a *silver bullet*: for instance, a number of security risks (e.g., sybil attack, double spending attack, 51% attack and other) are among the frequently observed ones in the literature [4]. We plan to compare different solutions to mitigate them in future research.

As a part of the future work, we plan to develop a blockchain-based comprehensive security risk reference model in order to systematically evaluate the overall security of the blockchain-based application. The model would not be dependent on the specific blockchain type or blockchain platform. It would be generic enough to cover the other security risks and blockchain platforms.

Acknowledgement. This research has been supported by the Estonian Research Council (grant IUT20-55).

References

1. Sato, T., Himura, Y.: Smart-contract based system operations for permissioned blockchain. In: 2018 9th IFIP International Conference on New Technologies, Mobility and Security, NTMS 2018 - Proceedings 2018-Janua, pp. 1–6 (2018)
2. Chen, L., Lee, W.K., Chang, C.C., Choo, K.K.R., Zhang, N.: Blockchain based searchable encryption for electronic health record sharing. Future Gener. Comput. Syst. **95**, 420–429 (2019)
3. Tosh, D.K., Shetty, S., Liang, X., Kamhoua, C.A., Kwiat, K.A., Njilla, L.: Security implications of blockchain cloud with analysis of block withholding attack. In: Proceedings of 17th IEEE/ACM International Symposium on Cluster. Cloud and Grid Computing, CCGRID 2017, pp. 458–467 (2017)
4. Iqbal, M., Matulevičius, R.: Blockchain-based application security risks: a systematic literature review. In: Proper, H., Stirna, J. (eds.) CAiSE 2019. LNBIP, vol. 349, pp. 176–188. Springer, Cham (2019). https://doi.org/10.1007/978-3-030-20948-3_16
5. Microsoft: Transaction Integrator Threat Mitigation (2017)
6. Study.com: What is Data Tampering? - Definition & Prevention
7. Fimin, M.: Five early signs of data tampering (2017)
8. Khan, M.A., Salah, K.: IoT security: review, blockchain solutions, and open challenges. Future Gener. Comput. Syst. **82**, 395–411 (2018)
9. Ruffy, F., Hommel, W., Eye, F.V.: A STRIDE-based security architecture for software-defined networking. In: ICN 2016, The Fifteenth International Conference on Networks, no. c, pp. 95–101 (2016)
10. Chen, J., Ma, X., Du, M., Wang, Z.: A blockchain application for medical information sharing. In: TEMS-ISIE 2018–1st Annual International Symposium on Innovation and Entrepreneurship of the IEEE Technology and Engineering Management Society, pp. 1–7 (2018)

11. Gallo, P., Quoc Nguyen, U.: BlockSee: blockchain for IoT video surveillance in smart cities Suporn Pongnumkul NECTEC Thailand. In: 2018 IEEE International Conference on Environment and Electrical Engineering and 2018 IEEE Industrial and Commercial Power Systems Europe (EEEIC / I&CPS Europe), pp. 1–6 (2018)
12. Dubois, É., Mayer, N., Heymans, P., Matulevičius, R.: Intent. Perspect. Inf. Syst. Eng. **2010**, 1–384 (2014)
13. Matulevičius, R.: Fundamentals of Secure System Modelling, 1st edn. Springer, Heidelberg (2017). https://doi.org/10.1007/978-3-319-61717-6
14. Pradeepkumar, D.S., Singi, K., Kaulgud, V., Podder, S.: Evaluating complexity and digitizability of regulations and contracts for a blockchain application design. In: 2018 ACM/IEEE 1st International Workshop on Emerging Trends in Software Engineering for Blockchain, no. 1, pp. 25–29 (2018)
15. Ali, S., Wang, G., White, B., Cottrell, R.L.: A blockchain-based decentralized data storage and access framework for PingER. In: Proceedings - 17th IEEE International Conference on Trust, Security and Privacy in Computing and Communications and 12th IEEE International Conference on Big Data Science and Engineering, Trustcom/BigDataSE 2018, pp. 1303–1308 (2018)
16. Cha, S.C., Chen, J.F., Su, C., Yeh, K.H.: A blockchain connected gateway for BLE-based devices in the Internet of Things. IEEE Access **6**, 24639–24649 (2018)
17. Li, H., Zhu, L., Shen, M., Gao, F., Tao, X., Liu, S.: Blockchain-based data preservation system for medical data. J. Med. Syst. **42**, 1–13 (2018)
18. Lin, C., He, D., Huang, X., Choo, K.K.R., Vasilakos, A.V.: BSeIn: a blockchain-based secure mutual authentication with fine-grained access control system for industry 4.0. J. Netw. Comput. Appl. **116**(February), 42–52 (2018)
19. Alcarria, R., Bordel, B., Robles, T., Martín, D., Manso-Callejo, M.Á.: A blockchain-based authorization system for trustworthy resource monitoring and trading in smart communities. Sensors **18**(10), 3561 (2018)
20. Hjalmarsson, F.P., Hreioarsson, G.K., Hamdaqa, M., Hjalmtysson, G.: Blockchain-based e-voting system. 2018 IEEE 11th International Conference on Cloud Computing (CLOUD), pp. 983–986 (2018)
21. Pop, C., et al.: Decentralizing the stock exchange using blockchain an ethereum-based implementation of the Bucharest stock exchange, pp. 459–466 (2018)
22. Yu, B., Liu, J.K., Sakzad, A., Steinfeld, R., Rimba, P., Au, M.H.: Platform-Independent Secure Blockchain-Based Voting System, vol. 2433. Springer, Heidelberg (2018)
23. Sylim, P., Liu, F., Marcelo, A., Fontelo, P.: Blockchain technology for detecting falsified and substandard drugs in distribution: pharmaceutical supply chain intervention. J. Med. Internet Res. **20**(9), e10163 (2018)
24. Bhuiyan, Z.A., Wang, T., Wang, G.: Blockchain and big data to transform the healthcare, pp. 2–8 (2018)
25. Li, J., Wu, J., Chen, L.: Block-secure: blockchain based scheme for secure P2P cloud storage. Inf. Sci. **465**, 219–231 (2018)
26. García-Magariño, I., Lacuesta, R., Rajarajan, M., Lloret, J.: Security in networks of unmanned aerial vehicles for surveillance with an agent-based approach inspired by the principles of blockchain. Ad Hoc Netw. **86**, 72–82 (2019)
27. Dai, H., et al.: TrialChain: a blockchain-based platform to validate data integrity in large. Biomed. Res. Stud. 1–7 (2018)
28. Ray, S.: Blockchains versus Traditional Databases (2017)
29. Dexter, S.: How Are Blockchain Transactions Validated? Consensus VS Validation (2018)

30. Owasp: Top 10–2017 A10-Insufficient Logging & Monitoring (2017)
31. Domain, C.P.: From Yahoo to Uber, major hacks of data
32. Mellado, D., Blanco, C., Sánchez, L.E., Fernández-Medina, E.: A systematic review of security requirements engineering. Comput. Stand. Interfaces **32**(4), 153–165 (2010)
33. Rao, U.H., Nayak, U.: Understanding Networks and Network Security, pp. 187–204. Apress, Berkeley (2014)
34. Dagan, G.: The Actual Networking behind the Ethereum Network: How It Works (2018)
35. Pozo, A.: Ethereum: Signing and Validating (2017)

License Chain - An Identity-Protecting Intellectual Property License Trading Platform

Julian Kakarott$^{(\boxtimes)}$, Katharina Zeuch, and Volker Skwarek

Hamburg University of Applied Sciences, Ulmenliet 20, 21033 Hamburg, Germany
{julian.kakarott,katharina.zeuch,volker.skwarek}@haw-hamburg.de
https://www.haw-hamburg.de/

Abstract. This paper proposes a design for privacy-critical blockchain applications with a focus on license trading: Observing parties shall neither know about the licenses nor the identity of the parties involved. On the other hand trading partners, themselves shall only get the information disclosed after the deal is completed. The proposed platform-concept enables trading intellectual property licenses while simultaneously decreasing transaction costs. The manuscript contains a concept analysis regarding privacy and security issues.

Keywords: Blockchain · Hyperledger Fabric · License trading · Privacy critical application · Identity protected transactions · Channels

1 Introduction

Intellectual property (IP) nowadays has to be seen as a managerial resource [30]. As a resource, it is desirable for every given company to be able to monetize it with marginal transaction costs. [13] shows that intellectual properties can be seen as intangible assets that entail payments in the form of fees. However, the market for IP licenses is unstructured and contains countless obstacles that obstruct effortless transactions. Looking at the structure of this particular market, the decision criteria of [4] identifies this as a reasonable use case for blockchain technology.

This paper proposes a blockchain based IP trading platform which is supposed to reach a large customer group, by being open and simultaneously identity-protecting. The sold licenses of the IPs shall be traceable and immutable - indicators for the usage of a blockchain-protocol [29].

The architectural concept of this platform will be called "License Chain". The paper describes the general idea of the concept as well as the licensing process of intellectual properties and evaluates the security of the concept. The decentralized scheme is based on Hyperledger Fabric. This enables the setup of so-called channels - independent ledgers each with its own set of participants, rules, and chaincodes. There are separate channels for the information stacks *IP*

© Springer Nature Switzerland AG 2019
C. Di Ciccio et al. (Eds.): BPM 2019 Blockchain and CEE Forum, LNBIP 361, pp. 29–42, 2019.
https://doi.org/10.1007/978-3-030-30429-4_3

specific data, user data and *transactions*. The transactions are solely stored as hash values on the blockchain. The original contracts, including the hash value saved on the ledger of one of the three channels, are separately stored at the contractual partners. This ensures secure and anonymous trading.

2 Concept

The License Chain concept relies on a simple premise. Intellectual properties generate value through licensing.

Licenses are contracts that allow the licensee to use a specific product, service or technology in exchange for a license fee. As the licensing process is the main function of the License Chain, the process will be described in detail. Functionalities exceeding the pure license trading feature will be discussed in a following paper.

Generally speaking, market participants are willing to license IPs, if the agreement raises the profit of licensor and licensee. Despite its importance, Gans and Stern [11] and Hagiu and Yoffie [14] showed that the IP license market is tremendously inefficient. To understand what this means, it is worth it to look at a paper of Eugene Fama [9]. He described in his paper "Efficient Capital Markets: A Review of Theory and Empirical Work." how efficient markets work and which characteristics they have. Fama [9] names three criteria of market efficiency. According to his paper, a market is efficient, if

1. "all agree on the implications of current information for the current prices",
2. "all available information is costlessly available to all market participants",
3. "there are no transaction costs" [9, p. 387].

The first criterion describes a natural property of a functioning market. Therefore, it is assumed that this market mechanism will set in as soon as the other two criteria are fulfilled. Therefore this mechanism will not be discussed in this paper. As mentioned before, intellectual properties come in all kinds of forms. Some might not be as confidential as others, but in order to create a platform for all possible IPs, the highest possible level of confidentiality should be met. To some companies, it might be crucial to keep the IPs they are working with a secret. If their competitors knew which properties they have licensed, they might get an insight into the firm's strategy. Therefore, it is absolutely essential for the network to limit the access to contractual data to as few parties as possible. That being said, Famas criterion number two has to be weakened. Not all information should be available to all participants, but rather all information that is essential to make a sell or buy decision.

Whenever two parties engage with each other on equal terms, transaction costs occur [5]. This problem is especially severe for intellectual properties like technologies and inventions [20]. It becomes obvious that the transaction costs of IP licenses are significantly higher than the transaction costs of other financial products like stocks. In the stock market, it is much easier to find a trading partner because of brokers who act as intermediaries. Moreover, the valuation of the asset is transparent. That being said, transaction costs in the stock market consist of fees for the brokerage service. Most importantly, these fees are profit related. Therefore, neither the buyer (licensee) nor the seller (IP owner) has initiation costs prior to the trade. Usually, when trading IP licenses, both parties have initiation costs regardless of whether a deal is made or not. The License Chain concept makes the IP license market more efficient by limiting transaction costs to profit-related fees. It is hoped that this stimulates IP owners and potential licensees to join the market as initiation costs are dramatically reduced.

2.1   Trusted Partners

Due to the fact that the application possibilities for a particular intellectual property might be incomprehensible for the owner and the potential licensee might not know what to look for, there is an intermediary needed. They are only needed if the transacting partners do not detect the opportunity by themselves. The intermediary has to have broad knowledge about specific areas and branches. Brokers are considered as potential sales partners. The operator of the License Chain would name brokers as "trusted partners" based on their know-how and ability to consult firms in certain branches or fields. The partners would then be equipped with certified hardware in order to participate as peers within the License Chain network. They play an important part in the transaction process which will be described below.

2.2   System Architecture

To raise data security the information set is split into three subsets. The first one includes information about the intellectual property, the second one consists of the identities of the contractual partners and the third one includes the licenses. Those subsets are implemented in Hyperledger Fabric as separate channels. In the following, these channels will be described in detail.

IP Channel

Channel number one contains information regarding the intellectual properties. In order to simplify the search for potential buyers, most IPs should be presented publicly on a web platform. This will further reduce transaction costs. The key information regarding the registered IP will be written on the ledger of the IP Channel. This includes a hash value of the property and the public key of the owner. It is not necessary to save the entire IP on the ledger. It just has to be unambiguously identifiable.

Identity Channel

Identities are more confidential than IP information. Therefore, they will be treated in a different way. The identities of all participants are only known by the operator of the License Chain Platform and the trusted partners. Partners need to have access to the identities to fulfill their broker functions. The identities are saved on a separated certified off-chain server. The public key of every user is needed for a successful transaction and is saved on this channel for reference purposes.

License Channel

When designing the License Chain concept, it seems intuitive to use Hyperledger Fabric private data collections to store contracts. For instance, the data could be stored on the peers of brokers who negotiated the license agreement.

However, the private data collection seemed to create unnecessary risks for the contractual partners. There is no strict necessity to store the contracts on third-party servers. As shown below, the License Chain concept has no need for storing the contracts at all. As the information of licensing agreements should remain between the involved parties, other participants of the network neither know which IPs have been licensed nor who bought the licenses. Thus, only a hash value of the agreement is stored on the ledger of the license channel for every transaction. The transaction data is not stored within the network or on License Chain servers. It is only sent to the contractual partners. Figure 1 shows a schematic overview of the License Chain architecture. As described above, the concept consists of three channels (IP, Identities, and Licenses). They all have their own ledger and consist of peers that have individual chaincodes. The user accesses the peers via the client application, which displays information to the user like a web interface.

2.3   Licensing Process

In the following, the process of licensing an IP through the License Chain is described, as it is by far the most frequent transaction. Over the course of this process, a deeper understanding of the functionality of the License Chain is conveyed.

All processes follow the mechanisms described in the Hyperledger Fabric Documentation [16] for Hyperledger Fabric Version 1.2. Nevertheless, the mechanisms are individualized in order to fit the purpose of the License Chain. The License Chain does not claim to create a high-frequency market comparable to the stock market or online retail. It is assumed that there is plenty of communication between buyer and seller before a licensing contract is made. Therefore, the platform does not have to execute transactions with abnormal speed.

After a potential license buyer has found an IP he wants to license, the terms of the agreement have to be negotiated. The buyer could have found the IP by himself using the online platform or he could have been helped by a broker. The first one is the easiest case which is why this case serves as a blueprint for the following transaction process. The parties will form an agreement including but not limited to the identities of the contractual partners, the IP identification number (ID) as well as price and duration of the agreement. After getting access to the platform via a web interface, the owner of the IP is able to propose the trade. Within their user account, IP owners are able to govern licenses of their properties. The website will offer a predetermined interface, in which the seller has to enter the parameters of the agreement. In order to identify the buyer

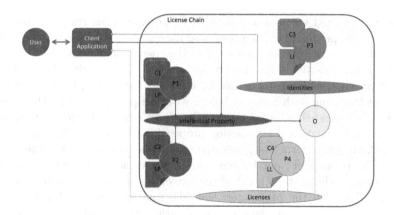

Fig. 1. Hyperleder Fabric based model of the License Chain Concept. P: Peer, C: Chaincode, L: Ledger, O: Ordering Node

distinctively, the seller has to state the public key of the buyer. After the seller has completed his entries, a message is created that is split into two parts. The first part includes the ID of the IP, which is also saved on the ledger of the IP Channel. This part of the message is readable for the application it is sent to. The second part of the message includes all other parameters that are necessary for the trade. This part is cryptographically signed with the private key that the user entered during the submission process. Both parts are sent to the client application.

In order to read the transaction parameters, the application will have to decrypt the second part of the message using the public key of the IP owner. In doing so, the application will look for the public key that is stored with the intellectual property ID within the IP Channel. This is redundancy in order to check whether the user was authorized to license the IP. Moreover, it will look for the public key of the buyer on the Identity Channel.

Now that the application has verified the message, it can process it. First of all, it will create a random value. The value and the parameters of the agreement will be hashed until only one hash value remains. A random value ensures by the principle of adding salt-and-pepper-noise that the transaction gets a unique hash even if a second transaction with the exact same parameters is transmitted. Moreover, if a third party would be interested in deducting the details of the agreement, it would not only have to guess the parameters and look for the right hash value in the License Channel but also guess the random value correctly. The required effort makes it unattractive to even try guessing. Afterward, the client application deposits the parameters and the random number in the user account of the buyer. The buyer logs into his account and gets the ability to review the information entered by the seller. If the information does not reflect the original agreement, the buyer can reject the offer and the seller is notified. In this case, all data regarding the original offer would be deleted and the seller has the ability to renew his offer. If the buyer agrees with the proposal, the process is continued towards a transaction. To express his consent, the buyer has to enter his private key. An automated message with a declaration of intent is signed with the private key and send to the client application.

The application should be able to decrypt the message with the public key of the buyer that was entered earlier by the seller. Moreover, it should be able to recreate the same hash value as before with the parameters and the random value that are included in the message of the buyer, as they should be the same as before. If this is the case, a transaction proposal is formed. The transaction will invoke a chaincode to write the generated hash value on the ledger of the License Channel. Therefore, both parties can refer to the value on the ledger if there is any discrepancy about the content of the agreement. Both are able to reproduce the hash value with the parameters and the random number that have been given to them. To prevent the client application itself from being fraudulent, it will not pass the hash value to the chaincodes, because it could have been manipulated, but rather the parameters and the random value itself, so that the chaincode, which is assumed to be working the way expected, will calculate the hash value on its own. In order to fool the system, the chaincodes on the majority of the peer would have to be manipulated. The invoked chaincode takes the parameters delivered by the transaction proposal as input and the chaincode gets executed against the current version of the ledger. The execution produces transaction results which include a response value, write set and read set. It is important to note that no update of the ledger was made up to this point. The peers sign their response and send it back to the client application, which collects the so-called "endorsements". Every partner and the operator has one peer in the License Channel. The License Chain concept assumes that all partners act as honest, impartial validators during the endorsement process. They are trusted to keep sensitive information confidential. If a majority of the peers respond with a proper endorsement, the transaction is submitted to the ordering service and the hash value is written on the ledger of the License Channel.

Finally, the client application is notified that the hash value has successfully been written on the ledger. The application creates a PDF printout that includes the parameters of the agreement, the random value, and the hash value and sends it to the seller and the buyer via email. The document serves as the official contract between the two parties. With this document, both parties can refer to the hash value stored on the ledger. As the licensing process is complete, the client application can delete all information regarding the transaction.

3   Licensing Process Security

Taking a look at the described licensing process shows several security issues.

3.1   Privacy

The first thing that comes to mind is the apparent loss of privacy due to the platform. Trusted partners and the License Chain operator only gain access to the plain data of the identity of all users. But due to the complexity of the market, this is not avoidable. Trusted partners are needed as brokers to match owners of intellectual property and potential buyers. They do not have access to information regarding agreements they have not initialized or assisted. Thus, it has to be stated that a loss of privacy exists but is necessary for the licensing market to work properly. But it is not a security risk for the users unless the trusted partners turn out to not behave trustworthily. If partners start to act untrustworthy that would also cause economical risks to License Chain and its users.

That leads to the next possible security thread. What happens if the assumption of honesty fails and trusted partners start behaving dishonestly?

This remains a single point of attack. To avoid this it is recommended to built up criteria that potential partners have to fulfill to become trusted partners. It is also assumed that all partners and the operator work as correctives for each other. This mechanism increases the trust in the affiliated partners.

3.2 Random Number Generation

A further security issue might be the random value creation. The applied random value generation algorithm is an important issue because every random number has to be unique. A suitable algorithm should meet the criteria mentioned by Stickler and Schachinger [27, p. 174]: producing pseudo-random numbers as close as possible to real random numbers, generate long periods so that the numbers do not repeat, be reproducible, be fast.

If these properties are not met, the random numbers might not remain unique. It is possible that the generated "random" numbers occur repeatedly. If a licensing contract expires, two parties might decide to trade the same IP again under the same contract conditions. To a certain probability, the random value generator could generate the same random value as before. Therefore two transactions could look exactly the same and create the same hash value. The uniqueness of transactions would no longer be given. To address this issue each generation of a random value is proposed to take the previous transaction's hash as seed.

3.3 Chaincode Security

One main aspect of a well functioning licensing process is the chaincodes used. Since chaincodes once deployed cannot be deleted, special attention has to be paid to accurate and error-free chaincode development. Although Hyperledger Fabric allows upgrading chaincodes [15] that does not mean deleting previous errors. It only enables activation of newer chaincode versions and thereby enables running multiple chaincode versions at the same time, which could cause security issues due to incompatibility. Faulty chaincodes like infinite loops [15, p. 4] should be avoided. A possibility to reduce chaincode errors to a minimum is presented by chaincode proving services. But it should be kept in mind that such services might thereby know the complete License Chain chaincodes and store that. This could be seen as a security issue because it enables the chaincode service provider to use potential security vulnerabilities that are not yet fixed.

3.4 Endorsement Policy

The endorsement policy of the License Chain is to be a majority decision. The majority can be gained comparatively easy if only a few peers have to endorse the transaction. If a trusted partner starts behaving dishonest or an attacker wants to compromise the network, only a few peers need to be convinced to act dishonestly for example by discussion or bribery. To make this more difficult it is recommended to keep the required percentage majority as high as possible, for the described security reasons, but also as low as necessary in order to keep the License Chain operational.

Taking another look at the licensing process and its chaincodes it is recognized that all chaincodes are triggered only by the website client application. That remains a single point of attack and causes the need for particular attention on frontend security.

4   General License Chain Security

In addition to the process, specific security issues the security of the underlying blockchain must also be analyzed. Figure 2 shows how mentioned security issues could be assigned to the blockchain stack layers proposed by Zhang and Jacobsen [31]. It includes attacks and security issues on the licensing process described above and also general concerns on the License Chain security discussed below.

It can be observed that there are possible attacks on all blockchain stack layers. Thereby it can be deduced that the usage of blockchain itself does not prevent upcoming attacks on the system.

Following several possible attacks and further security issues on the License Chain blockchain structure are discussed.

4.1   Selection of Hashing Algorithm

Hash values are used to compress data and uniquely represent it without revealing its content. According to [25, p. 303] hashing algorithms, also called hash functions, have to fulfill the properties of arbitrary message size, fixed output length, and efficiency. For security reasons they also have to provide preimage resistance, second image resistance, and hard collision resistance. Especially hard collision resistance and preimage resistance are very important regarding the License Chain concept in order to prevent trading of non-existing or wrong IP.

The most commonly known hashing algorithms are Message Digest 5 (MD5) and Secure Hashing Algorithm (SHA)-family. MD5 proposed by [26] is not collision free [6]. SHA-2, as well as SHA-3, seem to be secure hashing standards. Both are supporting output lengths longer then 200 bit as well as collision freeness [8, p. 9]; [6, p. 5]. Following the result of [6], the usage of SHA-3 is recommended

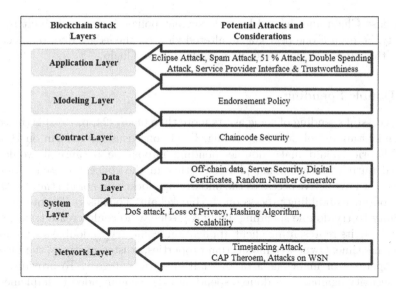

Fig. 2. Transfer of Security Concerns on License Chain to Blockchain Stack Layers (inspired by blockchain stack layers of [31])

for hashing data on the License Chain. Due to the possible future development of hashing algorithms, it is required to regularly control if the hashing algorithm is collision free.

4.2 51% Attack

One well known attack is the 51% attack described by [23,24] and [19]. Like described for License Chain a majority based endorsement rule is assumed, similar to mechanisms like Proof-of-Work. Therefore the system is vulnerable to 51% attacks. The License Chain concept works on the basis of a permissioned Hyperledger Fabric blockchain. Therefore only known partners are chosen to be network peers and enabled to participate in the consensus process. Thus it is assumed that there will be no incentive for them to try a 51% attack. All participating peers are interested in ensuring that the system works manipulation-free. Further, an attack is only sensible from an attackers point of view, if he has knowledge about a certain transaction. That is why the License Chain does not allow any partner to view plain contract information like the IP traded, the owner of it or the price paid. That means an attacker gaining access to the license channel does not automatically have access to data stored on the Identity and IP Channel which would give the information needed for an expedient attack.

4.3 Eclipse Attack

An eclipse attack like mentioned by [22] and [19] can end up in isolation of single client applications. Transactions are processed not only by one peer of the License Chain and defined by endorsement policy consensus is built by the majority. So even if one peer got an altered view on the ledger due to an eclipse attack, that does not lead to an inoperable License Chain.

4.4   Double Spending

"[...] successful spending of some assets more than once" [24, p. 1092] is the common understanding of double-spending. Used consensus mechanism on Hyperledger Fabric should make double-spending impossible because it would be detected during the endorsing phase. Further in the concept presented single users do not have active access to the underlying blockchain nor are they involved in the consensus-building process on the blockchain. Thus users do not have the possibility to try double spending. Only someone, who could create transaction proposals by its representing client application, could try to double spend an IP at the same time. Owners of intellectual properties, trusted partners, the License Chain operator or malicious attackers fall into this category. To provide additional security against such double spending it is recommended to implement a rule that only allows selling a license to the same buyer once.

4.5   Spam Attack

A spam attack, flooding a network with transactions so that the block creation gets delayed, is described by [22]. Transactions can only be invoked by client applications. The License Chain only has a limited number of client applications that can invoke chaincodes and thereby create transactions. These client applications are either representing trusted partners, the License Chain website or the License Chain operator.

A spam attack on the License Chain would only work if a trusted partner or an owner of IP decides to flood the network with trading proposals sent to potential buyers. This scenario could cause an overload on the processing peers. If proposals are accepted by buyers or maliciously cooperating client applications, transactions would be sent to their peers. The peers would process the transactions, which could cause the network to overload as well. That would lead to delayed processing of transactions and block creation. Another possibility to flood the network is to double spend licenses to one buyer, who is not recognizing the double spending. But security against such flooding is given by measures against double spending described above.

The limited number of client applications enabled to create transactions limits the possible number of spam attackers. Besides that, only an attacker who tampered the License Chain website could create transactions by controlling this client application. But this should be prevented by frontend security. Concluding a spam attack cannot be excluded, but seems unlikely on the License Chain due to the mentioned reasons.

4.6 Off-chain Data

Blockchain principles only affect on-chain matters. All data stored off-chain and not written on the chain is not protected by them [31]. Therefore this data has to be protected in other ways. Off-chain data storage will remain a single point of attack for sensitive data even if off-chain servers are made as secure as possible. As the [2] shows in its study, there are several weaknesses of servers working off-chain. To provide data security the License Chain should at least follow the solution approaches proposed by [2, p. 75–100] to secure their servers.

4.7 DoS Attack

A Denial of Service (DoS) attack aims to overtax the system so that it looses availability and is no longer able to work accurately [22,24]. Regarding blockchain systems, this implies an inability to process transactions any more. Although [4] state an infeasibility of DoS attacks for blockchains, due to its data redundancy by distribution, it is assumed that a blockchain network would become unable to process veritable transaction data like stated by [24, p. 1091]. For the License Chain, this could be weakened by an alteration of the used consensus mechanism following the approach of [28]. But DoS attacks cannot be excluded.

4.8 Considerations on Scalability

A blockchain network always bounces between the amount of throughput possible and the number of nodes the network can handle [18, p. 9]. Only trusted partners and the License Chain operator will maintain blockchain peers. Hyperledger based blockchain peers represent the nodes acting on the blockchain and joining the consensus process [17]. It can, therefore, be concluded, that this characteristic of scalability will not become a problem to the License Chain, because the number of peers on the License Chain will not grow big enough. Furthermore like stated by [31] transaction throughput is a characteristic of scalability. The trading of intellectual property licenses is a slow process. That is why the amount of upcoming transactions is not expected to be higher than a Hyperledger blockchain is capable of processing.

4.9 Considerations on CAP Theorem

Brewer [1] stated the CAP theorem in his keynote speech saying that any shared-data system "can have at most two" of the properties consistency, availability, and partition-tolerance. As [7, p.475] assume blockchain technology could provide consistency because the blockchain state should be the same at all participating blockchain nodes. Because blockchain networks only provide *eventual synchrony* [12, p. 32], the provided consistency can be assumed as also being *eventual consistency* [3, p. 24]. For the same reason - the distribution of the blockchain state - blockchain technology, and therefore also the License Chain, could provide partition-tolerance. The blockchain remains working even if parts of the network are split off. Taking into account the considerations of [21, p. 5] the Hyperledger Fabric blockchain technology also achieves availability. The situation could be different in the case of the License Chain web interface, through which users interact with the blockchain. This could, caused by error or attack, become unavailable.

4.10   Frontend Security

The web interface is an important part of the License Chain. It is the first impression potential users get to see and it is the access point for users to the License Chain. That is why high data traffic on the web interface is assumed. Included are also sensitive data needed to fill out registration forms or trading proposals. Therefore the website security should gain a high priority in the License Chain development process. It has a high impact on the overall License Chain security. Like [24, p. 1091] states the whole system "[...] could be compromised" by an insecure frontend. [10] recommends acting like "all clients connecting to you are potentially compromised or malicious". Therefore website users should not be given choices that enable malicious behavior like described by [10, p.81].

5   Conclusion

Today's license market for intellectual properties is inefficient due to unattractively high transaction costs. Those have been reduced by the creation of a trading platform that limits the transaction costs to profit-related fees. Because the participants can receive help from specialized brokers during all phases of the licensing process, it is possible for every IP owner to license their intellectual properties without initiation costs. This concept could have an impact on a variety of intellectual properties. Those range from common IPs like music or movies to extremely complex properties like patents.

Moreover, the security of the concept aspects has been analyzed by discussing several security issues. The blockchain technology backbone of the License Chain enriches the trading process by economic and technological security aspects. Conditions of a license trade are stored on-chain as a hash value, which enables the trading partners to proof their trade beyond doubt. This is provided while the privacy of licensees is guaranteed since no one else other than the License Chain operator and trusted partners have access to sensitive data. Transactions are not traceable since no transaction data is stored permanently. Although the License Chain increases security for IP license trading by using blockchain technology, some security issues remain. These cannot be completely ruled out, but are unlikely to happen due to the composition and structure of the License Chain based on a Hyperledger Fabric blockchain.

Acknowledgements. This research was conducted within the framework of the project HANSEBLOC and supported by Bundesministerium für Bildung und Forschung (BMBF-Förderung Nr. 03VNE2044D).

References

1. Brewer, E.A.: Towards robust distributed systems (abstract). In: Proceedings of the Nineteenth Annual ACM Symposium on Principles of Distributed Computing - PODC 2000, Portland, Oregon, USA, p. 7. ACM Press (2000). https://doi.org/10.1145/343477.343502, ISBN 978-1-58113-183-3
2. Bundesamt für Sicherheit in der Informationstechnik (BSI). Absicherung eines Servers (ISi-Server) (2013)
3. Bundesamt für Sicherheit in der Informationstechnik (BSI). Blockchain Sicher Gestalten - Konzepte, Anforderungen, Bewertungen, March 2019
4. Chowdhury, M.J.M., et al.: Blockchain versus database: a critical analysis. In: 2018 17th IEEE International Conference on Trust, Security and Privacy in Computing and Communications/12th IEEE International Conference on Big Data Science and Engineering (TrustCom/BigDataSE), New York, NY, USA, vol. 00186, pp. 1348–1353. IEEE, August 2018. https://doi.org/10.1109/TrustCom/BigDataSE.2018.00186, ISBN 978-1-5386-4388-4
5. Coase, R.: The nature of the firm. Economica 4(16), 386–405 (1937)
6. Debnath, S., Chattopadhyay, A., Dutta, S.: Brief review on journey of secured hash algorithms. In: 2017 4th International Conference on Opto-Electronics and Applied Optics (Optronix), pp. 1–5, November 2017. https://doi.org/10.1109/OPTRONIX.2017.8349971
7. DeCusatis, C., Zimmermann, M., Sager, A.: Identity-based network security for commercial blockchain services. In: 2018 IEEE 8th Annual Computing and Communication Workshop and Conference (CCWC), Las Vegas, NV, pp. 474–477. IEEE, January 2018. https://doi.org/10.1109/CCWC.2018.8301713, ISBN 978-1-5386-4649-6
8. Dworkin, M.J.: SHA-3 standard: permutation-based hash and extendable-output functions. NIST FIPS 202. National Institute of Standards and Technology, July 2015. https://doi.org/10.6028/NIST.FIPS.202
9. Fama, E.: Efficient capital markets: a review of theory and empirical work. J. Finance 25(2), 383–417 (1970)
10. Robert Fly: Detecting fraud on websites. IEEE Secur. Priv. Mag. 9(6), 80–85 (2011). https://doi.org/10.1109/MSP.2011.161, ISSN 1540–7993
11. Gans, J., Stern, S.: Is there a market for ideas? Ind. Corp. Change 19(3), 805–837 (2010)
12. Gilbert, S., Lynch, N.: Perspectives on the CAP theorem. Computer 45(2), 30–36 (2012). https://doi.org/10.1109/MC.2011.389, ISSN 0018–9162
13. Günter, M., Gisler, M.: Intellectual properties as intangible goods. In: Hawaii International Conference on System Sciences (2000). ISBN 0-7695-0493-0/00
14. Hagiu, A., Yoffie, D.B.: The new patent intermediaries: platforms, defensive aggregators, and super-aggregators. J. Econ. Perspect. 27(1), 45–66H (2013)
15. Hyperledger Foundation. Chaincode for Operators (2017). https://hyperledger-fabric.readthedocs.io/en/release-1.2/chaincode4noah.html. Accessed 28 Sept 2018
16. Hyperledger Foundation: Hyperledger Fabric Documentation (2017). https://hyperledger-fabric.readthedocs.io/en/release-1.2/. Accessed 02 Sept 2018
17. Hyperledger Foundation: Peers (2017). https://hyperledger-fabric.readthedocs.io/en/release-1.2/peers/peers.html. Accessed 21 Sept 2018
18. Li, et al.: Towards scalable and private industrial blockchains. In: Proceedings of the ACM Workshop on Blockchain, Cryptocurrencies and Contracts - BCC 2017. The ACM Workshop, Abu Dhabi, United Arab Emirates, pp. 9–14. ACM Press (2017). https://doi.org/10.1145/3055518.3055531, ISBN 978-1-4503-4974-1

19. Li, X., et al.: A survey on the security of blockchain systems. Future Gener. Comput. Syst. (2017). https://doi.org/10.1016/j.future.2017.08.020, ISSN 0167739X
20. Merges, R., Nelson, R.: On the complex economics of patent scope. Columbia Law Rev. **90**, 839–916 (1990)
21. Moubarak, J., Filiol, E., Chamoun, M.: Comparative analysis of blockchain technologies and TOR network: two faces of the same reality? In: 2017 1st Cyber Security in Networking Conference (CSNet), Rio de Janeiro, pp. 1–9. IEEE, October 2017. https://doi.org/10.1109/CSNET.2017.8242004, ISBN 978-1-5386-1332-0
22. Moubarak, J., Filiol, E., Chamoun, M.: On blockchain security and relevant attacks. In: 2018 IEEE Middle East and North Africa Communications Conference (MENACOMM). Institute of Electrical and Electronics Engineers (2018). OCLC: 1048269446, ISBN 978-1-5386-1254-5, 978-1-5386-1253-8, 978-1-5386-1255-2
23. Nakamoto, S.: Bitcoin: a peer-to-peer electronic cash system (2008)
24. Ogiela, M.R., Majcher, M.: Security of distributed ledger solutions based on blockchain technologies. In: 2018 IEEE 32nd International Conference on Advanced Information Networking and Applications (AINA), Krakow, pp. 1089–1095. IEEE, May 2018. https://doi.org/10.1109/AINA.2018.00156, ISBN 978-1-5386-2195-0
25. Paar, C., Pelzl, J.: Understanding Cryptography. Springer, Heidelberg (2010). https://doi.org/10.1007/978-3-642-04101-3, ISBN 978-3-642-44649-8, 978-3-642-04101-3
26. Rivest, R.: The MD5 Message-Digest Algorithm, April 1992
27. Stickler, B.A., Schachinger, E.: Basic Concepts in Computational Physics, 377 p. Springer, Cham (2014). OCLC: 869872006, ISBN 978-3-319-02435-6, 978-3-319-02434-9
28. Ulybyshev, D., et al.: Blockhub: blockchain-based software development system for untrusted environments. In: 2018 IEEE 11th International Conference on Cloud Computing (2018)
29. Richter, S., Witt, J.: Ein problemzentrierter Blick auf Blockchain - Anwendungsfälle. Lüneburg (2018)
30. Xia, H.: Industrial-Design-Centered Intellectual Property Strategy of the Company. In: Institute of Electrical and Electronics Engineers (2010). ISBN 978-1-4244-5161-6/10
31. Zhang, K., Jacobsen, H.-A.: Towards dependable, scalable, and pervasive distributed ledgers with blockchains. In: 2018 IEEE 38th International Conference on Distributed Computing Systems (ICDCS), Vienna, pp. 1337–1346. IEEE, July 2018. https://doi.org/10.1109/ICDCS.2018.00134, ISBN 978-1-5386-6871- 9

Defining and Delimitating Distributed Ledger Technology: Results of a Structured Literature Analysis

Maik Lange[✉], Steven Chris Leiter[✉], and Rainer Alt

Leipzig University, 04109 Leipzig, Germany
{mlange, leiter}@wifa.uni-leipzig.de,
rainer.alt@uni-leipzig.de

Abstract. There are currently different views in the scientific community on how the distributed ledger technology (DLT) relates to the blockchain technology. Some view them as synonyms, whereas others view DLT as the umbrella term for all blockchain related technologies. This paper approaches this topic by deriving definitions and core characteristics of DLT and blockchain technology. By using these definitions and an additional market research, a categorization for DLT and blockchain can be created. This categorization will operate as an additional component for IT-architects to decide on appropriate DLT solutions for their specific distributed ledger use cases.

Keywords: Digital ledger · Distributed ledger technology · DLT · Blockchain · Directed acyclic graph · Sharded ledger

1 The Origin of Distributed Ledger Technology

Fueled by the highly volatile development of cryptocurrencies, like bitcoin, the distributed ledger technology (DLT) has gained attention from technology experts across industries. Currently, DLT is following the Gartner [1] innovation hype cycle and is in the *"phase of disillusionment"*. By following this cycle, it is expected to reach a stable level of maturity in the future [2].

The technology of distributed ledgers and blockchain (BC) is built on the concept of ledgers. These initially come from the accounting sector and are a collection of a group of similar accounts in double-entry bookkeeping. Accounting ledgers summarize financial information as debits and credits and show the current balances of single accounts. Therefore, bookkeeping processes are building the foundation for most of the transactions of current economies [3].

The introduction of the internet and the connection of digital ledger to network systems, like enterprise planning systems, led to another increase in efficiency and enabled automated transactions across companies. Today, nearly every company, but especially the E-Business sector, uses some kind of digital ledgers in their IT

M. Lainge and S. C. Leiter—Equally contributed. R. Alt—Parentally contributed.

C. Di Ciccio et al. (Eds.): BPM 2019 Blockchain and CEE Forum, LNBIP 361, pp. 43–54, 2019.
https://doi.org/10.1007/978-3-030-30429-4_4

landscape. While the value generation happens through cooperation across companies, each company keeps its own record of transaction between partners. This happens in each company in specific central databases. The rise of distributed ledger technologies allows the use of shared digital ledgers for value generation. Through these new technologies, a more efficient use of each companies' capabilities can be enabled [4]. As like many emerging technologies, there is some confusion what the technology exactly covers and what its boundaries are. Based on the expected importance for economic transaction processes, a clear understanding of what the BC technology and the related DLT entail and how they could be classified is necessary and will support efficient implementation of market use cases. This generally valid clarification has not been settled by researchers, regulators or general accepted experts yet.

The first examples of these technologies were BCs like Bitcoin [4] and further developments enhanced it. As the applicable use cases evolved the technology evolved with it to a point where the earlier definitions do not fit the current state of the technology. For this reason, there are currently varying opinions in the scientific literature what BCs are, and where the borders to DLTs are. This also influences the practical applicability, as many practitioners manly think of cryptocurrencies when speaking about DLT and BC technology.

Therefore, this paper aims to determine a common understanding by deriving characteristics of both terms. By this, the research addresses scientists and practitioners at the intersection of DLT use case applications and IT architects, in addition to that the research delivers a benefit for the whole DLT community. To derive the common understanding, a scientific literature review was conducted, which focused on the used definitions in current scientific publications in the area. These definitions were then split into their single components resulting in a quantitative analysis of the mentioned characteristics. Using these, definitions for both terms were derived. To additionally understand how the terms relate to each other, a market research was conducted to either identify BCs that not fulfill the DLT definition or DLTs that not fulfill the BC definition and therefore to understand if both technologies are on the same level, or one is the umbrella term of the other. Afterwards the importance of DLTs for e-business is explained and an outlook with further research topics will be given.

2 Analysis of the Terms DLT and BC

2.1 Scientific Literature Review for DLT and BC

A systematic literature review was conducted following the vom Brocke et al. [5] approach. After the definition of the review scope and the conceptualization of the topic, the literature search, an analysis and synthesis led to a final research agenda.

The search was limited to results starting from 2008, as this is the year Nakamoto [6] released the bitcoin white paper that started the surge of BC solutions. The search was also limited to peer-reviewed, full-access papers and focused on the search terms *"Distributed Ledger"*, *"DLT types"*, *"DLT ecosystem"*, *"distributed ledger types"*, *"distributed ledger ecosystem"* and *"DLT"* in the databases IEEE xplore, Springer Link, ACM and EBSCO host. For each search term the databases were analyzed, and a set of papers selected. After this procedure, a total of 74 relevant papers remained, which then were examined.

The analysis of the literature is split into two parts, each of which focuses on either DLT or BC. The goal is to create a quantitative analysis for the core characteristics of each term. The expectation behind this quantitative analysis is that core characteristics are mentioned in most of the definitions. On the other hand, characteristics that are only mentioned a few times are not considered to be as important and are not central aspects of the term [7].

2.2 Shared Identity and Characteristics of DLT and BC

The research revealed different views regarding the relationship between DLT and BC. Some authors suggest that the terms are synonyms and represent the same concept [8]. Some view DLT as the umbrella term for concepts like BC and similar technologies [9, 10] and, additionally, there is a third group that views DLTs and BCs as related but independent technologies [11]. To ascertain which view may be considered the most reliable, it is necessary to first determine the characteristics that define DLTs and BCs.

In each of the selected papers, either the term DLT (22 definition attempts), BC (44 definition attempts) or both were defined (8 definition attempts) or shortly described. The number of analyzed papers has been raised until the ranking of optional and core features has stabilized. The said definitions were then extracted and split into their components for each term. These components were then grouped into related features and each of the mentioned characteristics counted. Depending on the number of mentions, the characteristics were split into two groups: core characteristics that must all be fulfilled in order to be classified as a DLT or BC; and optional features that may be fulfilled but are not mandatory. Characteristics mentioned by less than 20% of the sources were categorized as optional [7]. The complete list of mentions for each component can be found in the appendix (Fig. 1).

The **core characteristics** for DLT are described in detail in Table 1 and visualized in Fig. 2.

From these core characteristics, a definition for the term DLT can be created:

"Distributed Ledger Technologies are one type of distributed database shared over a peer-to-peer network, where transaction data is synchronized between nodes of the network and the data is immutably stored and secured through cryptographic techniques. Decisions in the network are managed through consensus algorithms."

Additional to the characteristics shared between DLTs and BCs, there are some core characteristics of BCs that are only optional features of DLTs (Table 2).

Based on these additional characteristics mentioned by the authors, a new definition for the BC term can be created:

"A blockchain is a transaction based, chronologic, immutable and synchronized distributed ledger shared over a peer-to-peer network. In a BC, transactions are stored in interlinked transaction sets, referred to as blocks. They execute and record single transactions using consensus algorithms and bundle them into transaction sets using cryptographic techniques."

When comparing the core characteristics of both terms it becomes clear that all of the DLT core characteristics are also core characteristics of BCs (cf. Fig. 3).

Table 1. Description of the DLT characteristics

Characteristic	Description
Consensus algorithms	• Consensus algorithms are "algorithms that help a distributed or decentralized network to unanimously take a decision whenever necessary" [12] • They create a consensus between the network participants of the current and past states of the ledger [9, 13] • Best-known examples are "Proof-of-Stake (PoS)" and "Proof-of-Work (PoW)" [11]
Database	• A database is a structured set of data, which is managed by a database management system (DBMS) • They efficiently manage persistent data and define a database model [14] • DLTs and BCs store and manage data. They offer functions to read and write said data and can therefore be defined as a type of database [15]
Peer-to-peer network	• DLTs and BCs are built on top of a network of nodes, which all help to manage the full network [14] • The peers participate in the consensus algorithms, store and share the data and, if available, execute smart contracts [11]
Immutable	• Data in a DLT or BC is unalterable [16, 17] • New data can only be appended to the record but not changed or deleted [16] • Incorrect data can only be corrected through a new transaction [18, 19]
Distributed	• In DLTs there is no central entity that has control over the network [20] • Following Baran [37], DLTs are not only decentralized but distributed because they also do not rely on a small set of important nodes
Shared	• In a DLT or BC network there is no information that is only stored in a single node [11, 16, 21] • Information is always shared between multiple nodes [9]
Synchronized	• In public BCs like bitcoin, every node permanently stores a copy of the complete chain [16] • Changes to the chain will then be synchronized through the complete network [16] • There are DLTs where it is not required that all nodes have all the information [9] • In DLTs like Corda, only nodes that are associated with a transaction see, verify and store the data of the transaction [22]
Transaction	• A transaction is a bundling of multiple database actions into a unit of work, which will either be fully executed or rolled back to the state prior to the transaction [14, 23] • Transactions transfer rights or values between economic subjects [3] • Opposite to relational databases which store the current state of the data, DLTs store the deltas in transactions [18]
Cryptography	• Data in DLTs and BCs is secured from changes using hash values and hash functions [24] • To secure new data from changes, hash values of previous data are used as an input to generate the hash value of the new data. If previous data is altered, the hash values for all subsequent data would change [25] • Cryptographic techniques are also used in the public-key-algorithm for the execution of transactions [24, 25]

Table 2. Additional BC characteristics

Characteristic	Description
Linked list of blocks	• The transactional data is stored in transaction sets often called blocks [13, 26] • Data in a BC is added by appending new blocks to the end of the chain [27] • The link is established through the use of the previous blocks hash value for the calculation of the new block [28] • On the other hand, data in DLTs does not have to be packed into blocks, as transactions can be directly linked to one or more predecessor transactions, e.g. in directed acyclic graphs [29]
Transparency	• In a public ledger, all the information is visible for all participants and each node is involved in the management of the data and everyone is able to join and leave the network [12, 30] • However, this does not necessarily apply to consortium or private BCs, where access, participation in the consensus algorithm and data visibility can be limited [31] • As such, BCs are only transparent to nodes with the sufficient rights [30]
Anonymity	• Nodes in a BC are only visible to the network through a network address [32] • Transactions between nodes only contain data related to the sending address, the receiving address and the asset or value that is transferred [32] • These characteristics only lead to "pseudo-anonymity" as the actual IP-addresses can be acquired through forensic methods [32] • In private BCs, there is also no anonymity as the participants have to authenticate themselves prior to accessing the network [31]

DLT		Blockchain	
Characteristic	**Mentions**	**Characteristic**	**Mentions**
Network	16	Transaction based	43
Consensus	15	Distributed	42
Record of trans. / Database	14	Ledger	38
Peer-to-Peer	13	Consensus	36
Immutable	11	Immutable	33
Decentralized	9	Block	28
Shared	9	Cryptography	28
Synchronized	8	Peer-to-Peer	27
Transaction based	8	Synchronised	23
Distributed	6	Chained / Linked (Blocks)	21
Cryptography	6	Decentralized	19
Chronologic	3	Chronological	14
Block	3	Transaprency	10
Chained / Linked (Blocks)	3	Public	10
PoW	1	Record of trans. / Database	9
PoS	1	Anonymous	8
Globally	1	Smart Contracts	6
Resistance to Cencorship	1	Digital ledger	5
Elimination of Trusted Third Party	1		
Smart Contracts	1	Core Characteristic	
		Optional Feature	

Fig. 1. Number of mentions for each characteristic of DLT and BC

Fig. 2. Characteristics of DLT based on the quantitative analysis

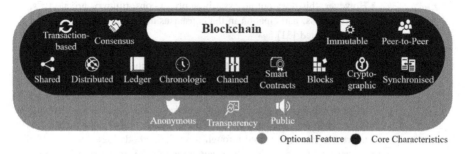

Fig. 3. Characteristics of DLT based on the quantitative analysis

On the other hand, some of the BC core characteristics (chained blocks) are only optional features of DLT. This leads to the conclusion that BCs are a specialized form of DLT. On this basis, the statement can be made that, "Blockchains are a subtype of DLT". To prove this, there must be DLT types that fulfill the DLT core characteristics but not those of BCs and the opposite situation should not exist.

2.3 DLTs Besides BCs

The previous literature search identified papers that focused on initial BC implementations like Ethereum, on certain DLT aspects (e.g. consensus algorithms, smart contracts) or their applicability to certain use cases, but not on the overall structure of DLT concepts. To gain this information, an online market research for current "DLT" solutions in the BC community is necessary. This approach will use a framework created by Cambridge University [33] during a DLT market research. To obtain data of smaller DLT-framework projects, a search for postings on non-scientific media like blockchain news websites, e.g. coindesk and coinhero, or in topic specific DLT and BC community boards and blogs similar to where the idea for the first BC bitcoin started, was executed. The goal of the market research is to check if there are projects that fulfill the DLT criteria and not the BC. For this reason, only a small sample of different projects were analyzed and clustered into groups. Further research is needed to gain a complete overview of the current DLT market.

Seven projects (IOTA, peaq, Hashgraph, Corda, ThunderChain, Radix DLT, Hyperledger) were selected for further evaluation and clustered into four groups (directed acyclic graphs (DAG), sharded ledgers (SL), hybrid ledgers (HL) and BC). One example of each group can be found in Table 3. These groups represent a snapshot of the current DLT market without any claim to completeness.

Table 3. Analysis of DLTs besides BCs

DLT	Protocol layer	Network layer	Application layer
DAG: Tangle (used by IOTA and peaq) [38]	• Transactions are directly linked without blocks • Each transaction verifies two existing transactions • Data structure is a directed acyclic graph	• Nodes do not have to be totally in sync (with an eventual consistency algorithm) • Nodes verify the two previous transactions and attach the result using a PoW algorithm • Nodes need to resolve conflicting transactions	• More scalable than a standard BC like bitcoin • Conflicting transactions can exist • Usage in internet of thing (IoT) solutions and high-volume transaction cases • Not open source
SL: Tempo Ledger (used by Radix DLT) [39]	• Uses data packages called atoms which contain a payload (some kind of data), sender and receiver address and is signed by the sender • Owned items are called consumables • Transactions of consumables are contained in transfer atoms • The history of ownership can be viewed through a list of connected consumables	• Uses a gossip algorithm to propagate transactions • Relies on eventual consistency • Not all nodes must have all the information • Data is only shared among interested parties (shards) • Atoms can be part of multiple shards	• Offers a high scalability compared to BCs like Ethereum • Designed for IoT use cases
HL: Thunder-Chain [40]	• Uses a hybrid approach of two protocols at the same time • A fast protocol for fast transaction handling • A traditional BC protocol as a backbone • Both protocols use blocks to package transactions	• For the fast protocol, a central entity (accelerator) gathers all transactions and assigns them sequence numbers • For the fast protocol, ¾ of a committee of trusted nodes have to verify the transactions • For the traditional protocol, the committee members ignore the messages from the accelerator	• Offers a high scalability compared to BCs like Ethereum • Fast protocol can be recovered in case of an error from the traditional BC

While this is only a small sample of DLTs besides BC, it allows the creation of clusters of the different approaches. The goal of these new approaches is to mitigate the issues that exist with current BC solutions. One is the difficult scalability of classic BCs. Another issue is the limited bandwidth for transactions which is the result of the synchronicity of all nodes. New blocks can only be created in the same speed as a block needs to be propagated through the network. To counter this, *directed acyclic graphs* (DAGs) use an asynchronous and non-deterministic way of structuring data. Instead of interlocking blocks into a chain, DAGs use a treelike data structure where a transaction can have multiple predecessors. This allows a higher bandwidth and increased scalability. Another cluster can be built for DLTs that do not share all the information with all nodes. These *sharded ledgers* only share between nodes that have an interest in the information. This is useful in cases where data privacy has to be protected and only certain nodes have the right to see the information. Another approach is the combination of a BC with other technologies. ThunderChain combines a fast protocol with a central service (accelerator) with a decentral BC as a backup. These *hybrid solutions* use the advantages of BCs and expand them with other technologies for different use cases. The following Fig. 4 shows a categorization of these subtypes and their characteristics.

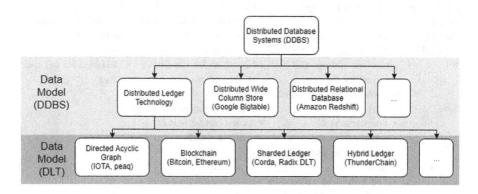

Fig. 4. Categorization of DLTs

The categorization is based on the overview of Hileman and Rauchs [33] and part of the IEEE reference framework for DLT/BC [34]. It is extended by the defined subtypes of DLT as well as examples for each category. While the four DLT subtypes cover a wide range of the existing DLT concepts, they may not cover all of them. Newer concepts will extend the range of DLTs and offer new possibilities for future use cases.

3 Relevance of DLTs for E-Business

Within the line of argumentation in Sect. 2, it was shown that all of the categorized DLT-solutions have an impact on all kinds of networked E-Businesses. The goal of the E-Business economy is the connection of different demanders and suppliers for uninterrupted trade. The E-Business sector has evolved from direct business-to-business interactions to a worldwide-decentralized connected transaction network. DLTs are especially designed to connect different economical units over a network without the need for a trusted third party and, as such, DLTs will influence market environments [4, 20]. So far, market platforms in an e-commerce sense are mostly managed by single platform holders that have full control over the said platform (e.g. Amazon marketplace). In a DLT environment, market rules are determined at the beginning and afterwards can only be changed in a decentralized way through the consent of the majority of market participants. There is no longer a central entity to control the market. The single point of failure can be deleted as DLTs are distributed across a node network. As shown, DLTs can also help to reduce the necessity for intermediaries in general, e.g. as part of business transactions. Therefore, DLT solutions will reduce transaction costs in an E-Business environment [35]. Current information technologies can lower the transaction costs because they ease access to information and past transactions and also lower the barrier of interaction between the companies [36]. DLTs have the ability to further lower these costs by eliminating intermediaries and thereby lowering the cost of manual labor. They also provide the opportunity to model relationships through the use of smart contracts (even though not all DLTs support smart contracts).

4 Conclusion

The paper has shown that a maturing level of development of BCs and DLTs can impact future economies and reduce the inherent transaction costs. Therefore, the importance of a clear understanding of the technology has been stated and this issue has been addressed through a scientific literature review that explored 74 definition attempts.

During this process, key characteristics of the BC technology and the DLT itself were identified and the overarching position of the DLT ascertained. It was indicated that the BC and DLT community has grown into a serious industry, which further develops specialized solutions and tools to improve established business transaction processes and tries to reorganize centralized ledger systems by improving the way transactions are handled and connected ledgers communicate, synchronize and update. As shown, some DLTs that are labeled as BC solutions do not fulfill the identified core characteristics and are therefore not BCs. This issue was resolved in a new hierarchical categorization of the DLT solutions. Further updates of this categorization will be necessary in the future, when standardization boards, e.g. ISO, DIN, ASX, will release their own DLT definition. Additionally, new technological solutions will enhance the spectrum of DLTs. As the categorization (Fig. 3) does not claim to be complete, further research is necessary to obtain a fully comprehensive view.

This future research should update the categorization of Fig. 4 in regular (e.g. annual) research loops and should include a backward comparison. This is necessary if new DLT data models have occurred on the market and therefore could impact the DLT or BC definitions or expand the DLT categorization on a horizontal view. This research expands the volume of underlying information and will therefore raise the quality of the definitions and the categorization even more. It should include additional criteria's, which address especially business scientists.

Additional research should focus on extending the DLT categorization for practical usage. The extension needs multiple perspectives. First, by going deeper into each category and analyzing their architecture and additional information for each DLT type. Second, by extending the number of existing DLT types with new developed types. The mentioned future research could be handled by additional systematic literature and market analysis and should be proved by qualitative expert interviews.

References

1. Gartner (ed.): 5 Trends Emerge in the Gartner Hype Cycle for Emerging Technologies. https://gtnr.it/2vTTphv. Accessed 10 Apr 2019
2. Jabed, M., Chowdhury, M., Colman, A., Kabir, M. A., Han, J., Sarda, P.: Blockchain versus database: a critical analysis. In: 2018 17th IEEE International Conference on Trust, Security and Privacy in Computing and Communications, pp. 1348–1353 (2018)
3. Barnett, R., Neple, T., Hassall, J.: Developing a global standard for interoperable accounting systems. In: Proceedings of the International Symposium on Distributed Objects and Applications, Edinburgh, UK (1999)
4. Marsal-Llacuna, M.-L., Oliver-Riera, M.: The standards revolution: who will first put this new kid on the blockchain. In: 2017 ITU Kaleidoscope: Challenges for a Data-Driven Society, pp. 1–7 (2017)
5. vom Brocke, J., et al.: Reconstructing the giant: on the importance of rigour in documenting the literature search process. In: 17th European Conference on Information Systems, vol. 9, pp. 2206–2217 (2009)
6. Nakamoto, S.: Bitcoin: A Peer-to-Peer Electronic Cash System, 9 (2008). www.Bitcoin.Org
7. Risius, M., Spohrer, K.: A blockchain research framework - what we (don't) know, where we go from here, and how we will get there. Bus. Inf. Syst. Eng. 59(6), 385–409 (2017)
8. Ibáñez, L.D., Simperl, E., Gandon, F., Story, H.: Redecentralizing the web with distributed ledgers. IEEE Intell. Syst. 32(1), 92–95 (2017)
9. Yu, F.R., Liu, J., He, Y., Si, P., Zhang, Y.: Virtualization for distributed ledger technology (vDLT). IEEE Access 6, 25019–25028 (2018)
10. Filipova, N.: Blockchain – an opportunity for developing new business models. Inf. Technol. 75–93 (2018)
11. Trump, B.D., Lorin, M.A.A.F., Matthews, H.S., Sicker, D., Linkov, I.: Governing the use of blockchain and distributed ledger technologies: not one-size-fits-all. IEEE Eng. Rev. 46(3), 56–62 (2018)
12. Sankar, L.S., Sinduh, M., Sethumadhavan, M.: Survey of consensus protocols on blockchain applications. In: 2017 International Conference on Advanced Computing and Communication Systems (2017)
13. Dai, M., Zhang, S., Wang, H., Jin, S.: A low storage room requirement framework for distributed ledger in blockchain. IEEE Access 6, 22970–22975 (2018)
14. Elmasri, R., Navathe, S.B.: Fundamentals of database systems, 6th edn. Addison-Wesley, Boston (2011)
15. Treleaven, P., Brown, R.G., Yang, D.: Blockchain technology in finance. Computer 50, 14–17 (2017)
16. Magazzeni, D., Mcburney, P., Nash, W.: Validation and verification of smart contracts: a research agenda. Computer 50(9), 50–57 (2017)

17. Paavolainen, S., Nikander, P.: Security and privacy challenges and potential solutions for DLT based IoT systems. In: 2018 Global Internet of Things Summit (GIoTS), pp. 1–6, June 2018
18. Niranjanamurthy, M., Nithya, B.N., Jagannatha, S.: Analysis of blockchain technology: pros, cons and SWOT. Clust. Comput. 5(2), 1–15 (2018)
19. Singi, K., Pradeepkumar, D.S., Kaulgud, V., Podder, S.: Compliance adherence in distributed software delivery: a blockchain approach. In: 2018 IEEE/ACM 13th International Conference on Global Software Engineering, pp. 126–127 (2018)
20. Bencic, F.M., Zarko, I.P.: Distributed ledger technology: blockchain compared to directed acyclic graph. In: 2018 IEEE 38th International Conference on Distributed Computing Systems (ICDCS) (2018)
21. Mitra, S., Bose, S., Gupta, S.S., Chattopadhyay, A.: Secure and tamper-resilient distributed ledger for data aggregation in autonomous vehicles. In: 2018 IEEE Asia Pacific Conference on Circuits and Systems, pp. 548–551 (2018)
22. Khan, C., Lewis, A., Rutland, E., Wan, C., Rutter, K., Thompson, C.: A distributed-ledger consortium model for collaborative innovation. Computer 50(9), 29–37 (2017)
23. Sheth, A., Rusinkiewicz, M.: On transactional workflows. IEEE Comput. Soc. 16(2), 37–40 (2001)
24. Dunphy, P., Petitcolas, F.A.P., Innovation, O.: Blockchain security and privacy - a first look at identity management schemes on the blockchain. IEEE Secur. Priv. 16, 20–29 (2018)
25. Anjum, A., Sporny, M., Sill, A.: Blockchain standards for compliance and trust. IEEE Cloud Comput. 4(4), 84–90 (2017)
26. Lemieux, V.L.: A typology of blockchain recordkeeping solutions and some reflections on their implications for the future of archival preservation. In: 2017 IEEE International Conference on Big Data (2017)
27. Alexopoulos, N., Daubert, J., Mühlhäuser, M., Habib, S.M.: Beyond the hype: on using blockchains in trust management for authentication. In: IEEE Trustcom/BigDataSE/ICESS (2017)
28. Kim, K., Justl, J.M.: Potential antitrust risks in the development and use of blockchain. J. Tax. Regul. Financ. Inst. 31(3), 5–17 (2018)
29. Poplawski, P.K., Szczypiorski, K.: Blockchain-based smart contracts for sustainable power investments. In: Second World Conference on Smart Trends in Systems, Security and Sustainability, pp. 105–112 (2018)
30. Caro, M.P., Ali, M.S., Vecchio, M., Giaffreda, R.: Blockchain-based traceability in agri-food supply chain management: a practical implementation. In: IoT Vertical and Topical Summit on Agriculture – Tuscany (2018)
31. Lundbaek, L.N., Huth, M.: Oligarchic control of business-to-business blockchains. In: Proceedings - 2nd IEEE European Symposium on Security and Privacy Workshops. EuroS and PW 2017, pp. 68–71 (2017)
32. Kuzuno, H., Karam, C.: Blockchain explorer: An analytical process and investigation environment for bitcoin. In: ECrime Researchers Summit, ECrime, pp. 9–16 (2017)
33. Hileman, G., Rauchs, M.: Global blockchain benchmarking study, 122. Cambridge Centre for Alternative Finance, University of Cambridge (2017)
34. Lima, C.: Developing open and interoperable DLT - blockchain standards. Computer 51, 106–111 (2019)
35. Coase, R.: The nature of the firm. Economica 4(16), 386–405 (1937)
36. Tan, Z., Zhou, W.: The impact of enterprise information technology construction on enterprise cost. In: IEEE, Beijing (2014)
37. Baran, P.: On distributed communications networks. IEEE Trans. Commun. Syst. 12(1), 1–9 (1964)

38. Popov, S.: The tangle. In: IOTA Whitepaper (2017)
39. Pass, R., Shi, E.: The thunder protocol. In: ThunderChain Whitepaper (2016)
40. Hughes, D.: Radix - Tempo. In: Radix DTL Whitepaper (2017). https://papers.radixdlt.com/tempo/. Accessed 19 Nov 2018

Trusted Artifact-Driven Process Monitoring of Multi-party Business Processes with Blockchain

Giovanni Meroni$^{(\boxtimes)}$, Pierluigi Plebani, and Francesco Vona

Dipartimento di Elettronica, Informazione e Bioingegneria, Politecnico di Milano,
Piazza Leonardo da Vinci 32, 20133 Milan, Italy
{giovanni.meroni,pierluigi.plebani}@polimi.it,
francesco.vona@mail.polimi.it

Abstract. Multi-party business processes are characterized by the lack of a central coordination, as each participant controls only a portion of the process. Nonetheless, organizations often need to know how the whole process is performed, especially when artifacts belonging to an organization are manipulated by the other participants. This requires a monitoring system able to collect and share in a trusted way data about the status of the activities performed by the different parties. To achieve this goal, in this paper we combine artifact-driven monitoring with blockchain. The former, introduced in previous work, can determine how the process is executed, while the latter enables a trusted data exchange among the participants of the business process to reduce the possibility for a fraudulent organization to alter monitoring data. The feasibility and the impacts on costs of the proposed platform is validated via a prototype based on the Ethereum blockchain implementing a real-world use case.

Keywords: Blockchain · Distributed ledger · Ethereum ·
Artifact-driven monitoring · Trusted process monitoring ·
Cyber-physical systems

1 Introduction

Business process monitoring holds a fundamental role in the Business Process Management life-cycle. In fact, monitoring does not only allow checking the compliance of the running process with respect to the expected behaviour, but also collecting data that are useful to improve the process model for future enactments. Especially in case of multi-party business processes, process monitoring becomes very difficult. This is due to the fact that each party has visibility on a portion of the whole process. Therefore, is up to the party involved in the possibly failing activities to notify issues to the other parties. This is particularly crucial when the failing activities operate on resources that belong to another party. For instance, in the logistic domain, the sender of a product wants to be

C. Di Ciccio et al. (Eds.): BPM 2019 Blockchain and CEE Forum, LNBIP 361, pp. 55–70, 2019.
https://doi.org/10.1007/978-3-030-30429-4_5

informed about the way its package is manipulated by the shippers involved in the delivery until it arrives at destination. To cope with this issue, current solutions usually rely on a centralized architecture, assuming that a specific entity is in charge of supervising the entire process execution by collecting all the relevant information on the status of the tasks and on the resources given by the parties [4].

In this scenario, artifact-driven process monitoring is an approach that has been proposed to monitor business processes [9]. It does not require any central authority as the monitoring is performed from the standpoint of the resources, i.e., the artifacts, managed by the parties during the execution of the process. Instead of relying on explicit notifications sent by human operators, artifact-driven process monitoring relies on the conditions of the physical objects (i.e., artifacts) participating in a process to determine when business activities are executed. Together with the Internet of Things (IoT) paradigm, which turns physical objects into smart entities aware of their conditions and of the process they participate in, artifact-driven process monitoring allows to autonomously monitor the process, regardless of the organization or the person in charge of executing it. In addition, artifact-driven process monitoring relies on a declarative representation of the process to monitor. This makes the monitoring more flexible, and able to handle deviations and violations that may occur at runtime without interruptions or human intervention. Moreover, flexibility is also improved because a central authority – which could became a bottleneck – is no longer required.

To this aim, artifact-driven process monitoring solves the issue of knowing the conditions of the physical objects, and the execution of the process. However, it requires the organizations to *trust* each other. In fact, a malicious organization may intentionally alter monitoring information collected by the smart objects, and then it may claim that the process was executed differently than what it actually was. While a previous work investigated the possible connections between artifact-driven monitoring and blockchain [11], this paper investigates the trade-off between the assurance of having persistent monitoring data and the minimization of the data written on the blockchain, which has been validated through a prototype based on Ethereum [17]. Real-world processes – and the related monitoring data – are also used to evaluate issues related to the cost of public blockchains in terms of cryptocurrency.

The remainder of this paper is structured as follows: Sect. 2 outlines the requirements that a trusted monitoring platform should fulfill. Section 3 presents and compares the architecture of the two possible blockchain-based solutions. Section 4 validates the proposed architectures against a real-world use case. Section 5 surveys related work. Finally, Sect. 6 draws the conclusions of this work and outlines future research plans.

2   Trusted Process Monitoring

Like in every multi-party business process, no organization has full control on the whole process. Instead, each organization is responsible only for the activities

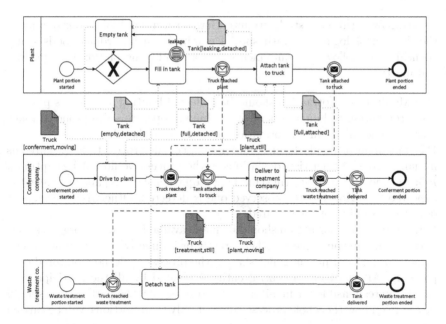

Fig. 1. BPMN diagram of the dangerous goods shipment process.

assigned to it. Consequently, being able to monitor the whole process becomes critical for organizations to be sure that the process is executed as expected and, if not, to identify who is responsible for such an inconsistency.

To better understand the importance of a reliable and trusted process monitoring solution, a case study concerning the shipment of dangerous goods is presented. An industrial plant P, to dispose of chemical waste, relies on the conferment company C. In turn, C relies on the waste treatment company T to neutralize the waste. The disposal process, which is represented in Fig. 1 using Business Process Model and Notation (BPMN), is organized as follows. Firstly, P stores the chemical waste inside a tank and waits for C to reach its plant. If the tank has a leakage, to avoid the chemical to be spread and pollute the environment, C has to immediately empty it and use another tank. Once C arrives, the tank is attached to its truck, then C leaves the plant and delivers the tank to T. Finally, T detaches the tank.

Concerning the trust, imagine that the tank is not properly disposed. Instead, it is abandoned in the woods and, after some time, it is found by the forest rangers. Without knowing how the process was actually performed, it would be impossible for them to know who is responsible for this crime. Firstly, P may have completely skipped the conferment part, and abandoned the tank on its own will. Alternatively, C may have cheated P by having made no deal with T. Thus, it may have abandoned the tank instead of delivering it to T. Finally, T may have correctly received the tank. However, to cut costs, it may have abandoned it instead of neutralizing its contents.

Starting from this case study, we interviewed several organizations operating in the domain of logistics - with special emphasis on hazardous goods - and we identified the following requirements that a monitoring platform, in general, should meet:

- **R1:** Monitoring information should be collected limiting as much as possible the intervention of human operators as human operators are prone to make mistakes and misleading information could be introduced.
- **R2:** The monitoring platform should not expect the process to be executed as initially agreed. Otherwise, deviations in the process would not be captured.
- **R3:** The monitoring platform should not stop when a discrepancy between the expected behavior and the observed one is detected. Otherwise, subsequent deviations would not be captured.
- **R4:** Monitoring information should be made available to all the organizations participating in the process, either directly or indirectly (i.e, as an observer). If monitoring information is not shared, the process could be monitored only partially. Alternatively, a central entity – trusted by all the participants – should be responsible for monitoring the process. All the participants should be aware on how the whole process, and not only their portions, will be carried out.
- **R5:** Monitoring information should be consistent and sent timely to all the participants. If different organizations have different monitoring information, then it would be difficult to know who has the right information.
- **R6:** If needed, organizations that did not take part in the process (e.g., a public prosecutor) should be allowed to access monitoring information even after the process completed.
- **R7:** Nobody should be able to alter monitoring information. Otherwise, if an organization incorrectly performed part of the process, it may alter monitoring information either to blame somebody else or to prove that they were compliant.
- **R8:** Nobody should be able to send monitoring information on behalf of somebody else. Otherwise, an organization may impersonate another one and send fraudulent information in order to blame somebody else.

The artifact-driven monitoring approach [9] can address some of these requirements. In fact, artifact-driven monitoring detects when activities are executed based on the conditions of the physical objects (i.e., artifacts) in the process. For example, the conclusion of activity Attach tank to truck can be detected when the artifact Tank is full and attached to the truck. Therefore, if these objects are made smart with the IoT paradigm, they can autonomously provide this information, thus addressing *R1*. Also, by relying on the artifact-centric language Extended- GSM (E-GSM) to represent the monitored process, artifact-driven monitoring can transparently deal with variations in the control flow, thus addressing *R2* and *R3*. For example, by modeling the process presented in Sect. 2 in E-GSM, control flow dependencies are considered descriptive rather than prescriptive. This way, artifact driven monitoring can detect – even though such an occurrence violates the control flow dependencies – if the tank was leaking and P did not emptied it. For further details on E-GSM and the advantages it provides for monitoring, we invite the reader to consult [2]. Finally, an artifact-driven monitoring platform can run entirely on top of physical objects exchanging monitoring information with each other, thus addressing $R4$.

However, as artifact-driven monitoring was not designed with trust in mind, it presents some limitations in this regard. Firstly, monitoring information is stored in the memory of each smart object. Consequently, anyone who has physical access to a smart object can potentially alter monitoring information and make it inconsistent. Secondly, no mechanism to verify either the origin or the correctness of monitoring information exchanged by smart objects was put in place. Therefore, any smart object that participates in the process can send monitoring information on behalf of any other smart object. Also, a compromised smart object may send monitoring information that does not reflect the actual state of the smart object. Finally, an artifact-driven monitoring platform relies on a centralized message bus to distribute monitoring information to the smart objects. Thus, a failure on that component would prevent the monitoring platform to correctly work.

3 Adopting Blockchain to Improve the Trust in Monitoring

To implement a fully trusted monitoring platform, thus addressing $R5$, $R6$, $R7$, and $R8$, we investigated the possible adoption of a blockchain. A blockchain [13] is a distributed ledger in which information is stored in a safe, verifiable and permanent way. Every time a new piece of information has to be made available to other participants, a new transaction is created. Transactions are then grouped into a block that references the previously stored block, hence the name "blockchain". Once a new block is created, it is validated and then made available to all the participants in the blockchain. This mechanism allows a blockchain to provide the following features:

- **Distributed consensus:** Multiple participants are responsible for validating information written on a blockchain. Therefore, as long as the validation mechanism is correctly implemented, it is impossible for a single participant to introduce incorrect information. Also, when a new participant joins the blockchain, it can obtain its own copy of the blockchain and participate in the validation process. This way, $R5$ and $R6$ can be addressed.
- **Persistence:** Each block in the blockchain directly references the previous one via a hashing mechanism. Therefore, it is impossible for a single participant to alter or delete a transaction once it has been written in a block. In addition, as the validation mechanism requires information on the previous blocks, every participant that performs this task holds a complete copy of all the data stored in the blockchain. Thus, even if a participant loses its copy of the blockchain, multiple copies of the data are still available, and $R7$ can be addressed.

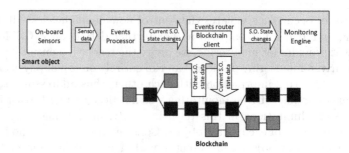

Fig. 2. Architecture of the fully blockchain-based platform.

- **Auditability:** When a new transaction is created, it contains a timestamp and a signature identifying the participant who created it. Therefore, it is impossible for a participant to create a transaction on behalf of another one. This way, *R8* can be addressed.

To provide a fully trusted monitoring solution, in Sects. 3.1 and 3.2 we present the architecture of two alternative platforms that, respectively, treat the enforcement of persistent monitoring information and the reduction of the information written on-chain as first-class citizens. In particular, the first platform fully guarantees that monitoring information will never disappear in exchange for a variable computational effort to be performed on-chain. Instead, the second platform makes the amount of information written on the blockchain independent on the amount of monitoring information produced. However, it does not enforce the persistence of monitoring information.

3.1   Fully Blockchain-Based Platform

The first platform relies entirely on a blockchain to store and forward monitoring information. As shown in Fig. 2, we take the architecture of an artifact-driven monitoring platform as a starting point. In particular, the physical characteristics of a smart object are collected by *On-board Sensors* and, thank to the *Events Processor* module, they are discretized into a finite set of states representing its conditions. Then, changes in the state of the smart objects participating in the process are notified to the *Monitoring Engine* module, which detects when activities are executed and identifies possible violations.

However, to let smart objects exchange information on their current state, we re-engineered the *Events Router* module, which implements information exchange mechanisms and policies, by integrating it with a *Blockchain Client*. The *Blockchain Client* is responsible for initiating a new transaction whenever the current smart object changes state, and for sending a notification to the *Monitoring Engine* whenever a new block containing a transaction from the other smart objects is added to the blockchain. Each smart object acts as a specific participant, and it has a unique address.

```
1   contract Blockclient {
2     string processModel; //process model
3     struct State { //event
4       uint id;
5       address sender;
6       string artifact;
7       string status;
8       string timestamp;
9       string data; }
10    mapping(uint => State) public states; //list of events
11    uint stateCounter;
12    struct participant {
13        bytes32 encodedArtifact; }
14    mapping(address => participant) public participants; //participants
15
16    function Blockclient(string _processModel, address[] _addrs, bytes32[]
          _encodedArtifacts) payable public {
17      for (uint p = 0; p < _addrs.length; p++) { //add participants
18        participants[_addrs[p]].encodedArtifact = _encodedArtifacts[p]; }
19      processModel = _processModel;} //store process model
20
21    function writeState(string _artifact, string _status, string _timestamp,
          string _data) payable public {
22      if (participants[msg.sender].encodedArtifact == stringToBytes32(_artifact
          ) { //check identity of sender and ownership of artifact
23        stateCounter++; //increment state counter
24        states[stateCounter] = State(stateCounter, msg.sender, _artifact,
            _status, _timestamp, _data); //store state data
25        LogWriteState(stateCounter, msg.sender, _artifact, _status, _timestamp,
            _data); }}} //emit a new event
26
27    function getProcessModel() public view returns(string) {
28      return processModel;} //retrieve process model
29  }
```

Fig. 3. Excerpt of smart contract supporting the fully-blockchain based platform.

Since a blockchain does not guarantee that monitoring data are recorded in the same chronological order as when they are produced, a reorder buffer has been introduced in the *Events Router*. In fact, transactions can be stored in reverse chronological order if the later ones are included into a block before the earlier ones are validated. Consequently, if the chronological order is not respected, the *Monitoring Engine* may incorrectly monitor the process. By buffering transactions until five subsequent blocks have been written on the blockchain, and then reordering them based on the timestamp when data were collected by sensors, it is possible to minimize the occurrence of monitoring errors caused by transactions violating the chronological order of monitoring data.

Before the process starts, the smart contract shown in Fig. 3 is deployed on the blockchain[1]. This smart contract contains the serialized model of the process to monitor (line 2) and a list of the smart objects participating in it (lines 12–14), which are instantiated once the contract is deployed (lines 16–19). It also defines a data structure to store monitoring information (lines 3–11), as well

---

[1] Smart contracts are implemented in Solidity. However, they can be easily ported to other languages.

methods to append new information (writeState, lines 21–25) and to retrieve the serialized process model (getProcessModel, lines 27–28). In particular, monitoring information is represented as a mapping (line 10), whose items (lines 4–9) contain an unique identifier, the identity of the smart object communicating the change, the type of smart object, the state currently assumed by the smart object, a timestamp indicating when it changed state, and the sensor data used to infer the state.

Once the smart contract is deployed, the *Blockchain Client* of all the smart objects referenced in that contract configures the *Monitoring Engine* with the provided process model. In addition, the *Blockchain Client* subscribes to the LogWriteState, which is emitted whenever new monitoring information is added to the blockchain (line 25). When the *Events Processor* of one of these smart objects detects a change in its state, the *Blockchain Client* invokes the writeState method by passing the monitoring information, thus initiating a new transaction. The other participants in the blockchain validate the transaction, which is then written in a new block. Meanwhile, if the *Blockchain Client* is notified about a new occurrence of LogWriteState, it extracts the smart object and the new state assumed by it and forwards this information to the *Monitoring Engine*.

It is worth noting that every participant that joins the blockchain can validate transactions from the smart objects and collect monitoring information. This allows third parties, such as external auditors, to monitor the process. When some information, especially on the structure of the process and on the state assumed by the smart objects, should not be publicly disclosed, it is still possible to encrypt it by putting in place a Public Key Infrastructure (PKI) and traditional key distribution mechanisms. This way, only entitled participants can read this information, and confidentiality can be guaranteed.

In addition, monitoring information can be easily accessed after the process finished, even if the smart objects are no longer present. This makes possible for entitled third parties to determine how the process was performed simply by replaying monitoring information. For example, still referring to the case study, the authorities can easily identify the organization responsible for having improperly disposed the tank, even if its memory was damaged. In fact, authorities can simply query the blockchain to obtain the process and all the changes in the state of the smart objects, being sure that this information was not altered once it was written on the blockchain. Then, they can instruct a *Monitoring Engine* with the E-GSM model, and replay the state changes to detect which portion of the process was incorrectly executed.

The main disadvantage of this platform is the potentially high amount of information that is written on the blockchain, which limits its applicability in conjunction with a public blockchain. Since a public blockchain requires a fee to be paid for each invocation of the smart contract, and the fee is dependent on the amount of information that is passed, the more information has to be written, the more expensive the monitoring platform will be. For example, as long as the state is simply represented by a label, the cost will be quite low. However, if the participants would like to know how the state was determined, then also the

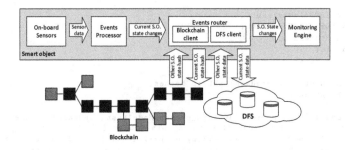

Fig. 4. Architecture of the DFS-blockchain hybrid platform.

historical values collected by sensors and the rules adopted to derive the state should be written on the blockchain, thus significantly increasing the cost of the platform.

3.2 DFS-Blockchain Hybrid Platform

To address the limitations of the fully blockchain-based platform, the cost associated to each transaction must be reduced and, possibly, made independent of the amount of information that is written. To this aim, we propose a second platform that relies both on a blockchain and on a publicly accessible Distributed File System (DFS). Like in the fully blockchain-based platform, this one relies on a blockchain to notify the smart objects on the process to monitor and on changes in their state. However, monitoring information is not stored inside the blockchain. Instead, information is stored as a file in the DFS, and only a reference to the file is stored in the blockchain.

To support this platform, the reference architecture shown in Fig. 4 is proposed. In this case, the *Events Router* integrates both a *Blockchain Client* and a *DFS, Client.* Like in the previous architecture, the smart contract shown in Fig. 5 is deployed on the blockchain before the process starts (portions identical to the one shown in Fig. 5 are omitted). However, this smart contract does not directly contain the serialized process model (line 2). Instead, the process model is stored in the DFS as a file, and a hash of that file is computed and stored in the smart contract. This way, once the smart contract is deployed, the *Blockchain Client* retrieves the hash of the process model by invoking the getProcessModel-Hash method. Then, it obtains the process model by asking the *DFS Client* to retrieve the file whose hash matches the one specified in the smart contract and, once received, it configures the *Monitoring Engine.*

Similarly, the data structure in this smart contract (lines 3–8) does not store the states assumed by the smart objects. Instead, it stores the hash computed from this information. This way, when the *Events Processor* detects a change in its state, the *Blockchain Client* asks the *DFS Client* to write the new state in a file, then it invokes the writeHash method by passing the hash of the newly created file, thus initiating a new transaction. Then, once the *Blockchain Client*

```
1   contract IPFSblockclient {
2      string processModelHash;
3      struct StateHash {
4         uint id;
5         string mHash;
6      }
7      mapping(uint => StateHash) public hashes;
8      uint hashCounter;
9
10     function IPFSblockclient(string _processModelHash, address[] _addrs,
              bytes32[] _encodedArtifacts) payable public {
11        for (uint p = 0; p < _addrs.length; p++) { ... } //add participants
12        processModelHash = _processModelHash; } // store process model hash
13
14     function writeHash(string _artifact, string _mHash) payable public {
15        if (participants[msg.sender].encodedArtifact == stringToBytes32(_artifact
              )) { //check identity of sender and ownership of artifact
16           hashCounter++; //increment state counter
17           hashes[hashCounter] = StateHash(hashCounter, _mHash); //store state
                 hash
18           LogWriteHash(hashCounter, _mHash); }}} //emit a new event
19
20     function getProcessModelHash() public view returns(string) {
21        return processModelHash;} //retrieve process model hash
22  }
```

Fig. 5. Excerpt of smart contract supporting the DFS-blockchain hybrid platform.

is notified on a change in the state of a smart object (event LogWriteHash), it receives the hash of the new state and then asks the *DFS Client* to retrieve the file matching that hash. Since the hash computed for each invocation of the smart object has a fixed length, the cost of each transaction is independent from the amount of data that is produced. Therefore, information on the state of a smart object can be enriched with historical sensor data and discretization rules without increasing the cost of the transaction. This allows to implement more sophisticated (off-chain) validation mechanisms, to ensure that monitoring information was not originated by a faulty or compromised smart object.

As in the case of the fully blockchain-based one, this platform guarantees the immutability of monitoring information. In fact, altering monitoring information would require one or more files stored in the DFS to be changed. However, a minimal modification in a file would completely change its hash, preventing it to be retrieved by the other participants. As files are not stored in a central location, and each file can be replicated an arbitrary number of times, decentralization is also guaranteed. However, this solution does not enforce persistence of monitoring information by design. In fact, unlike a blockchain, a DFS does not force participants to have a copy of all the stored information. Therefore, unless data retention policies are enforced by the organizations, nobody prevents the participants from deleting information stored inside the DFS once the process ends. Thus, if nobody keeps a copy of this information, it is lost.

Table 1. Comparison of the two proposed platforms.

Platform	Enforces distributed consensus	Enforces persistence	Enforces auditability	Permissioned blockchain	Public blockchain
Fully BC-based	Yes	Yes	Yes	Yes	Not recommended
DFS-BC hybrid	Yes	Not automatically	Yes	Yes	Yes

3.3 Comparision

Table 1 summarizes the most significant aspects of the two proposed platforms. In particular, both platforms enforce distributed consensus and auditability, and they both can be easily implemented using a permissioned (i.e., private) blockchain, which does not require a fee to be paid for each transaction. Only the fully blockchain-based platform automatically enforces persistence of monitoring information, as it stores this information on the blockchain. However, this increases the operational cost of the solution when it operates on a public blockchain, making such a combination not recommended.

4 Validation

To demonstrate the applicability of our solution on a real-world use case, we built a prototype of the two platforms described in Sect. 3[2] starting from the source code of the SMARTifact platform [1]. For the implementation of the Events Router module, we chose the Ethereum [17] blockchain and the Inter-Planetary File System (IPFS)[3] DFS due to both the availability of several tools, libraries, and testing infrastructures (e.g., testnets). In addition, a node implementing an Ethereum client can participate both in a private instance of the Ethereum blockchain and in the public one (i.e., the mainnet). As in the case of the original SMARTifact platform, also this one was entirely run on a Single Board Computer (SBC), in this case a Raspberry Pi[3]. To reduce the workload on the SBC, we configured the *Blockchain Client* as an Ethereum lightweight node. Lightweight nodes do not execute smart contracts, validate transactions, or require a complete copy of the whole blockchain to be downloaded. Therefore, their computational and storage requirements are low enough to be fulfilled by an SBC.

We then tested the two prototypes against a dataset provided by a European logistics company[4], which was also used in [10] to validate artifact-driven

---

[2] Source code at https://bitbucket.org/polimiisgroup/ethereumclient.

[3] http://www.raspberrypi.org.

[4] The (anonymized) dataset is available at http://purl.org/polimi/martifact/ logisticsds-anon (password: GM-CDC-JM-dataset).

Table 2. Results of the validation for the fully blockchain-based platform.

Process name	Executions per process	Correctness (%)	Completeness (%)	Median transactions per execution	Contract deployment cost (gas)	Median cost per transaction (gas)	Median cost per execution (gas)
AMS-BRU		100.00	77.78	5.67	3276717	724547	4472261
AMS-CDG		100.00	87.50	8.88	3298198	724611	6846820
AMS-FRA		75.00	100.00	10.75	3277485	724529	8608058
AMS-LHR	12	91.67	58.33	10.58	3766963	724564	7979801
BRU-AMS	10	90.91	90.91	5.80	3298710	724609	4532603
CDG-AMS	10	100.00	60.00	11.00	3298710	724486	8299217

Table 3. Results of the validation for the DFS-blockchain hybrid platform.

Process name	Executions per process	Correctness (%)	Completeness (%)	Median transactions per execution	Contract deployment cost (gas)	Median cost per transaction (gas)	Median cost per execution (gas)
AMS-BRU	9	100.00	77.78	5.67	1155343	116235	787424
AMS-CDG	8	100.00	87.50	8.88	1155343	116235	1176585
AMS-FRA	4	75.00	100.00	10.75	1155343	116235	1538362
AMS-LHR	12	91.67	58.33	10.58	1155343	116235	1326045
BRU-AMS	10	90.91	90.91	5.80	1155343	116235	789697
CDG-AMS	10	100.00	60.00	11.00	1155343	116235	1394119

monitoring. This dataset contains: *(i)* a model of 6 delivery processes with a total of 53 execution traces; for each execution, *(ii)* logs containing the position and the speed of the involved trucks. Following the artifact-driven approach, we enriched the process model by associating to each activity a finite set of states representing the conditions on the truck required for the activity to start or finish. Then, we defined rules to derive the state of the truck from logs, in order to autonomously monitor the process. Finally, we configured both platforms with the model and rules, and we replayed logs simulating the actual execution of the process. A new transaction was initiated every time a rule detected a change in the state of the truck. The transaction contained the new state, together with the most recent changes in the position and speed of the truck, amounting of 800 Byte of data. The prototype was tested with both a private instance of the Ethereum blockchain, and the Rinkeby public testnet[5]

Tables 2 and 3 summarize the results of the test using the fully blockchain-based and the hybrid platform, respectively. With respect to the artifact-driven monitoring platform described in [10], both platforms were capable of correctly monitoring the same process instances, as shown in columns *correctness* and *completeness*. Therefore, requirements *R1*, *R2*, *R3*, and *R4* were satisfied by both platforms. Also, thank to smart contracts, both platforms were able to satisfy requirements *R5*, *R6*, *R7*, and *R8* as well. Based on the complexity of the smart contract, i.e., the amount of data that has to be written and the operations

---

[5] http://www.rinkeby.io.

performed on the data, a value, named *gas*, is determined for each transaction. It is worth noting that the DFS-blockchain hybrid platform requires less than a third of the gas required by the fully blockchain-based platform. In fact, monitoring a process execution with the former requires between 787424 and 1538362 gas units, while with the latter it ranges between 4472261 and 8608058 gas units. In addition, every transaction initiated by the hybrid platform will store on the blockchain always the same amount of data, corresponding to the hash of the monitoring information. Therefore, the gas units required per transaction will always be the same, regardless of the amount of monitoring information that has to be stored. On the other hand, the amount of information written on the fully blockchain-based platform equals to the monitoring information collected by the platform. Therefore, if the amount of information generated per transaction will increase, the gas units per transaction will increase as well. It is worth noting, as already discussed in the previous section, that this higher gas requirement for the fully blockchain-based platform is compensated by the guarantee of persistence.

To use our prototype in conjunction with the public Ethereum blockchain, a fee directly proportional to the amount of gas consumed by the transaction has to be paid. However, the *gas price*, that is, the fee per gas unit, is not fixed and it can be defined when the transaction is initiated. In general, the higher the gas price is set, the faster the transaction will be processed. When carrying out the experiment, we had to set the gas price to 5 GWei (5×10^{-9} Ether), that is, circa 5.9×10^{-7} €[6]. As a consequence, the operational cost of the fully blockchain-based platform would range between 2.64 € and 5.08 € per process execution, and the one of the hybrid platform would range between 0.46 € and 0.91 €. Such a difference in terms of cost is even more pronounced if we consider larger and more complex processes, such as the ones included in the datasets of the 2014-2015-2017-2018 BPI Challenges[7]. For each process execution in these datasets, the number of transactions is on average up to six times the one considered in our dataset[8]. Thus, for the fully blockchain-based platform, the maximum cost would be at around 30 € per process execution, whereas for the DFS-blockchain hybrid platform it would stay under 5 € per process execution.

Such an high price makes reasonable to adopt the public Ethereum blockchain only in conjunction with the DFS-blockchain hybrid platform, and only when processes manipulating very dangerous (e.g., nuclear waste) or highly valuable goods have to be monitored. In the other cases, a private instance of the Ethereum blockchain, internally used by the participants and which does not require any fee to be paid, is probably more advisable. However, we expect the upcoming introduction of the proof-of-authority consensus algorithm in the public Ethereum blockchain to sensibly decrease the operational cost. In fact, proof-of-authority will significantly decrease the computational effort required to generate a new block, causing the high value of gas price to no longer be justified. In such a scenario, gas price would drop and, consequently, a monitoring

---

[6] The conversion rate was checked on March 15, 2019.

[7] https://www.win.tue.nl/bpi/doku.php?id=2018:challenge.

[8] We assumed a transaction to be initiated every time an event is produced.

platform relying on the public Ethereum blockchain would become affordable also for general purpose business processes.

5 Related Work

Traditionally, business-to-business communications have been performed with the Electronic Data Interchange (EDI) standard [6]. However, EDI has been conceived with commercial transactions in mind. In addition, it requires participants to join a dedicated commercial network, which requires participants to pay a subscription in order to be admitted. Finally, EDI does not implement any mechanism to archive transactions, nor to certify the identity of the sender. To improve trust in information systems, the adoption of blockchain has been investigated as a valuable solution [14, 16]. More specifically, [8] presents an exhaustive analysis of the implications of introducing a blockchain in inter-organizational processes and, among the others, the need for developing a diverse set of process monitoring frameworks on a blockchain. Also, [7] outlines the potential advantages of the synergy between blockchain and business artifacts.

To this aim, [12] exploits the Bitcoin blockchain to monitor and verify process choreographies. Starting from a BPMN collaboration diagram, a set of smart contracts is derived. Similarly, [5] proposes an approach to derive smart contracts from multi-party processes modeled as Petri nets, which is validated with respect to cost. [15] proposes supply chain traceability system relying on blockchain and on the IoT. Finally, [18] proposes a framework for coordinating and monitoring transportation processes based on several private blockchain installations, globally managed by a public blockchain. However, none of these works allow deviations in the execution order of activities. Consequently, the execution of activities that do not follow control flow dependencies is not detected. In addition, neither [12] nor [5] take into consideration the conditions of the physical objects (i.e., the artifacts) participating in the process. Such conditions are useful to determine if an event has occurred for real or it has been incorrectly reported.

6 Conclusions and Future Work

This paper presented how to provide a trusted monitoring platform for multiparty business processes. Starting from the benefits of the artifact-driven monitoring approach, the impact of blockchain adoption to provide a trusted environment has been analyzed. In particular two configurations of the proposed platform have been implemented and their pros and cons have been evaluated with a set of experiments. The results show that a DFS-blockchain hybrid platform is significantly less expensive than a fully blockchain-based one. Nevertheless, the second is preferable when monitoring information must be persistently stored.

A limitation of this approach consists in relying on off-chain software modules, like the *Events Processor* and the *Monitoring Engine*, to monitor the process. Consequently, the E-GSM model and the rules to determine the state of the smart objects cannot be formally validated by the blockchain. To improve this situation, future work will investigate the adoption of oracles to ensure the correct execution of these modules. Also, although the adoption of blockchain has the merit of increasing the trust in monitoring, the proposed solutions do not provide any type of control for possible malicious modification of the data before they are sent to the blockchain. For this reason, tamper-proof systems must be considered in the up-link, i.e., between the sensors and the chain. At the same time, the adoption of a blockchain brings the current disadvantages of this technology in terms of performances. In fact, writing, approving, and distributing a new block to all the participants takes seconds for a permissioned blockchain, or even several minutes for a public one. Nevertheless, research efforts to speed up operations on a blockchain are currently being taken by both academics and the industry, so we expect this issue to be eventually solved or scaled back.

Acknowledgments. This work has been funded by the Italian Project ITS Italy 2020 under the Technological National Clusters program, and by the DITAS project funded by the European Union's Horizon 2020 research and innovation programme under grant agreement RIA 731945.

References

1. Baresi, L., Di Ciccio, C., Mendling, J., Meroni, G., Plebani, P.: mArtifact: an artifact-driven process monitoring platform. In: Clarisó, R., et al. (eds.) Proceedings of the BPM Demo Track and BPM Dissertation Award co-located with 15th International Conference on Business Process Modeling (BPM 2017), CEUR Workshop Proceedings, Barcelona, Spain, 13 September 2017, vol. 1920. CEUR-WS.org (2017). http://ceur-ws.org/Vol-1920/BPM_2017_paper_188.pdf
2. Baresi, L., Meroni, G., Plebani, P.: Using the guard-stage-milestone notation for monitoring BPMN-based processes. In: Schmidt, R., Guédria, W., Bider, I., Guerreiro, S. (eds.) BPMDS/EMMSAD -2016. LNBIP, vol. 248, pp. 18–33. Springer, Cham (2016). https://doi.org/10.1007/978-3-319-39429-9_2
3. Benet, J.: IPFS-content addressed, versioned, P2P file system. arXiv preprint arXiv:1407.3561 (2014)
4. Dumas, M., La Rosa, M., Mendling, J., Reijers, H.A.: Fundamentals of Business Process Management, 2nd edn. Springer, Heidelberg (2018). https://doi.org/10.1007/978-3-642-33143-5
5. García-Bañuelos, L., Ponomarev, A., Dumas, M., Weber, I.: Optimized execution of business processes on blockchain. In: Carmona, J., Engels, G., Kumar, A. (eds.) BPM 2017. LNCS, vol. 10445, pp. 130–146. Springer, Cham (2017). https://doi.org/10.1007/978-3-319-65000-5_8
6. Hsieh, C., Lin, B.: Impact of standardization on EDI in B2B development. Ind. Manag. Data Syst. **104**(1), 68–77 (2004)
7. Hull, R., Batra, V.S., Chen, Y.-M., Deutsch, A., Heath III, F.F.T., Vianu, V.: Towards a shared ledger business collaboration language based on data-aware processes. In: Sheng, Q.Z., Stroulia, E., Tata, S., Bhiri, S. (eds.) ICSOC 2016. LNCS, vol. 9936, pp. 18–36. Springer, Cham (2016). https://doi.org/10.1007/978-3-319-46295-0_2
8. Mendling, J., et al.: Blockchains for business process management - challenges and opportunities. ACM Trans. Manag. Inf. Syst. **9**(1), 41–416 (2018)

9. Meroni, G., Baresi, L., Montali, M., Plebani, P.: Multi-party business process compliance monitoring through IoT-enabled artifacts. Inf. Syst. **73**, 61–78 (2018)
10. Meroni, G., Di Ciccio, C., Mendling, J.: An artifact-driven approach to monitor business processes through real-world objects. In: Maximilien, M., Vallecillo, A., Wang, J., Oriol, M. (eds.) ICSOC 2017. LNCS, vol. 10601, pp. 297–313. Springer, Cham (2017). https://doi.org/10.1007/978-3-319-69035-3_21
11. Meroni, G., Plebani, P.: Combining artifact-driven monitoring with blockchain: analysis and solutions. In: Matulevičius, R., Dijkman, R. (eds.) CAiSE 2018. LNBIP, vol. 316, pp. 103–114. Springer, Cham (2018). https://doi.org/10.1007/978-3-319-92898-2_8
12. Prybila, C., Schulte, S., Hochreiner, C., Weber, I.: Runtime verification for business processes utilizing the bitcoin blockchain. Future Gener. Comput. Syst. (2017). ISSN 0167-739X. https://doi.org/10.1016/j.future.2017.08.024, http://www.sciencedirect.com/science/article/pii/S0167739X1731837X
13. Swan, M.: Blockchain: Blueprint for a New Economy. O'Reilly Media Inc., Newton (2015)
14. Tai, S.: Continuous, trustless, and fair: changing priorities in services computing. In: Lazovik, A., Schulte, S. (eds.) ESOCC 2016. CCIS, vol. 707, pp. 205–210. Springer, Cham (2018). https://doi.org/10.1007/978-3-319-72125-5_16
15. Tian, F., Taudes, A., Mendling, J.: A supply chain traceability system for food safety based on HACCP, blockchain & Internet of Things. In: ICSSSM 2017, pp. 1–6. IEEE (2017)
16. Weber, I., Xu, X., Riveret, R., Governatori, G., Ponomarev, A., Mendling, J.: Untrusted business process monitoring and execution using blockchain. In: La Rosa, M., Loos, P., Pastor, O. (eds.) BPM 2016. LNCS, vol. 9850, pp. 329–347. Springer, Cham (2016). https://doi.org/10.1007/978-3-319-45348-4_19
17. Wood, G.: Ethereum: a secure decentralised generalised transaction ledger. Ethereum Proj. Yellow Pap. **151**, 1–32 (2014)
18. Wu, H., Li, Z., King, B., Ben Miled, Z., Wassick, J., Tazelaar, J.: A distributed ledger for supply chain physical distribution visibility. Information **8**(4), 137 (2017)

Mining Blockchain Processes: Extracting Process Mining Data from Blockchain Applications

Christopher Klinkmüller[1]([✉]), Alexander Ponomarev[1], An Binh Tran[1],
Ingo Weber[2,3], and Wil van der Aalst[4]

[1] Data61, CSIRO, Level 5, 13 Garden Street, Eveleigh, NSW 2015, Australia
{christopher.klinkmuller,alex.ponomarev,anbinh.tran}@data61.csiro.au
[2] Technische Universitaet Berlin, Berlin, Germany
ingo.weber@tu-berlin.de
[3] University of New South Wales, Sydney, NSW 2052, Australia
[4] RWTH Aachen University, Aachen, Germany
wvdaalst@pads.rwth-aachen.de

Abstract. Blockchain technology has been gaining popularity as a platform for developing decentralized applications and executing cross-organisational processes. However, extracting data that allows analysing the process view from blockchains is surprisingly hard. Therefore, blockchain data are rarely used for process mining. In this paper, we propose a framework for alleviating that pain. The framework comprises three main parts: a manifest specifying how data is logged, an extractor for retrieving data (structured according to the XES standard), and a generator that produces logging code to support smart contract developers. Among others, we propose a convenient way to encode logging data in a compact form, to achieve relatively low cost and high throughput for on-chain logging. The proposal is evaluated with logs created from generated logging code, as well as with existing blockchain applications that do not make use of the proposed code generator.

Keywords: Process mining · Blockchain · Smart contracts · Logging · XES

1 Introduction

Blockchain technology has been gaining popularity as a platform for developing *decentralized applications* (DApp) [14] that are, amongst others, used to execute cross-organisational processes [3,7,10,13]. In such cases, *process mining* [1] can assist developers in (i) understanding the actual usage of the DApp, (ii) comparing it to the intended usage, and (iii) adapting the DApp accordingly. A prerequisite for the application of process mining technology is the availability of *event data*, e.g., stored in the form of XES logs. Yet, extracting such data from DApps is surprisingly hard, as demonstrated by Di Ciccio et al. [2] on the

© Springer Nature Switzerland AG 2019
C. Di Ciccio et al. (Eds.): BPM 2019 Blockchain and CEE Forum, LNBIP 361, pp. 71–86, 2019.
https://doi.org/10.1007/978-3-030-30429-4_6

attempt of extracting meaningful logs from the Caterpillar on-chain BPMS [5]. The challenges derive from a mismatch between the *logged data* and the event data required for analysis, e.g., minimising logged information keeps the cost and data volume manageable. Challenges also arise from the underlying technology itself, e.g., Ethereum's block timestamps refer to the time when mining started, not to the block production. Moreover, as the DApp's source code is by default not shared, process participants are potentially left with cryptic information that is hard to decode.

To alleviate this pain, we propose a framework for extracting process event data from Ethereum-based DApps that utilize Ethereum's transaction log as a storage for logged data. The framework comprises three main parts:

- The *manifest* enables users to capture and share their view of how data logged by a DApp should be interpreted from a process perspective. It is input to all other parts and is processed without access to the source code. Thus, our framework eliminates the need to share DApp code. To support users in developing a manifest, our framework includes a *validator*, which checks if a particular manifest adheres to the rules outlined in this paper.
- The *extractor* retrieves logged data from the Ethereum transaction log, applies the rules from the manifest to transform the logged data into event data, and formats this data according to the XES standard [4]. As a consequence, the extracted data can readily be imported into process mining tools from academia and industry (e.g., ProM, Celonis, ProcessGold, Disco, Minit, QPR, Apromore, and RapidProM).
- The *generator* automatically creates logging functionality from the manifest. It further includes proposals for several optimisations, such as a means for encoding logged data in the compact form of a bitmap, which helps in achieving relatively low cost and high throughput for on-chain logging.

The proposal is evaluated with logs created from generated logging code, as well as with an existing DApp. It was created by developers other than the authors of this paper and thus demonstrates the universal applicability of the framework.

In the following, we first introduce relevant background information on process mining, blockchain and logging in Sect. 2. The approach is introduced in Sect. 3 and evaluated in Sect. 4, before Sect. 5 concludes.

2   Background

2.1   Process Mining and Process Event Data

Process Mining. The roots of process mining lie in the *Business Process Management* (BPM) discipline where it was introduced as a way to infer workflows and to effectively use the audit trails present in modern information systems. Evidence-based BPM powered by process mining helps to create a common ground for business process improvement and information systems development.

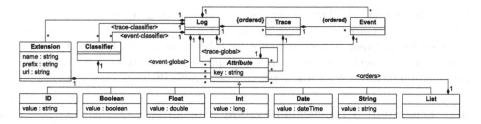

Fig. 1. XES meta-model (cf. [4])

The uptake of process mining is reflected by the growing number of commercial tools including Celonis, Disco, ProcessGold, Minit, myInvenio and QPR. Examples like Siemens where over 6,000 people are using process mining to improve operations in many areas attest the value of process mining for businesses.

Process mining is widely used to diagnose and address compliance and performance problems. There are three main types: (i) *process discovery*, (ii) *conformance checking*, and (iii) *model enhancement*. Starting from raw event data process discovery creates process models that reflect reality and that include all or only the most frequent behavior. Conformance checking combines modeled and observed behavior. By replaying event data on a process model (modeled or automatically learned) one can diagnose and quantify deviations, e.g., to find root causes for non-compliance. Model enhancement is used to improve or extend a process model using event data. Process mining can also be used in an online setting and to predict compliance or performance problems before they occur. There are hundreds of process discovery, conformance checking, and model enhancement techniques that rely on model representations like Petri nets, directly-follows graphs, transition systems, process trees, BPMN and statecharts.

Event Data. Event data is represented as an event log which provides a view on a process from a particular angle. Each event in an event log refers to (i) a particular *process instance* (ii) an *activity*, and (iii) a *timestamp*. There may be various other attributes referring to costs, risks, resources, locations, etc. The XES standard [4] defines a format for storing such event logs. Due to its widespread use and tooling support, it is a suitable target format for blockchain logged data, enabling analysts to examine DApps using process mining.

Figure 1 shows the XES meta-model as specified in [4]. The meta-model is oriented towards the general notion of *logs*, *traces*, and *events*. A log represents a process and consists of a sequence of traces which record information about individual process instances. Each trace contains a sequence of events referring to activities executed within the process instance. Logs, traces and events are described by attributes that have a *key*, a *type*, and a *value*. Attributes can also be nested, i.e., an attribute can contain other attributes. The XES standard does not prescribe terms for the keys and is thus free of domain semantics. However, to assign meanings to attribute keys, *extensions* can be included that define the meaning and the type associated with specific keys. Moreover, *global* values can be specified for any attribute at the event or trace level. Setting the global value v for the event (trace) attribute a means that if the value of attribute a is not specified for an event (trace), it implicitly takes value v. Finally, event (trace) *classifiers* comprise one or more attributes and each event (trace) with the same combination of values for these attributes belongs to the same class.

2.2   Ethereum: A Blockchain System

Blockchain. A blockchain is an append-only store of transactions, distributed across computational nodes and structured as a linked list of blocks, each containing a set of transactions [14]. Blockchain was introduced as the technology behind Bitcoin [8]. Its concepts have been generalized to distributed ledger systems that verify and store any transactions without coins or tokens [11], without relying on any central trusted authority like traditional banking or payment systems. Instead, all participants in the network can reach agreement on the states of transactional data to achieve trust.

A smart contract is a user-defined program that is deployed and executed on a blockchain system [9,14], which can express triggers, conditions and business logic [13] to enable complex programmable transactions. Smart contracts can be deployed and invoked through transactions, and are executed across the blockchain network by all connected nodes. The signature of the transaction sender authorizes the data payload of a transaction to create or execute a smart contract. Trust in the correct execution of smart contracts extends directly from regular transactions, since (i) they are deployed as data in a transaction and are thus immutable; (ii) all their inputs are through transactions and the current state; (iii) their code is deterministic; and (iv) the results of transactions are captured in the state and receipt trees, which are part of the consensus.[1]

Ethereum. Ethereum is a specific blockchain system that allows users to deploy and execute smart contracts. We focus on this system as it is the longest-running blockchain with expressive smart contract capabilities. It provides an interface to store information in the transaction log. In general, smart contracts can only write information to the log, but not retrieve information from it. However, applications connected to an Ethereum node can query the log for information. This enables the implementation of an event-driven DApp architecture where smart contracts share information and applications react to published information.

Smart contracts for Ethereum are typically written in *Solidity*. This language provides write access to the transaction log via so called *events*. Events are specified through their signature including the event's name and a list of typed parameters (as of Solidity version 0.5.x only fixed-length types can be used), but no return type. Events also do not have an implementation. Instead, when an event is emitted, the event's signature and parameter values are automatically written to the transaction log as a structured *log entry*. There is also a low-level interface that allows developers to flexibly define the structure of log entries, but the burden for retrieving those entries is increased. In practice this interface is rarely used as revealed by our analysis of 21,205 different real-world smart contracts which we downloaded from Etherscan[2], covering a period of 10 months

---

[1] Summary adapted from [12].
[2] http://etherscan.io.

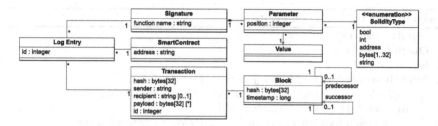

Fig. 2. EVM logging meta-model

starting in June 2018. Within these smart contracts, we found more than 300,000 event emissions, but only 127 calls to the low-level interface. Hence, we decided to focus on extracting log entries whose structure follows that of the Solidity events and leave the full support for the low-level interface to future work.

The conceptual schema of the data from the transaction log is shown in Fig. 2. A *log entry* represents an emitted event. We use the term log entry instead of event to avoid confusion with XES events (see Sect. 2.1). A log entry is associated with its *signature*, the *smart contract* that emitted the log entry and the *transaction* from which the log entry originated. The *id* of a log entry is only unique within the transaction and a smart contract is identified by its *address*. The signature contains the *function name* and a list of *parameters* defined by their *position* and *type*. Moreover, the transaction log contains the *value* for each parameter. For the transaction, we can retrieve its *hash*, the *payload*, the *sender* of the transaction, and the *recipient*, if available. Similar to the log entry, the *id* of a transaction is unique within the *block* that included the transaction. For such a block, we can load the *hash* and the *timestamp* as well as the *predecessor* and *successor* (which do not exist for the first and the latest block, respectively).

3   Approach

A high-level overview of our framework for extracting event data from Ethereum's transaction log is presented in Fig. 3. The *extractor* is a rule-based transformation algorithm that converts a set of log entries from the transaction log into files containing XES logs. The transformation rules can be flexibly

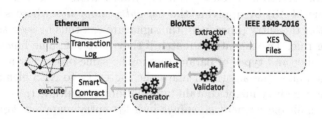

Fig. 3. High-level overview of the components

Algorithm 1. Extraction algorithm

Input: $manifest$
Output: $xesFiles$
1 $logs = \{\}$
2 **foreach** $smartContractMapping$ in $manifest$ **do**
3      $logEntries \leftarrow$ SelectLogEntries($smartContractMapping$)
4   **foreach** $logEntry$ in $logEntries$ **do**
5   **foreach** $logEntryMapping$ in $smartContractMapping$ **do**
6   **if** $logEntryMapping.signature = logEntry.signature$ **then**
7   **forall the** $elementMapping$ in $logEntryMapping$ **do**
8                      $attributeMappings = elementMapping.mappings$
9                      $attributes \leftarrow$ Extract($entry, attributeMappings$)
10   **if** $isEventMapping(elementMapping)$ **then**
11   AddEventAttributes($attributes, logs$)
12   **else if** $isTraceMapping(elementMapping)$ **then**
13   AddTraceAttributes($attributes, logs$)
14 $xesFiles \leftarrow$ CreateXesFiles($logs$)

---

adapted via the *manifest* which e.g., specifies which smart contracts to consider, how to filter events, which timestamps to include and where to find the concept (activity) name. The extractor can generate XES logs from any smart contract, given a fitting manifest, and given the required information has been logged in the first place. The *validator* supports the creation of a manifest by checking if it follows the rules of the manifest specification. Moreover, from a given manifest the *generator* automatically produces Solidity code for logging, which can then be integrated into smart contracts. This is particularly useful when using the feature mentioned in the introduction: compact encoding of data in a bitmap (details in Sect. 3.2). Following, we outline the different elements in detail.

3.1 The Extractor and the Manifest

The extraction Algorithm 1, takes the manifest as input and first initializes an empty set of logs (line 1). This set can be viewed as the root of a *log hierarchy* where each child is a log that, according to the XES standard (see Fig. 1), contains traces and events. Next, the algorithm iterates over the *smart contract mapping*s from the manifest (lines 2–13) and for each such mapping *selects the log entries* from the transaction log (line 3). Information is extracted from each log entry (lines 4–13) by applying the *log entry mappings* whose signature is equal to that of the entry (lines 5–6); the signature can thus be seen as the head of a mapping rule. Two signatures match if they have the same function name, the same number and types of parameters in the same order. For all matching log entry mappings, the algorithm maps the log entry to XES elements (lines 7–13). As one log entry might contain information for multiple traces or events, there can be multiple *element mappings* in a log entry mapping. For each element mapping (line 7–13) the algorithm extracts the attributes from the log entry according to the respective *attribute mappings* (lines 8–9). If the element

Table 1. Support for casting solidity into XES types ('+' = cast supported; '!' = cast supported, runtime exception possible; '-' = cast not supported)

Solidity types	XES types						
	int	float	date	string	boolean	id	list
int	!	!	!	+	-	-	-
string	-	-	-	+	+	!	-
address	-	-	-	+	-	-	-
byte	+	+	-	+	+	-	-
bytes	-	-	-	+	+	-	-
boolean	-	-	-	+	+	-	-
array	-	-	-	-	-	-	!

mapping is a *trace mapping* (*event mapping*) the algorithm *adds the attributes* to a new or an existing trace (event) in the log hierarchy (lines 10–13). Lastly, the algorithm *creates the XES files* from the logs (line 14) and returns the files. Below, we describe the steps of the algorithm and explain how the steps can be configured using the manifest. Further, we discuss exception handling. We also present a consolidated manifest meta-model and details of the validator.

Selecting Log Entries. For a smart contract mapping, log entries are selected based on two criteria. First, the log entries must have been written by a transaction that is included in a block from a specified block range $[fromBlock, toBlock]$. If no block range is defined, the log entries of the 1000 most current blocks are retrieved. Second, the log entries must have been emitted by a smart contract whose address is in a set of predefined *addresses* and there must be at least one address. Note that by specifying multiple addresses, a developer can apply the same transformation rules to different smart contracts. Finally, log entries are retrieved in the order in which they were written into the transaction log and the created XES elements follow this ordering.

Extracting Attributes. For every attribute mapping, the developer needs to specify the attribute's *name* and a *value builder*. A value builder is a function that (i) takes a log entry, (ii) returns a value, and (iii) is applied to each log entry the element mapping is executed for. A value builder is configured by specifying its *function name* and the return *type*, an XES type that becomes the type of the attribute. Moreover, the builder's *parameters*, a list of key-value pairs, must be set. *Static parameters* have a fixed value, whereas *value builder parameters* specify another value builder. We provide the following value builders:

- A *static value* is a fixed value that is assigned to the attribute. We support static values for all XES types except lists.
- *Parameter casts* access a log entry parameter or attributes of the associated block or transaction identified by their name and cast the value of the respective Solidity type into the XES type.

Table 1 lists the supported type casts. Some type casts might result in a runtime exception, if the parameter value violates the range of allowed values, e.g., only string values that represent UUIDs can be cast into ID attributes [4].

- A *string concatenation* returns a formatted strings that joins the values of value builders that return a string, int or id.
- *Value dictionaries* map the value returned by another value builder to attribute values. Value maps can be specified for arbitrary XES type combinations and must include a default value.
- *Bit mappings* are used when data from the smart contracts is compressed before being written into the transaction log. This is typically achieved by assigning bit ranges of a single log entry parameter to certain variables. We support the decompression of such bit ranges. To this end, the value of a specified bit range of length l is at runtime mapped to an integer value p from the interval $[0, 2^l)$. Then, p is converted into a meaningful value based on a value array with 2^l elements from which we return the pth value.

Table 2. XES extension for identity attributes (name: "Identity", prefix: "ident", URI: "https://www.data61.csiro.au/ident.xesext")

Key	Definition	Type	Cardinality	Element
pid	Identifies a particular process	string	0-1	event, trace
piid	Identifies a particular process instance	string	0-1	event, trace
eid	Identifies a particular event	string	0-1	event

Appending Attributes to the Log Hierarchy. The processing of an element mapping for a log entry results in a set of attributes which belongs to the same XES element. We determine the identity of this element, add the attribute set to it, and integrate it into the log hierarchy in the following way. Each attribute set is considered to contain identity attributes. In particular, we defined three identity attributes within our custom *ident* XES extension (see Table 2). The *ident:pid* attribute identifies the process that an event or a trace belongs to and each distinct pid-value results in a separate log element. The *ident:piid* attribute determines the identity of a trace element within a certain log element, i.e., the global identity of a trace element is determined by its pid and piid-values. Finally, the *ident:eid* attribute establishes the identity of an event within a trace, i.e., the global identity of an event is given by the pid, piid, and eid-values. If the extracted attribute set does not include any of the identity attributes, we add those attributes and set their values to a default value.

We then use these attributes to add the entire attribute set to the log hierarchy. First, we select the log element with the respective pid-value. If such a log element does not exist, we create a new one with the respective pid-value, add it to the hierarchy, and select it. Next, we look for the trace element with the respective piid-value within the selected log element. Again, if we cannot find such an element, we create a new one, add it to the log element, and select it.

If the element mapping is a trace mapping, we append the attribute set to the trace. Otherwise, we select or create an event element within the selected trace element based on the specified eid-value and append the attributes to this element. Following this strategy, we can integrate log entries from different smart contracts within the same log hierarchy. If no ident-attributes were specified, the algorithm generates one log element, containing one trace element and all log entries are mapped to individual event elements under this trace element.

Creating XES Files. The last step is to create XES files. Here, we create one XES file per log in the log hierarchy and set the file's name to the log's pid-value. To fully support the XES standard [4] and to relieve developers of having to edit the generated XES files, we allow users to specify XES extensions, global values and classifiers within the manifest. Each of these elements can be bound to a range of pids. If pids are specified for an element, the element is only included in the XES files corresponding to one of those pids. Otherwise, the element is added to all XES files. The inclusion of those features requires developers to adhere to the constraints that they impose on XES attributes. We discuss those constraints in more detail in the context of the validator (see below).

Runtime Exceptions. Some of the operations can result in runtime exceptions. The first exception type can occur when casting Solidity to XES types and was already discussed above. The second type refers to situations where the value of a certain XES attribute is set multiple times. While we restrict developers to set the value for an attribute only once within an element mapping, the problem can occur when adding attributes to existing elements. To circumvent this problem, the user can specify one *duplicate handling* strategy per attribute mapping. There are three different strategies: (i) *throw an exception*, (ii) *replace* the old value, and (iii) *ignore* the new value. Lastly, an *extension exception* is thrown in cases where an XES extension attribute is added to the log hierarchy, but the extension is not defined for the respective pid. Hence, extensions should only be restricted to certain pid-values, if the pid values are known in advance.

Developers can select one of three *exception handling* strategies for the entire manifest: (i) *determine* the algorithm (default option), (ii) *ignore* exceptions, and (iii) *write* exceptions to the XES logs. When the last option is selected, exceptions are converted into attributes. In case of a type cast exception and an extension exception, the algorithm creates a list with the key "error" and adds it to the attribute set. The exception information is added as a separate string attribute to the list's values section and the attribute's key is set to the key of the attribute that caused the exception. If there are multiple exceptions when processing one attribute mapping, the exceptions are grouped in the same error list. In case of a duplicate handling exception, we also create an error list which contains a string attribute per exception. In contrast to the other exceptions, we add the list to the attribute for which the value is set multiple times.

The Manifest. A consolidated view of the manifest which has been introduced throughout the introduction of the extraction algorithm is presented in Fig. 4.

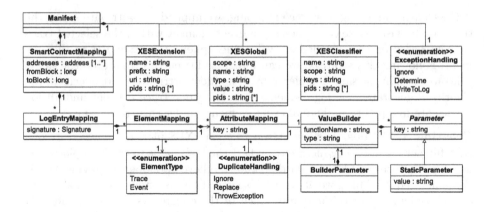

Fig. 4. Manifest meta-model

The Validator. The validation of a manifest is a two-step process. First, we check whether the manifest's structure adheres to the meta-model from Fig. 4. To this end, we ensure that (i) all manifest elements are structured according to their meta-model type, (ii) the relationships between the model elements adhere to those specified in the meta-model, (iii) all required elements, relationships and attributes are present, and (iv) that specified values have a valid format, e.g., that the specified Solidity types or XES types are known.

Second, we investigate the definition and usage of attributes as well as log entry parameters. To this end, we check that all combinations of attribute keys and types specified in attribute mappings, extensions and global values are consistent. We also verify that for each attribute that contains a prefix there is an extension that defines this attribute. Following the XES standard [4], we validate that there is a global value for all attribute keys used within classifier definitions. Further, we check the validity of the value builder specifications including their parameters. If a static value is specified, its string representation from the manifest must be castable into the specified type. For parameter casts, we check that they reference a valid parameter or attribute and that the type cast is supported (see Table 1). For all other value builders, we recursively verify that the return type of its child value builders is compatible with the expected input types, e.g., the concatenation value builder only allows the use of *xs:string*, *xs:id*, and *xs:int*.

While the validator verifies that the generated XES documents adheres to the XES standard, it cannot be guaranteed that all log entries can be processed, as discussed above in the context of runtime exceptions.

3.2 The Generator

We support developers of new smart contracts by generating logging functionality from the manifest. First, we use the signatures specified in the log entry mappings to generate Solidity events. This step is straightforward, as the signature specification in the manifest corresponds to the representation of events in

Solidity's *contract application binary interface specification*, or *ABI*, the interface specification of smart contracts which is shared with users that want to interact with the respective smart contracts.

Additionally, we implemented the generation of logging functionality for value dictionaries or bit mapping builders specified in the manifest. As mentioned in Sect. 2.2, smart contract developers can log various information via Solidity's event parameters. On the public Ethereum blockchain, there is a cost involved for emitting smart contract events, which is proportional to the size of event parameters values being emitted (for example, a parameter of type *string* may cost more to log than an *int* parameter, if the string value is longer than 32 bytes). Therefore, developers can choose to log smart contract event parameters of a smaller type, such as *int*, then define a value dictionary in the manifest to map the Solidity event parameter values to a corresponding description of the value. In such cases, the generator produces (i) the Solidity event signature, (ii) an *enum* of the dictionary values which are mapped to the event parameter, and (iii) a logging function which accepts an *enum* value, then emits the Solidity event with the corresponding parameter value. An example of Solidity code generated from a manifest value dictionary is provided in Listing 1.1.

```
1  contract XESLogger {
2      event GitCommit(uint authorId, bytes32 sha);
3      enum Author {FIRST, SECOND, THIRD, FOURTH};
4      uint[] enumValsAuthor = [1000, 2000, 3000, 4000];
5      function logCommit(Author author, bytes32 sha) internal {
6          uint authorId = enumValsAuthor[uint8(author)];
7          emit GitCommit(authorId, sha);
8      }
9  }
```

Listing 1.1. Solidity generated from manifest with value dictionary builder

Another pattern that developers can use to further reduce the smart contract event log size is to encode multiple pieces of information into one log entry parameter with a small type such as *int*. To do this, they can specify a *bitmap* value builder in the manifest, which maps a subset of consecutive bits in a log entry parameter to a range of values. This is essentially a generalization of the bitmapping strategy adopted in earlier works of one author [3,6]. To effectively encode multiple pieces of information, multiple bitmap value builders can be defined on separate bit ranges of the same parameter.

As an example, assume we define a manifest for extracting events from *Shirt-Produced* log entries, which are emitted each time a new shirt is produced in a *textile factory*. Three attributes related to a shirt, *Size*, *Fabric* and *Quality* are extracted from the same parameter, *encodedAttributes*. The first 3 bits (offset 0 to 2) are used to encode eight size classifications, bits 3–5 encode six shirt fabric types, and bits 6–7 represent four quality classes. Table 3 shows the bit mapping definitions for this example. From the respective value builder, the generator can produce a Solidity logging function which takes *Quality*, *Fabric* and *Size* input parameters as enums, and emits an event whose value correctly encodes the above information according to the mapping defined (see Listing 1.2).

```
1   contract XESLogger {
2       enum Quality {LOW, NORMAL, HIGH, EXCELLENT};
3       enum Fabric {COTTON, LINEN, WOOL, SILK, POLYESTER, BLEND};
4       enum Size {XXS, XS, S, M, L, XL, XXL, XXL};
5       event ShirtProduced(uint256 shirtId, uint256
            encodedAttributes, uint256 batchId);
6       function logShirtProduced(uint256 shirtId, Quality q,
            Fabric fabric, Size size, uint256 batchId) internal {
7           uint256 qMask = uint256(q) * (2**(6));
8           uint256 fabricMask = uint256(fabric) * (2**(3));
9           uint256 sizeMask = uint256(size) * (2**(0));
10          uint256 encodedAttributes = qMask | fabricMask |
                sizeMask;
11          emit ShirtProduced(shirtId, encodedAttributes, batchId)
                ;
12      }
13  }
```

Listing 1.2. Solidity generated from manifest with bit mapping builders

Table 3. Encode info in Solidity event parameter with bit mapping builders

Quality - bit range: 6..7		Fabric - bit range: 3..5		Size - bit range: 0..2	
Key	Value	Key	Value	Key	Value
00	Low	000	Cotton	000	2× small
01	Normal	001	Linen	001	Extra small
10	High	010	Wool	010	Small
11	Excellent	011	Silk	011	Medium
		100	Polyester	100	Large
		101	Blend	101	Extra large
				110	2× large
				111	3× large

4   Implementation, Evaluation, and Discussion

4.1   Implementation

We implemented the framework. The extractor and generator have been written in JavaScript for node.js, and manifests are specified in JSON format. The extractor takes several parameters as command line inputs:

- **rpc**: the URL of the blockchain node to query through the RPC interface

– m: manifest specification
– output: folder for storing extracted XES files

The complexity of the manifest file strongly depends on the complexity of the analyzed contracts. The manifest for our case study below has approximately 230 lines; the one for the code generation evaluation has about 65 lines.

4.2 Code Generation Evaluation

We tested the generator of logging code with a proof-of-concept demonstration of the *textile factory* example from Sect. 3.2. To this end, we first wrote the manifest specification, used it to generate logging code, then wrote a simple smart contract using this logging code and deployed it on a Geth Ethereum client using Ganache (a test mode that simulates an Ethereum blockchain in memory, but is otherwise identical in behavior). We then ran a test script against this Geth client, to 'produce' shirts according to a 'production schedule' which generated Solidity logs, and finally used the extractor to extract XES logs.

In this part of the evaluation, we tested the functional correctness of the generator and the extractor, which we found to be operating as per the design: the XES logs contained the same data in the same order as the production schedule. The tests of value and bit mapping functionality were successful as well: data was encoded as assumed, in 8 bits per shirt.

4.3 Case Study: CryptoKitties

CryptoKitties is "a game centered around breedable, collectible, and oh-so-adorable creatures we call CryptoKitties"[3]. While not Ethereum's most serious application, it is a well-known example of a DApp (that is primarily based on smart contracts), has been used heavily at times (likely due some of the kitties being sold for thousands of dollars), and has been in operation since December 2017. It also was developed without involvement of any of the paper's authors, making it a suitable candidate for demonstrating the framework's applicability.

```
1  event Birth(address owner, uint256 kittyId, uint256  matronId,
        uint256 sireId, uint256 genes);
2  event Transfer(address from, address to, uint256 tokenId);
3  event Pregnant(address owner, uint256 matronId, uint256 sireId,
        uint256 cooldownEndBlock);
4  event AuctionCreated(uint256 tokenId, uint256 startingPrice,
        uint256 endingPrice, uint256 duration);
5  event AuctionSuccessful(uint256 tokenId, uint256 totalPrice,
        address winner);
6  event AuctionCancelled(uint256 tokenId);
```

Listing 1.3. Event definitions in the CryptoKittie contract

---

[3] https://www.cryptokitties.co/, accessed 30/5/2019.

A CryptoKitty is the Ethereum version of a Tamagotchi. It is a digital asset owned by an Ethereum account and it can be traded. A CryptoKitty can breed new CryptoKitties. To this end, the owner can trigger the impregnation of a cat when having access to a second cat (either by owning it or by having the permission of the cat's owner). After a cat becomes pregnant, the owner must publish a "birth helper request" asking an independent account to trigger the birth in exchange of a certain amount of Ether. A CryptoKitty is represented by an identifier and its DNA, from which its features and appearance are derived. The source code of the CryptoKitties smart contracts is available on etherscan[4] and Listing 1.3 summarizes the event definitions from the source code.

We extracted two logs from these smart contracts with our framework and implementation[5]. The *genesis* log stems from the first 3000 blocks after creation of the smart contract at block 4605167. The *everyday* log is based on log entries from a random block range containing 13000 blocks, starting from block 6605100. In both cases, we only extracted information about the lifecycle process of the cats. Thus, we grouped all process instances in the same log and the ID of a cat is used as the process instance ID, i.e., the lifecycle of each cat is viewed as an independent process instance. Moreover, each log entry is mapped to individual events. Per auction and transfer-related log entry, we created one event in the trace of the cat represented by the tokenId. The birth and pregnant log entries involve multiple cats (matronId, sireId, kittyId) and are hence mapped to events in each cat's lifecycle. Note that choosing the pid, piid and eid-values is critical and a general concern for process analytics, on blockchain data or otherwise. For example, in our case study, we take the viewpoint of an individual kitty, but this may not be suitable for analysing the complete population. To generate different views, our framework allows analysts to materialize their choice of identity attributes in the manifest, and for some applications multiple manifests with different choices might be required to obtain the desired views.

We mined the extracted event flows from both logs as depicted in Fig. 5. Figure 5a shows that the developer started with two kitties initially, and bred them 3000 times for bootstrapping the game. The behavior during the everyday use Fig. (5b) shows considerably more variation and includes all types of events.

While we could delve into a deep analysis of kitty behaviour, the purpose of the case study in this paper was to test if the proposed framework can be applied to existing smart contracts – which we deem to be the case. We successfully extracted event logs, stored them in the XES format, and loaded them for analysis in both ProM and Disco.

5   Conclusion and Discussion

In this paper, we addressed the problem of applying process mining to smart contracts and focused on extracting meaningful event data from blockchain sys-

---

[4] https://etherscan.io/address/0x06012c8cf97bead5deae237070f9587f8e7a266d#code, Accessed: 17/05/2019.

[5] Generated XES files and manifest available under https://doi.org/10.25919/5d242b0be3384.

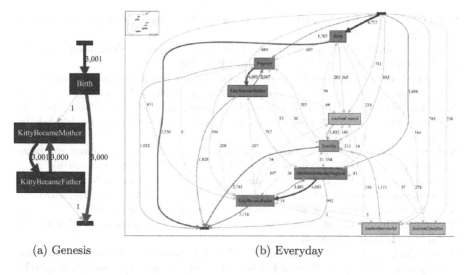

(a) Genesis   (b) Everyday

Fig. 5. Directly-Follows Graphs (DFGs) generated using ProM from both logs

tems, in particular from Ethereum transaction logs. Our proposed framework includes (i) the manifest specification for defining transformation rules that are automatically validated; (ii) the extractor that transforms log entries from a transaction log to XES logs; and (iii) the generator that produces high-level logging functionality for user-defined DApps. We showed that the generator produces logging functionality adhering to the log entries and data compression rules from the manifest. Further, we successfully applied the extractor to logs created from generated code, as well as logs from a pre-existing, long running and heavily used DApp, demonstrating its broad applicability.

There are a few limitations that impact the applicability of our framework. First, we focused on Ethereum and disregarded other blockchain systems which might use different logging mechanisms, potentially requiring a generalization of our framework. Second, our framework only offers a certain set of functionality; e.g., there are currently five types of value builders; complex conditions for filtering attributes and elements are not supported; and we do not fully support the low-level logging interface. While this emphasizes the need for further generalization, we also plan to improve the extensibility of the framework and to release it as open source, enabling users to adapt it to their needs. Further, process mining can be used for many purposes; here we only used it for exploration of the data, to demonstrate the feasibility of our framework. In future work, we will apply the tool to more use cases and purposes.

References

1. van der Aalst, W.: Process Mining - Data Science in Action. Springer, Heidelberg (2016). https://doi.org/10.1007/978-3-662-49851-4

2. Di Ciccio, C., et al.: Blockchain-based traceability of inter-organisational business processes. In: BMSD (2018)
3. García-Bañuelos, L., Ponomarev, A., Dumas, M., Weber, I.: Optimized execution of business processes on blockchain. In: BPM (2017)
4. IEEE standard for extensible event stream (XES) for achieving interoperability in event logs and event streams. IEEE Std 1849–2016, November 2016
5. López-Pintado, O., García-Bañuelos, L., Dumas, M., Weber, I., Ponomarev, A.: Caterpillar: a business process execution engine on the Ethereum blockchain. Softw.: Pract. Exp. **49**, 1–32 (2019)
6. López-Pintado, O., Dumas, M., García-Bañuelos, L., Weber, I.: Dynamic role binding in blockchain-based collaborative business processes. In: CAISE (2019)
7. Mendling, J., Weber, I., Van Der Aalst, W., et al.: Blockchains for business process management - challenges and opportunities. ACM TMIS **9**(1), 41–416 (2018)
8. Nakamoto, S.: Bitcoin: a peer-to-peer electronic cash system (2008)
9. Omohundro, S.: Cryptocurrencies, smart contracts, and artificial intelligence. AI Matters **1**(2), 19–21 (2014)
10. Prybila, C., Schulte, S., Hochreiner, C., Weber, I.: Runtime verification for business processes utilizing the Bitcoin blockchain. Future Gener. Comput. Syst. (2017). https://doi.org/10.1016/j.future.2017.08.024. ISSN 0167-739X
11. Tschorsch, F., Scheuermann, B.: Bitcoin and beyond: a technical survey on decentralized digital currencies. IEEE Commun. Surv. Tutor. **18**(3), 2084–2123 (2016)
12. Weber, I., Lu, Q., Tran, A.B., Deshmukh, A., Gorski, M., Strazds, M.: A platform architecture for multi-tenant blockchain-based systems. In: ICSA (2019)
13. Weber, I., Xu, X., Riveret, R., Governatori, G., Ponomarev, A., Mendling, J.: Untrusted business process monitoring and execution using blockchain. In: International Conference on Business Process Management (BPM) (2016)
14. Xu, X., Weber, I., Staples, M.: Architecture for Blockchain Applications. Springer, Heidelberg (2019). https://doi.org/10.1007/978-3-030-03035-3

Balancing Privity and Enforceability of BPM-Based Smart Contracts on Blockchains

Julius Köpke[✉], Marco Franceschetti, and Johann Eder

Department of Informatics Systems, Alpen-Adria-Universität Klagenfurt,
Klagenfurt, Austria
{julius.koepke,marco.franceschetti,johann.eder}@aau.at
https://www.aau.at/isys/

Abstract. Blockchains are a promising enabling technology for inter-organizational processes in untrusted environments and for the implementation of smart contracts in general. Smart contracts aim at three major objectives: observability, online enforceability and privity. Privity strives for limiting the sharing of information within a contract to those parties of a contract who have a contractual need to know. However, current BPM-based systems operating on blockchains do not address privity. The approaches deal with enforceability and privity as mutual exclusive properties. We show that the trade-offs between privity and enforceability can be considered in fine details and propose means to balance privity and enforceability in the design of smart contracts according to the application requirements. Besides this conceptual basis, we introduce patterns for encryption and key exchange allowing different levels of privity and for supporting proactive online enforceability in the presence of encrypted on-chain data.

Keywords: Inter-organizational business processes · Blockchain · Smart contracts · Privity · Confidentiality

1 Introduction

Blockchains are a powerful basis for applications in untrusted environments without requiring a trusted third party [18]. In particular, smart contracts [22] as counterparts of classical legal contracts in the digital world are assumed to strongly benefit from blockchain technology. The interest in blockchain technology in the BPM community is twofold. On the one hand, blockchain technology allows to overcome current limitations in business process management [15]. In particular inter-organizational business processes could be designed in different ways, if blockchains reduce the need for trusted mediators and their implementation could benefit from blockchain technologies. On the other hand, methods and techniques from the BPM community are promising technologies

© Springer Nature Switzerland AG 2019
C. Di Ciccio et al. (Eds.): BPM 2019 Blockchain and CEE Forum, LNBIP 361, pp. 87–102, 2019.
https://doi.org/10.1007/978-3-030-30429-4_7

for modeling and executing smart contracts [9]. Szabo defined three major objectives of smart contracts in [22]: observability, online enforceability, and privity. Existing approaches [5, 8, 14, 16, 19, 21, 23, 25] for executing business processes on blockchains emphasize on the aspects of observability and enforceability, but none of the approaches provides means for privity. However, the lack of privity is considered as a major factor limiting the practical application of blockchain based smart contracts in organizations [24].

Privity is a legal term and describes the property of a (smart) contract that knowledge of and about the contract should be shared only with those parties of a contract who have a contractual need to know. This property is hard to provide on current blockchains, where transactions are either entirely public or visible for all permissioned users in case of permissioned blockchains. This problem is currently mostly ignored in current BPM based blockchain approaches, and only general and static solutions like proposing to use a permissioned chain, using off-chain data, or generally using encryption without providing details are proposed. The usage of encryption of on-chain data is considered challenging as keys need to be shared between participants secretly [26].

In this paper we show that encrypted on-chain data storage and key exchange can be realized on current public blockchains such as Ethereum. Our aim is to extend process models with encryption and key exchange primitives to provide privity support for blockchain based BPM solutions. Our contributions are the following:

- Encryption and key exchange patterns for business processes supporting different levels of privity.
- Patterns for achieving enforceability in the presence of encrypted data.
- Strategies for balancing privity and enforceability based on application requirements.

The paper is structured as follows: Sect. 2 briefly introduces blockchain technology and presents messaging patterns on blockchains. In Sect. 3 we introduce patterns for implementing encryption and key exchanges in business processes for various privity requirements and discuss optimizations. Sect. 4 introduces patterns for supporting enforceability in the presence of encrypted data. In Sect. 5 we discuss the need to balance the objectives privity and enforceability. Contrast with related work (Sect. 6) and conclusions (Sect. 7) complete the paper.

2   Preliminaries

2.1   Public Blockchains

Blockchains as introduced with the Bitcoin-protocol [17] can be considered as distributed append-only databases where new data is appended in cryptographically linked blocks. Adding blocks and therefore the decision over the contents of the shared database is realized by a consensus protocol. Typically, *miners* are responsible for adding new blocks and for the verification of the included transactions. Only verified transactions (e.g. sender has sufficient funds) are added to the chain and every node in the network can verify all blocks/transactions. Therefore, the correctness of transactions is proactively enforced. The authentication of participants on blockchains is realized by public/private key encryption schemes: the sender of a transaction has to digitally sign the transaction and every participant in the network can verify the authenticity of the sender.

This architecture implies that all transactions are inherently public. Encryption or off-chain data storage of blockchain based applications can provide privity, however then transactions cannot be validated by miners based on the encrypted or off-chain data, leading to limited degrees of enforceability.

While first generation blockchains like Bitcoin focused on transactions which are specific for digital currencies and had only little support for custom transactions, more recent approaches like Ethereum [1] allow to implement custom transactions in Turing complete languages. Here the term smart contract is used for code executed on the blockchain. In the remainder of the paper we will distinguish between general smart contracts as proposed by Szabo in [22] and custom code on blockchains by referring to custom code as smart contract code.

2.2 Messaging Patterns via Blockchains

Blockchains can provide a single source of truth without requiring a trusted third party. Especially inter-organizational processes can benefit from this property. Inter-organizational processes are typically modeled in form of protocols of message exchanges (choreographies). We will therefore show how different messaging patterns can be implemented on blockchains. We base our patterns on the general data patterns presented in [26]. However, we add on-chain key exchange and discussions on enforceability.

Non-encrypted Message Exchange. *1:1 or 1:n:* The sender S signs a transaction T with data payload M. The smart contract code stores M on the chain and all recipients can retrieve the data from the chain either by querying [4] the (anyhow public) chain, or by calling specific smart contract code methods.

Benefits: The authenticity of the sender and of the message content is guaranteed by the blockchain. The message content is accessible by smart contract code. Therefore, verification of the current or of future transactions by the blockchain network can be based on the message content.

Drawbacks: No privity. The message content M is publicly available.

Encrypted Message Exchange. We require that the participants of the choreography have access to the public keys of each other. In addition, we require that it is possible to encrypt data for some receiver using her public key. Both assumptions are reasonable due to the architecture of blockchains. For example, in Ethereum [1], the public key of some address can be derived if the address was used for at least one previous transaction. Encryption of data based on the public key of the recipient is supported by DHKM [20]. This allows to implement the following patterns:

1:1: The sender S signs a transaction T with payload M. M is encrypted by S off-chain using the public key of the receiver R. R can read the data and decrypt it off-chain with her private key.

1:n: The sender S first encrypts the payload M off-chain with some newly generated symmetric key k. One encrypted version of the key is created off-chain for each recipient r in R using the recipient's public key. Finally, S signs a transaction with payload M', where M' contains the encrypted version of M and the encrypted key of each recipient. A variant is to use the *1:n* scheme also for *1:1* interactions. This is especially useful, if M is large and the actual implementation of public key encryption on the blockchain does not scale.

Benefits: Privity and Authenticity. Only recipients can read the message content.

Drawbacks: The message content is not accessible by smart contract code. Therefore, verification of the current or of future transactions by the blockchain network cannot be based on the message content.

Off-Chain Message Exchange. *1:1:* The sender S computes the hash value h of the message M and creates a blockchain transaction including h. The message content is sent to the recipient R using another communication channel.
1:n: Like *1:1*, but the message content is stored at some location where the recipients have access to.

Benefits: Like for encrypted message exchange but no (expensive) on-chain data storage, access can be revoked, encryption is optionally possible. In this case, keys can either be stored on-chain as before or off-chain.

Drawbacks: Like for encrypted message exchange and additionally data is not secured against modification or deletion.

3   Privity Preserving Data Exchange for Business Processes via Blockchain

The previously discussed messaging patterns on blockchains can be used to provide privity support for business processes executed on blockchains. A naive solution is the following: when a process instance is started, a session key is generated by one participant. Then one encrypted version of the session key is stored on-chain for each participant using the participant's public key. Consequently, each participant can decrypt the key and use it for encrypting and decrypting data during the course of the process instance. However, this approach has a major drawback: all participants get access to all data of the process. This can still be considered as a low degree of privity.

Therefore, more advanced techniques for encryption and key distribution are required. After introducing an example, we define privity spheres and present patterns for key distribution considering the different privity spheres.

In the remainder of the paper we will focus on on-chain encrypted data. However, the proposed strategies can also be used for off-chain encrypted data, where the keys are stored on-chain. This strongly limits the problems discussed in [26] of compromised keys, the lack of access revocation, and immutable data.

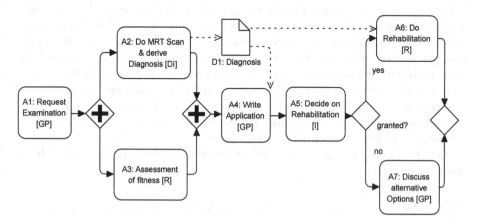

Fig. 1. Example inter-organizational process

3.1   Example Process

Similar to Caterpillar [19], we model inter-organizational cooperations as single Business Process Diagrams. For each task we specify the read and written data objects. Further, since the participant binding may differ for each process instantiation, and the actual binding is known at instantiation time, we consider design time specifications of participants as placeholders for blockchain user accounts/public keys.

An example process in BPMN notation is shown in Fig. 1. For a compact notation, we denote the participant or organization who is responsible to execute some task in square brackets. In the process model, first a general practitioner GP requests examinations ($A1$). Then in parallel an MRT image is taken and a diagnosis (Data object $D1$) is derived ($A2$) by a diagnosis institute DI and an assessment of fitness is created ($A3$) by a rehabilitation specialist R. Then the general practitioner GP writes an application for rehabilitation ($A4$) based on the results. Finally, a decision for granting the rehabilitation ($A5$) is taken by an insurance company I. If the rehabilitation is granted the rehabilitation is performed ($A6$) by the rehabilitation specialist R. Otherwise, the general practitioner discusses alternative options with the patient in task $A7$. For simplicity, we have included only one data object $D1$ in the process. The data object is created by the diagnosis institute. It is later required as an input for the tasks $A4$ and possibly $A6$. Depending on the required level of privity, we might allow every participant to read the diagnosis, only those who might need it, or only those who will definitely need it.

3.2   Privity Spheres

Privity requirements of smart contracts may differ. On the one end of the scale it might be reasonable, that all participants have access to all data and only third parties should not have access. On the other end of the scale we might take privity very seriously and only participants that certainly need some data value should be able to gain access to it. We have previously addressed a similar issue in the context of distributing data in inter-organizational processes via messages in [10,11]. Here we adapt and extend the notions of spheres for inter-organizational data-flow of [11], and define privity spheres and safeness classes for business processes executed on blockchains.

Let A be a step in a process model M writing to some variable v; let P be a process participant.

Global Sphere: P is in the global sphere of M, if M contains any step assigned to P.

Static Sphere: P is in the static sphere for variable v, if M contains any step assigned to P that reads or writes to v.

Weak-Dynamic Sphere: P is in the weak-dynamic sphere for variable v written by activity A, if there exists a continuation of the process starting at A, where P executes a task requiring v from A.

Strong-Dynamic Sphere: P is in the strong-dynamic sphere at some position l for variable v written by activity A, if for every possible continuation of the process starting at l, P will execute a task requiring v from A.

Example: Regarding the example in Fig. 1: the global sphere contains all participants (GP, DI, R, I). The static sphere of $d1$ contains DI, GP and R. The weak-dynamic sphere of $d1$ at position $A2$ contains GP and R. The strong-dynamic sphere of $d1$ at $A2$ contains only GP. R is in the strong-dynamic sphere only after the decision is taken.

Safeness Classes: Based on the different privity spheres, we can now define classes of encryption and key distribution implementations. Such an implementation is globally-/statically-/weak-dynamically-/strong-dynamically- safe if each participant has only access to data values if she is a member of the corresponding sphere for the data.

3.3 Augmentation of Processes

We start from process models where each step may read or write to data variables and is assigned to a participant in charge. Our goal is now to augment the process model with declarations for generating keys and encrypting/decrypting data, and with additional activities for exchanging keys between participants. We follow the basic principles for data encryption discussed in Subsect. 2.2. While we can assume that a task writing or reading some data variable can always be extended/wrapped with additional code for encryption/decryption and key generation, additional activities are required for key exchange (key exchange steps) and partially for generating keys. A key exchange step is a tuple $S = (l, A, D)$, where l is a label, A specifies the participant executing the step and D is a set of tuples of the form (k, R, c), specifying that A encrypts the key k with the public key of participant R under condition c and stores it on-chain. This realizes a transmission of k from A to R.

3.4 Encryption and Key Exchange Patterns

We now present encryption and key exchange patterns for the augmentation of processes for the different safeness classes. Figure 2 shows the original process on top and augmentations for each safeness class are shown below. Key exchange steps are decorated with a key symbol and include the set of tuples (k, R, c) for denoting the individual key transmissions of key k to participant R under condition c. Usual activities that are extended with declarations for key generation, encryption or decryption are depicted using usual data objects including a key symbol. The connections between nodes and encrypted data objects have additional labels specifying the key used for symmetric encryption of the data object. When the *new* keyword is used, a new key is generated by the participant writing the data.

Global: A key is generated at process start and it is subsequently transmitted to each participant. All later data encryptions and decryptions are realized with this key.

Example 1. The augmentation A in Fig. 2 contains an additional task KG executed by A for the creation of the key k and a subsequent key exchange step of A for the distribution of the key k to the participants B and C.

Static: One key is generated at process start for each data object. The keys are subsequently transmitted to the participants of each sphere. The key generation must be done by some member of the sphere.

Example 2. In augmentation B in Fig. 2, the initial step KG by participant A generates key k_x for data object x and k_z for data object z, respectively. Subsequently, k_x is transmitted to B and C, while k_z is transmitted only to C since B executes no step reading or writing z.

Weak-Dynamic: Whenever some participant writes to some data variable d, a new key k_d is generated and d is encrypted with this new k_d. The key k_d is immediately transmitted to each participant of the weak-dynamic sphere.

Example 3. In Augmentation C Fig. 2 we show an implementation of the weak-dynamic strategy. Partner A writes to the data objects x and z in step A. Consequently, she generates the keys k_x and k_z and transmits them to participant C since only C potentially reads x and z. Later on participant B writes to x in activity B without reading it. Therefore, B generates a new key k_x and transmits it to partner C.

Strong-Dynamic: Whenever some participant writes to some data variable, a new key k is generated, and the data is encrypted with k. The key is submitted by the participant writing to the data object at the latest possible time. Therefore, a key exchange step is added before each activity needing the data. The condition of the transmission needs to be included such that only keys are exchanged that are certainly needed.

Example 4. In Augmentation D in Fig. 2, partner A encrypts x and z with keys k_x and k_z. The transmission of the keys is performed immediately before executing C. In addition, the transmission of k_x to C is only performed if the condition c is *true*. Otherwise C must not gain access to k_x of A since B overwrites x and we cannot allow C to gain access to the old value via the blockchain. Similarly, B encrypts x with a new key k_x and this key is transmitted immediately before executing C only if the condition c is not *true*.

3.5 Optimization

Given the patterns for encryption and key exchange, we now discuss possible optimizations that go beyond the strict application of the patterns. Optimization can address two dimensions

(1) limiting the number of additional transactions for transmitting keys, and
(2) keeping the local processes of the participants as simple as possible.

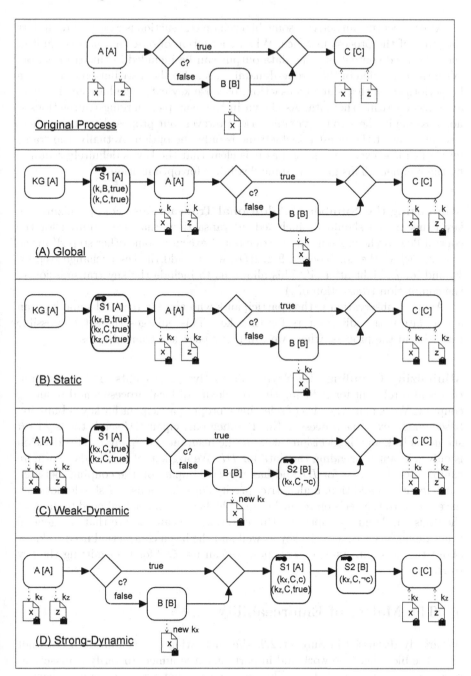

Fig. 2. Augmentation patterns for key generation and key exchange

After executing an activity some blockchain transaction is executed to update the state of the process instance. When encryption of on-chain data is applied, the encrypted content of some data output can be included in this transaction. With the exception of the strong-dynamic case, also the distribution of keys can be performed in that same transaction, because key exchange happens immediately after writing the data. As shown in the example, merging transactions is not possible in the strong-dynamic case. However, our proposed strategy where keys are sent at the latest possible time is only one option. Actually, the transmission can be executed as soon as it is clear that the key is definitely required by the recipient. This gives us some flexibility for optimization.

Minimizing the Number of Additional Transactions. For optimizing (1), key transmission should be included in transactions that are required for the control-flow anyhow. Assuming participant A executes some other step A' in the *true* branch of the xor-block in Fig. 2(D), we can add the key exchange step for k_x and for k_z right after A'. This allows us to include the key transmission in the completion transaction of A'.

Another observation is that participants who already received some key can act as alternative distributors for that key. This enlarges the set of possible activities in the process, where we can piggy-pack key transmissions.

Minimizing Coupling. Employing alternative participants for key distribution is also relevant for reducing the complexity of local processes and reducing coupling. We explain the idea of selecting a proper participant for key submission based on the example process in Fig. 1. When participant DI sends the key to R she needs to know the decision taken by the insurance company I. This decision is only relevant for sending the data for DI. We argue that this leads to a more complex local process for DI and has negative impact on the coupling between participants. In addition, under strict privity considerations, DI should not even have access to the decision result because she has no contractual need to know of the decision. Aiming to optimize this criterion, we can observe that the general practitioner has access to the key as well and she has a contractual need to know about the decision. As a consequence, we can use GP for transmitting the key to R.

4   The Matter of Enforceability

As already discussed in Subsect. 2.2, the encryption of on-chain data does not allow the blockchain network and in particular the miners to verify transactions based on the encrypted data. This also means that proactive enforcement is limited. We discuss the issue based on an example in Fig. 3. The process is executed by three participants. Each partner performs some task. Finally, partner C decides whether E or F is executed. Assuming the decision task is based on an expression over publicly available on-chain data, the correctness of the decision can be proactively enforced by smart contract code as all nodes and miners have access to the data. E.g., a decision by C not following the rules is not accepted. Alternatively, the decision can be taken automatically by smart contract code.

However, if the decision is based on encrypted data, then C is free to decide. Using currently applied public blockchain approaches, there is no way of validating or proactively executing the decision by the blockchain network. Therefore, the very strong proactive enforcement as known from crypto currencies is impossible. However, we propose that the problem can be limited by applying voting strategies between participants. Therefore, every participant who has access to the variables of a decision can execute the decision and record the result on the chain. When all votes are performed the actual decision smart contract code is executed (automatically). Miners can now verify or even automatically execute the decision by using the output of the participants. In particular, smart contract code and therefore the miners can check if the decision followed a specific decision mode. Viable decision modes are "all participants must decide in the same way" or "majority vote". etc. A rewritten process model following this strategy is shown in the lower part of Fig. 3. Providing some degree of enforceability by employing other participants is similar to the endorsement of partners for role binding proposed in [13] and the endorsement policies for forming consensus applied in the permissioned blockchain Hyperledger Fabric.

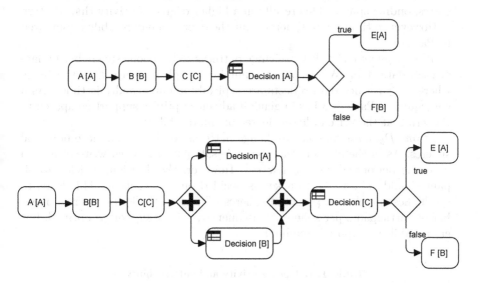

Fig. 3. Enforceable decisions over encrypted data

5   Balancing Privity and Enforceability

Current public blockchain approaches provide built-in enforceability only if no encryption is applied and on-chain data is used. In this case the blockchain network can verify all transactions. Enforceability over encrypted data can either be realized in a proactive way as supposed in Sect. 4 or it can be realized in a reactive way where participants might need to uncover encrypted data for dispute resolution. Obviously, the goals enforceability and privity are in conflict. The more participants in a privity sphere, the higher the degree of enforceability and the lower the degree of privity. The less participants in a sphere, the higher the degree of privity and the lower the degree of enforceability.

Aiming at privity, we can follow different patterns as proposed in Sect. 3. The approaches differ in the number of spheres and consequently in the average number of participants in each sphere.

We compare the different key distribution patterns from Sect. 3 in Table 1 based on the dimensions privity support, enforceability support, and number of spheres.

0: No Encryption The entire public has access to all data. This results in maximum enforceability and no privity.

1: Global-Safe There is only one sphere containing all participants of the process instance. This results in still good enforceability and a minimal degree of privity.

2: Static-Safe key exchange patterns lead to one sphere per variable leading to n spheres. Only participants accessing that variable are members of the corresponding sphere. This results in a higher degree of privity than Pattern 1. However, n times more spheres limit the degree of enforceability compared to Pattern 1.

3: Weak-Dynamic-Safe key exchange patterns result in one sphere per update of each data item. We denote this number of spheres with n' in the table, where $n' \geq n$ since data objects are typically updated multiple times. As a consequence, Pattern 3 has in general advanced privity support compared to Pattern 2 at the price of lower degree of enforceability.

4: Strong-Dynamic-Safe key exchange patterns result in even more potential spheres. As in the case of weak-dynamic-safe patterns, each write to a data object is performed with a new key. However, the decision, which participant should gain access to a key is decided only at runtime. This leads to the highest number of potential spheres n'' and to the lowest average number of participants per sphere. Consequently, privity support is optimal, but enforceability support is minimal.

Table 1. Balancing privity and enforceability.

Key exchange pattern	#Spheres	Privity	Enforceability
0: No encryption	0	o	+++++
1: Global	1	+	++++
2: Static safe	n	++	+++
3: Weak dynamically safe	$n' \geq n$	+++	++
4: Strong dynamically safe	$nn'' \geq n'$	++++	+

As a conclusion, designers should be empowered to balance the trade-offs between privity and enforceability individually for each data item or for each update of a data item based on application/contractual requirements.

6 Related Work

Blockchain technology has gained interest in the BPM community in recent years. Research challenges arising from blockchain technology from the business process modeling perspective were identified in [15]. A primer field of application of blockchain technology are smart contracts [22]. In [9] a modeling language for smart contracts based on data-centric BPM was proposed.

First systems based on classical activity-centric process models typically using subsets of BPMN models as input were presented in [5,7,8,14,16,19,21,23, 25]. We will now briefly discuss the most prominent solutions in more detail. The work in [25] introduces a method for monitoring choreographies via blockchains. The work in [19] goes one step further by aiming at providing an entire BPM engine on the blockchain. The work in [16] extends [19] with role-based access restrictions of transactions and the very recent work in [13] addresses dynamic role-binding at runtime. The work in [7] addresses the execution of DMN decision models on-chain. The work [23] follows the approach of [5] and [25] for translating BPMN models and integrates it in an MDA toolkit. Finally, the recent work in [21] addresses the question of resource allocation for processes which are executed on the blockchain.

However, none of the existing approaches [5,7,8,14,16,19,21,23,25] provide advanced solution for confidentiality. Only static approaches like no-encryption or off-chain data exchange are applied. We see our work as an extension of these works. Basically, we can enrich some process model based on our proposed key exchange strategies and enforceability patterns presented in Sect. 5 and then execute the resulting code on a slightly modified existing engine.

Optimizing key distribution for business processes executed on blockchains is strictly related to our previous works on generating optimized data-flow implementations for inter-organizational processes in [10,11]. We propose that an algorithm for the automatic generation of optimized key exchange and key distribution implementation as proposed in this paper can be implemented similar to our optimization approach for inter-organizational data-flow in [11].

The aim of this work was to provide privity support for business processes executed on currently available public blockchains such as Ethereum. For this scenario, we applied data encryption. One alternative option is to use permissioned blockchains such as Hyperledger[1] or Quorum[2]. In particular Hyperledger Fabric supports channels, which are technically private blockchains only accessible for specific participants. While we assume this to be very beneficial for static-safe implementations, we see challenges in the more restrictive privity classes. Another potential alternative to encryption is to use off-chain communication

---

[1] https://www.hyperledger.org/.
[2] https://consensys.net/quorum-2/.

which is in turn secured on-chain as applied in the Perun project[3] using state channels. We see generating augmentations for privity preserving data access of processes based on permissioned chains (e.g. by generating channels) or based on off-chain interactions (state channels) as interesting future work.

Another option is the application of alternative blockchain architectures such as proposed in Hawk [12], where zero-knowledge proofs [6] are used for validating private transactions. However, Hawk requires a trusted setup with an intermediary entity, which is typically not wanted for applications in untrusted domains as targeted by public blockchains. In [2] a blockchain-architecture providing confidential transactions is proposed. However, it focuses on specific requirements of the banking domain, and requires the active participation of intermediaries (banks) for the execution of transactions. Nevertheless, such blockchain architectures have the potential to limit the toll of encryption for proactive enforceability. However, for reactive enforceability, where participants might need to uncover the decrypted data for dispute resolution, the need to balance privity and enforceability remains.

7   Conclusion and Future Work

Privity, the containment of information proliferation to those who have a contractual need to know, is an essential property of (smart) contracts but not supported by existing blockchain based BPM approaches, partly because it is conflicting with enforceability. We argue that balancing privity and enforceability is a major task in designing smart contracts and we introduced the notion of privity spheres to represent different privity requirements. We have provided key exchange patterns respecting the spheres and have discussed possible optimizations. However, encryption limits the possible degree of online enforcement as data-based decisions cannot be verified by all blockchain nodes. Nevertheless, we proposed methods for achieving higher degrees of enforceability by securing decisions by other participants using voting schemes.

The proposed patterns and optimization strategies extend BPMN models with key exchanges and such that the resulting processes can be executed on some existing blockchain based BPM system [5,8,14,16,19,21,23,25]. While we have focused on key exchange for on-chain data in this paper, the same principles can also be applied for encrypted off-chain data, where only the keys are shared on-chain.

The presented approach leads to model driven development of smart contracts [3], where the user requirements for proactive or reactive enforceability and privity are described in a declarative way and then the system automatically generates an implementation with optimized decision taking, encryption, and key distribution.

---

[3] https://www.perun.network/.

References

1. Buterin, V.: Ethereum: a next-generation smart contract and decentralized application platform (2014). https://github.com/ethereum/wiki/wiki/White-Paper. Accessed 16 May 2019
2. Cecchetti, E., Zhang, F., Ji, Y., Kosba, A.E., Juels, A., Shi, E.: Solidus: confidential distributed ledger transactions via PVORM. In: SIGSAC CCS, pp. 701–717 (2017)
3. Di Ciccio, C., et al.: Blockchain support for collaborative business processes. Informatik Spektrum **42**, 182–190 (2019)
4. Di Ciccio, C., et al.: Blockchain-based traceability of inter-organisational business processes. In: Shishkov, B. (ed.) BMSD 2018. LNBIP, vol. 319, pp. 56–68. Springer, Cham (2018). https://doi.org/10.1007/978-3-319-94214-8_4
5. García-Bañuelos, L., Ponomarev, A., Dumas, M., Weber, I.: Optimized execution of business processes on blockchain. In: Carmona, J., Engels, G., Kumar, A. (eds.) BPM 2017. LNCS, vol. 10445, pp. 130–146. Springer, Cham (2017). https://doi.org/10.1007/978-3-319-65000-5_8
6. Goldwasser, S., Micali, S., Rackoff, C.: The knowledge complexity of interactive proof systems. SIAM J. Comput. **18**(1), 186–208 (1989)
7. Haarmann, S., Batoulis, K., Nikaj, A., Weske, M.: DMN decision execution on the ethereum blockchain. In: Krogstie, J., Reijers, H.A. (eds.) CAiSE 2018. LNCS, vol. 10816, pp. 327–341. Springer, Cham (2018). https://doi.org/10.1007/978-3-319-91563-0_20
8. Härer, F.: Decentralized business process modeling and instance tracking secured by a blockchain. In: ECIS 2018 (2018)
9. Hull, R., Batra, V.S., Chen, Y.-M., Deutsch, A., Heath III, F.F.T., Vianu, V.: Towards a shared ledger business collaboration language based on data-aware processes. In: Sheng, Q.Z., Stroulia, E., Tata, S., Bhiri, S. (eds.) ICSOC 2016. LNCS, vol. 9936, pp. 18–36. Springer, Cham (2016). https://doi.org/10.1007/978-3-319-46295-0_2
10. Köpke, J., Eder, J.: Equivalence transformations for the design of interorganizational data-flow. In: Zdravkovic, J., Kirikova, M., Johannesson, P. (eds.) CAiSE 2015. LNCS, vol. 9097, pp. 367–381. Springer, Cham (2015). https://doi.org/10.1007/978-3-319-19069-3_23
11. Köpke, J., Franceschetti, M., Eder, J.: Optimizing data-flow implementations for inter-organizational processes. DAPD 1–45 (2018)
12. Kosba, A.E., Miller, A., Shi, E., Wen, Z., Papamanthou, C.: Hawk: the blockchain model of cryptography and privacy-preserving smart contracts. In: IEEE Symposium on Security and Privacy, pp. 839–858. IEEE Computer Society (2016)
13. López-Pintado, O., Dumas, M., García-Bañuelos, L., Weber, I.: Dynamic role binding in blockchain-based collaborative business processes. In: Giorgini, P., Weber, B. (eds.) CAiSE 2019. LNCS, vol. 11483, pp. 399–414. Springer, Cham (2019). https://doi.org/10.1007/978-3-030-21290-2_25
14. Madsen, M.F., Gaub, M., Høgnason, T., Kirkbro, M.E., Slaats, T., Debois, S.: Collaboration among adversaries: distributed workflow execution on a blockchain. In: 2018 Symposium on Foundations and Applications of Blockchain (2018)
15. Mendling, J., Weber, I., van der Aalst, W.M.P., et al.: Blockchains for business process management - challenges and opportunities. ACM Trans. Manag. Inf. Syst. **9**(1), 4:1–4:16 (2018)
16. Mercenne, L., Brousmiche, K., Hamida, E.B.: Blockchain studio: a role-based business workflows management system. In: IEMCON 2018, pp. 1215–1220, November 2018

17. Nakamoto, S.: Bitcoin: a peer-to-peer electronic cash system (2009). http://www.bitcoin.org/bitcoin.pdf
18. Peck, M.E.: Blockchain world - do you need a blockchain? This chart will tell you if the technology can solve your problem. IEEE Spectr. **54**(10), 38–60 (2017)
19. Pintado, O., Garcia-Banuelos, L., Dumas, M., Weber, I., Ponomarev, A.: CATERPILLAR: a business process execution engine on the ethereum blockchain. Softw. Pract. Exp. **49**, 1162–1193 (2019)
20. Rescorla, E.: Diffie-Hellman key agreement method. RFC 2631, RFC Editor, June 1999. http://www.rfc-editor.org/rfc/rfc2631.txt
21. Sturm, C., Scalanczi, J., Schönig, S., Jablonski, S.: A blockchain-based and resource-aware process execution engine. Future Gener. Comput. Syst. **100**, 19–34 (2019)
22. Szabo, N.: Formalizing and securing relationships on public networks. First Monday **9**(2) (1997)
23. Tran, A.B., Lu, Q., Weber, I.: Lorikeet: a model-driven engineering tool for blockchain-based business process execution and asset management. In: Proceedings of the Dissertation Award, Demonstration, and Industrial Track at BPM 2018, pp. 56–60 (2018)
24. Udokwu, C., Kormiltsyn, A., Thangalimodzi, K., Norta, A.: The state of the art for blockchain-enabled smart- contract applications in the organization. In: The Ivannikov ISPRAS Open Conference sections, November 2018
25. Weber, I., Xu, X., Riveret, R., Governatori, G., Ponomarev, A., Mendling, J.: Untrusted business process monitoring and execution using blockchain. In: La Rosa, M., Loos, P., Pastor, O. (eds.) BPM 2016. LNCS, vol. 9850, pp. 329–347. Springer, Cham (2016). https://doi.org/10.1007/978-3-319-45348-4_19
26. Xu, X., Pautasso, C., Zhu, L., Lu, Q., Weber, I.: A pattern collection for blockchain-based applications. In: Proceedings of the 23rd European Conference on Pattern Languages of Programs, EuroPLoP 2018, pp. 3:1–3:20 (2018)

Performance and Scalability of Private Ethereum Blockchains

Markus Schäffer, Monika di Angelo$^{(\boxtimes)}$ ⓘ, and Gernot Salzer ⓘ

TU Wien, Vienna, Austria
{markus.schaeffer,monika.di.angelo,gernot.salzer}@tuwien.ac.at

Abstract. Smart contracts provide promising use cases for the public and the private sector by combining cryptographically secure blockchains and the versatility of software. In contrast to public blockchains, private ones can be tailored by configuring blockchain-specific parameters like the time passing between two consecutive blocks, the size of blocks, the hardware of the nodes running the blockchain software, or simply the size of the network. However, the effects of parameters on the performance of private smart contract platforms are not well studied.

In this work, we systematically examine to which extent the performance of private Ethereum blockchains scales with various parameters, and which parameters constitute bottlenecks. We introduce a concept for measuring the performance and scalability of private Ethereum smart contract platforms, as well as a framework for the automatic deployment of differently configured private Ethereum blockchains on the cloud. Based on the collected performance-related data, we visualize the impact of parameter changes on performance. Our results show that the effect of variations in one parameter is highly dependent on the configuration of other parameters, especially when running the system near its limits. Moreover, we identify a structure for the bottlenecks of current private Ethereum smart contract platforms.

Keywords: Blockchain · Ethereum · Evaluation · Performance

1   Introduction

For blockchain systems, there is currently a trade-off between decentralization, security, and scalability. This is known as the scalability trilemma [9], which states that a blockchain can only have two of the three properties.

For the most prominent smart contract platform Ethereum, each mining node stores the entire state (i.e. for each account its balance, code and storage) and also processes all transactions sequentially. This approach provides a high amount of security, yet greatly restricts scalability. Since there is no parallel processing in Ethereum mining, the throughput is currently capped at around 15 transactions per second in the public network [9].

This paper is a condensed version of the measurements described in [19].

© Springer Nature Switzerland AG 2019
C. Di Ciccio et al. (Eds.): BPM 2019 Blockchain and CEE Forum, LNBIP 361, pp. 103–118, 2019.
https://doi.org/10.1007/978-3-030-30429-4_8

In order to drastically increase scalability of Ethereum, its key developers focus on a combination of two approaches: sharding [9] and side-chains [7]. The former approach requires only a small percentage of nodes to see and process every transaction of the network, thereby allowing transactions to be processed in parallel by means of horizontal partitioning. The latter involves creating additional chains for transactions to be executed off the main chain.

For private networks, the scalability trilemma can also be tackled by choosing non-default values for the chain parameters (e.g. block size, block interval, or power of a mining node) to improve performance. The choice of these blockchain parameters affects throughput and latency. Even though Ethereum is comparatively well studied, there has been only little discussion about the effects of the different chain parameters on performance in a private setting so far (see Sect. 2).

Goals and Methods. The overall aim of this work is to further extend the understanding of the effects of different parameters in private Ethereum smart contract platforms with respect to performance and scalability. In this context, we specifically address the following research questions:

- What are suitable means for measurements?
- What are the effects of different parameter settings?
- Which parameters represent bottlenecks?

In order to answer these questions, we first devise a concept for measuring the performance of differently configured Ethereum networks. This includes the identification of relevant parameters, the definition of evaluation metrics, and the development of a deployment mechanism. After the implementation of the formulated concept as a measurement framework, the actual performance measurements are carried out to collect data. For the data analysis, we visualize the effects of parameters on performance, and we provide interpretations. Furthermore, we identify a bottleneck structure for the measured parameters. Finally, we re-examine findings reported in related work.

Roadmap. Section 2 summarizes related work. Our measurement concept is detailed in Sect. 3, and we analyze the collected data in Sect. 4. Identified bottlenecks are presented Sect. 5. In Sect. 6, we discuss our results in relation to related work, while we draw our conclusions in Sect. 7.

2   Related Work

In the most closely related work [4,5], the authors present an evaluation framework where private blockchains can be benchmarked against pre-defined workloads. In order to compare different blockchains, four abstraction layers (application, execution engine, data model and consensus) and according workloads are defined. The evaluation of Ethereum used only the proof of work (PoW) consensus algorithm, while the configuration of the nodes was not varied.

The performance and limitations of Hyperledger Fabric and Ethereum with varying numbers of transactions are studied in [17]. Metrics measured execution time, latency, and throughput. However, the consensus mechanism was disabled and the analysis was performed on a single-node network. In addition, the configuration of the node was not varied, and other parameters such as the mining difficulty of Ethereum were not investigated either.

The effect of different Ethereum clients (Geth and Parity) with respect to performance was studied in [18]. Even though the analysis was conducted with different types of nodes (different amount of RAM is mentioned), there is no information about the consensus algorithms and its parameters (e.g. mining difficulty or block frequency) used. Apparently, the number of nodes was not varied during the experiments.

A comparison of blockchain and relational databases is presented in [2]. For testing purposes, Ethereum and MySQL were chosen. Although seven differently configured machines have been used, no information is provided on how the configuration of the machine affects the measured metrics. While it is stated that results vary from computer to computer, results are provided for a single configuration only. In addition, the configuration of the machines resembles consumer machines such as laptops. Moreover, the size of the private Ethereum blockchain was fixed to six nodes and not varied. Consensus algorithms and their parameters were not included in the study.

Overall performance metrics and a performance monitoring framework are proposed in [24]. The authors provide detailed metrics for measuring performance on the Ethereum blockchain. Still, their analysis lacks some parameters: only one consensus algorithm (PoW) is covered; mining difficulty or block size are not varied; the configuration of nodes is not addressed.

A quantitative framework for analyzing the security and performance trade-offs of various consensus and network parameters of PoW blockchains is presented in [12]. However, it contains neither other consensus variants and their parameters nor any other number and type of node. A model predicting the performance and storage of executing contracts based on the transaction volume is proposed in [23]. It consists of formulas which were derived via regression analysis. The major drawback of this approach is that it only depends on the amount of transactions. The formulas do not include other variables such as consensus algorithm, or amount and configuration of the nodes. The authors of [11] deal with Bitcoin's scalability limits via proposing a new blockchain protocol which is designed to scale. Variables such as block frequency and block size were varied to make suggestions for a better blockchain protocol. For Hyperledger, there are a few tools and studies [13,16,21] that use similar ideas as already presented.

Bottlenecks in Bitcoin that limit throughput and latency are addressed in [3]. The results show that a re-parametrization of block size and block intervals may have a positive effect on performance and scalability. The authors of [22] proposed to improve scalability by optimization of block construction, block size and time control optimization, and transaction security mechanism optimization. Experiments were conducted that studied the relationship of block size and block construction. The authors of [15] state that existing Byzantine tolerant permissioned blockchains only scale to a limited number of nodes. A different design of blockchains is proposed in [14] where the authors argue that, for improving the performance and scalability of blockchains to a significant level, simply tweaking blockchain parameters such as block size is not enough.

In conclusion, previous work primarily focused on block frequency and block size for blockchain systems in general. However, other parameters such as node configuration or network size were hardly studied. For Ethereum in a private setting, only very few researchers reported performance measurements with differently configured networks, while none included results with the proof of authority (PoA) consensus variant. As PoA may be better suited for private blockchains than PoW, an important part is missing in the existing literature.

3   Concept

For presenting our concept in this section, we first identify parameters that affect the performance and scalability of Ethereum in a private setting. Then, we define the metrics used in our analysis, and finally we introduce the experimental setup.

3.1   Identified Parameters

Table 1 lists the identified parameters, where the ones used for our experiment are set in bold. The increase of block frequency may have a positive effect on performance [3], while the block propagation time imposes a lower bound. Regarding the effect of the block size on performance, the related work provides contradictory statements. While a positive effect of block size increase on performance is reported in [3], no positive effect is implied in [5]. Concerning workload, different smart contracts may show different runtimes according to their instructions and storage access. For example, [5] and [24] report a difference in performance. The parameter characterizing the computational power of a node is called node

Table 1. Identified performance and scalability parameters

Parameter	Description
Block frequency	Time between two succeeding blocks
Block size	Amount of transactions fitting in a block
Workload type	Smart contract
Node configuration	CPU, RAM, network speed
Network size	Number of nodes
Network structure	Structure of the blockchain network
Workload quantity	Amount of transactions to be processed
Amount of miners/sealers	Actively participating nodes
Blockchain client and API	E.g. Geth or Parity, web3.js or web3.py

configuration; it includes hardware configuration like the amount and type of CPU and RAM. This parameter was studied only to some extent in [18] and [2]. Again, only a few sources [5,24] discuss the effects of network size.

3.2 Evaluation Metrics

Nearly all studies (see Sect. 2) share the concept of throughput measured in 'transactions per second' (tps), but no other metrics beyond that. Table 2 defines the metrics for our analyses. Due to the large number of parameters in Sect. 3.1, we keep the amount of metrics low and focus on simple and high-level metrics. Hence, metrics regarding the hardware layer (like the utilization of CPU or memory) and the security of blockchains were excluded.

Table 2. Evaluation metrics

Metric	Description
Throughput	Number of successful transactions per second (tps)
Latency	Time difference in seconds between submission and completion of a transaction
Scalability	Changes of throughput and latency when altering a parameter (e.g. the network size or the hardware configuration of a node)

3.3 Experimental Setup

We employed the architecture in Fig. 1 to collect measurement data in an automated way. According to [18], the Parity client processes transactions significantly faster than the Geth client. Nevertheless, we decided to use the latter one as it is Ethereum's default client [8] and still is used more frequently than Parity [10]. For interaction, Geth offers an interactive JavaScript console, a JavaScript API for inclusion in applications and processes, and JSON-RPC[1] endpoints. The web3.js API [6] is the de facto standard for interacting with Ethereum clients. As a runtime environment for the application we selected Node.js since it is the most commonly used framework of all technologies included in the 2018 Stackoverflow developer survey [20].

As computing environment, we chose Amazon Web Services (AWS). Via the Elastic Compute Cloud (EC2) service one can rent computing power for different purposes on demand. Since the experiments required an Ethereum network with more than one node, we used AWS Cloudformation to start the nodes and install our mesaurement software in an automated manner. An additional

---

[1] JSON-RPC is a stateless, light-weight Remote Procedure Call (RPC) protocol that uses JavaScript Object Notation (JSON) as data format.

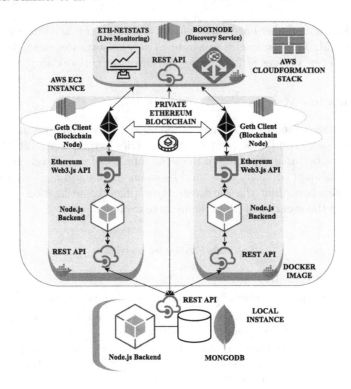

Fig. 1. Experimental setup

node ran the bootnode (a peer discovery service) and the monitoring software ETH-Netstats[2]. A local master node served as the command center for the experiments. The communication between the various nodes was done in REST-style (Representational State Transfer). For decoupling the major components, we used the Model-View-Controller design pattern. For storing the measurements for later analysis, we opted for MongoDB[3].

4   Data Analysis

In our experiments, we collected 4 000 data points ('measurements'), each corresponding to the average over several runs of the network with specific parameter settings. Each run comprised 1 000 transactions. In total, 4 million transactions were processed, which is roughly the volume of eight days on the Ethereum main chain. The computation time for all EC2 nodes and experiments was 380 h.

To measure the influence of node configuration and network size, we used the EC2 instances listed in Table 3. Unless stated otherwise, we varied only one variable at a time while the others were set to the default values in Table 4. The

---

[2] ETH-Netstats for the public Ethereum is available at https://ethstats.net/.

[3] MongoDB is a NoSQL database that uses JSON-like documents with schemata.

Table 3. EC2 instance types used for node configuration

Label	# CPUs	Speed	Memory	Network
c5.large	2	3 GHz	4 GB	10 Gbit
c5.xlarge	4	3 GHz	8 GB	10 Gbit
c5.2xlarge	8	3 GHz	16 GB	10 Gbit
c5.4xlarge	16	3 GHz	32 GB	10 Gbit
t2.xlarge	4	2.3 GHz	16 GB	Moderate

default values for difficulty and block period are those proposed by puppeth, the configuration utility of Geth.

Table 4. Default values for the variables included in the measurements

Difficulty	Block period	Gas limit	Workload	Instance type	# Nodes
524 288	15 s	4 700 000	Account	c5.xlarge	5

4.1 Block Frequency

Block frequency is inversely proportional to the time between blocks. In case of PoW, we varied the mining difficulty to obtain average block periods between 1 s and 2.5 s (0.25 to 4 times the default difficulty). For PoA, we used block periods of 2, 4, 8, 12, and 15 s. The experiments confirmed: throughput decreases and latency increases linearly with increasing block period.

4.2 Block Size

Ethereum uses the concept of gas to control the size of a block. Gas measures the resources (computation time and memory) consumed by a transaction. The total amount of gas in a block is capped by the block gas limit, which indirectly determines the number of transactions fitting into a block. In our experiments, the default value for the block gas limit results in blocks with 146 transactions of the default workload (account contract). We varied the number of transactions in a single block between 74 and 1 168 (gas limit factor 0.5 to 8).

As expected, we observe that as the block size increases, throughput increases while latency decreases in the same proportion, at least when the block period is large enough. For PoW and the default node configuration, the smallest considered block period approaches the time needed for creating, signing, and executing the transactions of a block. Here, throughput and latency will not improve when further increasing the block size.

4.3 Workload

For simulating different workloads, we used one of two smart contracts as the recipient of the transactions. The contracts differ in the state changes they perform: The first one ('account') changes the balance of two addresses, while the other one ('ballot') only accesses its own state. A transaction directed towards 'account' requires 32 k gas, while a call to 'ballot' needs only 27 k gas.

The observed effect of different workloads is depicted in Fig. 2. Surprisingly, there seems to be no difference between the two workloads for PoW, while there is a difference in the case of PoA. Welch's t-test with a significance level alpha of 5% shows that there is no significant difference for throughput and latency for PoW. For PoA however, the null hypothesis (no significant difference of the mean

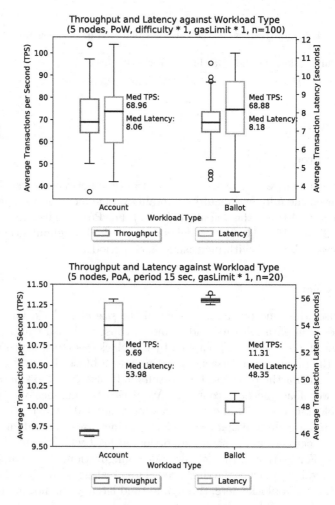

Fig. 2. Throughput and latency against workload type PoW (upper) and PoA (lower)

values of throughput and latency for the two workloads) can be strongly rejected, meaning that the difference is statistically significant. Throughput differs by 17%, which corresponds to the difference in transaction size (32 k vs. 27 k gas).

We argue that the different results obtained for PoW and PoA are due to the different block periods used. In case of PoW, the time needed for generating and processing the transactions is comparable to the block period. We noticed that the blocks were not always filled to their maximum. For PoA, on the contrary, the low block frequency allowed the nodes to generate and process the transactions within the block period. Hence, the effect of the workload on the performance was only observable when the nodes were not operating at their limits.

4.4 Node Configuration

To investigate the influence of computational power on performance, we specified four types of EC2 instances, each with a doubled amount of memory and cores (cf. Table 3). The parameters of the consensus algorithms were set to not limit performance: The gas limit was set so that the entire workload of 1 000 transactions could fit into a single block. Moreover, the parameters determining the block frequency were set to a maximum, i.e. the mining difficulty in case of PoW and the block period in case of PoA were set to their respective minimum.

Table 5. Scalability: increase of performance between successive node types

		large to xlarge	xlarge to 2xlarge	2xlarge to 4xlarge
Throughput	PoW	60.3%	48.9%	31.2%
	PoA	49.9%	35.6%	17.2%
Latency	PoW	37.8%	24.1%	18.9%
	PoA	29.0%	1.1%	22.1%

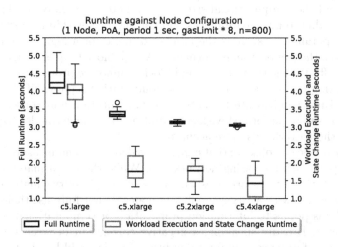

Fig. 3. Runtime analysis of different node configurations

As expected, the time required to complete the workload decreases as computing power increases. Table 5 shows the performance changes between successive node types. While the effect of doubling memory and CPUs is still noticeable, it becomes less apparent with more powerful node types. For PoA, this is illustrated in Fig. 3. The changes are more significant for PoW than for PoA.

Next to the reduced runtime for workload execution and state changes, transactions are also generated and signed faster when the computational power of a node is increased. By querying the number of transactions per block, we found that with less powerful node configurations, nodes are unable to pack the entire workload into a single block, even though the block size (the gas limit) is large enough. This is presumably due to a combination of slow workload generation, slow workload execution, and high block frequency. In such a case, at least one more complete block period is required for the rest of the workload, which aggravates the effect of slow generation and execution of the workload.

4.5   Network Size

Sometimes, increasing the number of machines is a reasonable approach to increase performance. However, factors such as network communication and consensus costs also play a crucial role in the context of blockchains. The time needed to propagate blocks to the majority of the nodes simply cannot be reduced by adding nodes to the network. In fact, communication and consensus efforts rather increase. On the other hand, information propagation is faster in a private setting than in the public Ethereum network due to the much smaller number of nodes in the network. For PoA, our measurements indicate that the performance does not change significantly with different network sizes. We assume that this is due to our experimental setup.

For PoW, however, the picture is different, and the effect of the network size also depends heavily on other parameters. The two major factors are block frequency and the computational strength of a node. Generally speaking, if the nodes are unable to propagate blocks and transactions within a short period of time, other parameters such as the number of nodes or a high block frequency cannot unfold their impact on performance. A high block frequency does not have the desired effect if the transactions and blocks cannot be propagated within the network during one block period. As the computational power of the t2.xlarge nodes could not compensate for network communication and consensus costs, measurements were performed with computationally stronger nodes (c5.4xlarge) to analyze these overheads more accurately.

In Table 6, one can observe that expected (calculated) and measured throughput drift apart with increasing network size. While there is a match of around 90–100% with smaller network sizes, larger networks only show a match of around 60–75%. Networks with a larger number of nodes do not fully use their available resources. This points to information propagation or computational power as a limiting factor. Broadly speaking, a negative correlation between the network size and the performance gain for an additional node could be identified.

Table 6. Calculated vs. Measured Throughput (PoW, 10× $difficulty$, c5.4xlarge)

Network size [nodes]	Block period [s]	Calculated runtime [s]	Throughput [tps]	Measured throughput [tps]
2	3.8	26.9	37.2	33.3 (89%)
4	2.3	15.8	63.5	63.2 (99%)
6	1.6	11.3	88.7	65.9 (74%)
8	1.3	9.2	108.8	75.6 (70%)
10	1.2	8.1	124.1	76.6 (62%)

5 Bottlenecks

The effect of a parameter may also depend on the settings of other parameters. When altering one parameter of the system, another one may become the bottleneck. In contrast to related work, we therefore argue that beyond discussing single parameters, information on the order of the bottlenecks is needed.

Bottleneck Structure. For private Ethereum networks using Geth, we derived the hierarchy of bottlenecks as depicted in Fig. 4. Parameters higher up in the hierarchy become a bottleneck as soon as the underlying ones no longer represent a bottleneck.

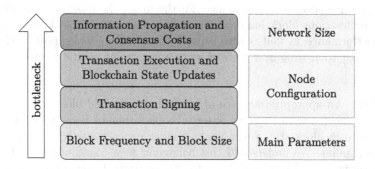

Fig. 4. Hierarchy of bottlenecks

Block Frequency and Block Size. The performance of a blockchain is, by definition, mainly a function of these two parameters, which according to our experiments are at the bottom of the hierarchy. With block frequencies at the limit of one block per second and large-sized blocks, processes such as transaction signing, transaction execution, changing the blockchain state, and propagating information become bottlenecks.

Node Configuration. The computational power of the nodes becomes the bottleneck as soon as the nodes in the network can no longer generate, sign, propagate and execute the transactions during the block period.

Network Size. Due to the overhead inflicted on the network when adding a node, the network size is at the top of the bottleneck hierarchy. When operating a network at its limits, parameters such as block frequency, block size, and node configuration restrict performance before performance is further reduced due to a larger network.

6 Discussion

The parameter settings of a private Ethereum network have a tremendous impact on performance. The values for throughput reported in literature range from a maximum of 284 tps in [5] to a minimum of 0.5 tps in [2]. Our experiments show that with a block period of 1 s, a block size large enough to fit 1 000 transactions into the block, an AWS EC2 instance of type c5.4xlarge, and a network of a single node, the throughput can be as high as 328 tps on average.

Block Frequency. When increasing the mining difficulty, the block frequency decreases, throughput decreases as well and latency rises. This is to be expected and consistent with more general findings already reported elsewhere. Our results confirm the results of [3], who show that an adjustment of the block interval may have a positive effect on performance. Furthermore, the results are in line with the move of various blockchain communities to increase the block frequency for better performance, as well as with Buterin who stated in a blog post [1] that the block propagation time in a network puts a constraint on the maximum block frequency.

Block Size. An appropriate choice of block frequency and block size is crucial. As to be expected with PoA, we observed a performance boost proportional to the increase in block size. Surprisingly, similar experiments with PoW show a saturation point. We understand this behaviour as a consequence of the work load being generated too slowly and the transactions being processed not fast enough. The most important finding is that an increment in block size substantially affects performance only if the block period is larger than the time needed for creating, signing, propagating, and executing the transactions as well as reaching consensus.

Unlike [5], we argue that an increase in block size has the potential to boost the performance of a private Ethereum network if the above-mentioned prerequisites are fulfilled. Our results agree with [22] who advocate the optimization of block size as a strategy for improving the scalability of blockchains to a certain extent. However, we were unable to confirm their observation that as the block size increases, the performance first increases, but decreases when it reaches a certain level. It may be that the block size was not chosen large enough in our experiments to trigger this effect. Finally, we want to emphasize that similar to block frequency, the block size may change over time if the value of target-GasLimit in the Geth client and the value of gasLimit in the genesis block do not match. It is not clear whether other authors have taken this issue into account.

Workload. The experiments regarding workload show differences between PoW and PoA that we attribute to the different block periods used (1 s for PoW vs. 15 s for PoA). Our observations are in line with previous findings [5,24] that report a dependency of performance on the type of smart contract used. In our experiments a throughput difference of around 17% was measured.

Node Configuration. When operating a private Ethereum blockchain at its limits by choosing a high block frequency and large block size, node configuration becomes more important. In a network with five nodes, throughput almost tripled and latency halved when increasing the computational power of the nodes by a factor of four. In our opinion, the marked difference between the our node configurations can be attributed to the fact that stronger machines feature faster transaction generation and signing, better network communication and consensus handling, quicker execution of the transactions, and faster state changes.

An analysis of the time needed solely for executing the transactions and changing a node's blockchain state confirmed previous work [18] that reported a decrease by 25% for processing transactions when increasing the memory of a node from 4 GB to 24 GB. Indeed, when changing the node configuration from c5.4xlarge (8 GB RAM) to c5.4xlarge (32 GB RAM), we observed an improvement by roughly 26%. Another finding is that computationally weak nodes may have troubles propagating transactions to the network.

Network Size. With the standard PoA settings, no significant performance difference could be observed when changing the network size. This is due to our experimental setup where all nodes seal blocks in a pre-assigned and static time interval. On the other hand, when adding nodes in the PoW setting, our results show that the performance rises at first but starts to decrease once a peak has been reached. Although it may seem puzzling that more power can actually reduce the performance of a network, these results are in line with previous work [5]. We found that additional network communication and consensus costs are the main limiting factor for the scalability of the network. Moreover, the effect of adding more nodes to a network also depends on block frequency, node configuration, and the current size of the network. Nodes may get out of sync and uncle blocks may be created if the time needed for propagating information in the network is larger than the block period.

Bottlenecks. Our results confirm the findings in [24]. We also observed that information propagation and consensus costs are the main factors limiting the scalability of private Ethereum networks. However, the bottleneck may actually shift from one parameter to another. The combined effect of block frequency and block size as well as of the node configuration may limit the scalability before information propagation and consensus costs become relevant.

7 Conclusions

We investigated the effects of various parameters on the performance and scalability of private Ethereum blockchains. To this end, we conducted 4 000 measurements and visualized the impact of parameter changes in several charts and tables. More details can be found in [19].

Summarizing, we conclude that the effects of different parameters are intertwined such that the optimal setting of one parameter often depends on the setting of the others as well. Our results indicate that scaling is only possible to a limited extent due to the current design of Ethereum. As a specific contribution, we identified a hierarchy of bottlenecks.

Limitations. Our experimental setup contains several sources for potential errors. First, the process of measuring itself might have influenced the system under observation. We ran a Node.js instance on each node that shared the resources with the Ethereum client. Likewise, the additional services needed for peer discovery (Bootnode) and live monitoring (ETH-Netstats) might have influenced the system. It is also unclear if and to which extent the chosen virtualization on the level of the operating system (Docker) produces results that differ from nodes running on physically separate machines. Finally, the way we generated and distributed the transactions may have affected the results.

It is unclear to which extent our observations can be generalized. Our work was exploratory and descriptive by nature. Inferential approaches may be needed to confirm, explain, and extend the findings. For some results, it may turn out that the experiments have been carried out on too small a scale. Although the volume of generated transactions equals eight days of transactions on the Ethereum main chain, the test data may not fully reflect the variability of real data.

Future Work. This study provides insights into the effects of different parameters on performance and scalability in private Ethereum networks. Still, further research is needed. Security considerations were beyond the scope of the present paper. Hence, future work should address for instance trade-offs between security and performance.

Our experimental setting can readily be used to collect data on further combinations of parameters. In particular, it may be worthwhile adding multivariate to our bivariate analyses to gain a better understanding of the interaction of parameters.

The current setup is tailored to the Geth client and the web3.js API. These technologies, the blockchain client and the used API, represent further parameters to be analyzed. It may well be that a client like Parity exhibits different performance characteristics.

Finally, a layer could be introduced that facilitates the addition of new workload types to the framework.

References

1. Buterin, V.: Toward a 12-second Block Time. https://blog.ethereum.org/2014/07/11/toward-a-12-second-block-time/. Accessed 19 Nov 2018
2. Chen, S., Zhang, J., Shi, R., Yan, J., Ke, Q.: A comparative testing on performance of blockchain and relational database: foundation for applying smart technology into current business systems. In: Streitz, N., Konomi, S. (eds.) DAPI 2018. LNCS, vol. 10921, pp. 21–34. Springer, Cham (2018). https://doi.org/10.1007/978-3-319-91125-0_2
3. Croman, K., et al.: On scaling decentralized blockchains. In: Clark, J., Meiklejohn, S., Ryan, P.Y.A., Wallach, D., Brenner, M., Rohloff, K. (eds.) FC 2016. LNCS, vol. 9604, pp. 106–125. Springer, Heidelberg (2016). https://doi.org/10.1007/978-3-662-53357-4_8
4. Dinh, T.T.A., Liu, R., Zhang, M., Chen, G., Ooi, B.C., Wang, J.: Untangling blockchain: a data processing view of blockchain systems (2017). http://arxiv.org/pdf/1708.05665.pdf
5. Dinh, T.T.A., Wang, J., Chen, G., Liu, R., Ooi, B.C., Tan, K.L.: BLOCKBENCH: a framework for analyzing private blockchains. In: International Conference on Management of Data, SIGMOD 2017, pp. 1085–1100. ACM (2017)
6. Ethereum: web3.js. https://web3js.readthedocs.io/. Accessed 21 Dec 2018
7. Ethereum 2.0. https://github.com/ethereum/eth2.0-specs. Accessed 20 Feb 2019
8. Ethereum Repository. https://github.com/ethereum. Accessed 19 Nov 2018
9. Ethereum Sharding. https://github.com/ethereum/wiki/wiki/Sharding-FAQs. Accessed 20 Feb 2019
10. Ethernodes.org. https://www.ethernodes.org/network/1. Accessed 19 Nov 2018
11. Eyal, I., Gencer, A.E., Sirer, E.G., Renesse, R.V.: Bitcoin-NG: a scalable blockchain protocol. In: 13th Conference on Networked Systems Design and Implementation, NSDI 2016, pp. 45–59. USENIX Association (2016)
12. Gervais, A., Karame, G.O., Wüst, K., Glykantzis, V., Ritzdorf, H., Capkun, S.: On the security and performance of proof of work blockchains. In: SIGSAC Conference on Computer and Communications Security, CCS 2016, pp. 3–16. ACM (2016)
13. Hyperledger. https://www.hyperledger.org. Accessed 14 Oct 2018
14. Kan, J., Chen, S., Huang, X.: Improve blockchain performance using graph data structure and parallel mining (2018). http://arxiv.org/abs/1808.10810
15. Li, W., Sforzin, A., Fedorov, S., Karame, G.O.: Towards scalable and private industrial blockchains. In: Workshop on Blockchain, Cryptocurrencies and Contracts, BCC 2017, pp. 9–14. ACM (2017)
16. Nasir, Q., Qasse, I.A., Abu Talib, M., Nassif, A.B.: Performance analysis of hyperledger fabric platforms. Secur. Commun. Netw. **2018**, 1–14 (2018)
17. Pongnumkul, S., Siripanpornchana, C., Thajchayapong, S.: Performance analysis of private blockchain platforms in varying workloads. In: 26th International Conference on Computer Communication and Networks, ICCCN 2017 (2017)
18. Rouhani, S., Deters, R.: Performance analysis of ethereum transactions in private blockchain. In: 8th International Conference on Software Engineering and Service Science, ICSESS 2017, pp. 70–74. IEEE (2017)
19. Schäffer, M.: Performance and scalability of smart contracts in private ethereum blockchains. Master's thesis, TU Wien (2019)
20. Stackoverflow: Developer Survey Results (2018). https://insights.stackoverflow.com/survey/2018#technology. Accessed 19 Nov 2018

21. Thakkar, P., Nathan, S., Viswanathan, B.: Performance benchmarking and optimizing hyperledger fabric blockchain platform. In: 26th International Symposium on Modeling. Analysis, and Simulation of Computer and Telecommunication Systems, MASCOTS, pp. 264–276. IEEE (2018)
22. Xin, W., Zhang, T., Hu, C., Tang, C., Liu, C., Chen, Z.: On scaling and accelerating decentralized private blockchains. In: 2017 IEEE 3rd International Conference on Big Data Security on Cloud (bigdatasecurity), IEEE International Conference on High Performance and Smart Computing (HPSC), and IEEE International Conference on Intelligent Data and Security (IDS), pp. 267–271 (2017)
23. Zhang, H., Jin, C., Cui, H.: A method to predict the performance and storage of executing contract for ethereum consortium-blockchain. In: Chen, S., Wang, H., Zhang, L.-J. (eds.) ICBC 2018. LNCS, vol. 10974, pp. 63–74. Springer, Cham (2018). https://doi.org/10.1007/978-3-319-94478-4_5
24. Zheng, P., Zheng, Z., Luo, X., Chen, X., Liu, X.: A detailed and real-time performance monitoring framework for blockchain systems. In: 40th International Conference on Software Engineering: Software Engineering in Practice, ICSE-SEIP 2018, pp. 134–143. ACM (2018)

Executing Collaborative Decisions Confidentially on Blockchains

Stephan Haarmann$^{(\boxtimes)}$, Kimon Batoulis, Adriatik Nikaj, and Mathias Weske

Hasso Plattner Institute, University of Potsdam, 14482 Potsdam, Germany
{stephan.haarmann,kimon.batoulis,adriatik.nikaj,mathias.weske}@hpi.de

Abstract. Decisions are an important aspect of enterprise operations. Decisions cross the boundary of a single enterprise, if multiple business partners collaborate in the decision making. To ascertain that all the participants behave as expected, blockchains can support collaborative decision making by storing relevant data and executing crucial decision logic in a tamper-proof and transparent manner. However, current blockchain technologies require the participants to publish the decision logic and are, therefore, not suited for sensitive data. This paper addresses this issue by proposing an approach that does not need to reveal sensitive data for supporting decision making. However, in case of a conflict, any participant can call for a blockchain-based conflict resolution at the cost of revealing the decision. To counter false claims that purposely reveal the decision, we provide a blockchain-enforced mechanism that discourages malicious behavior. We implement the approach using the Ethereum blockchain and evaluate the costs of resolving conflicts on a large set of decision models.

Keywords: Blockchain · Decision models · Collaboration · Privacy

1 Introduction

Organizations deploy business processes, which are essentially procedures for reaching business goals. A process consists of activities as well as their interdependencies, data requirements, and an embedding in an organizational and technical environment [20]; a process model captures this information, for example, using Business Process Model and Notation (BPMN) [14]. Some activities represent decisions. A decision can comprise multiple sub-decisions, and it can involve multiple processes that interact with each other. Decision Model and Notation (DMN) [15] is complementary to BPMN and provides the means to model decisions, their requirements, and their dependencies separately from processes.

While companies often collaborate by linking their processes through interactions, decision models are usually limited to one organization. However, many decisions are relevant to multiple parties. These cases require a common understanding of the decision logic and of the data inputs to decisions [13].

© Springer Nature Switzerland AG 2019
C. Di Ciccio et al. (Eds.): BPM 2019 Blockchain and CEE Forum, LNBIP 361, pp. 119–135, 2019.
https://doi.org/10.1007/978-3-030-30429-4_9

Recently, blockchains have been proposed as an implementation platform for interacting business processes [19]. Blockchains offer a new paradigm for supporting collaborations. They implement a tamper-proof ledger, which represents a shared, single source of truth and provides transparency and integrity protection. These technologies have been used to implement collaborative business processes [9,18] and decisions [7]. However, popular blockchain implementations bear two disadvantages: all data is public, and the execution is costly. In this paper, we propose a novel solution that addresses the former problem.

The approach is split in two main phases: an *operation phase* and a *conflict resolution phase*. By relying on cryptographic commitment schemes [6], the data and the decision logic is kept confidentially between the involved participants during the operation phase. In case of a disagreement, any of the involved participants can ask for a conflict resolution by invoking blockchain-based smart contracts. The contracts automatically resolve the conflict, at the cost of revealing the data and the decision logic, by verifying the decision inputs, executing the decision logic, and verifying the output. To prevent misconducts by participants (e.g., purposely revealing the decision logic), we propose a mechanism to punish false claims that trigger a conflict resolution and to reward righteous claims based on predetermined commonly agreed terms.

The remainder of this paper is organized as follows. In Sect. 2 we provide required background knowledge, followed by an overview of related work (Sect. 3). Section 4 comprises the concepts of our solution before we evaluate our approach with an Ethereum-based implementation regarding technical feasibility and costs (Sect. 5). The final section concludes our work with a discussion.

2   Preliminaries

This section provides preliminary background information. We provide an overview of DMN for decision modelling, explain the necessary concepts of blockchains, and present initial work on blockchain-based execution of decisions.

2.1   DMN

DMN is a modelling standard for operational decisions. A DMN model consists of two layers: requirements and logic. The requirements of a decision comprise sub-decisions and input data and are represented in a graph. Regarding the logic layer, DMN proposes decision tables as a standardized means. We explain these two concepts further with an example of a collaborative decision.

This decision is about a service level agreement between a retailer and a logistic contractor. Depending on the type of service level, if some percentage of the delivered items are damaged, the logistic contractor must pay a certain penal damage. The requirements graph (depicted in Fig. 1a) shows the decisions (i.e., *Service Level* and *Penal Damage*) and their respective inputs. An input is either data provided externally (i.e., *years as customer* and *number of shipments*

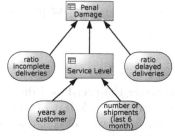

(a) Decision requirements graph for a service level agreement in logistics to determine penal damages

(b) Decision logic for the decision *Service Level* assigning service levels based on the time as a customer and the number of shipments

F	Inputs			Output
	years as customer	number of shipments		Service Level
	Number		Number	{Silver, Gold, Platinum}
1	≤	1		—	Silver
2	∈	[1..5]	≤	1000	Silver
3	∈	[1..5]	>	1000	Gold
4	>	5	≤	5000	Gold
5	>	5	>	5000	Platinum

F	Inputs			Output
	ratio delayed deliveries	ratio incomplete deliveries	Service Level	Penal Damage
	Number	Number	{Silver, Gold, Platinum}	Number
1	= 0%	= 0%	—	0%
2	—	—	Silver	1%
3	—	—	Gold	2%
4	≤ 1%	—	Platinum	2%
5	—	≤ 1%	Platinum	2%
6	—	—	Platinum	5%

(c) Decision logic for the decision *Penal Damage* assigns a penalty based on the ratio of flawed deliveries

Fig. 1. Decision model comprising the requirements graph (a), the logic (b) for the decision *Service Level*, and the logic (c) for the decision *Penal Damage*

for the decision *service level*) or outputs of other decisions (i.e., the *Service Level* for the decision *Penal Damage*).

The logic level defines rules for taking the decisions. The example uses Fig. 1b for the *Service Level* decision and Fig. 1c for the penal damage decision. Each table consists of rows/rules mapping a combination of input values to an output value. For example, each rule of Fig. 1b maps some combination of *years as customer* and *number of units* to a *Service Level*. However, the rules of a table can overlap, i.e., they match for the same combinations of inputs. Such conflicts are resolved by the table's hit policy. In this paper, we employ a *first* hit policy (i.e., indicated by the letter *F* in the upper left corner of the tables) for these cases, such that decision tables are evaluated one rule at a time from top to bottom until the first match is found. Any table with overlapping rules can be (with respect to its hit-policy) transformed into an equivalent non-overlapping (unique) one [2]. Unique tables lead to the same result for any hit policy.

This paper focuses on collaborative decision; we distinguish between two collaborative cases: 1. an output of a decision is required by multiple parties, 2. different inputs are provided by different parties. In the example, both participants are interested in the outcome of the *Penal Damage* decision: the logistic contractor must pay the damage to the retailer, who wants to confirm the amount. The inputs are mostly known by both participants; however, the number of incomplete deliveries is reported by the retailer while the logistic contractor provides the inputs for the decision *Service Level*.

2.2 Blockchain Technology

Nakamoto proposed the blockchain technology to power the peer-based digital currency bitcoin [12]. Blockchains offer a novel way to store a ledger of transactions decentralized: all information is shared among a network of equal peers (no central control). Transactions spread through the network and each node verifies and stores them into sequences called blocks. Under certain conditions (e.g., when providing the solution to a cryptographic puzzle), a node appends the block to the ledger (i.e., the blockchain) and propagates it to its peers.

Since the ledger is shared among nodes, its history is practically immutable: changing the ledger requires the majority of nodes to adopt the change. Furthermore, peer-based verification of transactions and cryptographic principles enable digital identities, which, for example, can be used to realize cryptocurrency systems. Such systems are the foundation for incentives and payments.

Blockchains focusing on asset transfers (e.g., Bitcoin) are considered members of the 1st blockchain generation. The 2nd generation of blockchains (e.g., Ethereum) has capabilities to store and execute custom code artifacts by the peer-to-peer network. Those programs are called smart contracts (a term coined in [17]) and implement escrows, business processes, and more. Smart contracts inherit the properties of the ledger: they are immutable, and their execution is tamper-proof. Thus, smart contracts are guaranteed to run as specified. Some are used as accountable representations of real world contracts and must be secured against attacks. Atzei et al. summarize some common vulnerabilities [1].

2.3 Blockchain-Based Decision Execution

Collaborative decisions require that all involved participants have a common understanding of both the decision logic and the inputs. At runtime, the successful collaboration depends on all participants coming to the same conclusion. However, in general participants may communicate faulty information.

For this reason, in [7], we presented a way to execute decisions on blockchains, acting as a central but neutral entity that can store information tamper-proofed. In that work, logic and inputs are published to the chain and the decision-making process for the example decisions (Fig. 1) is implemented as depicted in Fig. 2: each participant publishes a different part of the required inputs. Eventually, all data is available and the contractor triggers the blockchain-based execution of the decision *Service Level*. The correct decision output is stored on-chain and works as an input for the next decision triggered by the retailer. However, every piece of information (i.e., logic, inputs, and output) is stored publicly, limiting the applicability of this approach to non-sensitive data.

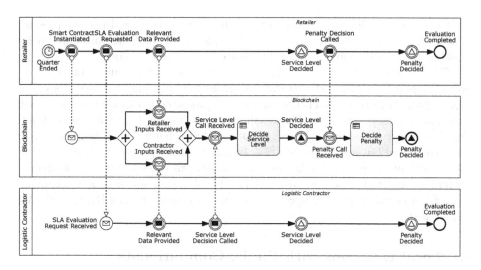

Fig. 2. Collaborative decision making by storing and executing decisions (logic and instance data) on a blockchain

3 Related Work

Recently, blockchain technologies have received high attention from academic and industrial communities. Among others, the BPM community acknowledges the opportunities and challenges of this technology [10]. Business to business interactions are based on contracts; technologies that guarantee the execution of such contracts offer ways of automating collaborations and preventing conflicts. As shown by Weber et al., blockchain-based applications can monitor and mediate the execution of business process choreographies without relying on a trusted third party [19]. García-Bañuelos et al. build up on this idea: they suggest to formalize BPMN models as Petri nets while minimizing the number of transitions to optimize the execution of the smart contracts respectively [5]. The work is the foundation for the blockchain-based process engine Caterpillar by López-Pintado et al. [9]. That approach considers that a blockchain is shared among all participants; thus, collaborative processes are local processes of the blockchain. Such processes require no communication with other processes. Other works follow this line, for example, Lorikeet by Tran et al., which additionally supports data models (i.e., registries) [18], and the work by Sturm et al., which enables flexibility by changing the model already deployed to the blockchain [16].

Besides procedural constraints (e.g., the order is shipped after the payment), contracts contain declarative rules (e.g., if the order is not shipped within 7 days, the shipment costs will be refunded); decision models can capture these and improve the models' comprehensibility [4]. So far, only few works consider collaborative decisions and decision models. The collaborative execution of decisions requires a common understanding of data and logic. Nikaj et al. propose a central REST-full decision services to address this requirement [13]. However, the solution requires all participants to trust the service provider. In [7] we present a blockchain-based solution: the service is deployed on the Ethereum blockchain making data, logic, and execution transparent and tamper-proof.

The mentioned works are aware of a major limitation: public blockchains are transparent because all data and logic is stored publicly; hence, they are not applicable to privacy-sensitive data. The presented works list two potential solutions: privacy preserving blockchains such as HAWK [8], which are not yet feasible, due to slow performance; and private blockchains, which keep data and logic concealed but are less secure [22]. In this work, we propose a different solution based on commitment schemes [6]. Commitment schemes allow participants to publicly commit to secret data without revealing it. They are one mechanism used to incorporate data privacy in blockchain systems such as HAWK [8] and zerocoin [11].

4   Local Decisions with Public Commitments

Collaborating enterprises usually specify the terms for the joint work in contracts. Details of the contract are often confidential for multiple reasons: they may contain sensitive data or put participants in an adverse position (e.g., for future negotiations). However, if a participant breaches the contract, others may disclose the contract and provide proofs of the violation at court to enforce penalties and receive compensation. In this paper, we present an approach, in which the role of the court is performed by blockchain-based smart contracts.

Figure 3 provides an overview of our approach. It consists of a *preparation phase* and two main phases: the *operation phase* and the *conflict resolution phase*. During the *operation phase*, participants execute decisions locally but commit publicly to secret inputs and outputs via cryptographic commitment schemes. If and only if a conflict occurs during this phase, the *conflict resolution phase* is entered. Additionally, a *preparation phase* is executed before the *first* instance.

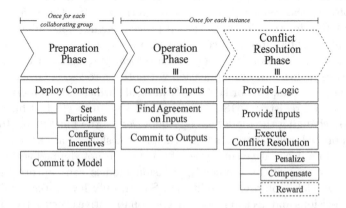

Fig. 3. The approach comprises three phases with multiple steps: a preparation phase, an operation phase, and a conflict resolution phase. Dashed elements are optional

Collaborative decisions require a common understanding of the decision logic and the instance data between all participants. During the *preparation phase*, all participants publicly commit to a secret decision model (only known by the participants) comprising all input and output variables (i.e., with a name and a value range) as well as the decision logic (i.e., a set of decision tables). Additionally, the terms for handling frauds are set. However, this is a onetime procedure performed for each group of collaborating parties (each contract). In the example, the logistics contractor and the retailer negotiate the terms of the service level agreement. Afterwards, both commit to the decision model: by comparing their hashes, they can determine whether they agree. The means of commitment are discussed further in the following sections.

4.1 Operation Phase

During the *operation phase*, decisions are executed locally. Thus, we can only enter the *operation phase* once a common understanding of the decision model exists and has been verified during the *preparation phase*. An instance of a collaborative decision is successful if all collaborators come to the same conclusions. This is the case if participants agree on the data—all inputs and all outputs.

If relevant knowledge is distributed, then participants must first establish common ground. To this end, the collaborators need secure means of communication, which authenticates collaborators, keeps messages confidential, and protects the messages integrity. In general, the message exchange should be performed off-chain (e.g., via snail mail). However, protocols, such as the peer-based shh[1], can be tools to exchange encrypted messages via the blockchain network. We assume that a suited communication tool exists, without specifying or relying on its nature.

Once a participant knows all the input values $(i_1, i_2, \ldots, i_n)$, he or she can derive the decision's output o. Next, the participant publicly commits to the confidential values using a cryptographic commitment scheme. We use a *cryptographic* hash function h to calculate the hashes $(h(i_1), \ldots, h(i_n), h(o))$. The hashes are submitted to (and stored in) the smart contract via signed transactions. A commitment is public since it is stored on a blockchain that can be accessed by anyone, but, at the same time, it conceals the true value. Since the commitment is conveyed by a signed transaction, its origin can be verified. Only those who know the value (i.e., the collaborators) can verify the commitment.

In the service level agreement example, knowledge is considered to be shared by the logistic contractor and the retailer. Both participants first commit to the input values to verify their common understanding of the inputs. Afterwards, they execute the decisions locally (one decision at a time) and commit to the outputs (any third party is incapable of distinguishing commitments to inputs from commitments to outputs). Only once the logistics contractor and the retailer committed to the same value for a certain variable, it is safe to use

---

[1] The shh implementation for Ethereum is called whisper (https://github.com/ethereum/wiki/wiki/Whisper accessed 11/29/2018).

it for decision making. This forces both participants to complete the decision *Service Level* before *Penal Damage*. If they do not agree on an output, each of them can trigger the conflict resolution.

4.2 Conflict Resolution Phase

In case the participants dissent on a decision's output, the proposed smart contracts can resolve the conflict automatically. The participants already have claimed to have a common understanding of the decision model as well as the decision inputs and have proved this by agreeing on the respective hash values. Thus, each participant is able to provide the values corresponding to the hashes. Given a value and the secret the smart contract verifies them against their hash. In case of success, the smart contract interprets the decision and derives corresponding outputs, which in turn are verified against the corresponding hashes. If inputs or decision logic are invalid, then the claimant did not provide the right information and can try again. If the outputs do not match the respective hashes, a fraud was rightfully reported; else, the claim was misplaced.

Based on the verification of outputs, the smart contract assigns blame. If the verification uncovers fraudulent outputs, all participants that provided the respective hashes are penalized, the claimant is rewarded, and all collaborators who did not sign the values are compensated for the disclosure of the confidential information (namely the decision logic and instance data). If the outputs do match the hashes, the claim is a fraud itself and the claimant is penalized for publishing the information and all other collaborators are compensated. The following list summarizes the incentive model:

reward. If a claimant reveals a fraudulent instance, he or she is rewarded for enforcing the terms of the agreement.

compensation. By disclosing the secret information honest participants may be harmed. Thus, all honest participants receive a compensation.

penalty. Two cases are penalized: 1. providing/signing wrong outputs for a decision and 2. declaring legitimate instances fraudulent.

In order to enforce penalties, rewards, and compensations the smart contract must have sufficient funds at disposal. For that reason, the smart contract manages an escrow for each participant.

The amounts paid as rewards, compensations, and penalties must be tailored to each use case and are part of the contract. During the *preparation phase* the smart contract is configured respectively. However, to automate the incentive mechanism (which is part of the conflict resolution) respective funds must be provided to the smart contract upfront. During the preparation phase, each participants provides the funds to pay the penalty for the worst-case scenario:

$$escrow(p) = penalty = (compensation \cdot (|participants| - 1)) + reward$$

The convicted parties must pay a compensation to the harmed participants and potentially the reward to the claimant.

The smart contract makes the enforcement of the incentives possible. Thus, making it practically meaningless for participants to commit a fraud since all "cards" will open and unequivocally reveal the fraud. The only risk is that revealing the decision brings benefits that outweigh the penalty from the fraud's perspective. Hence, it is very critical to model and agree on a fair incentive model that foresees any malicious behavior from each participant's point of interest.

If in our example (see Fig. 1a) both participants agree, that the retailer has a *Silver* service level agreement and not all deliveries have been complete/in time, then the logistic contractor must pay the retailer a penal damage of 1%. However, if the retailer committed to a value for the output penal damage that is unequal to 1, the logistic contractor can trigger the conflict resolution. The contractor provides all data—decision logic and inputs—in clear text. The smart contract verifies the data by matching the corresponding hashes to the respective commitments. If so, it derives the output *penal damage* = 1%, hashes it, and compares the hash to the retailer's commitment. Since the retailer committed to another value, the hashes do not match. The smart contract automatically rewards and compensates the logistics contractor and penalizes the retailer.

5   Implementation and Cost Analysis

In this section, we present our prototypical implementation based on the Ethereum blockchain[2] [21]. Ethereum is a blockchain of the 2nd generation, which can be deployed publicly and privately. We chose Ethereum since it is the most common public 2nd generation blockchain. However, any other blockchain with comparable capabilities (e.g., EOS[3] or Tezos[4]) can be used. Ethereum supports Turing-complete smart contracts usually written in the programming language *Solidity* (see Sect. 5.1 for implementation details).

However, to stop adversaries from executing smart contracts that put a high load on the network (e.g., by running indefinitely) each operation comes at a price [21]. When a participant calls a smart contract (via a transaction), he or she has to provide sufficient funds (called *gas*) to execute the call. An adaptable gas price maps gas to Ether—Ethereum's cryptocurrency. Nevertheless, even if a participant has a great amount of Ether, the execution is limited by the gas limits of the transactions and blocks, which vary over time. We evaluate the costs of our implementation, to show that it is affordable to run on public blockchain and that it is within the gas limits (see Sect. 5.2).

---

[2] Ethereum website: https://ethereum.org (accessed 11/26/18).

[3] EOS website: https://www.eos.io (accessed 11/26/18).

[4] Tezos website: https://tezos.com (accessed 11/26/19).

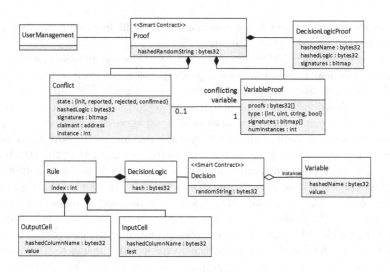

Fig. 4. High level structure of the implemented smart contracts

5.1   Ethereum-Based Implementation

Our implementation has two smart contracts (see Fig. 4). Each smart contract is responsible for one of the main phases. The contract `Proof` stores and compares the commitments during the *operation phase*. In the *conflict resolution phase*, the contract `Decision` verifies instances and resolves conflicts.

`Proof` stores the addresses of all collaborators. Additionally, it stores a set of variables (inputs and outputs) identified by their hashed name (32-bytes, when using keccak256/sha3). The smart contract stores a list of instances. Each instance assigns a hash and a bitmap to each variable. The bitmap encodes which participants have signed/committed to this hash. Since the domain of variables can be small (e.g., boolean values), the value should be enriched before hashing to prevent brute-force attacks. Therefore, participants agree on a random string, which is kept secret between them. All participants commit to the string during the preparation phase; it is stored in the proof contract. A value is appended to the hash of the random string before being hashed. Generally, we recommend to change the random string for every instance; else, inputs can be discovered by analyzing the value distributions. The `Proof` contract stores information of variables and proofs via mappings. The contract maps each hashed variable name (32-bytes) to a variable object that holds further information (see Listing 1.1). The hash of the kth instance is stored in the respective position k of the array `proofs`. At the same position in `signatures`, a bitmap is stored. Each participant is assigned to a certain position of the bitmap: when he or she signs/commits to the hash, then the respective bit is set to 1.

Listing 1.1. Solidity implementation of members via mappings and structs: `vars` maps each hashed variable name to a `Variable` object holding the type, the proofs (hashed values), the signatures for each proof, and the number of instances

```
contract Proof {
    struct Variable {
        TYPE t; // the type: boolean, (unsigned) integer, or string
        bytes32[] proofs; // each element is a hashed value
        uint8[] signatures; // bitmap marking signatures
        uin8 numInstance; // the number of instances
    }
    // Mapping of variables: hash(name) => Variable Object
    mapping(bytes32 => Variable) public vars;
}
```

Only once a conflict is reported, the contract `Decision` is deployed. During deployment the claimant provides the address of the `Proof` and the random string used for calculating the hashes. The contract has multiple responsibilities. For one, it stores the decision logic: each cell of the decision table's body is provided in a transaction. A respective cell in an input column is a test; in an output column, it is a value. Tests depend on the corresponding column's type.

Boolean. A boolean condition is given by an element of an enumeration: it is either T for true, F for false, or the wildcard $*$.

Integer. We support unsigned and signed integers. Corresponding conditions are represented by intervals with upper and lower bounds as well as two boolean flags to indicate whether a respective bound is included or excluded.

String. Strings must always be compared for equality with others [15]. Thus, the condition consist of a 32-bytes string which is compared to the input.

Another responsibility of the contract `Decision` is verifying the commitments. Firstly, it hashes the random string and verifies that it matches the commitments of the collaborators—if the random string is wrong, the conflict resolution is canceled (so far no sensitive data has been stored). Afterwards, the participant calling the contract resolution provides the decision logic: the contract `Decision` calculates the hash of the decision table and compares it to the respective one stored within the contract `Proof`. It calculates the hash incrementally whenever a new cell is provided to the smart contract (see Listing 1.2). All participants must agree on an order of the cells (i.e., from top left to the bottom right) to derive the same hash for the same logic. The hashes are chained, meaning that a hash is included in the calculation of the subsequent hash. Eventually, the final hash depends on all cells of the decision table.

Listing 1.2. Setting a boolean condition (cell of an input column of type boolean). The hashed decision table is stored in `verificationHash` and updated for each cell

```
function addBooleanCondition(bytes32 _varHash, uint8 _ruleNum, BOOL_TEST
    _test) public [...] {
        verificationHash = keccak256(verificationHash, rndmString, _varHash,
            _test);
        booleanTests[_varHash][_ruleNum] = test;
}
```

The instance information is verified similarly: the `decision` contract receives an input for a variable, hashes it, and compares it to the one in the `Proof` contract (see Listing 1.3). Only if the verification is successful, the data is stored.

Listing 1.3. Whenever an (integer) input is set, its hash is calculated with the random string and compared to the proof. For the value to be stored, the hashes must match

```
function setIntInput(bytes32 _varHash, uint8 _instanceID, int32 _value)
    public {
    require(proof.getValueHash(_varHash, _instanceID) ==
            keccak256(rndmString, _value), "Wrong Input");
    intInputs[_varHash][_instanceID] = _value;
}
```

Deploying an instance of a contract is expensive. Thus, reducing the number of required instances can reduce the overall costs of the implementation. In our implementation, the contracts `Proof` and `Decision` can handle up to 256 instances of a decision (an 8-bit unsigned integer). However, once a conflict occurred and the respective `Decision` has been deployed, future instances and data can be discovered by brute force attacks or analyzing the value distribution.

We refer the reader who is interested in further implementation details to the complementary online resources[5]. They comprise the complete source code as well as additional documentation. Among others, we discuss how we protect our implementation against common attacks [1], such as *reentry attacks*, *unpredictable states*, and *race-to-empty attacks*.

5.2   Cost Analysis

Executing Ethereum-based smart contracts costs Ether: every operation that a smart contract performs has a price, which must be paid by the one calling the contract. For one, execution costs limit the applicability of smart contracts because not all scenarios are viable. In general, the costs for the execution must be lower than the value gained by the blockchain. Second, the maximal number of operations is limited by the gas limit. Thus, smart contracts can reach a boundary that makes them impossible to execute. In this chapter, we provide an overview of the costs of our smart contracts[6].

As described above, this paper's approach follows three phases. In the first phase (preparation phase), the smart contract `Proof` is deployed and the variables are initialized. This is done only once for each collaboration. The costs only depend on the decision table's headers (number and type of inputs and outputs) and the number of participants. For each variable and for each decision, the name's hash is provided to the smart contract. Variables additionally have a type. Consequently, the initialization cost c_{init} depend linearly on the number of variables and decisions. The costs for a single decision with i variables are

---

[5] Source code, binaries, and documentation at https://owncloud.hpi.de/index.php/s/EZrGNPpsjBfHTJH.

[6] Based on the average gas price and the average Ether to Euro exchange rate on 11/26/2018 source https://etherscan.io.

$$c_{init}(i) = 28500 \ gas \cdot i + 109208 \ gas \quad (or \quad c_{init}(i) \approx 0.04724 \ \text{€} \cdot i + 0.18101 \ \text{€}).$$

Additionally, the deployment costs of the contract `Proof` must be paid (about 2.19 €). Even for 100 inputs, the costs of the *preparation phase* are fairly low (about 4.90 €+ 2.19 €). Since a single contract instance can be used for up to 256 instances, the *preparation phase* has a low impact on the overall costs.

During the *operation phase*, participants commit to values of certain variables. This again depends on the number of inputs and the number of participants only. We measure the costs for bilateral decisions with 5 to 100 inputs (in steps of 5). However, due to compiler optimization and conditional code the costs are only approximately linear. For two collaborators and i variables the costs c_{op2} can be approximated by the following linear regression:

$$c_{op2}(i,p) \approx 83967 \ gas \cdot i + 111618 \ gas \quad (or \quad c_{op2}(i,p) \approx 0.18493 \ \text{€} \cdot i + 0.13917 \ \text{€}).$$

This holds only for the second instance on-wards. The first instance is approximately 1.7 times more expensive.

The third phase, the conflict resolution, depends on the number of inputs as well as the number of rules: on the one hand, inputs and logic are provided directly to the blockchain (initialization); on the other hand, the interpretation of the decision requires sequential evaluation of the decision logic (conflict resolution). We empirically evaluate 400 randomly generated decision tables with $5, 10, 15, \ldots, 100$ rules and $5, 10, 15, \ldots, 100$ inputs. All columns have the type `integer` (32-bit). The initialization requires us to send a transaction for each cell of the decision table's body. Eventually, the complete decision table is stored in the contract `decision`. Thus, the costs depend mainly on the number of cells, which depend on the number of inputs and rules (see Fig. 5a and b). The initialization costs vary between 1,195,970 *gas* (1.98 €) for a 5 times 5 decision table and 380,517,400 *gas* (630.70 €) for a 100 times 100 decision table.

The conflict resolution depends on two parts: firstly, the instance data (true values of inputs) must be provided; secondly, the decision logic is interpreted for the inputs and the outputs are derived. One can see in Fig. 5c, that the costs mainly depend on the number of inputs, because we save one value for each input. When evaluating the decision logic, we successively evaluate each rule of the decision table from top to bottom. Hence, the costs increase with the number of rules as well. However, in general persisting data in a smart contract (changing its state) is more expensive than enacting logic that only reads data [21]—consequently, the number of rules has a lower impact compared to the number of inputs. The costs for the conflict resolution vary between 315,740 *gas* (0.52 €) for a 5 times 5 decision table and 5,526,013 *gas* (9.16 €) for a 100 times 100 decision table. Note, for the conflict resolution we randomly select a rule and generated inputs respectively; thus, it does not depict the worst case. The complete data, decision tables, and cost analysis results are provided online[7].

---

[7] Evaluated decision tables and results at https://owncloud.hpi.de/index.php/s/EZrGNPpsjBfHTJH.

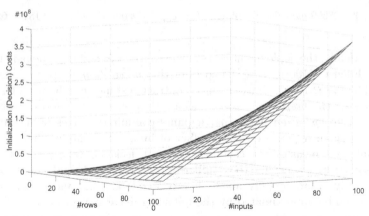

(a) Costs for initializing the contract decision (providing logic and inputs) dependent on the number of rules and inputs *(View 1)*

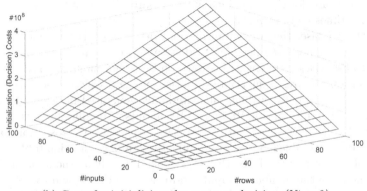

(b) Costs for initializing the contract decision *(View 2)*

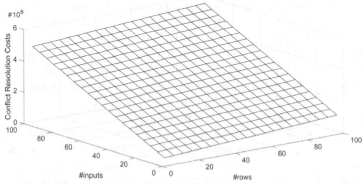

(c) Costs of the conflict resolution dependent on the number of rules and the number of inputs

Fig. 5. Costs of the overall conflict resolution consisting of the contracts initialization (a, b) and executing the resolution (c)

6 Discussion and Conclusion

Collaborative decisions are often important steps in inter-organizational processes: successful collaborations can depend on correct decision making. Therefore, participants are interested in enforcing correct behavior of all collaborators. To this end, they may rely on a trusted third party.

Previous research shows that at the cost of revealing all required information, such a third party can be replaced by a public blockchain. However, in many cases, decision logic and inputs are sensitive data. Therefore, our solution applies a blockchain and a cryptographic commitment scheme: it requires disclosure of relevant information only in case of a conflict (similar to legal procedures). Additionally, an incentive model deters all participants to misbehave.

Our approach relies on legally enforcable smart contracts: the blockchain community envisions

> [...] a future where legal agreements such as business contracts are recorded and automatically managed without error[...]

as described in the Corda white paper [3]. However, the current concept and implementation still bears some drawbacks compared to a centralized solution. Firstly, using public blockchains is more expensive, but our analysis shows that the execution costs are acceptable in many cases. Secondly, some operations have strict causal dependencies—even with an average block-time of a couple of seconds (Ethereum), it slows down automated decision making.

Future work should address some of the approach's limitations. The current incentive model is basic. Especially in settings of more than two collaborators, multiple participants can be penalized and compensated, but the current model treats all situations the same. A second conflict may be less harmful since the decision logic has already been revealed; the model should be adapted consequently. Other scenarios run multiple instances simultaneously. In such a case, escrows must be instance-based to be able to cope with all potential conflicts. Further, it is possible that a participant reveals most of the decision logic (and thereby harms collaborators) but never executes the conflict resolution (thus no compensation). Although such a behavior can be disincentivized, similar action can take place off-chain. Therefore, future research may investigate voting and/or reputation-based mechanisms to penalize participants.

Overall, our contribution enforces collaborative decisions via blockchains and minimizes the need for public disclosure. Thereby, we overcome one of the central limitations of public blockchains for inter-organizational settings: much of the involved data is confidential and must stay concealed if possible.

References

1. Atzei, N., Bartoletti, M., Cimoli, T.: A survey of attacks on ethereum smart contracts (SoK). In: Maffei, M., Ryan, M. (eds.) POST 2017. LNCS, vol. 10204, pp. 164–186. Springer, Heidelberg (2017). https://doi.org/10.1007/978-3-662-54455-6_8
2. Batoulis, K., Weske, M.: Disambiguation of DMN decision tables. In: Abramowicz, W., Paschke, A. (eds.) BIS 2018. LNBIP, vol. 320, pp. 236–249. Springer, Cham (2018). https://doi.org/10.1007/978-3-319-93931-5_17
3. Brown, R.G.: The Corda platform–an introduction, May 2018. https://www.corda.net/content/corda-platform-whitepaper.pdf
4. Calvanese, D., Dumas, M., Laurson, Ü., Maggi, F.M., Montali, M., Teinemaa, I.: Semantics and analysis of DMN decision tables. In: La Rosa, M., Loos, P., Pastor, O. (eds.) BPM 2016. LNCS, vol. 9850, pp. 217–233. Springer, Cham (2016). https://doi.org/10.1007/978-3-319-45348-4_13
5. García-Bañuelos, L., Ponomarev, A., Dumas, M., Weber, I.: Optimized execution of business processes on blockchain. In: Carmona, J., Engels, G., Kumar, A. (eds.) BPM 2017. LNCS, vol. 10445, pp. 130–146. Springer, Cham (2017). https://doi.org/10.1007/978-3-319-65000-5_8
6. Goldreich, O.: The Foundations of Cryptography - Basic Techniques, vol. 1. Cambridge University Press, Cambridge (2001)
7. Haarmann, S., Batoulis, K., Nikaj, A., Weske, M.: DMN decision execution on the ethereum blockchain. In: Krogstie, J., Reijers, H.A. (eds.) CAiSE 2018. LNCS, vol. 10816, pp. 327–341. Springer, Cham (2018). https://doi.org/10.1007/978-3-319-91563-0_20
8. Kosba, A.E., Miller, A., Shi, E., Wen, Z., Papamanthou, C.: HAWK: the blockchain model of cryptography and privacy-preserving smart contracts. In: IEEE Symposium on Security and Privacy, SP 2016, pp. 839–858 (2016). https://doi.org/10.1109/SP.2016.55
9. López-Pintado, O., García-Bañuelos, L., Dumas, M., Weber, I.: Caterpillar: a blockchain-based business process management system. In: Proceedings of the Demo Track at BPM 2017, Business Process Management (BPM 2017) (2017). http://ceur-ws.org/Vol-1920/BPM2017paper199.pdf
10. Mendling, J., Weber, I., et al.: Blockchains for business process management - challenges and opportunities. ACM Trans. Manag. Inf. Syst. **9**(1), 4:1–4:6 (2018). https://doi.org/10.1145/3183367
11. Miers, I., Garman, C., Green, M., Rubin, A.D.: Zerocoin: anonymous distributed e-cash from bitcoin. In: Proceedings of 2013 IEEE Symposium on Security and Privacy, SP 2013, pp. 397–411 (2013). https://doi.org/10.1109/SP.2013.34
12. Nakamoto, S.: Bitcoin: A peer-to-peer electronic cash system (2008). https://bitcoin.org/bitcoin.pdf
13. Nikaj, A., Batoulis, K., Weske, M.: REST-enabled decision making in business process choreographies. In: Sheng, Q.Z., Stroulia, E., Tata, S., Bhiri, S. (eds.) ICSOC 2016. LNCS, vol. 9936, pp. 547–554. Springer, Cham (2016). https://doi.org/10.1007/978-3-319-46295-0_34
14. Object Management Group: Business process model and notation (BPMN) version 2.0.2, January 2014. https://www.omg.org/spec/BPMN/
15. Object Management Group: Decision model and notation (DMN) version 1.2, August 2018. https://www.omg.org/spec/DMN/

16. Sturm, C., Szalanczi, J., Schönig, S., Jablonski, S.: A lean architecture for blockchain based decentralized process execution. In: Daniel, F., Sheng, Q.Z., Motahari, H. (eds.) BPM 2018. LNBIP, vol. 342, pp. 361–373. Springer, Cham (2019). https://doi.org/10.1007/978-3-030-11641-5_29
17. Szabo, N.: Formalizing and securing relationships on public networks. First Monday **2** (1997). https://doi.org/10.5210/fm.v2i9.548
18. Tran, A.B., Lu, Q., Weber, I.: Lorikeet: a model-driven engineering tool for blockchain-based business process execution and asset management. In: Proceedings of the Demo Track Track at BPM 2018, Business Process Management (BPM 2018), pp. 56–60 (2018)
19. Weber, I., Xu, X., Riveret, R., Governatori, G., Ponomarev, A., Mendling, J.: Untrusted business process monitoring and execution using blockchain. In: La Rosa, M., Loos, P., Pastor, O. (eds.) BPM 2016. LNCS, vol. 9850, pp. 329–347. Springer, Cham (2016). https://doi.org/10.1007/978-3-319-45348-4_19
20. Weske, M.: Business Process Management - Concepts, Languages, Architectures, 2nd edn. Springer, Heidelberg (2012). https://doi.org/10.1007/978-3-642-28616-2
21. Wood, G.: Ethereum: a secure decentralised generalised transaction ledger. Ethereum Project Yellow Paper **151**, 1–32 (2014)
22. Zheng, Z., Xie, S., Dai, H., Chen, X., Wang, H.: An overview of blockchain technology: architecture, consensus, and future trends. In: Proceedings of 2017 IEEE International Congress on Big Data, BigData Congress 2017, pp. 557–564 (2017). https://doi.org/10.1109/BigDataCongress.2017.85

Permissioned Distributed Ledgers for Land Transactions; A Case Study

Duneesha Fernando[✉] and Nalin Ranasinghe

University of Colombo School of Computing, Colombo, Sri Lanka
{dtf,dnr}@ucsc.cmb.ac.lk

Abstract. Considering the inefficiency and ineffectiveness of the current manual land registration systems being practiced in Sri Lanka and the emergence of the concept of blockchain based land registries as a successful replacement for badly kept, mismanaged and/or corrupt land registries from around the world, this research proposes and evaluates the applicability of a permissioned distributed land ledger solution for Sri Lanka. The final solution presents optimal content for the ledger (extracted from the current folio), preserves current land transactions, has reassigned duties to state validators and has got away with the folio system while ensuring derivation of the pedigree/folio tree for a land at a given time. A regional distributed land ledger representing the present regional ledger system and an island wide unified land ledger which addresses unequal regional land transaction density conditions across the island were proposed as solution models. The proposed models of the solution were implemented using Hyperledger Fabric v1.2. They were evaluated for performance on an AWS t2.large instance with 2 vCPUs, 8GiB memory, under different land transaction density conditions and node failure conditions. A community consisting of twenty-one peers belonging to nine organizations, was subject to evaluation. The island wide solution records higher throughput, lower latency and tolerance for fail-stop conditions than the regional distributed land ledger. Further, the island wide solution does not show a significant drop in throughput up to two crash failures out of seven Kafka brokers in production scale deployment.

Keywords: Permissioned distributed land ledger ·
Land transaction density · Fault tolerance · Transaction throughput ·
Latency

1 Introduction

Currently, two types of land registration systems are being practiced in Sri Lanka. They are (1) the Deed Registration System and (2) the Title Registration System ("Bimsaviya" national land titling project).

Regardless of all the efforts taken by its government, the administrative framework for land registration in Sri Lanka is not sufficiently effective and

© Springer Nature Switzerland AG 2019
C. Di Ciccio et al. (Eds.): BPM 2019 Blockchain and CEE Forum, LNBIP 361, pp. 136–150, 2019.
https://doi.org/10.1007/978-3-030-30429-4_10

efficient. There are many negative implications of the present land registration systems in Sri Lanka, such as existence of a large number of unsolved land disputes, litigation and unclear tenure leading to land encroachment, misuse and disuse of land.

Current land registration systems as well as newly proposed systems/strategies should enforce pragmatic decisions rather than relying on too standardized, bureaucratic and costly approaches [1]. While exploring for pragmatic approaches taken by other countries in the world in order to improve the efficiency and effectiveness of their land registration systems, it could be observed that some countries have turned their attention towards implementing blockchain based land registries. A badly kept, mismanaged and/or corrupt land registry could be successfully replaced by a blockchain based land registry, because of the added value of cryptographic auditability [2]. However, it could be observed that, not only countries with badly kept land registries (e.g.: Honduras, Ghana) but also countries with already well-functioning land registries (e.g.: Sweden, Georgia, Estonia) have reaped benefits by implementing and deploying blockchain based land registries [3–8].

As claimed by concepts of Distributed Systems, blockchain is one type of distributed ledger. A Distributed Ledger Technology (DLT) network is a collection of interconnected nodes where, each node maintains a copy of the same database, called the ledger. The process of updating the distributed ledger requires exchanging transaction information between nodes, achieving distributed consensus among nodes, followed by adding the validated transaction as a new ledger entry.

This research provides a distributed ledger solution for the Sri Lankan land transaction scenario. DLT is suitable for implementing a land ledger due to its advantages over traditional (centralized) databases, such as, providing a full audit trail of information history, accessibility to a common view of information to all nodes at the same time and high level of trustworthiness. DLT facilitates storing digital records of assets, when new information regarding a land asset is created (e.g.: when a new land is registered) as well as when existing information about a land asset changes (e.g.: when the owner of a land changes).

Out of the two main types of distributed ledgers; unpermissioned (permissionless) and permissioned, this research provides a permissioned DLT solution for the Sri Lankan land transaction scenario. A permissioned DLT network contains an authorized consortium of participants. In a permissioned DLT network distributed consensus is obtained through validation by a selected subset of 'trusted validating nodes'. Through analyzing content of current folio system, three main types of validators per a land transaction, recognized by the Sri Lankan government (i.e. Registrar General's Department) could be identified. They are the (1) Regional Land Registrar on behalf of Regional Land Registry, (2) Notary and (3) Surveyor. Considering this similarity with the real scenario and advantages of permissioned DLT over unpermissioned DLT in aspects such as speed of updating the ledger, energy consumption of the validation process, security and operational costs, it was inferred that a permissioned DLT solution is more suitable for implementing a distributed land ledger for Sri Lanka.

Thus, the aim of this research is to provide a permissioned distributed ledger solution for the Sri Lankan land transaction scenario, subsequent to a systematic performance evaluation of the proposed solution. Through this research, it is intended to find answers to the following research questions.

(A) What are the capabilities and limitations of adapting an open source solution for implementing a distributed land ledger for Sri Lanka?

(B) What is the performance difference between two proposed abstract models of the land ledger under different land transaction density conditions and node failure conditions?

(C) What are the future prospects and possibilities for implementing a large scale distributed land ledger model for Sri Lanka?

'Land transaction density' with respect to a Regional Land Registry (RLR) is the frequency of land transactions submitted to the particular RLR. RLRs such as Colombo, Galle generally have a higher land transaction density than RLRs such as Hambantota, Tangalle. Two Abstract Models are proposed based on the validation policies of Sri Lankan land transaction scenario and the heterogeneity of land transaction density across RLRs in Sri Lanka.

A consensus protocol is responsible of determining the order in which entries are appended to the distributed ledger. When individual nodes in a DLT network crash or behave maliciously, they would act against the common goal of reaching consensus. A fault tolerant consensus protocol must be established in the DLT network in order to detect and withstand such process failures. The crash (fail-stop) model of process failures, where a process can fail by stopping was considered during evaluation.

The research methodology required, designing the permissioned distributed land ledger to suit the Sri Lankan land transaction scenario based on features of a generic permissioned DLT platform, followed by its implementation using an open source permissioned DLT platform (Hyperledger Fabric v1.2) and finally evaluation of performance under different land transaction density conditions and node failure conditions.

Rest of the research paper is structured as follows. Section 2 presents a review of the literature on blockchain based land registries in other countries important towards design. Section 3 presents the design of the distributed land ledger. Section 4 explains the implementation details of the distributed land ledger solution using Hyperledger Fabric. Section 5 provides details of evaluation performed and interpretation of the results obtained. Section 6 provides the conclusion along with prospects for future work.

2   Literature Review

Blockchain-Based Land Registries of Other Countries. This section provides a review of features of blockchain-based land registries of other countries, important towards designing the Sri Lankan distributed land ledger based on [3–8].

Most of the countries listed in Table 1 have taken cross-chain exchange layer approaches across public and private blockchains rather than relying on only one type of DLT.

Table 1. Type of blockchain technology used by other countries.

Country	Type of blockchain technology
Georgia	Permissioned blockchain anchored to the Bitcoin blockchain
Sweden	Permissioned DLT network where trusted parties validate transactions while public could view details in the blockchain using an SSN based ID solution
Estonia	Public ledger
Chicago's Cook county	A colored coin (a bitcoin token) represents the land asset. Ownership change is recorded on a public ledger (the Bitcoin blockchain)
Honduras	Factom anchored to the Bitcoin blockchain
Ghana	Blockchain solution based on Bitcoin blockchain technology

In blockchain based land registries of all countries listed above, only the hash value of data is embedded in the blockchain, while actual data which is generally large in size and confidential, is kept off-chain (in a traditional server). Through this move, content of a land transaction remains irrefutable.

In all the countries reviewed, custom designed blockchain solutions have been developed. In Georgia, Sweden and Estonia, blockchain solution has been implemented to suit the title registration process exercised in those countries. In contrast, developers of Cook county's blockchain based land registry have implemented and deployed a "Blockchain deed protocol".

3 Design

This section provides the design of the DLT solution for a generic permissioned DLT platform. Since, majority of Divisional Secretariat divisions in Sri Lanka follow the deed registration system [1], the proposed solution would preserve properties of the deed system. Figure 1 presents the high level architecture of the proposed Sri Lankan distributed land ledger.

3.1 Design of Optimal Land Ledger Content

Details included in the current folio could be divided into two main sections (Fig. 2). They are (1) Fixed details regarding a land and (2) Transaction details. Section on transaction details store one record per each land transaction.

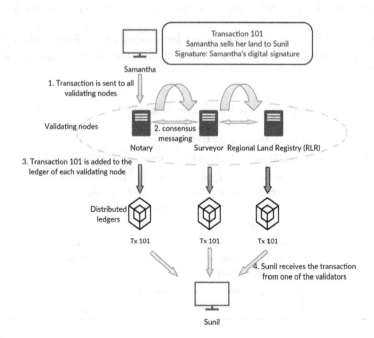

Fig. 1. High level architecture of the proposed Sri Lankan distributed land ledger

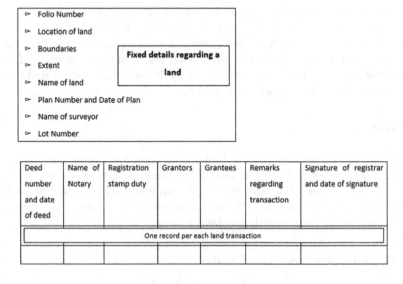

Fig. 2. Structure and details included in the current folio

The **ledger (L)** of a permissioned DLT platform (with blockchain as the underlying database structure) comprises of,

1. **World state (W):** Stores the state of the ledger at a given point in time.
2. **Transaction log:** Stores all transactions which have contributed towards current world state in **blockchain B.**

It could be observed that world state W is similar to the conjunction of section on fixed details regarding a land and details of the latest transaction regarding the land. Further, blockchain B is analogous to past transaction records included in transaction log of the folio.

Optimal ledger content was extracted from the current folio, by removing redundant details and adjusting attributes to suit a distributed ledger solution. Thus, the optimal ledger content included in the provided permissioned distributed land ledger consists of, *Land ID, Location of land, Boundaries of land (N, E, W, S), Extent, Hash of plan, Hash of deed, Registration stamp duty, Owner, Remarks regarding transaction & Parent Land ID.* The provided solution includes hash values of plan and deed in the optimal content of the land ledger, similar to other countries reviewed in Sect. 2.

3.2   Design of Transactions Against Distributed Land Ledger

In this research, "Land transactions", refer only to change of ownership right of a particular piece of land between two parties. At a given time, when the world state W of a land in the land ledger is queried, latest values corresponding to the attributes in optimal ledger content would be returned. If a client, inquires for the pedigree/folio tree of that land via his notary, the transaction log would return all past transaction records.

Figure 3 demonstrates the taxonomy of transactions in the proposed land ledger solution. queryLand query would facilitate clients to request details regarding a piece of land when the LandID is provided. queryAllLands query which facilitates retrieving details of all lands of the ledger would be useful for

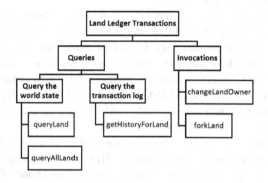

Fig. 3. Design of land ledger transactions

the land registrars at RLRs. Clients would be able to request for a change of ownership of an existing piece of land through changeLandOwner transaction. Furthermore, a client would be able to request to split an existing land and register newly created lands with new owners, updated extents and boundaries through forkLand transaction. Although, this research has got away with the folio system, since all transaction details which have contributed towards current world state are available in the blockchain B, it is possible to obtain the pedigree/folio tree which corresponds to a particular land at any given time through getHistoryForLand query.

3.3   Design of Two Abstract Models for the Sri Lankan Distributed Land Ledger

A RLR is identified by the district that it belongs to (One district may have one or more RLRs). A notary is identified by the RLR that he/she is registered with [9]. A surveyor is identified by the district [10].

Suppose a person from Colombo wants to buy a land in Galle which is located in the terrain of Galle RLR. Assume the buyer hires a notary from Colombo to perform all the legal undertakings related to the purchase of land. Notary's responsibilities include certifying the purchase consideration with a written deed until forwarding the deed to the land registrar of Galle RLR for registration. Since the land is located in Galle RLR's territory, the record pertaining to the land is included in the Galle RLR's land ledger. Suppose the buyer hired a surveyor who is registered in the Hambantota district. The surveyor prepares a plan which is annexed to the deed (prepared by the notary) with an affidavit by the surveyor certifying that he has prepared the plan correctly and truthfully. The land registrar in Galle RLR would consider all details and endorsements provided by the notary and the surveyor and provide his endorsement, thus successfully completing registration of the land transaction. Therefore, it is evident that, all 3 parties need to endorse a transaction pertaining to a particular land, in order for it to be successfully registered. Since the notary has been registered with the Colombo RLR in this scenario, a copy of the deed has to be sent to the Colombo RLR for future reference.

When the above scenario is considered, it could be observed that the extent of details accessible by each type of validator varies. Accordingly, each RLR stores details of lands in its territory, including deeds and plans of those lands. A notary possesses deeds of lands certified by him. A surveyor possesses plans of lands prepared by him. Notaries and surveyors could access details pertaining to lands belonging to a particular RLR through formal inquiry. RLRs have copies of deeds pertaining to lands (these lands could belong to other RLRs) certified by notaries registered with the particular RLR.

In the implemented solution, all three types of validators would have access to the optimal ledger content. In addition, RLRs would have access to deeds and annexed plans of lands in their terrain as well as those of lands certified by notaries registered with them. Notaries would have access to deeds certified by them and surveyors would have access to plans prepared by them. This approach has preserved the extent of details accessible by validators in the present traditional land transaction scenario.

As required by the second research question, two abstract models have been provided as permissioned DLT solutions for the Sri Lankan land transaction scenario. Abstract Model 1 (AM1) was designed such that it closely maps the current manual system. From the previously explained traditional scenario, four validators per a given land transaction could be identified. They are (1) Regional Land Registry where the land belongs to, (2) Notary, (3) Surveyor and (4) Regional Land Registry where the notary has been registered. Since, validators from at most 3 districts are involved in the validation process, implementation of a 'three district model' is acceptable for the purpose of evaluation.

In the present traditional system, each RLR maintains a ledger containing only details of lands belonging to that RLR. When this situation is adapted in AM1, each RLR holds an independent land ledger of its own lands.

In the real Sri Lankan scenario, each RLR has to endorse all transactions submitted for registration, regarding lands in its terrain. This requirement, emerges an issue with regards to workload distribution among RLRs. RLRs such as Colombo, Galle which have a high land transaction density may have a high overhead on performing validation of submitted transactions. Thus, when a set of transactions pertaining to lands situated island wide, are submitted to the permissioned DLT network concurrently, RLRs with low land transaction density (Hambantota, Tangalle) would complete validation earlier than RLRs with high land transaction density. This would reduce the overall transaction throughput of the provided solution. Transaction throughput is the rate at which transactions are committed to the distributed land ledger.

Abstract Model 2 (AM2) which is more suitable for a distributed system is proposed as a remedy to the above mentioned drawback of AM1. AM2 proposes a single island wide land ledger for the entire country. In AM2, all RLRs would access a single land ledger containing details of all lands across the island.

Now, since all RLRs have access to the same land ledger, RLRs having low land transaction densities would be able to validate transactions submitted to RLRs with high land transaction densities, thus sharing the workload. It was hypothesized that through this design approach of AM2, the overall transaction throughput would increase.

In order to prevent possible problems arising in AM2 due to the deviation from the real Sri Lankan scenario, the implemented solution requires clients to submit copies of deed and plan when a transaction is submitted to the DLT network. The hash values of deed and plan are generated by the system before sending the transaction to the validating nodes. The validators would perform validation based on the hash values of deed and plan. As a result of this approach, validators are prohibited from submitting forged transactions.

4   Implementation

4.1   Permissioned DLT Platforms and Hyperledger

Subsequent to eliminating DLT platforms specifically developed to support financial applications, those which lack clear explanation of protocol and formal review of properties as well as proprietary DLT platforms based on [11] and [12], Hyperledger was chosen for the implementation of the Sri Lankan distributed land ledger. Hyperledger is an open-source, permissioned DLT platform which facilitates implementation of generic applications [13–15]. Hyperledger project provides high degrees of confidentiality, scalability and security. Although Hyperledger has powered successful prototypes, Proofs of Concept and several production systems, across different industries and use cases (food-safety network [11], etc.), there is no published work on a distributed land registry solution implemented with Hyperledger for Sri Lanka or any other country in the world.

Fabric which is the most established framework out of the five frameworks provided by Hyperledger was chosen for the implementation of Sri Lankan distributed land ledger. Fabric could be identified as a distributed Operating System for permissioned blockchains [16]. This section provides the most important and relevant, high level implementation details of the distributed land ledger solution, provided using Hyperledger Fabric version 1.2.

4.2   Implementation of Optimal Land Ledger Content and Transactions

Hyperledger's chaincode is used to define assets and contain the rules for modifying the assets. During implementation, chaincode was written in go language, while land assets were modeled as JSON in chaincode (LandID is the key and remaining attributes listed in optimal ledger content comprise the values). CouchDB was used as the state database during implementation. Complex rich queries were implemented using the CouchDB JSON query language, to query against the data values in ledger.

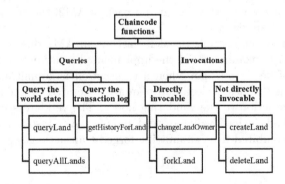

Fig. 4. Implementation of Chaincode functions

As shown in Fig. 4, two new non-directly invocable functions; createLand and deleteLand were implemented, in order to implement forkLand function. fork-Land transaction checks whether the sum of the extents of the new lands is consistent with the extent of original land and whether boundaries of newly created lands do not overlap with each other. If so, it will invoke deleteLand transaction which will delete the original land from ledger, and createLand transaction will be invoked n times to create n number of new lands as requested by the transaction proposal. It is ensured that the implemented solution preserves the consistency of the land ledger, before and after executing a set of transactions. getHistoryForLand chaincode function was implemented based on GetHistory-ForKey chaincode API function which facilitates data provenance in Hyperledger Fabric.

4.3   Implementation of the Two Abstract Models

The DLT network comprising of validators (peers) is implemented as a network of Docker containers in Hyperledger Fabric. Peers belonging to one trust domain are identified as members of a single organization.

As required by the design of two AMs, three types of organizations (RLR organization, Notary organization, Surveyor organization) were implemented. Figure 5 demonstrates that the implemented three district model has all three organizations per each district. Both AMs consist of nine organizations providing a community of twenty-one peers. The orderer organization (org 10 in green colour) in Fig. 5 is responsible of executing the consensus protocol.

Hyperledger Fabric's channel architecture was exploited in implementing the regional land ledgers of AM1 and island wide land ledger of AM2. All peers connected to a single channel can maintain a separate ledger which is embedded in a distinct chaincode.

In AM1, each RLR owns one channel, one chaincode for that channel and thus one land ledger (Fig. 5a). In contrast, AM2 contains a single channel to which all RLRs are connected, one chaincode for that channel and thus one land ledger representing all lands across the island (Fig. 5b).

In AM1, the RLR that the land belongs to, should certainly endorse the transaction. In AM2, if the RLR that the land belongs to is overloaded with requests for validation, a RLR with low land transaction density could perform validation on behalf of the RLR with high land transaction density. Fabric's endorsement policy specifies which validators or how many of them need to endorse a transaction proposal.

Thus the two endorsement policies for the two AMs are depicted as follows.

- **AM1:** AND (**org1**, OR(org1, org4, org7), OR(org2, org5, org8), OR(org3, org6, org9))
- **AM2:** AND (OR(org1, org4, org7), OR(org2, org5, org8), OR(org3, org6, org9))

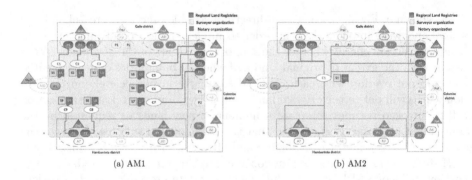

(a) AM1   (b) AM2

Fig. 5. Channel architecture of the Three District Model in the 2 AMs (Color figure online)

4.4 Implementation of Production Scale DLT Networks and Facilitation of Fault Tolerance

Implementation details stated up to the previous section were based on Solo ordering service which is a single-node implementation. Although Solo ordering service is recommended for development and testing of DLT networks, it does not suffice in real production, because of the inability of one ordering node to withstand crash faults. Hyperledger Fabric facilitates plugging Kafka-based ordering service which ensures CFT.

Implementation of Distributed Land Ledger with Kafka-Based Ordering Service. Kafka-based ordering service consists of Hyperledger Fabric Ordering Service Nodes (OSNs), an Apache Kafka cluster and a Zookeeper ensemble. Table 2 contains configuration details of Kafka-based ordering service which were implemented in order to evaluate performance up to two crashes for the distributed land ledger solution.

Table 2. Configuration of Kafka-based ordering service tolerating upto two crashes. (M; Minimum number of in-sync replicas, N; Default replication factor, K; Total number of Kafka brokers)

No. of crashes	M	N	K	Z (No. of Zookeeper nodes)	No. of OSNs
1	2	3	4	3	2
2	3	4	7	3	2

5   Results and Evaluation

This section presents a performance evaluation of the two AMs based on heterogeneous land transaction density conditions across RLRs and failure conditions.

Evaluation model followed in this section was devised based on [17,18]. Implementation and evaluation of the two AMs were performed on an AWS t2.large instance (64bit X86, 2 vCPUs, 8GiB memory) with Ubuntu 18.04.1, Docker version 18.06.0 and Docker Compose version 1.21.2.

Evaluation was performed for a scenario where one RLR has a higher land transaction density than others. Within a set of simultaneous transactions submitted to the DLT network, the ratio between changeLandOwner transaction invocations and forkLand transaction invocations is 3:2, unless stated otherwise. It was ensured that the execution of submitted transactions was not interrupted by queries.

Primary performance metrics of Hyperledger Fabric as stated in [17] are,

Throughput:- Rate at which transactions are committed to the ledger.
Latency:- Time taken from application sending the transaction proposal to the transaction commit.

5.1   Evaluation of the Two Abstract Models

AM1 and AM2 were evaluated for throughput and latency in Kafka-based ordering service under the first configuration in Table 2. Throughput of AM2 is higher than that of AM1 for all evaluated workloads. Although the latencies of both models increase with load, latency as well as rate of increase in latency of AM1 is always higher than that of AM2. AM1 has a higher latency due to the bottleneck of validation at the RLR with a higher land transaction density (Fig. 6).

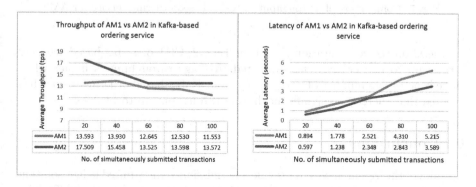

Fig. 6. Throughput and Latency of AM1 vs AM2 in Kafka-based ordering service

Evaluation for Crash Fault Tolerance (CFT). Fault tolerance of a Fabric network could be evaluated at two levels. They are at, (1) the level of validating nodes and (2) the level of ordering service.

Fault tolerance capabilities of the two AMs at the level of validating nodes (endorsing peers), is governed by their respective endorsement policies. In AM1, if the node representing the RLR that the land belongs to is crashed, none of the transactions could be endorsed and thus committed to the ledger. But, with AM2 even if the RLR node that the land belongs to is crashed, any other RLR could validate the transaction/s on behalf of the original RLR. Thus, AM2 is more suitable for implementing a distributed land ledger for Sri Lanka when fault tolerance at the level of validating nodes is considered.

Hyperledger Fabric mainly focuses on crash fault tolerance at the level of ordering service, i.e. crashing of Kafka brokers of the Kafka-based ordering service. Since AM2 is capable of tolerating crash faults at the level of validating nodes, crash fault tolerance at the level of ordering service was evaluated for AM2 (Fig. 7).

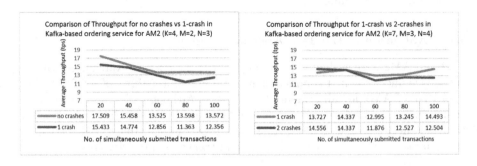

Fig. 7. Comparison of Throughput in Kafka-based ordering service for AM2

Based on the configuration models in Table 2, CFT of Kafka-based ordering service up to two crashes was evaluated. Average throughput is higher when there is no or less number of crashes. However, Kafka-based ordering service has ensured that there is no significant drop in throughput up to two crashes.

6 Conclusions

The aim of this research was to provide a permissioned distributed ledger solution for the Sri Lankan land transaction scenario, in order to overcome the inefficiency and ineffectiveness of the current manual land registration systems in practice. Through this research, a permissioned distributed land ledger for Sri Lanka was designed, implemented using Hyperledger Fabric and evaluated for performance in terms of transaction throughput and latency.

Since it was possible to provide all the queries and transaction invocations as suggested by the design, using Hyperledger Fabric, it could be stated that the capabilities of adapting Hyperledger Fabric for implementing a distributed land ledger for Sri Lanka is high. Most importantly, since we could get away with the folio system, while facilitating derivation of pedigree/folio tree from Fabric's transaction log, the fact that Hyperledger has high capabilities is confirmed. Fabric's concept of organizations, channel architecture and endorsement policies helped implement the real Sri Lankan validation policies as required by the two AMs. Thus it could be concluded that features provided by Hyperledger Fabric are ideal in implementing a distributed land ledger solution for Sri Lanka.

Due to the absence of an existing algorithm for checking overlapping boundaries for non-rectangular shaped lands, the implemented solution performs boundary checking for rectangular shaped lands only. Above identified limitation is **excluded** as a limitation of adapting Hyperledger for implementing a distributed land ledger for Sri Lanka, because, it is possible to improve Hyperledger's chaincode, once an algorithm for boundary checking of non-rectangular shaped lands is available.

As it could be interpreted in Sect. 5, AM2 performs better than AM1, due to its higher throughput & lower latency under heterogeneous land transaction density conditions and tolerance of crash faults of RLRs unlike AM1. Further, it was identified that Kafka-based ordering service provided by Hyperledger Fabric ensures that there is no significant drop of throughput in AM2 for a given configuration when one crash failure occurs. Thus, it could be concluded that AM2 is ahead of performance than AM1 under different land transaction density conditions and failure conditions.

6.1 Limitations and Implications for Further Research

This section presents future prospects and possibilities for implementing a large scale distributed land ledger model for Sri Lanka as required by the third research question.

During production scale deployment of the proposed solution, it is important to provide higher CPU power (by allocating multiple CPU cores) on peer nodes [17], followed by a resource allocation evaluation.

Since arrival rates of transactions in real world production systems would be following certain distributions, generating concurrent transactional proposals, while maintaining the land transactions density variation of the real Sri Lankan scenario via a workload generator, is suggested as essential future work towards evaluating a large scale DLT solution.

It is recommended that the large scale implementation of the distributed land ledger solution for Sri Lanka be deployed on an IaaS platform, similar to Honduras, where the blockchain based land registry application has been deployed on the infrastructure provided by a cloud service provider [7]. If the above recommended deployment is opted to in the future, a performance evaluation should be performed on instances in a datacenter.

During large scale implementation, evaluation on the effect of network latencies on throughput and further testing for both CFT and BFT (Byzantine Fault Tolerance) are recommended.

References

1. Perera, T.: Implementing land registration systems in Sri Lanka: being pragmatic. Sri Lankan J. Real Estate **4**, 74–96 (2011)
2. Vos, J.: Blockchain-based land registry: panacea, illusion or something in between? In: IPRA/CINDER Congress, Dubai. European Land Registry Association (ELRA) (2017)
3. Pipan, R.: Bitfury, 7 February 2016. https://bitfury.com/content/downloads/the_bitfury_group_republic_of_georgia_expand_blockchain_pilot_2_7_16.pdf. Accessed 7 Jan 2019
4. Lantmateriet (The Swedish Mapping cadastre and land registration authority), Telia Company, Chromaway and Kairos Future: The Land Registry in the blockchain. Kairos Future, Sweden (2016)
5. Estonian blockchain technology. https://e-estonia.com/wp-content/uploads/faq-a4-v02-blockchain.pdf. Accessed 7 Jan 2019
6. Mirkovic, J.: Blockchain Cook County-Distributed Ledgers for Land Records. https://illinoisblockchain.tech/blockchain-cook-county-final-report-1f56ab3bf89. Accessed 7 Jan 2019
7. Collindres, J., Regan, M., Panting, G.: Using Blockchain to Secure Honduran Land Titles. Fundacion Eleutra, Honduras (2016)
8. Real Estate Land Title Registration in Ghana, 27 March 2016. http://bitlandglobal.com/. Accessed 7 Jan 2019
9. Official website of the Registrar General's Department. http://www.rgd.gov.lk. Accessed 29 Jan 2019
10. Survey Department of Sri Lanka: Land Survey Council of Sri Lanka. http://www.landsurveycouncil.org. Accessed 29 Jan 2019
11. Whitepaper on Distributed Ledger Technology, vol. 1. Hong Kong Monetary Authority, Hong Kong, November 2016
12. Cachin, C., Vukolic, M.: Blockchain consensus protocols in the wild. In: 31st International Symposium on Distributed Computing (DISC 2017), Vienna, Austria (2017)
13. An Introduction to Hyperledger. The Hyperledger White Paper Working Group (2018)
14. Hyperledger Architecture, Volume 1 Introduction to Hyperledger Business Blockchain Design Philosophy and Consensus. Hyperledger Architecture Working Group (2017)
15. Hyperledger Architecture, Volume 2 Smart Contracts. Hyperledger Architecture Working Group (2017)
16. Androulaki, E., Cachin, C., Ferris, C., Muralidharan, S.: Hyperledger fabric: a distributed operating system for permissioned blockchains. In: EURO/SYS 2018, Porto, Portugal (2018)
17. Thakkar, P., Nathan, S., Viswanathan, B.: Performance benchmarking and optimizing hyperledger fabric blockchain platform. arXiv:1805.11390v1 [cs.DC] (2018)
18. Nasir, Q., Qasse, I., Talib, M., Nas, A.: Performance analysis of hyperledger fabric platforms. Secur. Commun. Netw. **2018**, 14 (2018)

Towards a Multi-party, Blockchain-Based Identity Verification Solution to Implement Clear Name Laws for Online Media Platforms

Karl Pinter[✉][iD], Dominik Schmelz[iD], René Lamber, Stefan Strobl, and Thomas Grechenig

Vienna University of Technology, Industrial Software (INSO), 1040 Vienna, Austria
{karl.pinter,dominik.schmelz,rene.lamber,stefan.strobl,
thomas.grechenig}@inso.tuwien.ac.at

Abstract. Online communication has increased steadily over the past decades. It has become common practice that the identities of content creators do not have to be revealed. The use of abbreviations or pseudonyms is a de facto standard in online communities. Real identities are hidden behind these and protocol-based identifiers such as Internet Protocol Addresses are difficult to assign to real persons. Due to the increase of fake news and hate postings, the obligatory use of "real names" has been and still is discussed worldwide. In some countries, a "clear name" respectively "real name" obligation has been implemented or such laws are in the process of being implemented. One example is South Korea which gained international fame in 2007 as a "clear name" obligation has been introduced by law. The law was repealed shortly afterward.

In Germany, the "Netzwerkdurchsetzungsgesetz 2017" was passed. In Austria, a draft of the "Bundesgesetz über Sorgfalt und Verantwortung im Netz" (SVN-G) was submitted for review in 2019. Newspaper platforms and large corporations such as Twitter or Google would be affected by the obligation to use "clear names". The architecture drafted in the SVN-G was analyzed by us and numerous weak points were identified. Thus, we propose a significantly improved architecture as well as an implementation outline using blockchain-based identity providers.

Keywords: Data retention · e-ID · eGovernment · Privacy · Data protection · Tracking · Blockchain

1 Introduction

The use of the Internet is growing worldwide [35]. So-called "hate postings" in social media brought Austrian politics onto the scene. The Internet has been described as a "legal vacuum" by senior government officials [6]. To be able to find the authors' "real names" of postings, the "digital ban on masking" was

© Springer Nature Switzerland AG 2019
C. Di Ciccio et al. (Eds.): BPM 2019 Blockchain and CEE Forum, LNBIP 361, pp. 151–165, 2019.
https://doi.org/10.1007/978-3-030-30429-4_11

discussed and sent for review in the form of the Bundesgesetz über Sorgfalt und Verantwortung im Netz (SVN-G) [37]. All statements in this paper refer to the draft of the SVN-G [37]. A comparable law in Germany is the Netzwerkdurchsetzungsgesetz (NetzDG).

The SVN-G is only directed at platforms, with

- either more than 100.000 users
- or 500.000 Euro annual turnover
- or who receive more than 50.000 Euro in press subsidies.

This means that Facebook, Twitter, and daily newspapers, among others, are affected. Service providers of online forums are to be obliged to register their users with "real names" and addresses. According to the present draft, service providers would not only have to disclose the first name, surname, and address of a user to the police, the public prosecutor's office and courts (in investigations in connection with a posting) but also to third parties [37, §4 Abs. 1]. This condition is fulfilled in case of defamation, slander or injuries to honor [37, §4 Abs. 2]. The service provider decides whether he transmits the data to the plaintiff. Another legal problem arises: the authority does not decide on the transmission. An offense [37, §7] is punishable with penalties up to 500.000 Euro. The present draft also mentions the obligation to transmit offenses of credit injury. This means that financially potent litigants will be superior to less financially potent litigants purely in terms of possible litigation costs. The planned law will come into force on September, 1st 2020 [37]. The SVN-G is seen by critics as another form of data retention [16]. A media lawyer described the project as "data retention of user data" [16].

In matters of data retention within the EU, Directive 2006/24/EC was adopted. This provided that certain data had to be retained nationwide and without cause. In addition to technical issues, this storage also entailed numerous legal areas of conflict [19]. Finally, data retention in Austria was abolished in 2014 [5].

The idea of the General Data Protection Regulation (GDPR) is to consolidate data protection laws within the EU. The EU Data Protection Directive 95/46/EC [12] adopted in 1995 has been replaced. In 2016, the EU Regulation (EU) 2016/679 came into force and has been implemented in the member states since May 2018. A core feature of the new regulation is the right to be forgotten [3] which means that a natural person has the right that his/her data is anonymized or deleted after the identification is not needed anymore for the processing. Another more general feature is privacy by design which means that systems must be designed in a way to minimize the amount of personal data processed [33].

We, therefore, propose a system that does not store user data with service providers and excludes any suspicion of data retention. Blockchain-based identity providers are presented as one possible solution to break up the identification monopoly and enhance both trust and availability of the overall solution.

The paper is structured as follows. We start the paper by discussing the current situation. Then we describe the related work in Sect. 2. In Sect. 3 the current problems are presented from social, technical and legal points of view. The architecture provided in the draft is reviewed in Sect. 4. An improved and much more detailed architecture is discussed in Sect. 5. Section 6 discusses the need for multiple identity providers and highlights the advantages of blockchain-based approaches. The conclusion in Sect. 7 summarizes the contributions of this paper and gives an outlook on planned future work.

2   Related Work

A secure electronic Government (eGovernment) Environment is described by Posch et al. [30]. eGovernment in Austria is summarized by Höchtl et al. [17]. Work on a privacy-preserving electronic ID (eID) was done by Zwattendorfer et al. [44]. A model for user-centric and qualified identity information was proposed by Lenz and Krnjic [24]. Performance and scalability evaluation in a Federated Identity Architecture was done by Carretero et al. [7]. uPort is an open identity system that is built on Ethereum [42]. Theuermann et al. worked on different issues in the field of mobile eID [41, p. 15f] and point to the necessity that eID concepts must be extended to purely mobile use. Postident procedures can be used to establish an eID [39]. Elsden et al. identify identity management as one out of seven classes of blockchain applications [13]. Chalaemwongwan and Kurutach have presented an "A Practical National Digital ID Framework on Blockchain (NIDBC)" including a practical example application in the context of national health care [8]. Takemiya and Vanieiev propose the "Sora identity system to manage decentralized, self-sovereign identities on the blockchain" [38]. Lee discusses Blockchain-based ID as a Service (BIDaaS) as a means of providing identity services in the cloud [23]. Moyano et al. propose a Know Your Customer (KYC) solution for the financial industry based on distributed ledger technology [29]. The EU Government Action Plan identifies key eGovernment issues to be implemented between 2016 and 2020 [10] [17, p. 3f].

Citizen Cards serve in eGovernment as a central element for identification. In Austria, there is no uniform authority issuing citizen cards, but rather a large number of issuing offices [31]. When we speak of a citizen card, strictly speaking, we mean a physical smart card on which the electronic identity is stored. A mobile phone signature, on the other hand, uses the smartphone to identify the citizen [41, p. 18ff]. In linguistic usage, however, the terms are often used synonymously. A qualified signature as provided for by the current law has personal data such as first name, surname, etc. in the certificate. Therefore, there is an area of conflict if one speaks of the obligation to use "real names" on the one hand, but on the other hand, also wants to remain anonymous [40]. On the one hand, security is provided by a two-factor authentication alone, on the other hand, the user can also be identified by a mobile phone number.

3   Problems

In South Korea, a "real name" obligation was already introduced in 2007 [9]. The law was later repealed. The danger of cyberattacks was pointed out [11].

Since the companies now stored user data, they were targeted by cyberattacks [21]. Among others, 35 million users of an SK Communications website portal were captured [22]. Google and YouTube refused to implement the "real name" requirement in their products [21]. A precise user tracking is not possible, but it was found that users switched to foreign (outside South Korea) websites to express their opinion there [21]. However, this also means that the law has led to discrimination between companies in and outside South Korea [21]. A study by Cho and Kim [9, p. 3047] shows that the "real name" requirement has a significant effect on behavior and reduces hate postings, the effect was highly visible in the group of power users, but not in the group of average users.

The observable effects in South Korea can, therefore, be summarized:[9]

- The Danger of cyberattacks increases
- Discrimination against companies
- Behavioral change through "real names" can be detected in certain user groups.

3.1   Social Issues

About Austria, the planned law is a type of data retention [16]. User data are to be retained in the storage sovereignty of companies. Historically, censorship goes back thousands of years, whereby in Austria the time around the year 1850 achieved a high degree of fame [28]. Data retention, as required by Directive 2006/24/EC, was ultimately overturned by the European Court of Justice (ECJ) in 2014. If the idea of data retention is brought to an end, numerous problems arise at different levels. On the one hand, a "scissors in the head" always arises when a user knows that he is being monitored. The results of [9] clearly show that the behavior of users changes in the case of monitoring. Another problem can be accuracy. In the case of a "real name" requirement, only heavy users seem to be affected [9, p. 3047]. As the example of South Korea shows the enforceability with foreign service providers is questionable [21]. Users also tend to switch to foreign services [21]. Furthermore, this can result in discrimination against companies [2,21]. If the "real name" obligation is implemented, the effort necessary for platforms becomes too high and they may hence cease operation. This has implications for freedom of the press and could represent a cut in freedom of expression. Similar, ensuring that data security measures are established could result in the discontinuation of a platform for cost reasons [9, p. 3047]. From the user's point of view, the hurdle of a separate registration process could stop some from registering in the first place. In extreme cases, there could be a danger that, for example, a change of government could result in postings being interpreted against the user.

3.2   Technical Issues

According to the draft, user data must be stored by the service provider [37]. This implies that the user must also go through a non-standard login process for each service provider. At the end of the login process, certain user data is kept in stock similar to data retention. A technical standard for data storage is not defined [37]. The avoidance of duplicate data between service providers will be impossible. It does not seem to be clear how and by whom obsolete data must be updated. The draft does not regulate how a user should identify himself or herself. In the worst case, this could also be done by a copy of an identity card via e-mail. If we summarize the points, we quickly conclude that user tracking would be possible. The danger of data leaks is imminent, the attractiveness for cyberattacks against service providers would be significantly higher [21]. This also increases the risk of a loss of reputation in the event of a data leak.

3.3   Legal Issues

In addition to the social and technical questions of implementation, legal questions also arise. The legal problems that could arise during the implementation of the draft are manifold [37]. As in South Korea [21], the principle of equality could be violated [2]. The E-Commerce Directive stipulates that no stricter requirements may be laid down than present in the country of origin of the respective operator [2]. Keeping data in stock, especially if it is nationwide and without cause, can be a serious encroachment on the basic right to data protection [2]. Furthermore, there is an interference in competition, which would not be compatible with the fundamental right to entrepreneurial freedom [2].

4   The Architecture According to Draft

A simplified representation of the solution sought in the draft law can be found in Fig. 1.

1. The user logs on to a service provider and must identify himself/herself there.
2. The service provider stores the user's data.
3. In the case of a request, the service provider releases the data.

The sensitive data is stored by the service provider. As a result, each service provider must operate its infrastructure. This model does not provide a query in competent authority database. The technical implementation is regulated differently by each service provider. It is difficult for the user to see how high the level of data protection at the respective provider is in detail [9, p. 3043ff]. How the identification process is to look like is only regulated rudimentarily [37].

5   Proposed Architecture

In Sect. 4 it was shown that the planned architecture lacks in preciseness and opens up possibilities for misuse and at least increases the danger of cyberattacks, as the example of South Korea showed [21]. We, therefore, propose the

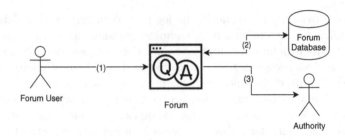

Fig. 1. Architecture as proposed by SVN-G

following more comprehensive functional architecture to give all affected stakeholders more guidance and to help mitigate some of the most prominent risks that were discussed in Sect. 3. We first lay out the involved stakeholders and then discuss in detail the use cases to be implemented to ensure a standardized and secure identification process. All use cases and accompanying descriptions use the Austrian Bundesministerium für Inneres - Federal Ministry of the Interior (BMI) as a concrete example. Since on the one hand the relevant civil registries and on the other hand the executive is located in this ministry, this means that it represents both the role of the identity provider and competent authority. However, the solution can be generalized to any suitable organization capable of running an eID service in the role of the identity provider and therefore possibly be separated from the role of a competent authority.

5.1   Stakeholders

The following stakeholders are involved in the subsequently presented use cases.

- User: wants to participate in online information exchange on one (or more) online media platforms.
- Service provider or Operator: operates the affected online media platform. Legally obligated to identify the users interacting with the platform.
- Identity provider: responsible for identifying an online user and matching him with a legal person (KYC). Vouches for the correctness of the provided identity information (or token).
- Competent authority: Requires a service provider to identify the person behind a posting in violation of the law.

5.2   Onboarding

The solution depicted in Fig. 2 incorporates a standardized registration process. Since the once-only principle is to be maintained, the registration of a user is only necessary once in total [10].

1. The user downloads a signed app from an App Store. The root certificate of the BMI is already included in the app, The user can now choose a Personal

Identification Number (PIN) or password. Other authentication methods such as fingerprint, face or voice recognition are also feasible [41, p. 18].

2. The user is verified via a strong verification service (e.g. citizen card).
3. The app then creates a private/public key pair. The public key is now sent to the server of the BMI.
4. The revocation key is now returned and the user can print it. Preferably a series of words or a Quick Response (QR) code is used here.
5. The public key of the user is signed by the BMI. In later steps, the signed public key can be used to prove the users' legitimacy to the forum.

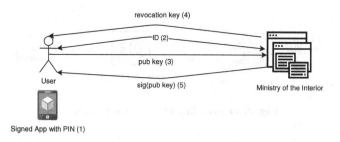

Fig. 2. A standardized registration process for onboarding a user

5.3 Revocation

In case the user has lost his smartphone, for some other reason, has no more access to the app, or the device or credentials are suspected to have been compromised, the following revocation procedure is provided. The user takes the printed revocation sheet and scans the QR code with any app. This contains a Uniform Resource Locator (URL) of the BMI server (contains revocation tokens). The website asks whether the user wants to invalidate his/her certificate. If so, the public key is included in a revocation list. This list will be fetched by the service providers regularly, for example at least daily. Optionally, the BMI server could notify them about new revocations. Technologies such as Bloom filters or cryptographic accumulators could be used to process queries more quickly [4, 18].

5.4 Onboarding of a Service Provider (Online Forum)

A service provider must comply with the legal requirements and ensure the measures for the identification of users. A number of steps are now required to implement this as shown in Fig. 3. It is important to note that any implementation should be designed and realized with the possibility for multiple identity providers in mind.

1. The legal entity operating the service (operator) must identify himself/herself, e.g. with a citizen card.
2. The BMI framework must now be downloaded and a private/public key pair created.
3. The public key is stored at the BMI server.
4. The forum needs additional storage (e.g. database table) with signatures, term/validity of these and an assignment to the user.

The revocations can be stored on the file system as they are append-only and as such can easily be updated. The private key must be stored securely. For larger installations an Hardware Security Module (HSM) is recommended [20].

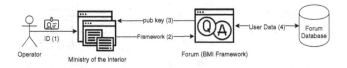

Fig. 3. Onboarding of a service provider

5.5   Online Identification Against "Digital Masking"

After the user has completed the onboarding procedure described in Sect. 5.2, he/she can register with a service provider that has also completed the onboarding process. When registering, it is sufficient to enter a pseudonym, i.e. only a nickname, which is then visible to other users of the service. The rules governing the choice of a nickname are open to the individual service provider. For the purpose of registration, the service provider displays a QR code. This code shall include at least a challenge with a random number [15], a signature, and a verification URL.

1. Now the user scans the QR code using the app and his PIN code defined in the app. The app now verifies the identity of the service provider with the BMI certificate and signs the challenge with the user's private key.
2. Then the verification URL stored in the QR code is opened with the signed response from the signature of the public key (BMI) including the public key of the user.
3. Now it is checked whether the revocation list of the BMI is up to date. For this, the website repeatedly calls a URL of the BMI and compares the hash value of the last received file (commit ID) with the current one. The difference between the new entries is reported back if there is a delta.
4. If the certificate is not in this list, the signature of the user and the signature of the public key of the BMI are checked and, if successful, the signature of the user is stored. This contains the reference to the user's public key.

The service provider knows from the process described, that the user is known to the BMI. The service provider does not have to verify with the BMI whether the user is valid. This consideration was chosen to make tracking or profiling by the BMI impossible.

5.6   Incident Handling, Pseudonymization, and Identification

In the event of a criminal complaint, the BMI contacts the service provider and identifies itself with a signed message. The service provider verifies whether the message really originates from the user and whether the request is justified. Once the BMI request has been verified, the signature of the user suspected of having sent an infringing message is transmitted to the BMI. The BMI verifies the signature using the public key stored by the BMI and identifies the user. Now the identified user is known. Subsequently, the service provider could be informed that the account must be blocked or the offending posting deleted. The user will be informed electronically about the identification as well as further steps are taken. It is important to mention that the service provider does not know the identity of the user at any time. This is known only to the BMI. It should be noted that there can be no de-anonymization at all, one must correctly speak of identification and pseudonymization.

5.7   Remarks

The procedure ensures that users can identify themselves online, as well as offline without the BMI being able to constantly track the users' processes but identify them if necessary. When a user registers with a service provider, zero-knowledge proofs (ZKP) [14] could be used. The identity information of users is not stored with the forum operator. In the event of a break-in with the forum operator, the identities of the users cannot be used for other services. The users have the possibility to withdraw their electronic identity from the BMI if it is stolen or no longer accessible. If the BMI is broken into and all public keys of the users are stolen, no critical information is revealed. If, however, the private key of the BMI is stolen, all certificates must be revoked and recertification of the users must be performed. By the definitions of the GDPR, a public key or a signed challenge represents personal data since it is directly related to a natural person. In this context, this is a legal requirement and therefore a goal. The executive must be able to find the originator of a posting. A forum operator or a data thief, on the other hand, could not track down a user with "real names". With shown architecture (without Blockchain) the service provider does not need to communicate with the BMI regarding each user. Only a recurring update of the blacklist is necessary. This cannot be correlated to the user. Therefore the BMI does not know which user is registered at which service. To prevent a service provider from impersonating a user at another service provider, features like an "audience" field or the use of "self-assessed OpenID providers" [32] could be purposeful. The present draft law leaves open whether only persons residing in Austria are to be included, or further groups of persons could be affected. Since the explanatory notes mention the possibility of a link with mobile phone numbers, it can be assumed that only persons resident in Austria are affected. The eIDAS Regulation (EU) No 910/2014 is currently in force, which also regulates the cross-border exchange of IDs [40].

6 Identity Providers

The draft SVN-G suggests storing the personal information of the natural person on each service provider's server. This could be mitigated by storing the information on the servers of a KYC provider. Identity providers play a crucial role in the realization of "real name" requirements. Placing the responsibility of identifying a user with the competent authority at first seems like a natural fit and will be discussed in Sect. 6.1. However, this comes with all the downsides of a classic monopoly. In today's world, multiple organizations already perform identification of customers due to respective legal requirements. To break up the monopoly we provide a blockchain-based architecture that enables these organizations to act as (alternative) identity providers. In addition, a blockchain would provide for diversification in KYC providers. The information stored on the blockchain is a public key and a signature on the public key by a KYC provider to proof trust in the identity of the natural person, usually after performing an offline identification. This enables the user to freely choose and possibly distribute his online activities to impede traceability.

6.1 eGovernment Architecture

In contrast to the architecture presented in Sect. 5, one approach could be using the existing citizen card solution: a login process using the competent authority as an identity provider to pass data to a service provider. This in itself already represents an initial slight improvement in architecture and data quality compared to the proposal of "real name" laws. The user does not log on to the service provider itself but identifies himself using a citizen card [30, p. 263ff]. After login, the data is stored at the service provider, if one proceeds analogously to the planned law. This means that data is passed on to the service provider. From the user's point of view, the handling is now simpler and many different user accounts can be handled without redundant data entries. This approach is naive because data from the citizen card is simply passed on to the service provider. With this variant, the user would have more comfort with the registration, more security and on the other hand, higher data quality would be ensured. However, the negative side is that user data would still be stored by the service provider. This also means that they would be ideally suited as targets for cyberattacks, as the example of South Korea has shown [21]. To mitigate the shortcomings of the naive SVN-G approach, the solution can be extended by implementing the proposed architecture as outlined in Sects. 5 and 6.2. By doing this the competent authority becomes one of possibly many equal (and interchangeable) identity providers that compete for users through the quality of service. At the same time, the universality of the service is ensured to guarantee that every citizen has access to at least one provider.

6.2 Blockchain Architecture

Blockchain technology can help in the context of eGovernment and eID [27,36]. An identity blockchain can dissolve the monopoly of identification of users by a central authority (like BMI). The identification monopoly means that only one entity has the possibility to identify natural persons. Furthermore, it adds a security layer against Denial of Service (DoS) attacks against the ID Provider, as shown in Fig. 4 [8,13,38]. Data protection needs to be considered separately with these blockchain solutions, because personal data is stored directly on the public blockchain. A typical data-protected approach is to only store a technical reference to the personal data on-chain. The remaining data is stored locally with the identity provider and can, therefore, be deleted under the requirements of the GDPR. In the context of Privacy by Design, each entity should be able to have as many identities as necessary (as designed by [43]). This ensures that identities, personas, and contexts are separated. With a blockchain solution, there can be multiple KYC vendors in parallel that can determine the identities of a users and confirm them by publishing the signature of their public keys [29]. It's up to the forum operator to express trust in one or more KYC providers [25]. In real terms, this could mean that e.g. post offices, supermarkets or banks could identify natural persons at their locations for a fee and, if the result is positive, publish the signed public key of the user on the blockchain.

1. The user logs on to an ID portal.
2. The user chooses between KYC providers and identifies himself.
3. The KYC verified information (or reference) is stored on the public blockchain.
4. The user receives the signature of the identity from the KYC provider.
5. The user can log on to the services that trust the KYC provider without revealing personal information.
6. The service provider can verify the user without communicating with the KYC provider.
7. In the event of a violation law enforcement needs to combine the information of the service provider and the KYC provider to identify the user.

The mapping from the public keys to the offline identifications (e.g. ID card number) is stored in a private database with the KYC providers. In case of a criminal complaint, this information is passed on to the authorities. Requests against a KYC provider can be protected against DoS by the use of blockchain in the KYC process. With the advantages of blockchain technology on one hand, this solution could on the other hand enable the analysis of the users' behaviour by the service provider [25, p. 540f]. Furthermore, the visible correlation between a KYC provider and the user can make sensible information such as the approximate location public.

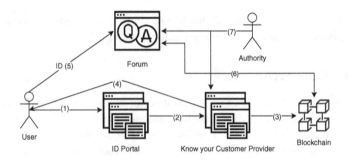

Fig. 4. Blockchain architecture

7 Conclusion

As the example of South Korea showed, "real name" laws, while effective to a certain degree, carry some inherent social and legal risks that cannot be mitigated with technical measures [9]. Most prominently any such solution is regionally limited to the area of jurisdiction and can, therefore, be easily circumvented by using foreign services, pushing the user data and content into the hands of less regulated service providers. This in itself should be reason enough to carefully reconsider the implementation of such laws. However, the implementation as proposed in the draft SVN-G also entails significant risks in the space of data protection and security. This situation can and should be, improved by relatively simple means.

We, therefore, propose a functional architecture that clearly specifies the processes involved in the onboarding and identification of users as well as revealing their identity to a competent authority in case of violations against applicable laws. Identity providers play a key role in this scenario. To hold up the "once-only" principle of eGovernment [1] and ensure universal access we propose that an eGovernment eID solution acts as a primary, but not the only identity provider. Ideally, this solution is constructed on a blockchain-based solution. This step already greatly improves data protection and as an added benefit promotes the use and therefore increases the reach of eGovernment services. Alternative, third party identity providers are necessary to break up the identification monopoly. We propose to use blockchain-based identity solutions in order to improve security and availability. Verifying a KYC transaction on a blockchain locally furthermore addresses the risk of an identity provider tracking the interactions of a user with service platforms. By using multiple identity providers the user has the possibility to impede illegal tracking and profiling attempts.

Future work will be directed towards the possibilities of storing not only the results of a KYC process on the blockchain but also the registration with a service provider. This would provide provable traceability between the original identification of a user and his association with a certain service. On the one hand, this represents a significant improvement for the service provider, on the other hand, it also opens up attack vectors when it comes to profiling the users' interaction patterns with different platforms. Attack vectors like man-in-the-middle attacks [15,26], Distributed Denial of Service (DDoS) [34], compromised devices or emerging technologies such as Decentralized Identifiers (DIDs) are part of future work. On a technical level a standardized Application Programming Interface (API) for interacting with an identity provider would significantly improve interoperability.

References

1. Akkaya, C., Krcmar, H.: Towards the implementation of the EU-wide "once-only principle": perceptions of citizens in the DACH-region. In: Parycek, P., et al. (eds.) EGOV 2018. LNCS, vol. 11020, pp. 155–166. Springer, Cham (2018). https://doi.org/10.1007/978-3-319-98690-6_14

2. Al-Youssef, M.: Postings: Aufhebung der Anonymisierung könnte gegen EU-Recht verstoßen. https://derstandard.at/2000101118088/Postings-Aufhebung-der-Anonymisierung-koennte-gegen-EU-Recht-verstossen. Accessed 09 Apr 2019

3. Ambrose, M.L., Ausloos, J.: The right to be forgotten across the pond. J. Inf. Policy **3**, 1–23 (2013)

4. Bloom, B.H.: Space/time trade-offs in hash coding with allowable errors. Commun. ACM **13**(7), 422–426 (1970). https://doi.org/10.1145/362686.362692

5. Bundesgesetzblatt: 44. Kundmachung: Aufhebung von Bestimmungen des Telekommunikationsgesetzes 2003, der Strafprozeßordnung 1975 und des Sicherheitspolizeigesetzes durch den Verfassungsgerichtshof (2014). Ausgegeben am 30. Juni 2014

6. Bundeskanzleramt: Bundesminister Blümel: 'Der digitale Raum darf kein rechtsfreier Raum sein'. https://www.bundeskanzleramt.gv.at/-/bundesminister-bluemel-der-digitale-raum-darf-kein-rechtsfreier-raum-sein-. Accessed 10 Apr 2019

7. Carretero, J., Izquierdo-Moreno, G., Vasile-Cabezas, M., Garcia-Blas, J.: Federated identity architecture of the European eID system. IEEE Access **6**, 75302–75326 (2018). https://doi.org/10.1109/ACCESS.2018.2882870

8. Chalaemwongwan, N., Kurutach, W.: A practical national digital id framework on blockchain (NIDBC). In: 2018 15th International Conference on Electrical Engineering/Electronics, Computer, Telecommunications and Information Technology (ECTI-CON), pp. 497–500, July 2018. https://doi.org/10.1109/ECTICon.2018.8620003

9. Cho, D., Kim, S., Acquisti, A.: Empirical analysis of online anonymity and user behaviors: the impact of real name policy. In: 2012 45th Hawaii International Conference on System Sciences, pp. 3041–3050, January 2012. https://doi.org/10.1109/HICSS.2012.241

10. Communication from the Commission to the European Parliament, the Council, the European Economic and Social Committee and the Committee of the Regions: EU eGovernment Action Plan 2016–2020. https://eur-lex.europa.eu/legal-content/EN/TXT/PDF/?uri=CELEX:52016DC0179&from=EN. Accessed 10 May 2019

11. Digital Chosun Inc.: Real-name online registration to be scrapped. http://english.chosun.com/site/data/html_dir/2011/12/30/2011123001526.html. Accessed 30 Dec 2011

12. European Union Directive: 95/46/EC of the European Parliament and of the Council of 24 October 1995 on the protection of individuals with regard to the processing of personal data and on the free movement of such data. Official J. EC **23**(6) (1995)

13. Elsden, C., Manohar, A., Briggs, J., Harding, M., Speed, C., Vines, J.: Making sense of blockchain applications: a typology for HCI. In: Proceedings of the 2018 CHI Conference on Human Factors in Computing Systems, CHI 2018, pp. 458:1–458:14. ACM, New York (2018). https://doi.org/10.1145/3173574.3174032

14. Feige, U., Fiat, A., Shamir, A.: Zero knowledge proofs of identity. In: Proceedings of the Nineteenth Annual ACM Symposium on Theory of Computing, STOC 1987, pp. 210–217. ACM, New York (1987). https://doi.org/10.1145/28395.28419

15. Gilad, Y., Herzberg, A., Shulman, H.: Off-path hacking: the illusion of challenge-response authentication. IEEE Secur. Priv. **12**(5), 68–77 (2014). https://doi.org/10.1109/MSP.2013.130

16. Hammer, D.: Viele offene Fragen zu Registrierungspflicht. https://orf.at/stories/3118452/. Accessed 11 Apr 2019

17. Höchtl, B., Lampoltshammer, T.J.: E-Government in Österreich: Ein Überblick, pp. 1–27. Springer, Wiesbaden (2019). https://doi.org/10.1007/978-3-658-21596-5_7-1

18. Kumar, A., Lafourcade, P., Lauradoux, C.: Performances of cryptographic accumulators. In: 39th Annual IEEE Conference on Local Computer Networks, pp. 366–369, September 2014. https://doi.org/10.1109/LCN.2014.6925793

19. Kunnert, G.: EuGH zur Vorratsdatenspeicherung: Außer Spesen nichts gewesen? Datenschutz und Datensicherheit - DuD **38**(11), 774–784 (2014). https://doi.org/10.1007/s11623-014-0303-6

20. Köppel, B., Neuhaus, S.: Analysis of a hardware security module's high-availability setting. IEEE Secur. Priv. **11**(3), 77–80 (2013). https://doi.org/10.1109/MSP.2013.56

21. Lam, O.: South Korea: Internet 'real name' law violates the constitution. https://advox.globalvoices.org/2012/08/28/south-korea-internet-real-name-law-violates-the-constitution/. Accessed 28 Aug 2012

22. Latif, L.: 35 million users are affected by a South Korea hack. https://www.theinquirer.net/inquirer/news/2097740/35-million-users-affected-south-korea-hack. Accessed 28 July 2011

23. Lee, J.: Bidaas: blockchain based id as a service. IEEE Access **6**, 2274–2278 (2018). https://doi.org/10.1109/ACCESS.2017.2782733

24. Lenz, T., Krnjic, V.: Towards domain-specific and privacy-preserving qualified eID in a user-centric identity model. In: 2018 17th IEEE International Conference on Trust, Security and Privacy in Computing and Communications/12th IEEE International Conference on Big Data Science and Engineering (TrustCom/BigDataSE), pp. 1157–1163, August 2018. https://doi.org/10.1109/TrustCom/BigDataSE.2018.00160

25. Mondal, P.C., Deb, R., Huda, M.N.: Know your customer (KYC) based authentication method for financial services through the internet. In: 2016 19th International Conference on Computer and Information Technology (ICCIT), pp. 535–540, December 2016. https://doi.org/10.1109/ICCITECHN.2016.7860255

26. Naher, N., Asaduzzaman, Haque, M.M.: Authentication of Diffie-Hellman protocol against man-in-the-middle attack using cryptographically secure CRC. In: Chakraborty, M., Chakrabarti, S., Balas, V., Mandal, J. (eds.) Proceedings of International Ethical Hacking Conference 2018. Advances in Intelligent Systems and Computing, vol. 811, pp. 139–150. Springer, Singapore (2019). https://doi.org/10.1007/978-981-13-1544-2_12

27. Niranjanamurthy, M., Nithya, B.N., Jagannatha, S.: Analysis of blockchain technology: pros, cons and SWOT. Cluster Comput. (2018). https://doi.org/10.1007/s10586-018-2387-5

28. Ogris, W.: Die Zensur in der Ära Metternich. In: Kern, B.R., Wadle, E., Schroeder, K.P., Katzenmeier, C. (eds.) HUMANIORA Medizin—Recht—Geschichte, pp. 243–256. Springer, Heidelberg (2006). https://doi.org/10.1007/3-540-28514-8_15
29. Parra Moyano, J., Ross, O.: KYC optimization using distributed ledger technology. Bus. Inf. Syst. Eng. **59**(6), 411–423 (2017). https://doi.org/10.1007/s12599-017-0504-2
30. Posch, K.C., Posch, R., Tauber, A., Zefferer, T., Zwattendorfer, B.: Secure and privacy-preserving eGovernment—best practice Austria. In: Calude, C.S., Rozenberg, G., Salomaa, A. (eds.) Rainbow of Computer Science. LNCS, vol. 6570, pp. 259–269. Springer, Heidelberg (2011). https://doi.org/10.1007/978-3-642-19391-0_19
31. Posch, R., Leiningen-Westerburg, A., Menzel, T.: Das Konzept Bürgerkarte und erste Ausprägungen. e & i Elektrotechnik und Informationstechnik **120**(7), a18–a20 (2003). https://doi.org/10.1007/BF03054890
32. Sakimura, N., Bradley, J., Jones, M., de Medeiros, B., Mortimore, C.: OpenID Connect Core 1.0 incorporating errata set 1. https://openid.net/specs/openid-connect-core-1_0.html#SelfIssued. Accessed 08 Nov 2014
33. Schaar, P.: Privacy by design. Identity Inf. Soc. **3**(2), 267–274 (2010)
34. Šimon, M., Huraj, L.: A Study of DDoS reflection attack on internet of things in IPv4/IPv6 networks. In: Silhavy, R. (ed.) CSOC 2019. AISC, vol. 984, pp. 109–118. Springer, Cham (2019). https://doi.org/10.1007/978-3-030-19807-7_12
35. Statista: Internet usage worldwide (2018). https://www.statista.com/study/12322/global-internet-usage-statista-dossier/
36. Sullivan, C., Burger, E.: Blockchain, digital identity, e-government. In: Treiblmaier, H., Beck, R. (eds.) Business Transformation through Blockchain, pp. 233–258. Springer, Cham (2019). https://doi.org/10.1007/978-3-319-99058-3_9
37. SVN: Entwurf - Bundesgesetz, mit dem ein Bundesgesetz über Sorgfalt und Verantwortung. https://www.ris.bka.gv.at/Dokumente/Begut/BEGUT_COO_2026_100_2_1631073/BEGUT_COO_2026_100_2_1631073.pdf. Accessed 02 May 2019
38. Takemiya, M., Vanieiev, B.: Sora identity: secure, digital identity on the blockchain. In: 2018 IEEE 42nd Annual Computer Software and Applications Conference (COMPSAC), vol. 02, pp. 582–587, July 2018. https://doi.org/10.1109/COMPSAC.2018.10299
39. Terboven, J.: Postident online with the new personal identity card. In: Pohlmann, N., Reimer, H., Schneider, W. (eds.) ISSE 2010, pp. 385–391. Vieweg+Teubner, Wiesbaden (2011). https://doi.org/10.1007/978-3-8348-9788-6_37
40. The European Parliament and the Council of the European Union: Regulation (EU) No 910/2014 of the European Parliament and of the Council of 23 July 2014 on electronic identification and trust services for electronic transactions in the internal market and repealing Directive 1999/93/EC. (2014), 23. Juli 2014
41. Theuermann, K., Zefferer, T., Lenz, T., Tauber, A.: Flexible und benutzerfreundliche Authentifizierungsverfahren zur Umsetzung transaktionaler E-Government-Services auf mobilen Geräten, pp. 1–30. Springer, Wiesbaden (2019). https://doi.org/10.1007/978-3-658-21596-5_36-1
42. uPort: Open Identity System for the Decentralized Web. https://www.uport.me. Accessed 11 May 2019
43. W3C: Decentralized Identifiers (DIDs) v0.13. https://w3c-ccg.github.io/did-spec/. Accessed 10 July 2019
44. Zwattendorfer, B., Tauber, A., Zefferer, T.: A privacy-preserving eID based single sign-on solution. In: 2011 5th International Conference on Network and System Security, pp. 295–299, September 2011. https://doi.org/10.1109/ICNSS.2011.6060018

Data Quality Control in Blockchain Applications

Cinzia Cappiello[1], Marco Comuzzi[2(✉)], Florian Daniel[1], and Giovanni Meroni[1]

[1] Politecnico di Milano, Milan, Italy
{cinzia.cappiello,florian.daniel,giovanni.meroni}@polimi.it
[2] Ulsan National Institute of Science and Technology, Ulsan, Republic of Korea
mcomuzzi@unist.ac.kr

Abstract. This paper discusses the problem of data quality in blockchain applications at three levels of abstraction, i.e., conceptual, logical and physical. Conceptually, it makes explicit the need for information of typical data quality metrics for their online assessment. Logically, it analyzes how the adoption of blockchain technology affects the availability of the data needed for quality assessment. Physically, it identifies a set of implementation options that take into account the information needs of metrics and the restrictions by the technology; special attention at this level is paid to Ethereum and Solidity. Two case studies put the identified patterns and abstractions into context and showcase their importance in real-world distributed applications and processes.

Keywords: Blockchain · Data quality · Smart contracts · Ethereum · Solidity

1 Introduction

A *blockchain* is a distributed ledger, that is, a log of transactions that provides for persistency and verifiability of transactions [12]. *Transactions* are cryptographically signed instructions constructed by a user of the blockchain [15] and directed toward other parties in the blockchain network, for example the transfer of cryptocurrency from one account to another. A transaction typically contains a pre-defined set of metadata and an optional payload. Transactions are grouped into so-called *blocks*; blocks are concatenated chronologically. A new block is added to the blockchain using a hash computed over the last block as connecting link. A *consensus protocol* enables the nodes of the blockchain network to create trust in the state of the log and makes blockchains inherently

This research was supported by the MSIT (Ministry of Science and ICT), Korea, under the ITRC (Information Technology Research Center) support program (IITP-2018-0-01441) supervised by the IITP (Institute for Information & communications Technology Promotion) and by the DITAS project funded by the European Union's Horizon 2020 research and innovation programme under grant agreement RIA 731945.

C. Di Ciccio et al. (Eds.): BPM 2019 Blockchain and CEE Forum, LNBIP 361, pp. 166–181, 2019.
https://doi.org/10.1007/978-3-030-30429-4_12

resistant to tampering [10]. *Smart contracts* [13] extend a blockchain's functionality from storing transactions to performing also computations, for example to decide whether to release a given amount of cryptocurrency upon the satisfaction of a condition agreed on by two partners.

After having emerged as the core technology for cryptocurrencies, blockchains are increasingly adopted as building blocks for information system implementation. In particular, in the context of inter-organisational business processes, they can be used to create a trusted repository of transactions executed among a set of parties that do not necessarily trust each other. When underpinning systems supporting inter-organisational business processes, the quality of the data stored in blockchains becomes particularly critical. While data quality is trivial to enforce on transactions representing exchanges of cryptocurrency (e.g., the value transferred cannot be missing from a transaction and it must not exceed the amount of currency that the originator of a transaction owns), assessing data quality may become elaborated when transactions represent business interactions among parties collaborating in the context of a complex business process.

Given their nature, blockchains natively already provide for some quality guarantees regarding the data stored on them: the use of hashes to link blocks prevents tampering with data, while the use of cryptographic signatures provides for provenance and non-repudiation. However, blockchains also come with severe limitations that hamper assessing the quality of data stored on them, i.e., of the payload of transactions. This, in fact, is not subject to analysis and approval by standard consensus protocols and is treated by blockchains like a black box.

Analyzing these data requires either extending the internal logic of the underlying *consensus protocol*, or implementing data quality assessment logic, i.e., the data quality *controls*, in the form of suitable *smart contracts* to be invoked when needed. The former approach makes the whole blockchain aware of the content of payloads, but it also produces a blockchain infrastructure that is tailored to and restricted by the specific quality controls implemented. That is, all transactions would have to comply with the chosen payload formatting convention or the consensus protocol would not be able to process them correctly. As a consequence, this solution would suit only limited, private blockchain scenarios, in which only selected (and informed) nodes can participate to the network. The use of smart contracts, instead, enables the implementation of multiple data quality controls on top of generic blockchain infrastructures and their flexible, domain-specific use by applications. Yet, smart contracts, too, are subject to strict limitations that distinguish them from generic software modules:

- Smart contracts implement *passive application logic*; that is, they must be invoked by a client to be enacted and able to process data. This means that smart contracts cannot be implemented as listeners that automatically react to the presence of given data items inside the payload of generic transactions;
- Smart contracts cannot directly *query the blockchain* to retrieve data stored in transactions recorded on it; they only have access to the payload of those transactions explicitly directed to them as addressees, to data stored in their

own, local variables, or to data held by other smart contracts and made available through suitable functions;

– Smart contracts cannot access *data outside the blockchain*. In order to guarantee the repeatability of the computations implemented by them, smart contracts cannot query external databases or Web APIs, as these might produce different results in different instants of time. In order to obtain data from the outside world, so-called oracle smart contracts (short "oracles") can be used, which enable external data sources to push data into the blockchain, e.g., upon explicit solicitation or periodically – however, using standard transactions that are recorded on the blockchain;

– Executing smart contracts has a *cost*. Invoking a smart contract means generating a transaction directed to the smart contract and sending possible input data in its payload. This transaction is distributed over all nodes of the blockchain network and is subject to consensus, which consumes computing resources that need to be payed for. Also saving data on the blockchain consumes storage space that has a cost. Storing large amounts of data on the blockchain is thus not advisable, if not prohibitively costly.

In this paper, we aim to assist developers in the design and implementation of blockchain applications that come with their own data quality control requirements. Each application may have its own, domain-specific rules and conventions that need to be supported. The extension of existing applications with data quality controls is out of the scope of this paper, as extending existing applications is generally not possible: once data or code are written on the blockchain, they cannot be modified any longer. Hence, there is little space for improvement, and it is generally easier to just deploy a new application or a new version of it to guarantee specific data quality levels. This paper thus makes the following contributions:

– It identifies four combinable *conceptual patterns* representing the information needs of typical data quality controls for standard data quality metrics and proposes a set of *policies* for handling situations where these controls detect critically low data quality;
– It studies the four patterns in the context of blockchain technology and provides a set of *logical and physical implementation alternatives*;
– It shows the applicability of the identified solutions in the context of two *application case studies* with original data quality control requirements.

The remainder of the paper is organised as follows. Section 2 introduces the problem of data quality assessment in software applications. Section 3 discusses the proposed patterns and contextualizes them to blockchain systems. Section 4 shows the applicability of the proposed options in two application scenarios, while conclusions are drawn in Sect. 6 after discussing related work.

2   Data Quality Control Requirements

This section provides a *conceptual* discussion of information needs for the assessment of typical data quality dimensions and possible reaction in response to quality issues. Note that, in this paper, we focus on *on-line* data quality controls, that is, assessing the quality of data as they are submitted to an information system by a client application. We do not consider the case of off-line quality control, such as checking the quality of data stored in a system periodically or upon request.

2.1 Information Needs for Data Quality Assessment

Data quality is often defined as data *fitness for use* [11] and, as such, it is captured by a large number of data quality dimensions, the relevance of which depends on the application context. In order to provide a focused discussion, this paper considers a limited number of data quality dimensions, i.e., accuracy, completeness, consistency and precision. The former three dimensions are considered relevant in the context of traditional information systems development. The latter is particularly relevant in Internet of Things (IoT) scenarios, in which data may be provided continuously to a system by sensors.

Accuracy is defined as a measure of the proximity of a data value v to some other value v' that is considered correct [11]. Operationally, there are different ways of defining the accuracy of a value v depending on the nature of the domain of v. In data streams, accuracy is often analyzed with precision, that is, the degree to which consecutive measurements or calculations show the same or similar results. *Precision* is often defined in terms of the standard deviation of the measured values. The smaller the standard deviation, the higher the precision. *Completeness* is defined as the degree with which a given data collection includes the data describing the corresponding set of real-world objects [4]. *Consistency* refers to the satisfaction of semantic rules defined over a set of data items [4].

Each data quality dimension may have one or more metrics that specify how it can be calculated. The definition of the data quality assessment algorithms depends on the type of sources and on the type of data and may require additional metadata or rules, such as consistency rules, or expected values v' when assessing accuracy. Focusing on information needs, i.e., additional data required to assess the quality of a variable value, Fig. 1 depicts four situations that may occur.

Figure 1(a) refers to the situation in which the evaluation of the quality does not require additional information and therefore it can be conducted by considering only the analyzed value. For example, the accuracy of a value can be assessed by considering a specified business rule, using constants, such as "a temperature value is accurate if it is between 18 and 22 Celsius degree." Moreover, completeness is usually assessed by considering only the analysed value, i.e., checking whether the value is present or missing.

Figure 1(b) refers to the situation in which the evaluation of the quality of a value relies on the availability of one or more values of the same variable registered in the past. For example, a temperature value registered by a sensor may be considered accurate only if it does not exceed the average of values registered in the past 3 h by more than 25%. Moreover, in an IoT scenario,

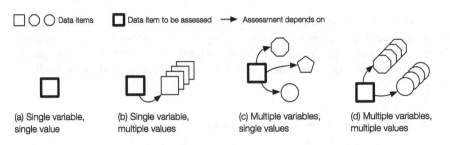

(a) Single variable,   (b) Single variable,   (c) Multiple variables,   (d) Multiple variables,
single value   multiple values   single values   multiple values

Dependencies among variables and values when assessing data quality: single variable, single value vs. multiple variables and time series of values

Fig. 1. Dependencies among variables and values when assessing data quality: single variable, single value vs. multiple variables and multiple values (history).

assessing the precision of a sensed value needs always to consider the results of the previous measurements.

Figure 1(c) refers to the situation in which the evaluation of the quality of a value relies on single values of a number of other variables. For example, the accuracy of a patient name may be checked against the values of names and social security numbers provided by a public government registry, or the consistency of a temperature value registered by a sensor may be assessed against values of other variables registered by other sensors, such as pressure and relative humidity.

Finally, Fig. 1(d) refers to the general case in which the evaluation of a value relies on multiple values of any number of other variables, possibly including the values of the variable which is being assessed. For example, a temperature value may be checked for consistency against historical values of temperature and pressure.

The next sections will show the way in which these different information needs may affect the implementation of data quality control in blockchains.

2.2   Quality Control Policies

Computing data quality measures on the fly allows an application to verify quality requirements at runtime, e.g., violations of consistency rules. This enables the implementation of data quality controls, if suitable reactions able to deal with identified issues are implemented. There may be different types of reactions in response to identified issues; deciding how to react is again an application-specific decision. In general, we distinguish five *policies* that may be adopted:

✚ *Accept value*: Sometimes, even though there is a clear violation of some data quality requirements, it may just be easiest to accept a value and just do nothing else. For instance, during the configuration of a sensor sending data to an information system, we may already know that the values communicated by the sensor during the configuration are not relevant to the system and hence, since they are not reliable, quality alerts can be ignored.

◎ *Do not accept value*: A possible decision may be to reject a low quality value and not write it into the system. For instance, in the case of sensor readings, this policy may apply when accuracy of data is important, that is, it may be preferable to have only highly accurate sensor readings instead of a complete series of readings of possibly low quality.

■ *Log violation*: In some cases, it may be necessary to accept a value while, at the same time, flagging it of low quality. The flag may be considered by other applications in future computations. For example, if a social security number provided by a patient does not match any record in a citizen registry, the system may be configured to accept it anyway, but with a flag to signal that a default quality control against a citizen registry has failed.

✹ *Raise event*: When a low quality value represents a critical situation that requires immediate reaction by an application or human actor, it may be necessary for a system to raise an event to notify someone or some other system. For example, low quality sensor readings may signal potentially critical issues when they concern an airtight container of dangerous goods being transported on public grounds.

↺ *Defer decision*: Finally, sometimes one single violation may not be enough to take a definite decision on how to intervene. In these cases, it may be an option to simply defer the decision for later re-evaluation.

Which of these policies are best depends on the application's data quality requirements, data retention obligations, expected reaction times, and similar. Each variable equipped with a data quality control may ask for a different policy. Policies may change during runtime, e.g., to react to different modes of execution, such as configuration vs. production. Ideally, the quality controls allow the application to dynamically switch or reconfigure policies as needed.

3   Data Quality Control on the Blockchain

Based on the analysis of information needs for data quality assessment provided in the previous section, we now discuss how data quality controls and reaction policies can be *logically* implemented in blockchains. Our assumptions underlying the rest of this paper are:

- Data quality controls are implemented using *smart contracts*, which provide the necessary flexibility to accommodate different quality control. We consider the extension of the consensus protocol, although feasible, not suitable to support application-specific quality controls.
- We focus on *on-line* data quality controls, i.e., on assessing the quality of data as they are added to the blockchain by a client via a suitable transaction and are to be stored by a smart contract.
- Client transactions always address a smart contract containing *application logic* of the distributed application that we want to equip with data quality controls. Transactions between parties without the involvement of a smart contract cannot be monitored from the inside of the blockchain, e.g., to prevent low quality data to be written.

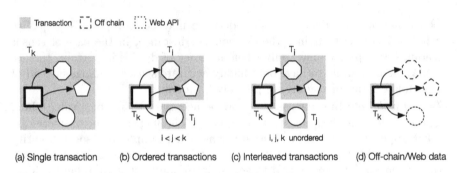

Fig. 2. Availability and correlation of data for quality assessment: transactions, transaction order, and on-chain/off-chain data. The figure uses the multiple variables/single values configuration for presentation purpose; other configurations are similar.

- We require developers to identify which of their data need quality control and, for those that do, to delegate quality control to external, *quality-aware smart contracts* with suitable setters, getters and quality control logic. Developers thus must cede control of some of their variables, however in exchange for readily available and reusable quality control logics.

Before discussing implementation options, we discuss in the next section blockchain-specific patterns to capture the information needs for data quality assessment introduced in the previous section.

3.1   Data Access for Quality Assessment in Blockchains

Figure 1 introduced the four core types of data needs that may arise when assessing any of the discussed data quality metrics. The highlighted dependencies are conceptual and, especially in the context of blockchain applications, require a proper technological grounding for a developer to understand how to implement concrete quality metrics. The fundamental question that must be answered is *when* and *where* each of the necessary data items is available for processing.

Figure 2 summarizes the situations that we may encounter in a blockchain application, proposing four patterns that may be combined in function of the application's requirements. Data items (values of variables) required to assess the quality of a specific variable value may be available for processing via:

- *A single transaction* carrying all necessary values in its payload. This represents the easiest situation in which all necessary values are grouped and synchronized. A quality metric for the value of interest involving the other values, e.g., satisfaction of consistency rules, can be computed instantly as soon as the smart contract receives the payload.
- *Multiple ordered transactions* each carrying a piece of the information needed to compute a quality metric, with the value we want to compute the metric for always being the last to arrive. This requires collecting data from multiple

transactions, but as soon as the value of interest arrives, the metric can be computed. An example could be checking the completeness of prior activities when reaching special milestone activities in a business process. Note that, owing to the distributed nature of blockchains, we cannot assume that transactions are received by all nodes in a network in the same order. However, this assumption may hold true in many practical cases if these transactions are sufficiently spaced in time.

- *Multiple interleaved transactions* where each transaction carries a piece of the information needed or the value of interest, but no specific order is guaranteed. Correctly computing a metric, in this case, requires correlating transactions and waiting till all correlated values have successfully been recorded by a smart contract. For example, it may be necessary to wait for multiple recommendation letters before assessing a job application.
- *External data sources*, such as off-chain data stored by one of the nodes of the blockchain network or web-accessible data. As explained earlier, data outside the blockchain require help from so-called oracles in order to push data from the outside into the blockchain. This of course complicates the computation of metrics, requiring the involvement of external actors, and increases cost. An example for this pattern is the evaluation of the precision of a given value as a function of its historical values stored off-chain.

Like for the patterns of the conceptual dependencies among data items in Fig. 1, also the above configurations may be arbitrarily combined in the context of specific applications to be developed. For instance, there may be a metric that requires both on-chain and off-chain data, or one that requires values that are distributed over multiple ordered transactions like a time series of values, e.g., temperature readings. Each of these combinations may thus require purposefully designed implementations of the respective quality metrics. Once implemented, their online application enables computing quality measures on the fly, discarding transactions, adding flags or raising events if needed, as specified by the relative quality control policies. Low quality flags or events raised, in turn, may trigger reactions according to application-specific policies.

3.2 Quality-Aware Smart Contracts: Implementation Options

The previous discussion provided a condensed view of logical considerations that must be made so as to correctly implement data quality controls in the blockchain using smart contracts. We have seen that some of the characteristics that make blockchain technology and smart contracts powerful in the first place, however, pose severe restrictions on how quality controls can be implemented – a task that typically does not provide major issues off-chain.

Based on the data access patterns introduced in Fig. 2 and our analysis of smart contract reuse options [7], we identify four core smart contract *implementation patterns* for quality controls:

```
1   contract HistoryDQContract {
2       uint16[10] vars;  // array holding values subject to quality control
3       uint8      index; // index of most recent value stored
4
5       function set(uint16 _var) public returns (int8){
6           if(index == vars.size) index = 0;   // update index
7               else index++;
8           vars[index] = _var; // store value, possibly overwriting oldest one
9           return check();
10      }
11
12      function get() public return (uint16) { // fetch latest value
13          return vars[index];
14      }
15
16      function getHistory() public return (uint16[]) { // fetch full history
17          uint16[10] result; // to hold chronologically ordered values
18          for (int8 i=index; i>=0; i--)
19              result[index - i] = vars[i];
20          for (int8 i=vars.size-1; i>index; i--)
21              result[index + vars.size - i] = vars[i];
22          return result;
23      }
24
25      function check() returns (int8){
26          ... // TODO: implementation of quality control logic over full array
27      }
28  }
```

Fig. 3. Solidity code fragment for single variable/multiple values quality controls based on a history of 10 values with no event raised upon detection of quality problems.

(a) *Stateless smart contract:* if all data items that are needed to assess a given value are present in the payload of the same transaction, a simple, stateless smart contract with one function accepting the data as input is enough to implement the necessary control logic. Two sub-options are available:
   - *Ad-hoc contract*: we can implement a contract that accepts as input the values to be checked, implements the quality control logic, and responds with a respective assessment. In Solidity, this type of contract would be invoked by an application's smart contract using a standard *message call*.
   - *Reusable library:* we can also opt for the implementation of a so-called library, such as SafeMath (https://bit.ly/2MRElXl), that does not require the explicit invocation of an external contract. The application smart contract could attach the library to the data types to be controlled using the Solidity command **using** *library_name* **for** *data_type*. This could for instance guarantee that no unwanted values are ever written into a variable of those types. Doing so means transparently invoking quality controls using *delegate calls*.
(b) *Stateful smart contract:* if the quality control to be implemented instead asks for values stemming from different, ordered transactions, we need a stateful smart contract with one or more functions able to provide for the persistent storage of values across different invocations. As storage on the blockchain

typically incurs a high cost, the objective should be to keep the data stored on-chain as small as possible. Again, there are two sub-options approaches:

- *Multi-variable contract:* in this case, only single values of different variables need to be stored persistently, and we know that as soon as the value to be assessed arrives, all other values are up to date. Ideally each variable is equipped with suitable setters and getters to be used by the application's smart contract, while the setter of the variable whose quality is to be controlled also implements the respective quality control logic to be evaluated at each invocation.
- *History contract:* in this case, also a history of values, e.g., using a simple array, by one or more of the variables stored in the quality control smart contract must be maintained. In order to keep the cost of storage low, it is of utmost importance that the smart contract is properly configured so as to keep the history as short as possible without however compromising the evaluation of the quality metrics. Figure 3 illustrates a possible template for a history contract monitoring one variable.

(c) *Stateful smart contract + correlation:* here we do not have any guarantee that by the arrival of the value to be assessed all other values necessary for the assessment are up to date, as there may be interleaved transactions setting these values. This type of configuration thus asks for the correlation of values to decide when the quality assessment can be performed. We distinguish two distinct ways of correlating data depending on the correlation needs:

- *Flagging contract:* if the problem is correlating independent transactions where each time we only need the latest value of all variables involved, it may be enough to have flags that track which values have been updated since the last assessment. At each setting of a new value by the application, a function of the contract can be called implementing the actual quality control; if all values are flagged, the control is executed and the flags are reset, otherwise the control is deferred. The code fragment in Fig. 4 provides an example of a flagging-based control.
- *Correlation contract:* if the contract is required to control multiple values of a given variable in function of respective sets of other values produced in independent but conceptually connected transactions (e.g., different business processes executed in parallel), it is necessary that the application itself provides additional metadata in the form of correlation identifiers for each new value that is set. This allows the quality control smart contract to properly correlate values as they arrive and to update independent counters for each value to be assessed. As soon as a counter reaches its target value, the respective value of interest can be assessed for quality and the counter reset again.

(d) *Smart contract + oracle:* in all those cases where there is a need for data from the outside of the blockchain, a simple smart contract is no longer enough. The help from a so-called oracle is needed, enabling the quality control smart contract to fetch data from the outside. In line with most of the literature, we distinguish two different types of data access requirements:

176   C. Cappiello et al.

```
1   contract FlaggingDQContract {
2       uint16 varA;        // monitored variable
3       bool    isUpdatedA; // update flag
4       uint32 varB;        // variable the control depends on
5       bool    isUpdatedB; // update flag
6
7       function check() returns (int){
8           if (isUpdatedA && isUpdatedB) { // if both variables are up to date
9               isUpdatedA = isUpdatedB = false; // reset flags
10              ... // TODO: apply quality control logic and return result
11          } else return -1; // return if check not applicable yet
12      }
13
14      function setA(uint _varA) public returns (int){
15          varA = _varA;
16          isUpdatedA = true;
17          return check(); // control quality if applicable
18      }
19
20      function setB(uint32 _varB) public returns (int){
21          varB = _varB;
22          isUpdatedB = true;
23          return check(); // control quality if applicable
24      }
25      ... // TODO: implementation of getters
26  }
```

Fig. 4. Solidity code fragment for multiple variables/single value quality controls correlating two variables using simple Boolean flags.

- *Off-chain data:* these are data that are stored on one of the nodes of the blockchain network, e.g., in a database hosted by the node. Presumably, this node is thus aware of the application and is configured to push off-chain data into the blockchain (using transactions directed toward a smart contract of the application) either periodically or upon request (e.g., in response to an event risen by the application smart contract).
- *Web-accessible data:* on the other hand, there may be the need for data that are not hosted by any of the nodes of the blockchain network and that are instead accessible via http calls over the Internet. In this case, the quality control smart contract may make use of an oracle smart contract to ask for external data, provide the oracle contract with a callback function for the notification of the result, and wait for the oracle to raise an event to external observers able to provide the requested piece of information. This is the typical use of Provable (formerly Oraclize, https://provable.xyz/), the use of which is exemplified in Fig. 5.

For those quality controls that raise an event that is meant to be intercepted by external actors for off-chain reactions, e.g., the re-calibration of a sensor, it may further be important to understand if the event was generated from the longest branch of the blockchain (the one that will survive) or from a fork. If the event is launched from a block included in a fork that eventually will be dismissed, that event may however already have been observed and processed by the external actor. Depending on the specific application's requirements, this

```
1   contract OracleDQContract {
2       OracleInterface oracle; // declaration of oracle contract
3       uint var; // variable to be monitored
4
5       event DQAssessmentDone(int result); // event for assessment notification
6
7       function set(uint _var) public {
8           var = _var;
9           bytes4 sig = bytes4(keccak256("callback(uint)")); // set callback
10          oracle.retrieveExtData(sig, this); // fetch external value
11      }
12
13      function callback(uint _extVar) public {
14          emit DQAssessmentDone(check(_extVar)); // assess and notify result
15      }
16
17      function check(uint _extVar) returns (int){
18          ... // TODO: implementation of quality control logic
19      }
20      ... // TODO: implementation of getter
21  }
```

Fig. 5. Solidity code fragment invoking oracle to fetch data for quality assessment. The contract emits an event `DQAssessmentDone` upon completed assessment. The assessment is executed asynchronously when the oracle invokes the `callback` function.

may pose issues. To be on the safe side, it would be advisable to wait for the specific blockchain's minimum number of block confirmations to know if the event stems from the longest branch or not before taking action.

4   Application Scenarios

4.1   Hazardous Goods Transportation

Let us consider the transportation of hazardous goods, such as liquids with a flash point of 23 °C carried in special temperature- and pressure-controlled, watertight tanks. For safety reasons, it is typically further necessary to track live also the position of the tanks throughout the whole movement – the tanks are typically equipped with a suitable GPS transponder – to be able to trigger fast interventions by police or fire brigades in case of emergency. In order to prevent the parties involved in the transportation (there may be multiple carries) to alter or delete monitored data, e.g., to hide liability in case of an accident, we assume a blockchain is adopted to store monitored data and to record the movement.

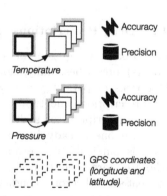

Fig. 6. Information needs, transactions and policies for hazardous goods monitoring.

The use of blockchain technology alone does not however prevent incorrect data to be stored in the first place. It may occur that one of the temperature sensors of the tank becomes defective, which could cause the reporting of inconsistent or inaccurate data. This in turn could lead to false alarms or, instead, to accidents that remain undetected. In the former case, the shipment might be stopped and emergency agencies deployed unnecessarily. In the latter case, emergency agencies might not be called in time. Either case would result in financial loss or damage.

To avoid these issues, mechanisms to evaluate the quality of sensor data before storing them permanently are required: the readings of both temperature and pressure can be checked for accuracy and precision before raising alerts. Accuracy can be checked against an interval of allowed values, e.g., temperature $T \in [0, 20]$, and precision against a maximum standard deviation computed over a range of historical values, e.g., $stdev(T) < \Delta T_{max}$ over 5 readings; same for pressure. Let us assume, in this scenario, that violations of accuracy requirements are considered as more severe than excessive variations of precision. GPS coordinates are stored merely for documentation purpose and do not require any specific quality control.

In terms of the patterns identified in this paper, the described scenario involves four variables as summarized in Fig. 6: temperature, pressure, longitude and latitude. Only the former two need to be stored on-chain and checked for quality; GPS coordinates can be kept off-chain. Accuracy is checked as soon as a value is available (synchronously, as proposed by the single transaction pattern in Fig. 2(a) for single variable/single value dependencies); precision is computed based on a history of 5 values (pattern 2(b)). In terms of implementation, all checks can be implemented using a single smart contract of type *history* with support for multiple variables/multiple values for both temperature and pressure that raises alerts for accuracy violations and logs excessive deviations in precision (in line with the defined quality requirements).

4.2   Drug Prescriptions

Each doctor (from general to specialized practitioners) prescribes, daily, dozens of medications to dozens of patients, each with different ongoing prescriptions and treatments. A typical error is the prescription of a drug that is incompatible with one already in use by a patient. This issue is particularly relevant for elderly people, who are more likely to need different medications to treat several chronic conditions. In order to prevent doctors from repudiating prescriptions, from tampering with their prescription record (e.g., to hide negligence) but also from false accusations by patients about treatments received or medications

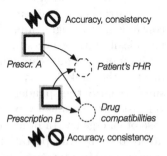

Fig. 7. Information needs, transactions and policies for drug prescription monitoring.

prescribed, a blockchain can be used to record prescriptions. To partly alleviate doctors from their burden we may want to implement a quality control that checks (i) if a prescription is correctly associated with a patient registered in a healthcare software system running off-chain and (ii) if the prescription is compatible with ongoing treatments by the patient (by consulting a suitable Web API provided by the Food and Drug Administration). This gives doctors a sense of responsibility but also helps them prevent errors.

The described quality checks refer to a functional requirement of the application that can be seen as a data quality control and supported by the approach described in this paper. Given the use of both off-chain data (patient's personal health record) and web-accessible data (drug compatibility), the implementation of the quality control requires a smart contract that makes use of an oracle to fetch data from the outside for the evaluation of the consistency of a prescription, which corresponds to pattern (c) in Fig. 1 (multiple variables/single values). The quality check verifies the presence of the patient's social security number (SSN) in the off-chain system (accuracy) and the absence of incompatibilities among the drugs currently prescribed to the patient on-chain (consistency). Next to a function to store prescriptions for patients (each prescription consists of one SSN and one drug), the smart contract must further implement a function that allows the application to delete prescriptions at their natural termination or upon request to keep only ongoing prescriptions on-chain and save storage. The configuration of the resulting quality control contract is summarized in Fig. 7, which can be easily implemented by extending the template in Fig. 5.

5   Related Work

The introduction of second generation blockchains, i.e., with smart contract capability, has triggered researchers to analyze smart contracts, providing best practices for their software quality. For example, Atzei et al. [1] survey smart contracts deployed in the Ethereum blockchain, classifying their code vulnerabilities. Wohrer and Zdun [14] outline security patterns for smart contracts. Bartoletti and Pompianu [3] identify common programming patterns in Ethereum smart contracts and classify them based on the type of application. Zhang et al. [16] propose software patterns to ensure interoperability of smart contracts in the healthcare domain.

Concerning data quality, it is worth to notice that some contributions (e.g., [6]) claim that, since theoretically the information stored in the blockchain should be the exact representation of the events occurred in the real world, the data integrity and quality increases with the adoption of blockchain technology. In fact, the adoption of blockchain offers an automated means for creating, processing, storing and sharing information, therefore reducing human errors and improving the accuracy, completeness and accessibility of data supporting operational and decisional processes [8,9]. For example, in [2], authors propose a medical record management system using blockchain technology. The authors claim that a benefit of the proposed system is the improved data quality and quantity for medical research. The availability of a greater data volume can be also a mean to compare data and correct errors, as described in [5]. This paper proposes, for the IoT scenario, a blockchain-based platform to assess and improve data quality of sensor data. However, none of the existing contributions provides a systematic approach to address data quality issues in blockchain.

6 Conclusions

This paper analyzes the issue of data quality in blockchain applications. Starting from a conceptual standpoint, in which we identify the information needs of data quality metrics, we propose a set of implementation options, focused on the Ethereum technology, to assist developers in crafting appropriate data quality controls in blockchain applications. Two case studies show the applicability of the proposed approach. The approach does not yet consider in depth the relation between data quality controls and smart contract validation lifecycles. Given the probabilistic nature of proof-of-work consensus, values required for controlling data quality may be submitted in transactions ending up in dead end forks of the blockchain; this could create data completeness issues. Reactions to events raised by quality controls may be problematic if not properly analyzed before acting.

Since usage of the Ethereum network must be paid using gas, future work will analyse the computational and, therefore, economical, overhead introduced by data quality controls and how it can be minimised in the context of different implementation options. We will also consider the applicability of the proposed implementation options in other blockchain technologies besides Ethereum, such as Hyperledger Fabric and Sawtooth.

References

1. Atzei, N., Bartoletti, M., Cimoli, T.: A survey of attacks on ethereum smart contracts (SoK). In: Maffei, M., Ryan, M. (eds.) POST 2017. LNCS, vol. 10204, pp. 164–186. Springer, Heidelberg (2017). https://doi.org/10.1007/978-3-662-54455-6_8
2. Azaria, A., Ekblaw, A., Vieira, T., Lippman, A.: MedRec: using blockchain for medical data access and permission management. In: OBD 2016, pp. 25–30 (2016)
3. Bartoletti, M., Pompianu, L.: An empirical analysis of smart contracts: platforms, applications, and design patterns. In: Brenner, M., et al. (eds.) FC 2017. LNCS, vol. 10323, pp. 494–509. Springer, Cham (2017). https://doi.org/10.1007/978-3-319-70278-0_31
4. Batini, C., Scannapieco, M.: Erratum to: data and information quality: dimensions, principles and techniques. Data and Information Quality. DSA, p. E1. Springer, Cham (2016). https://doi.org/10.1007/978-3-319-24106-7_15
5. Casado-Vara, R., de la Prieta, F., Prieto, J., Corchado, J.M.: Blockchain framework for IoT data quality via edge computing. In: BlockSys@SenSys 2018, pp. 19–24. ACM (2018)
6. Chen, S., Shi, R., Ren, Z., Yan, J., Shi, Y., Zhang, J.: A blockchain-based supply chain quality management framework. In: ICEBE 2017, pp. 172–176 (2017)
7. Daniel, F., Guida, L.: A service-oriented perspective on blockchain smart contracts. IEEE Internet Comput. **23**(1), 46–53 (2019)

8. Esposito, C., De Santis, A., Tortora, G., Chang, H., Choo, K.R.: Blockchain: a panacea for healthcare cloud-based data security and privacy? IEEE Cloud Comput. **5**(1), 31–37 (2018)
9. Kar, S., Kasimsetty, V., Barlow, S., Rao, S.: Risk analysis of blockchain application for aerospace records management. In: AeroTech Americas. SAE International (2019)
10. Mingxiao, D., Xiaofeng, M., Zhe, Z., Xiangwei, W., Qijun, C.: A review on consensus algorithm of blockchain. In: SMC 2017, pp. 2567–2572. IEEE (2017)
11. Redman, T.C.: Data Quality for the Information Age. Artech House, Boston (1996)
12. Satoshi, N.: Bitcoin: A Peer-to-Peer Electronic Cash System (2008)
13. Szabo, N.: Smart contracts: building blocks for digital markets. EXTROPY J. Transhumanist Thought (16) (1996)
14. Wohrer, M., Zdun, U.: Smart contracts: security patterns in the ethereum ecosystem and solidity. In: IWBOSE@SANER 2018, pp. 2–8. IEEE (2018)
15. Wood, G.: Ethereum: a secure decentralised generalised transaction ledger. Ethereum Proj. Yellow Pap. **151**, 1–32 (2014)
16. Zhang, P., White, J., Schmidt, D.C., Lenz, G.: Applying software patterns to address interoperability in blockchain-based healthcare apps. CoRR, abs/1706.03700 (2017)

Central and Eastern Europe Forum

Process Maturity of Organizations Using Artificial Intelligence Technology – Preliminary Research

Piotr Sliż[(✉)] [iD]

Institute of Organization and Management, University of Gdańsk,
Gdańsk, Poland
piotr.sliz@ug.edu.pl

Abstract. The main goal of the article was to present the results of the process maturity assessment of organizations using artificial intelligence technology on the Israeli market. As a result of the theoretical study, an empirical gap was identified, resulting from the lack of studies addressing the issues of process maturity in organizations using artificial intelligence. The research question was constructed in the work. RQ: What is the level of process maturity of the organization on the Israeli market that has declared the implementation of artificial intelligence technology? Empirical proceedings were carried out on a sample of 19 non-probabilistically selected organizations functioning in Israel. The multi-dimensional process maturity assessment model (MMPM) was used to assess the level of implementation of process solutions, adjusted to the specificity of the given sector. The study used research methods, such as: quantitative and qualitative bibliometric analysis, survey and statistical methods. The first chapter presents the results of the quantitative and qualitative bibliometric analysis. Then, the next chapter characterized the concept of process maturity and described the applied MMPM methodology. The third chapter describes the population of the surveyed organizations on the Israeli market. The next chapter presents the detailed results of the empirical proceedings. The last chapter contains the study results and discussion. The article ended with a summary, which included directions for further proceedings and outlined the limitations resulting from the adopted research methodology. As a result of the study, the vast majority of organizations were qualified to the first level, identified as a state in which the fragmentary occurrence of elements of the process approach in management was observed.

Keywords: Process maturity · Process management · Process approach · Artificial intelligence · AI organization

1 Introduction

Modern organizations, in order to flexibly respond to external impulses coming from a turbulent market environment, should make sure that their interior is also dynamic [1]. This requires building highly flexible systems, organizational structures, the use of modern technologies, IT methods and tools, and the need to understand the

© Springer Nature Switzerland AG 2019
C. Di Ciccio et al. (Eds.): BPM 2019 Blockchain and CEE Forum, LNBIP 361, pp. 185–202, 2019.
https://doi.org/10.1007/978-3-030-30429-4_13

presumption. This means the need to redefine the concept of the client from the recipient of the effect of processes towards the prosumer understood as a co-creator in modelling processes in the organization [2, 3, 19].

This article focuses on assessing the level of process maturity of organizations that produce hardware and software products using artificial intelligence technology, which is identified as "a subdivision of computer science, which deals with the investigation of different problem areas like robotic, speech and flow text recognition as well as image and video processing" [27]. Further clarifying, "the AI examines how to capture and understand the intelligent behaviour of computers, or how to solve problems by using computers that require interoperability" [27]. The functioning of modern organizations in the era of digitalization and the use of IT techniques and tools creates wide possibilities in the field of optimization and improvement of business processes. It may turn out that the use of artificial intelligence technology will reconstruct the labour market by redefining the desired role of the employee, who will interfere only in the states of entropy of the constructed information systems. In addition, the use of artificial intelligence, machine learning, virtual reality, IoT and robotics process automation will positively affect the process of digitizing contacts with clients of the organization, enabling dynamic improvement of processes through a faster diagnosis of their needs. Therefore, it may turn out that organizations that will be able to discount the benefits resulting from the implementation of IT tools in process management will achieve long-term supremacy on the market. The premise for the study was to review reports and research related to artificial intelligence and its impact on the organization and their market environment. The report published by Geospatial World saw a clear increase in the financing of organizations using AI technology in the world from 1.739 billion USD in 2013 to 15.242 billion USD in 2017 [4]. In turn, in a subsequent study carried out in 2016–2017, an attempt was made to estimate the size of the AI market worldwide. According to the results of the report presented by the authors in 2016, the market size was 3221.8 billion USD, 2017–4819.11 billion USD, while in 2018–7345.34 billion USD [5]. In turn, according to the AI report, the market revenue worldwide in 2025 is estimated at 89847.26 billion USD [5]. In addition to the economic dimension, the social dimension related to the implementation of artificial intelligence technology should also be emphasized. According to international proceedings, published by IPSOS, carried out in September 2018 on a sample of 18000 respondents aged 16–64, an attempt was made to answer the question about people's trust in artificial intelligence technology. The largest share of positive responses was recorded in China (70%), Saudi Arabia (64%), Mexico (56%) and India (50%). In turn, the most negative responses were obtained in Canada (55%), Germany (50%), Japan (50%) and the United States (47%) and Australia (46%) [6]. In turn, the report presented in June 2018 by CISTP identified 4635 organizations identified as AI companies. According to the report, the largest share of organizations was recorded in the USA (43,75%), China (21,81%), United Kingdom (8,46%) and Canada (6,15%) [7]. At this point, the shortage resulting from the lack of a clear definition of the term and determinants of the AI organization should be emphasized. According to the author, the report presented requires further clarification, as the analysis of the Israeli market in this study identified 885 organizations, and only 121 were qualified in the CISTP report [7].

The main goal of the article was to present the results of the process maturity assessment of organizations using artificial intelligence technology on the Israeli market.

2   Literature Review

2.1   Quantitative Bibliometric Analysis

The aim of the presented bibliometric analysis was to identify the theoretical gap, consisting of a small number of descriptive studies using artificial intelligence technology in the management of the process organization. The reason for undertaking the described problem of assessing the level of maturity of modern organizations using artificial intelligence (AI) technology was the literature research, consisting of quantitative and qualitative bibliometric analysis, performed based on the Web of Science database. The study used the *article title* search category. In addition, resources for all Web of Science categories were used (see Table 1).

Table 1. Results of the quantitative bibliometric analysis in 2000–2018

Query*	Number of documents	Times cited (with self-citations)	h-index (with self-citations)
"Process management"	8184	52857	90
"Process maturity"	328	2791	26
"Artificial intelligence"	4939	22793	57
"Process management" AND "Artificial intelligence"	2	8	1
"Process maturity" AND "Artificial intelligence"	0	0	0

*In the search of queries, instead of the artificial intelligence entry the *AI* abbreviation was used, for which no studies were found in connection with the entries of *process management* and *process maturity*.

Source: Own study based on Web of Science data (as of 25.01.2019)

The analysis of document types showed that in the vast majority of studies, they were submitted as an article or conference paper. The results of the quantitative analysis with the LOESS regression at the 50% base [8–10] are shown in Fig. 1a and b.

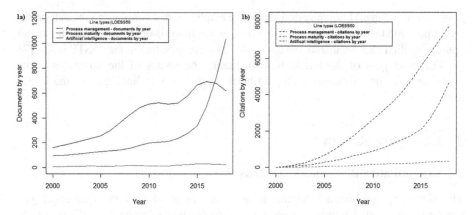

Fig. 1. A summary of the number of publications (1a) and the number of citations (1b) based on Web of Science. Source: own study based on Web of Science using the R programming language.

The results presented show a growing number of publications and citations for process management, process maturity and artificial intelligence in the studied time series (see Fig. 1a and b). The increasing number of documents and citations from 2000 of studies on queries of "process management" and "artificial intelligence" may indicate that researchers are becoming more and more interested in both issues (see Fig. 1a and b). However, noteworthy is the insignificant number of publications in which they were combined (Table 1).

The analysis of the "process maturity" entries showed that the number of studies oriented on the assessment of process maturity of the organization and the maturity of processes in the organizations is significant. In turn, the extension of the organization's process maturity assessment query with the entries "artificial intelligence" or "AI" made it possible to formulate a methodological gap based on the lack of centralized research on process maturity assessment of organizations declaring the use of AI technology.

2.2   Qualitative Bibliometric Analysis

Artificial intelligence is defined in the literature as "the theory and development of computer systems able to perform tasks normally requiring human intelligence (...)" [11, 20]. In addition, "the AI examines how to capture and understand the intelligent behaviour of computers, or how to solve problems by using computers that require interoperability" [11, 20]. Clarifying, artificial intelligence "is a complex of various research in computer science, as well as in technology, logic, psychology, linguistics and philosophy, which aim is, or which may have possible applications to create an autonomous, a thinking robot. It is not important whether someone believes, or not, in the achievement of this ultimate goal. The only thing is that the vision of such a robot determines the problems and directions of research (or at least it has determined so far), progress in particular directions are measured (or rather should be) the degree of approximation to this vision" [12].

In turn, the process maturity of the organization is identified in this article as "the state of the system, in which it the continuously discounts the benefits of the advancement of the applied process solutions that is an expression of the modern organization's aspiration to provide itself with the ability to respond to turbulent challenges requiring flexible solutions of the environment" [13]. Depending on their design function, prospective, descriptive and comparative models are distinguished [14]. The models enabling the assessment of the level of implementation of the elements of the process approach were presented, among others, by: Maull, Tranfield and Maull [15], Rosemann and de Bruin [16], Rosemann, de Bruin, and Power [17] and Lee, Lee and Kang [18].

At this point, it should be emphasized that in the quantitative analysis, no documents were identified regarding the assessment of the level of maturity of organizations declaring the use of artificial intelligence technology. Subsequently, among the analysed articles, in point 2.1. those that meet the criteria for the occurrence of process management and artificial intelligence at the same time were selected. As a consequence, two studies were identified. The first one presents the approach to optimization and management of processes using machine learning and artificial intelligence [19], while the second focused on the use of data processing to prepare e-prognosis and e-diagnosis purposes in production processes [20].

3 Review of Organizations Using Artificial Intelligence on the Israeli Market

For the needs of empirical proceedings, a register of organizations using artificial intelligence technology on the Israeli market was designed. The reason for choosing the Israeli market was the possibility of constructing the organization's register and the third position of the researched market in terms of global distribution of AI start-ups in the report of R. Berger entitled Artificial Intelligence – A strategy for European start-ups [28]. The list was created based on startuphub.ai [21]. In the prepared register, 885 organizations (as of October 2018), which declared on their websites that they use the AI technology in Israel were identified. Based on the data contained on the websites of the surveyed organizations, their structure is divided into groups (see Fig. 2). It should be emphasized here that the name of the grouping was made on the basis of the identified groups on the startub.ai site [28].

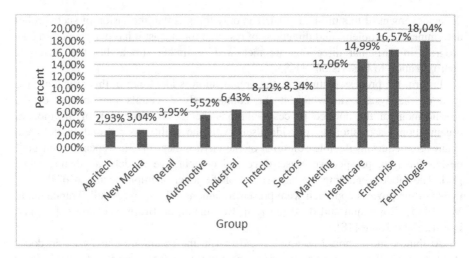

Fig. 2. Structure of the surveyed organizations due to the areas in which they offer products or services. Source: own study based on [21]

In turn, Fig. 3 shows the standardized distribution of three variables. The following was qualified among them: the year of commencing the activities of the organization using AI in Israeli, the number of documents for the entry of artificial intelligence in the world and the popularity of the entry: artificial intelligence in Israel using the Google

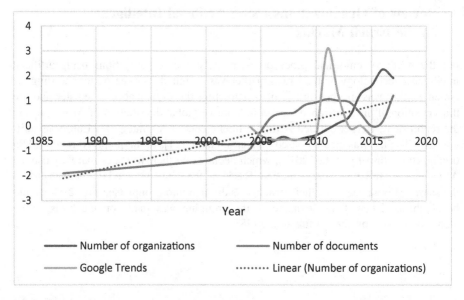

Fig. 3. A summary of commencing the operations by the AI organization, the number of documents regarding the issue of artificial intelligence and popularity of the AI entry in 1987–2017. Source: own study based on [21]. As of: 24.10.2018.

Trends tool [22, 23]. The graph depicts an increase in interest in the term of artificial intelligence and an increase in the number of new organizations since 2010 (see Fig. 3). At this point, it must be emphasized that the longest functioning organization in the registry was registered in 1987.

Then, the structure of recipients in the surveyed organizations was verified in the following relations: business to business (B2B), business to customer (B2C), business to government (B2G), business to business to customer (B2B2C) (see Fig. 4).

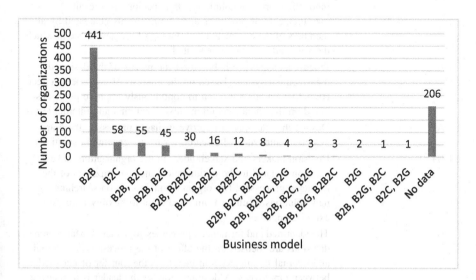

Fig. 4. Structure of recipients of organizations characterized in Table 2. Source: own study based on [21]. As of: 24.10.2018.

In addition, it was noticed that among 885 analysed units [21], the vast majority of them is focused on the production of software products (711). In a smaller number, the combination of both hardware and software was declared (136), while hardware alone (5) and for 33 organizations no information was found in this area.

4 Research Methodology

The study was carried out in the fourth quarter of 2018 using the opinion poll method. The research sample was selected using the non-probabilistic technique with a targeted choice. Out of 885 identified organizations on the Israeli market, only for 434 contact details were found for people at the position of the CEO or owners/founders. Invitations to participate in the study were sent first. The organization's register has been prepared on the basis of available data on organizations using AI in Israel at www. startuphub.ai. From among 1000 organizations in which it was confirmed that the

Table 2. Characteristics of the level in the long- and short-term dimension of the MMPM model

Marking the process maturity level	Process maturity level characteristics for the long-term dimension
L5 A+	The process organization, in which all the specified criteria were met, demonstrating the correctly identified, formalized and metered process architecture. In the long-term dimension, the organization is characterized by the improvement of the metered and manager processes, using management methods, IT tools and innovative, original solutions. Organization, as a result of measurements of processes and improvements generated by all members of the organization, is looking for a new space in which the value added can be generated
L5 A	Process management is based on the results of the designed measurement system. Based on the analysis of the process effect, corrective actions are taken to continuously improve processes based on the client's requirements, in external and internal terms
L5 A−	Despite the attempts to improve manager processes, there are no symptoms indicating the search for newer generation solutions
L4 B+	Decision-makers and stakeholders in the organization make decisions related to the optimization and dynamization of the managed processes. The organization focuses on searching for new solutions resulting from an attempt to flexibly influence external impulses
L4 B	The identified and formalized processes are metered. Management decisions are focused on the effect of the process. The external and internal training system facilitates the transfer of knowledge between employees. A desirable role of the leader is to manage the diffusion of knowledge in the established, interdisciplinary teams oriented on the implementation of tasks and solving problems in the space of the entire organization
L4 B−	The measures applied primarily concern the assessment of mega processes (main and central processes). There are no decisions regarding the reconfiguration of the system of meters for all identified processes. Functional managers are responsible for coordinating tasks in the subordinate division. In the long term, the organization exhibits symptoms characteristic of the P3 level
L3 C+	In organizations, management decisions are focused on results. This means that the organization attempts to synergize the measurement result in making management decisions
L3 C	Most of the identified processes in the organization are formalized. The trainings are carried out in accordance with the plan determined in advance (e.g., by the grantor). The lack of symptoms indicating the implementation of internal training. The defined state of the process architecture is metered

(continued)

Table 2. (*continued*)

Marking the process maturity level	Process maturity level characteristics for the long-term dimension
L3 C−	The developed system of measures mainly concerns the measurement of mega processes. Measurements are made for the needs of the top decisions (e.g., the grantor). Training is the motivational element of an employee. Their implementation does not support the exchange of views and development of the employees' competences
L2 D+	As a result of the formalized infrastructure of all identified processes, decisions are made regarding measurement of the selected processes in the organization. The simultaneous orientation towards the tasks and results prevents the overall measurement of all processes
L2 D	The organization uses the term 'process' correctly. This means that it is understood as a repetitive sequence of sequentially implemented actions which aim is to generate the added value. Only mega processes and some auxiliary processes are identified in the organization. This also applies to the formalization of processes in the form of maps
L2 D−	The organization uses the concept of the process, but it is identified incorrectly. It is often identified with the procedure, standard or task. Despite the identification and formalization of mega processes (or main processes), the orientation of management actions is focused on tasks
L1 E+	The organization is looking for new solutions in the field of management approach. The dominant functional management formula directs it towards functions and tasks. In the long-term dimension, there are measures to move away from the classical form of management through the bottom implementation of the quality management system, e.g., ISO, resulting from the internal needs of the organization.
L1 E	The organization has insignificant features of the implementation of the process approach. No identified factors that could change the orientation of the management approach in future management activities
L1 E−	An organization with strongly dominant elements of a functional approach in management. A multi-level hierarchical structure prevents horizontal pre-orientation. In the long-term dimension, there are no single symptoms that could indicate a change in orientation in management. The organization does not use the concept of a process

Source: [25, 26]

questionnaire arrived and was also opened, only 19 organizations took part in the survey. The research questionnaire was addressed only to respondents in positions of a chief executive officer (CEO) or the owner.

The research questionnaire presented in the MMPM methodology [25] was adapted to the specifics of the studied organizations and consisted of 12 questions, enabling the assessment of the level of maturity with the process-related symptoms [25, 26]. At this point, it should be emphasized that the author is aware of the existence of a broad spectrum of models of process maturity in the literature. The reasons that supported the use of the MMPM model were as follows: access to a model-adapted research questionnaire and the possibility of comparing the results in other sectors in which the study was carried out using the MMPM methodology.

The application of the MMPM model made it possible to assess the implementation status of the studied organizations in three dimensions: short-term, long-term and system-wide (see Table 2). This means that the results obtained made it possible to qualify the studied organizations to one of five levels of maturity.

In turn, the short-term dimension allows the organization to be assessed on each of the five levels in three dimensions: development, stagnation and atrophy. It should be understood that the analysis in the short- and long-term dimension allowed for assessment whether the studied process symptoms in the organization direct it towards increasing, stagnation or reduction of elements of the process approach in the management. In turn, the third systemic dimension allowed for the assessment of maturity from the perspective of selected four Aston features: specialization, standardization, formalization and centralization [25, 26].

The study was carried out using the CAWI technique (ang. computer-assisted web interviewing) [24]. Respondents' answers in accordance with the assumptions of the MMPM methodology have been transformed into a five-point Likert scale. Then, on the basis of the obtained number of points, the classification organizations were subjected to one of five levels. At this point, it should be emphasized that the organization could not be qualified to a higher level if it did not meet the criteria for assessing the lower level [25, 26].

At this point, it should be emphasized that the main axis of this study was not the assessment of the process maturity of individual processes in the surveyed organizations, but the assessment of the process maturity of the organization.

5   Results and Discussion

On the basis of responses given by the respondents, an attempt was made to assess the level of process maturity of the studied group of organizations. In the empirical investigation, question and answer questionnaire was used to assess the degree of implementation of management elements based on the symptoms of processability in the units under study [25, 26]. In the first question, respondents were asked about using the concept of "process" in the studied organizations. The distribution of responses is shown in Table 3.

Table 3. The distribution of answers to the question regarding the use of the concept of the process in the studied organizations

Class*	Number	Percent
The criterion determined in a "top-down" method, specifying required features of activities conducted by one organization's employee or a team of employees	7	36,84%
A group of sequentially conducted and planned activities as a result of which, from a certain baseline, that is from an outlay, a result is achieved, that means a transformed outlay is enriched with the value added	4	21,05%
A sequence of unique, combined and connected tasks with common aim, supposed to be performed in a defined time, up to the budget limit, in accordance with the agreed requirements	4	21,05%
An activity specified in job description or in organizational bylaw, conducted by a single employee or a team of employees	1	5,26%
The term "process" does not exist within the organization	3	15,79%
Total	19	100,00%

*Question with a single variant of the answer. The questionnaire contains definitions of such terms as: standard, process, project, task.
Source: own study based on [25] and a study implemented in 2018.

Based on the data presented in Table 3, it was noticed that the term process in the studied group of the organizations is associated in the vast majority with the definition of a standard and project (21.05%). What is noteworthy are the replies confirm that only 21.05% of the studied organizations correctly ≈identify the term process, and 15.79% of units do not use it at all.

Then, the respondents were asked about the direction of the management activities in the organization. In the vast majority of organizations (84.21%) the answer that was selected was that the activities are focused at the same time om the implementation of tasks and results. The second group were organizations in which activities were focused primarily on the implementation of tasks (15.79%), which may indicate a functional approach in management. t this point, it should be emphasized that no response desired from the perspective of the process-mature organization was observed, indicating that the actions are oriented towards the effect of the process [25].

In turn, the following answers were obtained only from 3 organizations to the open questions regarding the indication of the identified processes – O1: algorithm development, mobile development, operations and infrastructure software development. O2: employee evaluation, sales, project risk assessment and budget planning. O3: prospect treatment from the lead the meeting till we are engaging with him and he becomes our client.

The questionnaire asked respondents about a graphical presentation of the process architecture in the form of maps of the course of activities in processes. The distribution of responses was as follows: processes in organization are not formulated in the form of maps (52,63%), yes, in relation to chosen projects (36,84%), yes, regarding main processes (5,26%) and yes, in relation to all processes identified within the organization (5,26%).

Table 4. The distribution of the answers to the question about the desired role of an employee from the perspective of the organization's goals and strategies*

The role of the leader

The role of the employee	A leader is responsible for the transfer of knowledge between employees and is the one who intervenes when activities performed by employees are far from the agreed assumptions	Coordination of tasks of subordinated section, division or department and problems resolving during the process performance	Coordination of the tasks of subordinated section, division or department	Grand total
The role of a person performing assigned tasks and initiating of improvements within the held position	15,79% (3)**	26,32% (5)	–	42,11% (8)
The role of an autonomous team member performing tasks and stimulating the improvements within the entire organization	21,05% (4)	21,05% (4)	5,26% (1)	47,37% (9)
The role of multitask provider in the scope of organization's selected department	5,26%\ (1)	5,26% (1)	–	10,53% (2)
Grand Total	42,11% (8)	52,63% (10)	5,26% (1)	100,00% (19)

*The table presents a summary of responses for two questions contained in the research questionnaire. The questions were characterized by a single variant of the answer.
**The number of organizations is shown in the brackets.
Source: own study based on [25] and a study completed in 2018.

The next part of the questionnaire attempted to verify the role of the employee and the leader desired from the perspective of goals and strategy of the organization. The distribution of answers for two questions is summarized and presented in Table 4.

In turn, the distribution of responses to the question about the measurement of processes was as follows: process cost (44,44%), process flexibility - the ability of the process to introduce changes (55,56%), income generated by a process. (38,89%), level of the external customer's satisfaction (55,56%), level of the internal customer's

Table 5. The distribution of answers to the question about the type of training provided in the surveyed organizations.

Class*	Number	Percent
Trainings are organized pursuant to the training series "top-down" planned (by e.g. head office, importer, grantor)	4	21,05%
Additional trainings arising from the current needs are carried out by specialized external organizations	2	10,53%
Supplementary trainings, during which the presence of a trainee is not an obligation, are carried out in a way of online trainings (e-learning)	2	10,53%
There are internal trainings conducted in the organization	9	47,37%
There are no trainings scheduled	7	36,84%

*The question in the questionnaire was characterized by a multivariant response criterion. Of the listed responses, respondents answered "TRUE" or "FALSE".
Source: own study based on [25] and a study completed in 2018.

satisfaction (22,22%) and process quality (33,33%). At this point, it should be emphasized that in 11.11% of the studied units, measurements are not performed, while in one organization an open response was indicated – process time.

In the next step, it was verified how the knowledge transfer is carried out in the analysed organizations. To this end, respondents were asked about the types of training provided in the surveyed organizations (see Table 5), goals of external and internal training (see Fig. 5).

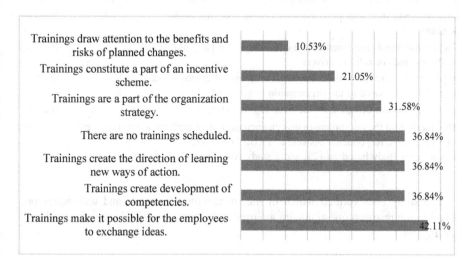

Fig. 5. The distribution of answers to the questions regarding the objectives of internal training. *The question in the questionnaire was characterized by a multivariant response criterion. Of the listed responses, respondents answered "TRUE" or "FALSE". Source: own study based on [25] and a study completed in 2018.

The following answers were obtained to the question regarding the objectives of training implementation in the surveyed organizations: they result from the employees' invention to share the knowledge obtained during external trainings (15,79%), they result from an own initiative e.g. the current changes in organization (26,32%), they are carried out in a planned and regular way (21,05%), they are organized in order to new employees' implementation to the organization (42,11%). Furthermore, 36,84% of respondents answered that internal training was not implemented at all (see Fig. 5).

Table 6 presents the distribution of answers to the question regarding the implementation of improvements in the studied group of organizations. The high share of answers is noteworthy, in which the respondents declared that improvements are generated by all employees. As a result of the comparison of data from Tables 3 and 5, it was noticed that all respondents who indicated the response desired from the perspective of the goals and strategies of the organization of the employee's ole as the autonomous team member performing tasks and stimulating the improvements within the entire organization marked the answer that improvements in the organization are generated by all employees.

Table 6. The distribution of answers to the question about the type of training provided in the studied organizations

Class*	Number	Percent
Improvements are generated by all employees	16	84,21%
Improvements are planned on the basis of customer's requirements	12	63,16%
Improvements are carried out during the process performance	10	52,63%
Improvements start with planning their course and establishing deadlines	7	36,84%
The improvements are based on the cost analysis of particular actions on the grounds of activity drivers	5	26,32%
Improvements are planned on the basis of identified external and internal threats posed to the organization (e.g. crisis)	3	15,79%
Improvements are designed by the planning department	2	10,53%

*The question in the questionnaire was characterized by a multivariant response criterion. Of the listed responses, respondents answered "TRUE" or "FALSE".
Source: own study based on [25] and a study completed in 2018.

The study also verified which of the management methods and techniques presented in the research questionnaire are used in business practice in the surveyed units (see Fig. 6).

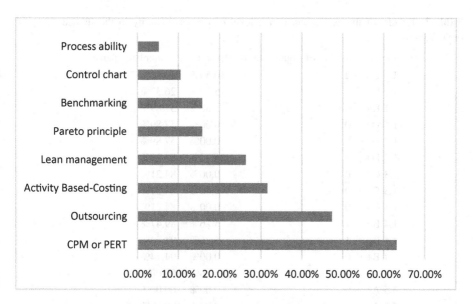

Fig. 6. The distribution of answers to the question regarding the use of selected management techniques and methods. *The question in the questionnaire was characterized by a multivariant response criterion. Of the listed responses, respondents answered "TRUE" or "FALSE". Source: own study based on [25] and study completed in 2018.

At this point, it should be emphasized that the largest share of positive responses was noted for the responses regarding the use of the CPM and PERT method, which may indicate that the surveyed organizations are primarily focused on the implementation of projects rather than processes.

As a result of the conducted research and analysis of the obtained results, the classification of the examined Organizations was made taking into account the short- and long-term variant. The results are shown in Table 7.

The second conclusion, the assessment of the level of process maturity of the examined organizations using the MMPM model, made it possible to formulate a proposal regarding the system dimension. The analysis of the responses indicated a high one, enabling the assessment of maturity of units from the perspective of four features: formalization, centralization, specialization and hierarchy [25, 26]. It was noticed that the highest arithmetic mean value was noted for the centralization and hierarchy features. The remaining values of arithmetic means for features of formalization and specialization make it possible for the studied units to achieve higher levels of process maturity of the organization [25].

Table 7. Results of the assessment of the level of process maturity in the studied group of organizations

Level*	Number of organizations	Percent	Accumulated percent
L1 E−	2	10,53%	10,53%
L1 E	3	15,79%	26,32%
L1 E+	6	31,58%	57,89%
L2 D−	0	0,00%	57,89%
L2 D	0	0,00%	57,89%
L2 D+	5	26,32%	84,21%
L3 C−	0	0,00%	84,21%
L3 C	0	0,00%	84,21%
L3 C+	0	0,00%	84,21%
L4 B−	1	5,26%	89,47%
L4 B	1	5,26%	94,74%
L4 B+	0	0,00%	94,74%
L5 A−	1	5,26%	100,00%
L5 A	0	0,00%	100,00%
L5 A+	0	0,00%	100,00%
Total	19	100,00%	

*Symbols were explained in Table 2.
Source: own study estimated based on [25] and study completed in 2018.

6 Conclusion

The results of the study obtained in this work allowed to formulate three conclusions of a general nature. Here they are:

Firstly, as a result of the analysis of the level of process maturity of the surveyed group of organizations, it was shown that the largest share of the surveyed units was qualified, in the short-term dimension to level 1 (L1) (57,89%), while in the long-term dimension to the level L1 E+ (31,58%).

The second, last, conclusion, as a result of a detailed analysis of partial results it was noticed that the studied group of the organization focused to a large extent on the implementation of projects rather than the improvement of business processes. It may mean that in the business area of organizations using modern IT technologies, process and project structures appear. This conclusion requires more extensive research and the preparation of a methodology and a research tool to assess both process and organization maturity.

The summary and conclusions presented in this article should be treated as a preliminary study. The developed results are an incentive to undertake broader considerations and research of the author on the issues of process maturity of organizations using modern information technologies. It should be understood that further research directions have been set, focusing on the analysis of business models of the surveyed organizations and the implementation of a quantitative and qualitative international study to confirm the following general conclusions about the empirical facts examined. The research presented in this article was preliminary in nature. The author's goal is to expand the quantitative research to other markets and the subsequent implementation of a qualitative research, the aim of which will be to compare organizations carrying out the same activity with and without using artificial intelligence technology in terms of the level of process maturity of the organization, evaluation of process effectiveness and their degree of automation.

The outline of the study's limitations results, first of all, from the adopted method and non-random sampling technique, therefore the presented results should be interpreted only for the examined group of 19 organizations. This means that the formulated conclusions should be confirmed for the empirical facts examined, using the methods of a survey opinion poll or observation that participates in a random sample of the organization.

References

1. Grajewski, P., Rybicki, J.: The paradox of a change radicalism on an example of the process organization [Paradoks radykalizmu zmiany na przykładzie organizacji procesowej]. Res. Pap. Wroclaw Univ. Econ. **422**, 275–286 (2016)
2. Czubasiewicz, H., Grajewski, P., Sliż, P.: Business process maturity of hotels and accommodation stablishments – report of empirical research [Dojrzałość procesowa hoteli i obiektów noclegowych w Polsce–wyniki badania empirycznego]. Sci. J. Poznan Univ. Technol. Ser. "Organ. Manag." 76, 243–258 (2018)
3. Brilman, J.: Nowoczesne koncepcje i metody zarządzania [Modern Management Concepts and Methods]. Polskie Wydawnictwo Ekonomiczne, Warszawa (2002)
4. Geospatial World. https://www.geospatialworld.net/blogs/13-artificial-intelligence-trends-2018/. Accessed 19 Feb 2019
5. Tratica. https://www.tractica.com/research/artificial-intelligence-market-forecasts/. Accessed 19 Feb 2019
6. IPSOS report. https://www.ipsos.com/sites/default/files/ct/news/documents/2018-10/entre preneurialism-2018-global-report.pdf. Accessed 19 Feb 2019
7. CISPT report. http://www.sppm.tsinghua.edu.cn/eWebEditor/UploadFile/China_AI_develop ment_report_2018.pdf. Accessed 19 Feb 2019
8. Cleveland, W.S., Devlin, S.J.: Locally weighted regression: an approach to regression analysis by local fitting. J. Am. Stat. Assoc. **83**(403), 596–610 (1988)
9. Cleveland, W.S.: LOWESS: a program for smoothing scatterplots by robust locally weighted regression. Am. Stat. **35**(1), 54 (1981)
10. Cleveland, W.S.: Robust locally weighted regression and smoothing scatterplots. J. Am. Stat. Assoc. **74**(368), 829–836 (1979)
11. Lämmel, U., Cleve, J.: Künstliche Intelligenz. Carl Hanser Verlag GmbH Co KG (2012)
12. Kisielewicz, A.: Artificial intelligence and logic. Summary of the scientific undertaking [Sztuczna inteligencja i logika. Podsumowanie przedsięwzięcia naukowego]. WNT, Warszawa (2011)
13. Grajewski, P.: A Process-Oriented Organization [Organizacja procesowa], 2nd edn. Polskie Wydawnictwo Ekonomiczne, Warszawa (2016)

14. Poppelbub J., Roglinger M.: What makes a useful maturity model? A framework of general design principles for maturity models and its demonstration in BPM. In: ECIS 2011 Proceedings, Paper 28 (2011). http://aisel.aisnet.org/ecis2011
15. Maull, R.S., Tranfield, D.R., Maull, W.: Factors characterising the maturity of BPR programmes. Int. J. Oper. Prod. Manag. 23(6), 596–624 (2003)
16. Rosemann, M., de Bruin, T.: Towards a business process management maturity model. In: Bartmann, D., Rajola, F., Kallinikos, J., Avison, D., Winter, R., Ein-Dor, P., et al. (eds.) Proceedings of the 13th European Conference on Information Systems, Regensburg (2005). https://eprints.qut.edu.au/25194/1/25194_rosemann_2006001488.pdf
17. Rosemann, M., de Bruin, T., Power, B.: A model to measure business process management and improve performance. In: Jeston, J., Nelis, J. (eds.) Business Process Management, London, vol. 27, pp. 299–315 (2006)
18. Lee, J., Lee, D., Kang, S.: An overview of the business process maturity model (BPMM). In: Chang, K.C.C., et al. (eds.) Advances in Web and Network Technologies, and Information Management. APWeb 2007, WAIM 2007. Lecture Notes in Computer Science, vol. 4537, pp. 384–395. Springer, Heidelberg (2007). https://doi.org/10.1007/978-3-540-72909-9_42
19. Paschek, D., Luminosu, C.T., Draghici, A.: Automated business process management–in times of digital transformation using machine learning or artificial intelligence. In: MATEC Web of Conferences, vol. 121, p. 04007. EDP Sciences (2017)
20. Bae, H., Kim, S., Kim, Y., Lee, M.H., Woo, K.B.: E-prognosis and diagnosis for process management using data mining and artificial intelligence. In: 29th Annual Conference of the IEEE Industrial Electronics Society (IEEE Cat. No. 03CH37468), IECON 2003, pp. 2537–2542. IEEE (2003)
21. Staruphub.au. https://startuphub.ai/. Accessed 25 Oct 2018
22. Google Trends. https://trends.google.com/trends/. Accessed 25 Oct 2019
23. Choi, H., Varian, H.: Predicting the present with Google Trends. Econ. Rec. 88, 2–9 (2012)
24. Kagerbauer, M., Manz, W., Zumkeller, D., Kagerbauer, M., Manz, W., Zumkeller, D.: Analysis of PAPI, CATI, and CAWI methods for a multiday household travel survey. In: Transport Survey Methods. Best Practice for Decision Making, pp. 289–304 (2013)
25. Sliż, P.: Dojrzałość procesowa współczesnych organizacji w Polsce [Process maturity of contemporary organizations in Poland]. Wydawnictwo Uniwersytetu Gdańskiego, Sopot (2018)
26. Sliż, P.: Concept of the organization process maturity assessment. J. Econ. Manag. 33, 80–95 (2018)
27. Lämmel, U., Cleve, J.: Künstliche Intelligenz. Publisher Hanser (2012)
28. https://asgard.vc/wp-content/uploads/2018/05/Artificial-Intelligence-Strategy-for-Europe-2018.pdf
29. https://www.startuphub.ai/israels-artificial-intelligence-startups-2018/

A Generic DEMO Model for Co-creation and Co-production as a Basis for a Truthful and Appropriate REA Model Representation

Frantisek Hunka[1(✉)] and Steven van Kervel[2]

[1] University of Ostrava, 701 03 Ostrava, Czechia
frantisek.hunka@osu.cz
[2] Formetis Consultants BV, Boxtel, The Netherlands
steven.van.kervel@formetis.nl

Abstract. DEMO (Design Engineering Methodology for Organization) has its foundation in the DEMO Enterprise Ontology (DEO), and provides a strong theoretical foundation and a generic platform for business process modeling. The REA (Resource-Event-Agent) ontology, which originates from accountancy systems, provides a domain-specific platform for value modeling business processes. Rather than traditional approaches to accountancy, REA captures the details of each resource under an enterprise's control, and thus is able to offer a wider, more precise, and more up-to-date range of reports. Despite its great potential, REA ontology suffers from anomalies which have their origin in the absence of rigorous theoretical foundations. These anomalies can be overcome either by introducing rigorous theoretical foundations for the current REA ontology, or by useful collaboration of REA ontology with an ontology that provides a strong theoretical foundation. The paper deals with the latter option. It not only contemplates different aspects of both ontologies, but also analyzes and proposes a possible way for collaboration between these modeling frameworks.

Keywords: DEMO Enterprise Ontology (DEO) · DEMO methodology · Co-creation co-production · REA ontology · REA model

1 Introduction

The DEMO methodology is based on *the theory of* DEMO Enterprise Ontology and provides a generic platform for business process modeling. DEMO is based on a generic ontology, e.g., enterprise ontology, which meets the strictest requirements provided by conceptual modeling theories. DEMO is further based on the social communication and language theories of Habermas and others, general systems theory, the design science paradigm [8], conceptual languages, native executing software engines [16], and has strong formal foundations. DEMO is a modeling methodology of prescriptive knowledge - that provides four so-called aspect models of an enterprise. More specifically, it provides prescriptive knowledge (for execution) and descriptive knowledge (facts) about the enterprise. These four DEMO models [1, 4] are propositions in a formal language, each with a precisely defined grammar and vocabulary. Due

© Springer Nature Switzerland AG 2019
C. Di Ciccio et al. (Eds.): BPM 2019 Blockchain and CEE Forum, LNBIP 361, pp. 203–218, 2019.
https://doi.org/10.1007/978-3-030-30429-4_14

to the high degree of abstraction, it is conceptually guaranteed that *any* imaginable enterprise that may exist in reality - the real world, can be modeled in one, and only one, way. Its strong formal foundations enable the design and implementation of a software engine that directly executes DEMO models. This approach eliminates any programming; the model is the executable specification. Once DEMO models have been accepted as "the best representation of the enterprise", these models can be executed in a production environment. DEMO model execution in production provides many valuable capabilities; complete workflow (-like) control of the actors in the enterprise; total knowledge of each atomic communication act of each actor, with complete audit trails, and process-mining (-like) analysis of daily business process execution.

DEMO Enterprise Ontology is a generic ontology in the formal sense [1, 2] which means that it strictly and exclusively captures the generic theoretical concepts within the domain ontology. These concepts are defined by the DEMO operation axiom [1]: (i) "there is a world of human actors that fulfill actor roles"; (ii) "there is a world of communication (coordination), of communicative acts and facts between actors"; and (iii) "there is a world of productions delivered by actors". In addition, the DEMO transaction axiom states that actors that communicate with each other following a specific transaction pattern [3]. They cannot deviate from the transaction pattern.

The REA modeling framework is a domain-specific approach, which originated from the accountancy domain. This ontology is called the REA Enterprise Ontology as three of the fundamental concepts are Resources, Events, and Agents [6, 12]. The main benefit of the REA approach is that it enables the keeping track of primary and raw data about economic resources. All accounting artifacts are derived from the data describing exchange and conversion REA processes [9]. All reports based on the accounting artifacts are always consistent, since they are derived from the same data.

The structure of the paper is as follows. Section 2 shortly describes the main features of the DEMO methodology. The REA model with commitments and claim entities is depicted in Sect. 3. Section 4 deals with factual information support for the REA model analysis. The DEMO CC-CP model and its possibilities are presented in Sect. 5. Section 6 illustrates a simple example of a practical cooperation between the two modeling approaches. Discussion is delivered in Sect. 7. Conclusions and future research are depicted in Sect. 8.

2   The DEMO Methodology – Main Features

According to the DEMO methodology [1], an organization is composed of people (social individuals) that perform two kinds of acts, *production* acts and *coordination (communication)* acts. The result of successfully performing a production act is a *production fact*. An example of a production fact may be that a payment has been paid *and accepted*, or that an offered service has been accepted. All realization-specific details are fully abstracted out. Only the acts and facts as such are relevant, not how they are achieved. The result of successfully performing a *communication act* is a *communication fact*. Examples of coordination acts include *requesting* and *promising* a production fact, which essentially constitutes a mutually binding obligation (contract).

The subsequent communication acts and facts "*state*" and "*accept*" of the production constitute the fulfillment of the obligation (contract), agreed on by both actors.

A fact is a proposition about the real world that can be either false or true, and can be validated by empirical observation. A fact may encompass a single object, or may encompass more objects. Depending on the number of objects that are involved in a fact, we speak of unary, binary, ternary, etc., facts. An example of a unary fact is: *the Vendor is a Person*. An example of binary fact is: *a Customer receives a Pizza*.

In DEMO modeling, enterprises are represented by discrete deterministic systems that may exist in a set of precisely defined allowed states; the so-called state space [5]. For each state, there is a set of allowed transitions to another state, the so-called state transition space. All other state transitions are forbidden and cannot occur. In general, a state is determined by the set of facts that exist at that moment. A state change or state transition consists of one or more facts starting or ending to exist. The occurrence of a transition at some moment is called an event.

Events are widely defined as "things that happen in the real world" and that cause some effects. In DEMO there are only (i) communication (coordination) acts - one actor communicating with another actor, following the transaction pattern; (ii) production facts that describe the production of a specific actor; and (iii) facts, that are caused by acts in the real world that may become true or false. Example (i): a pizza has been requested by a customer and promised by the pizza baker, a contract has come into being. Example (ii): the production *fact* of the pizza baker is a pizza margarita. Example (iii): the exchange rate between the US dollar and the euro is 1.234. By empirical observation of the real world, this fact is either true or false.

The results of the DEMO methodology are the Construction Model, the Process Model, the Fact Model, and the Action model (four aspect models). For the CC-CP model presentation, the Construction Model is utilized.

3   The REA Model – Main Features

The REA model is composed of two kinds of different transactions termed "increment" and "decrement" with respect to the view of one of the agents. The two kinds of transactions form a 'dual notion', e.g., the type sale for the enterprise agent (left side), and the type purchase for the customer agent (right side). The term "increment" means that the value of resource(s) in the corresponding transaction(s) will increase, and the term "decrement" means that the value of resource(s) in the corresponding transaction (s) will decrease after completion of the REA model describing an exchange process [6, 12]. In the case of the REA conversion process, the resource(s) in one kind of transactions are consumed or used, and the resource(s) in a different kind of transaction(s) is/are produced (created), or some of its/their features change.

Each REA transaction is comprised of *commitment* and *event* entities, forming the dynamic part of a transaction. Further entities of a transaction make up a pair of economic *agents* with different interests and a *resource* entity. Apart from an agent and resource entities, representing "physical items", an REA transaction can contain "category items" for resource and agent entities in the form of resource type entity, and agent type entity.

The commitment entity addresses the issue of modeling promises of future economic events, and the issue of reservation of resources. The reason for this solution is that economic events specify only actual increment or decrement in resource values, not the future increment or decrement in resource values. Commitment entities and their relationships with other entities are shown in Fig. 1. Each commitment is related to an economic resource by a *reservation* relationship that specifies which resources will be needed or expected by future economic events. A commitment entity is related to event entity/entities by the *fulfilment* relationship. The event entity represents the point in time at which actual change of property rights, or conversion of economic resources occurs.

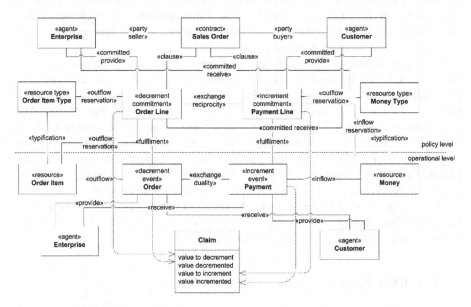

Fig. 1. REA model with commitments and claim entities. Source: [9]

Different kinds of transactions are related to each other by the *reciprocity* relationship, which relates different kinds of commitments, and by the *duality* relationship, which relates different kinds of economic events.

4   Factual Information Support for the REA Model Analysis

Both modeling frameworks utilize the notion of a transaction or transaction pattern, which, in general, contains common things such as the two human beings partaking in the transaction, the resulting product (in REA *economic resource*) for which the whole transaction takes place, a promise given by one human being to perform a production act, and an event representing the occurrence of the production act (activity). However, a DEMO transaction represents a precisely defined state machine, and transactions are ordered in a tree structure, utilizing production facts aggregation (*DEMO composition axiom*) to form a business process. In addition, the DEMO transaction contains complete possible states such as *decline* or *reject* etc., including revoking operations. The DEMO transaction "infrastructure" is robust enough to meet all real-world requirements, and thus forms a prescriptive system.

The REA framework assumes that a business process is composed of two kinds of transactions which are bound by the *reciprocity* and *duality* relationships see Fig. 1. In REA, one kind of transactions is performed in consideration of performing the other kind of transactions. In the view of one agent (actor role) one kind of transactions represents a decrement in value of economic resources, and the other kind of transactions represents an increment in value of economic resources. However, the REA approach does not provide a truthful state machine in the sense of the DEMO methodology, and represents a functional approach, thus forming a purely descriptive system.

In ontology collaboration, it must be taken into account that the DEMO methodology strictly distinguishes between the *coordination* and the *production* world, whereas the REA modeling approach only deals with the *production* world. It implies that the way in which DEMO captures real world phenomena is much broader and more comprehensive. The next step of collaboration concerns the locating and pinpointing of appropriate conceptual mapping between the modeling approaches.

A *top-down conceptual mapping from REA to DEMO* would require the expression of each REA concept to the DEMO primitives, which would fail because REA does not provide all concepts and primitives that are necessary in DEMO. As a result, the DEMO models would be largely undefined, and hence useless.

A *bottom-up conceptual mapping from DEMO to REA* is the alternative way, in which REA might provide an accounting and financial perspective on an enterprise, and the DEMO concepts would be mapped to the REA concepts. This approach guarantees that useful results may be achieved, as DEMO models capture everything that is happening in the real world, with good empirical evidence.

In DEMO, actors communicate about a production fact. DEMO "says" nothing about production facts except that there is a hierarchical structure (DEMO composition axiom) in which production facts are arranged. Human actors commit themselves to a production fact (DEMO *Request* and *Promise*), and agree by communication (DEMO *State* and *Accept*) that the production fact exists in the real world. So, by analyzing the communication acts and facts it is possible to derive factual propositions about production facts, such as "the actors agree that a product has to be delivered and has to be paid for", which is a mutually binding contract. The production facts "product X has been produced and accepted", and "payment Y has been made" are the fulfilment of a contract. Since every atomic communication act and fact is precisely known and recorded at production time, it should therefore be possible to provide complete and correct information about all REA events that occur in the real-world.

In DEMO, real-world states and state transitions are expressed in the form of facts. DEMO models are able to supply REA model with all the facts currently needed by the REA model and possibly supply the REA model with other facts that may increase their applicability.

The inclusion of a state machine inside a DEMO transaction enables us to distinguish two complementary REA views on each REA model in one DEMO transaction. In a simple case, which can be used to demonstrate the approach, the *purchase/sales* and *money receipt/money disbursement* are utilized. One DEMO transaction represents both REA dependent views of *purchase* and *sales* in one. The request and accept DEMO transaction steps stand for *purchase,* whereas the promise and state transaction steps represent *sales.* The same holds for *money receipt* and *money disbursement,* in which *money receipt* represents the request and accept DEMO transaction steps, whereas the promise and state DEMO transaction steps represent the *money disbursement* REA dependent views.

The product part contains production facts and their specifications. More specifically, it is composed of independent facts and dependent facts. The product consists of independent facts e.g.: "purchase 6145 is completed", and dependent facts e.g.: "article type is pizza Margherita" etc.

From the REA point of view, the most important coordination facts are e.g.: "sales 1658 is promised", and "purchase 6145 is completed", because they express a *committed* phase of transaction and a *fulfilled* phase of transaction.

However, the current DEMO Enterprise Ontology does not enable us to explicitly express all communication facts or to deal with any logic aggregated facts or dependent facts. The FAR (Fact, Agenda, Rule) Ontology [13], which is an extension to the current DEMO Enterprise Ontology, enable to support above mentioned issues.

In general, DEMO transactions are arranged in a tree structure with a parent-child relationship between them (utilizing the Composition axiom). The parent-child relationship is very effective and natural, but in some cases it is unable to capture all real world phenomena. By this we mean "the same level" transaction relationship, which is an inseparable part of a contract model, and must be signed by parties and evaluated in terms of contract fulfillment. The model of contract implicitly covers different kinds of transactions that are "on the same level" relationship. In order to solve the above described issues, the DEMO co-creation and co-production (CC-CP) model was conceived [10, 11].

5   The DEMO CC-CP Model

The FAR ontology [13] specifies that a fact is a proposition that may have a logic relation with other facts in a recursive way. A fact is a proposition that may have three values; true | false | undefined. To illuminate the previous, let us consider the following example. Fact: "the invoice (xyz) has been paid". Value true: the invoice has been paid, which can be validated empirically by checking the bank statement. Value false: the invoice has not been paid, also as shown by the bank statement. Value undefined: it is not known, probably because there is no access to any bank statements for empirical validation.

The FAR ontology enables the CC-CP model to utilize all communication facts and any logic aggregated facts. The DEMO CC-CP model captures all the facts relevant to the REA exchange process, and even other facts that are produced by REA information and business events. Its main asset is in its ability to uniquely distinguish and capture *a contract on the table*, *a signed contract*, and *a fulfilled contract*.

5.1 The DEMO CC-CP Construction Model

This model is not only designed for utilizing individual exchange processes between a Principal and a Contractor, but it can also be used in production chains as an elementary building block. Its name is derived from its usage in production chains. Many highly specialized enterprises do not have a well-defined portfolio of products with fixed prices but offer their capabilities to meet the specific requirements of their Principals. Here we offer the following definitions: *co-creation* captures the principal and the contractor(s) working together on the engineering of an acceptable artifact; *co-production* captures the shared production of the engineering artifact by both Principal and Contractor(s), including matching financial transactions. The DEMO CC-CP model was firstly introduced in [10] and further developed in [11].

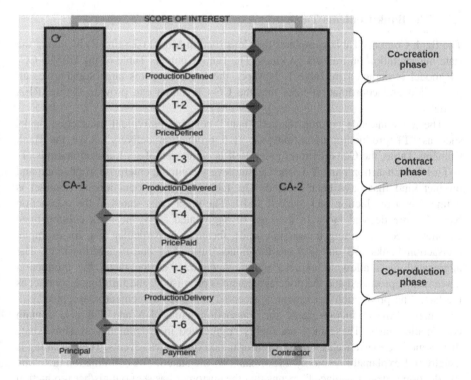

Fig. 2. The DEMO CC-CP construction model, Source: [11] (Color figure online)

The DEMO CC-CP construction model is illustrated in Fig. 2. This model is composed of three phases and each phase contains two DEMO ontological transactions. The *co-creation phase* represents a stage in which production (in REA resource types), as well as the price of production, are defined. When this phase is concluded, it means that the contract has been worked out but includes no obligations for the Principal and Contractor. The green color used in the drawings for T-1 and T-2 transactions indicates the *infological* layer, meaning that the production part and the price part of the contract are prepared but that the contract has not yet come into effect (business layer – the red color). The contract has not been signed in this phase.

The *contract phase* includes the signing of the contract by both parties (the contract comes into effect), which is represented by the reciprocity relationship in the REA model. This phase also involves fulfilment of the contract. The *co-production phase* addresses the individual production deliveries and individual payments for production deliveries. It follows from the nature of the exchange process that the products can be delivered in many sub-deliveries. Likewise, payment can be fulfilled by several partial payments.

5.2   The Bank Contents Table

The Bank Contents Table completes the Construction Model (see Fig. 2) by taking the state interpretation on transaction kinds. The Bank Contents Table of the DEMO CC-CP model is depicted in Table 1. In short, the Bank Contents table summarizes all production and coordination facts that the CC-CP model can provide for the REA model.

The left hand-side column marked "bank" contains individual transaction banks such as "T1 production definition", or "T-5 production delivery". Like the Bank Contents Table, the Construction model itself is composed of six transaction kinds (T-1–T-6). In transaction bank T-1, one can find every contract, enterprise, production and product kind that have been created. The fact that "the production of Contract is defined" is a production fact marked as P1. The other facts stated in the transaction bank T-1 are derived facts. In the case of aggregated facts, the bank column must encompass corresponding transaction kinds, meaning in particular that, for example, transaction banks T-3 and T-4 are mentioned instead of one transaction kind. The aggregated facts allow to express signing a contract as the fact: "the production agreement is promised and the price agreement is promised", and fulfilling a contract as the fact: "the production agreement is accepted and price agreement is accepted".

Apart from production facts, the transaction banks T-5 and T-6 also contain coordination facts. These facts are highly appreciated in accountancy systems, since they come into existence as a result of information or business events. Their meaning is usually self-explanatory, so only a few examples are stated. The coordination fact: "the [production order] was placed" means that the customer has sent out his/her production order to the enterprise. The coordination fact: "the [delivery order] was dispatched' represents the event during which the production contained in the delivery order was presented to the customer.

Table 1. The bank contents table of the DEMO CC-CP model

Bank	Independent/dependent fact
T-1 production definition	CONTRACT
	The principal **of** Contract
	The contractor **of** Contract
	ENTERPRISE
	The production **of** Contract
	PRODUCTION
	The product-kind of Production
	PRODUCT_KIND
	The volume **of** Product-Kind
	The price **of** Product-Kind
	The delivery day **of** Product-Kind
	The production **of** Contract is defined P1
T-2 price definition	PRICE
	The price **of** Contract
	MONEY_KIND
	The money kind of Price Line
	The amount **of** payment **of** Money-Kind
	The day **of** payment **of** Money-Kind
	The price **of** Contract **is** defined P2
T-3 production agreement, T-4 price agreement	CONTRACT_SIGNED
	The production_agreement is promised and The price_agreement is promised T3.pm and T4.pm
T-3 production agreement	PRODUCTION_AGREEMENT
	The production_agreement **is** fulfilled P3
T-4 price agreement	PRICE_AGREEMENT
	The price_agreement **is** fulfilled P4
T-3 production agreement T-4 price agreement	CONRACT_FULFILLED
	The production_agreement **is** fulfilled **and** The price_agreement **is** fulfilled P3 and P4
T-5 production delivery	PRODUCTION_DELIVERY
	The production delivery **of** Contract_Signed
	The product **of** Production_Delivery
	PRODUCT
	The actual volume **of** Product
	The actual price **of** Product (price per unit)
	The actual delivery day **of** Product
	The production order placed (sent) T5.rq
	The production order declined T5.dc
	The production order received T5.pm
	The delivery order handed over T5.st
	The delivery order receipt T5.ac (P5)

(continued)

Table 1. (*continued*)

Bank	Independent/dependent fact
	The delivery order rejected T5.rj
T-6 payment	PAYMENT
	The payment of Contract_Signed
	The money-kind of Payment
	MONEY_KIND
	The actual amount of payment of Money-Kind
	The actual day of payment of Money-Kind
	The invoice placed (sent) T6.rq
	The invoice declined T6.dc
	The invoice received T6.pm
	The payment made (sent) T6.st
	The payment receipt T6.ac (P6)
	The payment rejected – dispute T6.rj

The Bank Contents Table provides a detailed overview of all production and coordination facts that the DEMO CC-CP model is able to capture and deliver for further processing. In general, it also means that not all the facts may be needed by the REA model.

6   An Instance of the REA Model and Facts Identification

The Bank Contents Table, which is part of the CC-CP Construction Model expresses both production and coordination facts of a simple purchase/sales process, see Table 1. In order to get a deeper insight into REA semantics, an example of an REA instance model that describes a sales process is stated. The process represents a sales order between the customer (Adam) and the salesman (Mia's pizzeria). The customer orders two Margherita Pizzas and one Cola 0.5 l. The REA model can be described as a contract (Sales Order) which is composed of two kinds of transactions. These transactions are marked as increment or decrement transactions according to the value of the related resource entity. In the REA transaction, it is usually possible to distinguish between a physical item and category item. In this case, a resource entity represents a physical item and a resource-type entity represents a category item. The same holds for an agent entity and agent-type entity. Resource and resource-type entities represent domain-specific entities.

As is obvious from Fig. 3, the REA instance model consists of two decrement transactions and one increment transaction. The first decrement transaction includes the *commitment Line1*: Sales Line captures the liability of the salesman to sell two pizzas to the customer. The *event Line1*: Sales Line represents production itself, which means that two pizzas were delivered to the customer by the salesman. This transaction contains the resource type and resource of Margherita pizza and a pair of agents: the salesman and the customer.

The second decrement transaction includes the *commitment Line2*: Sales Line which captures the liability of the salesman to sell one Cola 0.5 l to the customer. The *event Line2*: Sales Line represents the delivery of Cola 0.5 l from the salesman to the customer. The transaction is accompanied by the resource type and the resource representing Cola 0.5 l, and a pair of agents.

The third increment transaction includes the *commitment Total*: Sales Line and captures the liability of the customer to pay the salesman for the ordered goods. The *event Total*: Payment Line represents the making of a payment by the customer, and the acceptance of it by the salesman. The resource type is represented by money.

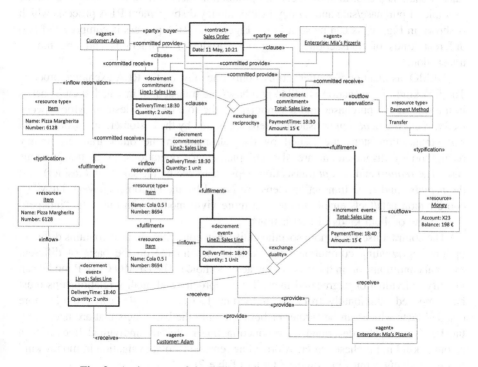

Fig. 3. An instance of the REA application model of a sales order

The core relationships in the REA model are relationships which relate the decrement commitments to increment commitments (the reciprocity relationship), and which relate the decrement event to the increment events (the duality relationship).

The reciprocity relationship represents signing a contract in which one kind of transactions (e.g., decrement transactions) is in consideration of the other kind of transactions (e.g., increment transactions). It means that the corresponding economic agents (actor roles) have agreed on the resource types, and their amount that will be exchanged for another amount of resource types, at the time and place promised in the commitment. This agreement also supposes that the promised amount of resource types will be available at the promised time.

Only a simple contract is considered, and therefore no further commitments reflecting, e.g., penalties, are stated. The duality relationship represents the fulfillment of individual transactions and the whole contract.

The process of fact identification will proceed from the Bank Contents Table, containing all production facts and necessary coordination facts, and the REA instance sales model. The coordination facts and production facts will be identified in a simple example of purchase/sale and money receipt/money disbursement REA process, which is shown in Fig. 3. As can be seen in the Figure, the REA process is composed of two different kinds of transactions: two goods (products) transactions and one money transaction.

DEMO, as mentioned earlier, utilizes only one view on the REA exchange process. The first kind of transaction is called purchase/sale transaction, in which a customer is in the role of the purchaser and a vendor is in the role of the salesman. More specifically, *request* and *accept* transaction steps are issued by the customer, and *promise* and *state* transaction steps are issued by the salesman. In the other transfer, money receipt/money disbursement are also complementary operations, as in the previous case. The *request* and *accept* transaction steps are issued by the salesman (cashier), and the *promise* and *state* transaction steps are issued by the customer (payer). DEMO's coordination acts/facts enable to create a more vivid model, with only one "independent" view on both kinds of transactions.

The contract itself is a more specific entity than commitment, as it contains different options representing commitment that will be instantiated on the basis of different external conditions, or on the basis of the actor's choice. The DEMO CC-CP model can identify individual or aggregated facts. The reciprocity and duality relationships must be composed additionally from the individual facts. The model can provide more detailed facts which can be further elaborated. Only the basic facts that are needed by the REA model are described. A production line represents individual lines with a resource kind in Purchase Order. A price line represents total evaluation in money kind for all production lines in Purchase Order (Table 2).

Table 2. Summary of facts that the CC-CP model can provide for the REA sales order model

Fact No	Fact description	REA model relationship
1	Contract [*sales order #132*] come into enforce on [*current day 18:15*]	
2	Contract of [*sales order*] has ID [*#132*]	
3	Customer of [*sales order #132*] is [*Adam*]	Party
4	Enterprise of [*sales order #132*] is [*Mia's Pizzeria*]	Party
5	Production line of [sales order #132] is [*Line1*]	Clause
6	Product kind of [*Line1*] is item [#6128]	Inflow reservation
7	Quantity of [*Line1*] is [2]	
8	Delivery day of [*Line1*] is [*current day 18:30*]	
9	Item [#6128] has name [*Pizza Margherita*]	
10	Price per unit of item [#6128] is [*9 €*]	
11	Production line of [*sales order #132*] is [*Line2*]	Clause
12	Product kind of [*Line2*] is item [#8694]	Inflow reservation
13	Quantity of [*Line2*] is [1]	
14	Delivery day of [*Line2*] is [*current day 18:30*]	
15	Item [*#8694*] has name [*Cola 0.5 l*]	
16	Price per unit of item [#8694] is [*1.5 €*]	
17	Price line of [*sales order #132*] is [*Total*]	Clause
18	Payment method of Price line [*Total*] is [*method*]	Outflow reservation
19	Payment time of [*Total*] is [*current day 18:30*]	
20	Money kind of [*Total*] is [*money kind #3541*]	
21	Total amount of [Total] is [*19.5 €*]	
22	Actual product delivery of [*Line1*] is product ID [*#6128*]	Fulfilment
23	Actual quantity of product delivery of [*Line1*] is [2]	
24	Actual delivery day of product [*Line1*] is [*current day 18:40*]	
25	Actual price per unit of product ID [#6128] is [*9 €*]	
26	Actual product delivery of [Line2] is product ID [*#8694*]	Fulfilment
27	Actual quantity of product delivery of [*Line2*] is [1]	
28	Actual delivery day of product [*Line2*] is [*current day 18:40*]	
29	Actual price per unit of product ID [#8694] is [*1.5 €*]	
30	Production agreement [*#3132*] was fulfilled	
31	Actual payment of [*Total*] is money [kind]	outflow
32	Actual payment amount of [Total] is [*19.5 €*]	
33	Actual payment day of [Total] is [*current day 18:45*]	
34	Price agreement [*# 4132*] was fulfilled	
35	Contract [*sales order #132*] was fulfilled on [*current day 18:45*]	

This section shows that the DEMO CC-CP model is able to capture and provide all facts (production, coordination, and aggregated) for the REA model representation. Software execution of the CC-CP model should provide all information needed for a REA compliant accounting system.

7   Discussion

There are two principal reasons for a truthful and appropriate REA model representation by a generic DEMO model for co-creation and co-production. The first reason is that the DEO (DEMO Enterprise Ontology) ontology is a generic foundational ontology and the REA ontology is a domain-specific ontology [1, 2, 14]. This implies that the generic ontology with DEO qualities and capabilities should support a domain-specific ontology. It can be emphasized that among other benefits that DEO provides, there is the capability of grasping all the phenomena that occur in reality with good empirical evidence [7, 15]. In general, this feature of DEO is worthful for the REA ontology because it could considerably extend its functionality.

The second reason potentially supporting cooperation is that the DEO provides also prescriptive information systems of the enterprise (not only descriptive information systems). If we apply the DEMO engine and execute the REA model in DEMO modeling language, then the generic transaction pattern gives the actor roles firm guidance from which they cannot be deviated; it is an enforcing business procedure. This feature may be highly useful for REA ontology since it only provides descriptive knowledge. The DEMO prescriptive capabilities can dramatically improve the rather "loose coupling" between the REA's commitment entity and economic event entity, thus forming a principal element of REA transactions. For REA, this would, in essence, entail a shift towards financial information systems with precisely defined relations between a commitment entity and economic event entity.

To realize collaboration between different ontologies, some kind of mapping between ontologies must be set up. Whereas the *top-down approach* (starting from accounting artifacts trying to capture the phenomena and things in the real world) proves to be ineffective, the *bottom-up approach* (to develop some DEMO model that captures all REA artifacts well and without anomalies) shows to be a passable means of potential collaboration. As can be seen from the previous text, collaboration of both ontologies doesn't represent a horizontal way of collaboration between two more or less equal sides. Collaboration utilized in the described approach represents a systematic hierarchical approach, in which the DEMO CC-CP model –the bottom part– supplies factual knowledge to the REA model –the upper part. The mapping itself is based on elementary parts - facts that can be transferred to the REA model.

Information contained in the form of facts would require some other (additional) operations to transfer these facts into the form of the REA information system. But this demand is less difficult than supplementing REA ontology with features described above.

8 Conclusions

The paper deals with the idea of a generic and a domain-specific ontologies collaboration in a *systematic hierarchical way*. This collaboration is designed and clarify in the form of facts (elements of information) that are produced by the DEMO CC-CP model and are intended for the REA model. The presented solution is based on systems engineering, the construction of a system, in such a way that a desired functional behavior of the system is realized. Two important quality criteria have been discussed; ontological truthfulness and ontological appropriateness.

All relevant real-world phenomena must be well captured by the DEMO CC-CP model; otherwise it is impossible to devise a working REA compliant accounting system. The DEMO CC-CP model together with the Bank Contents Table (Sect. 5) provide, in general, summary of all production and coordination facts that the proposed model is capable to capture and deliver in the area of reciprocal transaction modeling. In this way, a claim of appropriateness – execution of the DEMO CC-CP model provides all factual information for a REA accounting system – is provided. Failure to meet this quality criterion renders the DEMO CC-CP model totally useless.

Future research will be aimed at real-world verification and validation of the proposed DEMO CC-CP model towards REA model representation. The further goals of the future research will be analyze and modeling of a more complex and robust DEMO CC-CP model.

Acknowledgements. The paper was supported by the grant provided by Ministry of Education, Youth and Sports Czech Republic, reference number SGS06/PRF/2019.

References

1. Dietz, J.L.G.: Enterprise Ontology Theory and Methodology. Springer, Heidelberg (2006)
2. Dietz, J.L.G.: Architecture - Building strategy into design. Academic Service (2008)
3. Dietz, J.L.G., Hoogervorst, J.A.P.: The discipline of enterprise engineering. Int. J. Organisational Des. Eng. **3**(1), 86–114 (2013)
4. Dietz, J.L.G.: The Essence of Organization, 2nd edn. Sapio Enterprise Engineering, Delft (2015)
5. Dudok, E., Guerreiro, S., Babkin, E., Pergl, R., van Kervel, S.J.H.: Enterprise operational analysis using DEMO and the enterprise operating system. In: Aveiro, D., Pergl, R., Valenta, M. (eds.) EEWC 2015. LNBIP, vol. 211, pp. 3–18. Springer, Cham (2015). https://doi.org/10.1007/978-3-319-19297-0_1
6. Dunn, C.L., Cherrington, O.J., Hollander, A.S.: Enterprise Information Systems: A Pattern Based Approach. McGraw-Hill/Irwin, New York (2004)
7. Guizzardi, G.: Ontological foundation for structural conceptual models. Ph.D. thesis, University of Twente (2005)
8. Hevner, A.: A three cycle view of design science research. Inf. Syst. Decis. Sci. Scand. J. Inf. Syst. **19**(2), 87–92 (2007)
9. Hruby, P.: Model-Driven Design Using Business Patterns. Springer, Heidelberg (2006)

10. Hunka, F., van Kervel, S.J.H., Matula, J.: Towards co-creation and co-production in production chains modeled in DEMO with REA support. In: Aveiro, D., Pergl, R., Gouveia, D. (eds.) EEWC 2016. LNBIP, vol. 252, pp. 54–68. Springer, Cham (2016). https://doi.org/10.1007/978-3-319-39567-8_4
11. Hunka, F., van Kervel, S.J.H.: The REA model expressed in a generic DEMO model for co-creation and co-production. In: Aveiro, D., Pergl, R., Guizzardi, G., Almeida, J.P., Magalhães, R., Lekkerkerk, H. (eds.) EEWC 2017. LNBIP, vol. 284, pp. 151–165. Springer, Cham (2017). https://doi.org/10.1007/978-3-319-57955-9_12
12. McCarthy, W.E.: The REA accounting model: a generalized framework for accounting systems in a shared data environment. Account. Rev. **57**, 554–578 (1982). **2**(5), 99–110 (2016)
13. Skotnica, M., van Kervel, S.J.H., Pergl, R.: Towards the ontological foundations for the software executable DEMO action and fact models. In: Aveiro, D., Pergl, R., Gouveia, D. (eds.) EEWC 2016. LNBIP, vol. 252, pp. 151–165. Springer, Cham (2016). https://doi.org/10.1007/978-3-319-39567-8_10
14. van Kervel, S.J.H., Dietz, J.L.G., Hintzen, J., Meeuwen, T., van Zijlstra, B.: Enterprise ontology driven software engineering. In: Proceedings of ICsoft 2012 – 7th International Conference on Software Paradigm Trends, pp. 151–165. SciTePress (2012)
15. van Kervel, S.J.H., Hintzen, J., van Meeuwen, T., Zijlstra, B., Vermolen, J.: A professional case management system in production, modeled and implemented using DEMO. In: CBI 2014, 8th TEE Workshop: Transformation & Engineering of Enterprises, Geneva, Switzerland, pp. 205–210 (2014)
16. van Kervel, S.J.H.: Ontology driven enterprise information systems engineering, Ph.D. thesis, University of Technology Delft (2012)

Integration of Blockchain Technology into a Land Registration System for Immutable Traceability: A Casestudy of Georgia

Nino Lazuashvili, Alex Norta[(✉)], and Dirk Draheim

Department of Software Science, Tallinn University of Technology,
Akadeemia tee 15a, 12618 Tallinn, Estonia
ninalazuashvili@gmail.com, alex.norta.phd@ieee.org,
dirk.draheim@taltech.com

Abstract. Land as an immovable property represents an important asset for which such crucial aspects evolve as ownership rights, security of land records, possible disputes, corruption risks and sundry transparency matters of land registry processes. Critical issues are traceability of records, hazards of document forgery as well as vulnerability to various errors. Delivering accountable land registry systems and particularly increasing validity of land titles is vital for present-day governments in terms of suppressing corruption, eliminating red tape, enhancing transparency, improving speed of the stated public service and eradicating risks of possible disputes. Furthermore, integration of the blockchain technology into land registries leads to achieving a disruptive transformation of public-service provision systems. This Georgia focused casestudy-based research ascertains how blockchain technology resolves the issues above concerning contemporary land registry systems and examines determinants for a successful application of the digital novelty. The findings from semi-structured interviews and document studies we analyze and scrutinize the present blockchain model of the Georgian government. Additionally, we provide recommendations for administering the blockchain-based digital solutions present in the public land registry service-provision system.

Keywords: Blockchain · Land title · Registry · Property · NAPR · The Bitfury Group · Georgia

1 Introduction

Contemporary technologies are constantly evolving and challenging societies [1,2]. Artificial intelligence, blockchain, smart contracts, electronic identities and many other advancements are actively being integrated into day to day government-citizen relationships [3,4]. With the evolution of information- and

© Springer Nature Switzerland AG 2019
C. Di Ciccio et al. (Eds.): BPM 2019 Blockchain and CEE Forum, LNBIP 361, pp. 219–233, 2019.
https://doi.org/10.1007/978-3-030-30429-4_15

communication technologies (ICT), state authorities are challenged to provide more efficient and effective services to citizens, yet guaranteeing a high level of data security, transparency, auditability, and privacy. Acquisition of information, transparent diffusion, secure storage and proper communication have become essential parts of present-day public sectors and ICT in this regard plays an important role in supporting proper functioning of governments [5]. The digital roadmap of the twenty-first century is constantly progressing and ICT advancements heavily influence the performance of present-day governments. ICT spurs innovation and in this sense can play a transformative role as well [6]. In many aspects these digital novelties might determine the course of actions of countries' developments too. The application of contemporary electronic tools to governmental operations and e-service provision systems posses the ability to create platforms for providing fast, transparent, cheap and convenient solutions to citizen related concerns.

Blockchain technology is a disruptive innovation with the potential to revolutionize the way governments and other non-profit, or for-profit organizations handle themselves, as well as how they communicate with collaborating parties. Technology creates a platform for the distributed governance and affects in every aspect the stakeholders' relationships via affecting the full spectrum of document processing, data storage, information exchange, power distribution, transparency and other crucial aspects of business processes [4]. In this regard, blockchain technology creates novel opportunities for governments to succeed in all respects of government-citizen relationships and support the provision of highly advanced services within electronic platforms. Thus, identifying prevalent challenges regarding the application of the technology to state services, possesses vast potential to further contribute to the development of public service provision systems.

1.1   Research Objectives

Based on the extended version of this study [7], our casestudy in this paper focuses on the land title blockchain project of the National Agency of Public Registry[1] (NAPR) of Georgia[2,3] and examines the grounds of the given public service from various angles with the aim of providing wider insight about the project. Our research focuses on identifying challenges related to the application of blockchain technology to the Georgian state-service routine and discover recommendations. Thus, the main goals of the research are defined as follows:

- Evaluate the land-tiling blockchain project from the point of effectiveness and efficiency.
- Point out the project advantages and disadvantages.
- Propose a framework for the future development of blockchain technology within the same and any other state services.

---

[1] https://napr.gov.ge.
[2] https://europa.eu.
[3] https://www.consilium.europa.eu.

We deem it relevant to clarify for the reader, even though the state of art of the blockchain technology can be endlessly discussed, this paper does not focus on the thorough analysis of the blockchain technology as it is the subject to a bigger scale research. This work intends to examine the blockchain-based solution deployed by the Georgian government within the land registry system and generate a set of recommendations for the further expansion of the project.

1.2 Motivation

We identify factors for the successful administration of blockchain technology and discuss the world precedent of an early adopter country, Georgia. This research is motivated by ascertaining how blockchain works for the public sector, to what degree the technology benefits the land-title registry process and to find what lessons have been learned so far. Determining the next development steps for improving the system is an additional incentive for our research.

The remainder of the paper is structured as follows. Section 2 presents related work and Sect. 3 describes the execution of casestudy-based research for this study. Next, Sect. 4 presents the case selection, subject selection and results of this study. In Sect. 5, we discuss the results related to its context. Finally, Sect. 7 concludes this paper and gives future work.

2 Related Work

Blockchain technology is deemed as one of the most disruptive and promising technological solutions to today's state operations [8]. Even though the technology itself is still immature [9], as the new layer of prevailing e-governments blockchains provide better accountability, trust, integrity, and improved performance [8]. Citation [9] suggests that blockchain technology improves various state operations even in those cases where there does not exist a developed e-government and "adequate technical-, or institutional infrastructure in place" [9].

Study [9] asserts that "ICT systems based on blockchain technology, implying decentralized management and control, offer more robust and flexible solutions that cannot be corrupted. Still, lessons learned from earlier efforts to introduce new technology underscore the importance of following a realistic, systematic approach". Thus, in [10], it is pointed out that applying blockchain technology to developing countries is essential in terms of defeating corruption and malicious activities. Furthermore, study [10] also emphasizes the potential of blockchain technology in terms of data-security enhancement and to support solutions where blockchain technology reinforces business processes within government [10]. Furthermore, "blockchain has the potential to render government operations more efficient by improving the delivery of public services and increasing trust in public sectors" [10].

The essence of blockchain adoption into state services is motivated by the economic benefit and various data security and validity issues [11] where blockchain is a benefactor. The economically beneficial side for the state in case of administering blockchain technology for storing government records [12] is a promising secure tool along with offering cost-effective solutions for saving sensitive data. In comparison, administering blockchain technology might be very costly [11] and experimentation of the attractive operational solutions offered by blockchain might be inefficient for sole employment within the individual state agency context.

Blockchain can be applied to every area of the government operations where transaction processes take place [4] and as the one of most decently compelling arguments [4], "the fundamental characteristics of this technology enables an implementation in a wide range of processes for asset registry, inventory, and information exchange, both hard assets such as physical properties, and intangible assets such as votes, patents, ideas, reputation, intention, health data, information, etc."

The role of blockchain in the land registries is particularly useful [4] for reducing risks of corruption and manipulation of land registry transactions as long as land ownership data is a very sensitive in terms of ownership rights. Blockchain is a useful tool to protect the land transaction parties, provide trust among the owner of land and a seller and yields authenticity of the land title records. Blockchain technology is currently applied [13] to various state services such as energy markets, education, e-businesses, and so on. The application of blockchain technology to land registries [13] is a useful tool for conducting land-related transactions, including "transfer of land or the establishment of a mortgage". Thus, the capacity of blockchain-based solutions [14] facilitates providing the integrity of land records and data traceability for any audit purposes.

Paper [10] accentuates the empirical essence of blockchain-technology adoption as a government solution and argues that even though from the ICT perspective. The technological compatibility of blockchain to the existing information-technology systems are identified and beneficial aspects also are defined while less is known on the empirical challenges such as the regulatory frameworks of countries, managerial approaches, organizational studies, etc. Based on [10], empirical data shows blockchain-technology application to governmental and identifies the most applicable governmental sectors. The health sector is identified for applying blockchain to the management of patients' health records, followed by the education sector. Authors [10] similarly to [9] also identify the financial sector be a potential area for blockchain applications while, additionally, public-private relationship areas and supply chain also benefit from the technology. Nevertheless, empirical, or practical evidence about blockchain application to state services [10] is lacking while the majority of approaches are theoretical and lack practical support.

3   Research Methodology

We explain next the methodology applied to the research in Sect. 3.1, discuss data collection methods in Sect. 3.2 as well as draw the readers' attention to the sample selection process for the study. This section also cover the design of the questionnaires for the semi-structured interviews and logic behind the semi-structured questionnaire that follows the idea of the study's research questions for more comprehensive data collection purposes.

3.1 Casestudy

We choose casestudy-based research as the main method for attaining the empirical primary data about the study object as the passage [15] asserts that "empirical research implies to one's experience and observations often without due regard for system and theory". Such design helps in attaining a brief overview of the property-registry blockchain project of the Georgian government and gives an opportunity to analyze the topic based on this factual example. The unique nature of the casestudy design provides more opportunities for exploring the subject and as scholars [16] note, "case studies offer an approach that does not require a strict boundary between the object of study and its environment".

As long as the government of Georgia is a pioneer state in the successful application of blockchain technology in public services, casestudy design is a competent method for briefly exploring the implemented project. As research questions, we examine how blockchain technology contributes to the public service-provision process of Georgia in the context of the land-tiling project framework. Furthermore, our research follows the path of the main study question of how blockchain fits into the narrative of contemporary e-service provision systems of the Georgian government? What are the main criteria for evaluating the project? How does blockchain technology affect the public service provision system?

3.2 Data Collection

Our research is qualitative and entails data collection methods both from primary and secondary sources. Study [15] explains the primary sources refer to collecting data for the first time and is mainly deployed for studying of not yet researched topics. The secondary data-collection method, on the other hand, gives opportunities to explore topics that have already been studied once. On that account, the research applied to the primary data collection method via interviews and, in addition, for diversifying the data, we apply document analysis to the research as a secondary data collection method.

Interviews: Semi-structured interviewing style is applied to the paper as the means for the exploratory studies to help gain comprehensive information about the study topic and to understand the respondents' perspectives to the study object [17]. First-degree, primary data is acquired within the interviews and this feature stands out as a remarkable characteristics of the interview-based data collection method in terms of producing valuable output for the qualitative studies [18]. More enhanced explanations about questionnaire design, sample size determination and data analysis procedures are provided in the next sections.

Document Review: Alongside the interviews, document review as a secondary data collection method is also applied within the given paper in order to expand and diversify data. Such a method applies to different types of documents, in light of evidence from the study [19], and includes both printed and electronic sources. This process of data collection explores information for the study object via the content of the respective documentation. One of the main advantages of employing such a data collection method in parallel with the interviews is that documents related to study questions match with the agenda topics that are not mentioned by the interviewees. As quotation [19] suggests, "document analysis is often used in combination with other qualitative research methods as a means of triangulation with the combination of methodologies in the study of the same phenomenon". Therefore, more comprehensive results are expected to be attained within a combination of the interview and document review-data collection methods.

Survey-Sample Selection: The sample size for the data collection is eight respondents. Among the interviewees are the stakeholders of the land tilting project, both from NAPR and the Bitfury Group, who either used to work on or are currently implementing the project under investigation and include former head of the National Agency of Public Registry, current lead of the Project Management and Sales Department, present head of the Working Component of the Information and Communication Technology Development and a Software Maintenance and Development Engineer of the agency. Moreover, respondents from third parties such as experts researching blockchain technology and those developing technology in the private sector are interviewed to attain impartial and unprejudiced information. This eventually results in collecting the unbiased and more easily populated data. All the interviews are conducted remotely, between the period of March–April 2019 and for more detailed description we refer the reader to the master paper [7].

Questionnaire: In order to attain comprehensive answers to the study questions, the interview questionnaire is constructed based on the main research and sub research questions, respectively. For the logical flow of the interview process, questions are initially grouped into logical units such as the set of the open-ended questions related to understanding the respondents' backgrounds and their competency with regards to study object, as well as questions to attain respondents' evaluations of Georgia's prevalent public administration system. The set of questions are designed to specifically explore the preliminary researches conducted before launching blockchain into the land registry system. This part is followed by questions about the outcomes of the project and the respective metrics for measuring the results. The questionnaire also addresses the topic of stakeholders and their roles in the project, whilst the final set of questions draw attention to the prospective application of blockchain technology into state services. Furthermore, a semi-structured interview style we deploy for attaining the versatile insights on the study objects.

Finally, interview results are analyzed via elaborating tool-based data analysis method. Therefore, we employ one of the Computer Assisted/Aided Qualitative Data Analysis Software (CAQDAS) tools, such as the open-source R package qualitative data analysis tool - RQDA project[4].

4   Case Selection, Subject Description and Result Presentation

Given the extended version of this paper in [7], Sect. 4.1 provides insights towards the case subject and briefly describes it, whilst in Sect. 4.2 results of the research are presented into two main parts that draw attention to the identified requirements necessary for adoption the blockchain solution into land registry states-service systems. Hereby needs to be mentioned that even though the recommendations are drawn based on the reviewed documents and academic literature, our proposition still has to be tested and validated. Finally, but importantly, the second part of the chapter explains briefly how conventional blockchain solutions operate in realtime state land-title operations.

4.1   Case and Subject Description

The land-registration process in Georgia is fully administered by the NAPR. At the present time, the land-registration process takes from one to four days and is almost a fully digitized service. As the most IT advanced public authority in the country, NAPR constantly strives towards enhancing the services through accepting contemporary digital challenges. One of the main, yet fully unleashed technology is the blockchain and NAPR decided to adopt for the implementation of this digital platform to increase the overall performance of the agency and improve the quality of the e-services and particularly address improvement of the land title service. The agency started exploring the technology in 2015–2016.

Existing threats on data security, such as cyber-attacks and data breaches, are the incentives that play a major role for NAPR in adopting blockchain technology along with enhancing the existing registration model of land titles and eliminating the possible risks of corruption. Red tape and corruption in the state services are the legacy that Georgian public administration system is left with after the collapse of the Soviet Union and blockchain technology provides opportunities for addressing the aforementioned issues as well. Land titles are digitally provided since 2006, thus, a fair base for implementation of blockchain technology already exists. By integrating blockchains into the administration of land titles, NAPR discovers a way to move from a centralized model of data management to a decentralized one. In this regard, all advantages are inherited from the blockchain's essence of a distributed ledger technology, rendering transactions simultaneously available for peers to mine, check, save and validate.

---

[4] http://rqda.r-forge.r-project.org.

NAPR partners with the Bitfury Group[5], a worldwide blockchain development company. Specialists from both organizations, the Bitfury Group and NAPR develop the project whilst NAPR is responsible for the content provision and Bitfury for the implementation of the blockchain technology itself. In order to harmonize with the existing system of property registry along with the respective legislation, both organizations agree on the creation of the "add-on" layer over the existing system. Thus, the process of the immutable and traceable property registration remains unchanged, while one more layer of the blockchain is built on top to store land titles on the blockchain. At present, the entire process of land registration lasts up to four working days, while transferring the first-hand land titles from NAPR's database to the blockchain requires roughly 10 min.

4.2   Result Presentation

Requirements Necessary for Further Blockchain-Technology Adoption: We thoroughly analyze the data from various sources such as interviews and internal documentation as well as provide insights for the cases of Sweden, Dubai and The Netherlands [7]. Thus, general recommendations for adopting blockchains into land-registry systems we summarize as follows:

- Governments must focus on the goals and final outcomes they intend to reach by administering blockchains. Therefore, governments must initially decide the scope of the services where blockchain technology is applied and, based on the needs of the government, must initially determine which blockchain solution is preferably and the most suitable for the country.
- Public-private partnership is conducive for the successful application of blockchain technology. Therefore, agencies that are specifically working either on the development of blockchain technology, or on the development of digital ID systems, as well as agencies working on business-process automation processes, must be involved from the start.
- Legislative frameworks need to be reviewed and necessary amendments implemented to assure the compatibility of blockchains with local- and international regulations.
- Citizen awareness with respect to the technology must be raised before launching blockchain technology to ensure that customers, citizens trust such novel high-tech e-services.
- In order to eliminate present manual processes in land administration services, new operational schemes have to be defined where manual work is no more persistent.
- Governments must continuously investigate blockchain technology to accentuate the research and development side of such projects.

At the same time, major aspects identified within the research that support the adoption of blockchain technology specifically in the Georgian ecosystem, we categorize as follows:

---

[5] https://bitfury.com.

- Having a developed e-government is one of the biggest benefits to face the challenge of blockchain adoption. This element is also identified as a major support factor for the successful implementation of the Georgian land-titling project. Based on international rankings, Georgia shows significant results in the advancement of e-government development as also previously also discussed in the extended version [7] of this paper.
- Public-private partnership is a crucial aspect for blockchain-technology adoption. In case of Georgia, the Bitfury group develops the blockchain solution for the government and since then keeps providing the service. The same applies to other adopter countries as well where occasionally even several private-sector companies provide the solutions for integrating blockchain technology into existing land-registry systems.
- The legislative framework is a crucial aspect for the successful integration of blockchain technology. In case of Georgia, the project success is greatly determined by the flexibility of the respective regulations that do not hinder NAPR from saving the citizens' data on the blockchain. In cases of other countries such as Sweden or The Netherlands, for administering blockchain technology into the public service, major regulatory changes are required.
- Research and development activities are equally an important element for blockchain-technology adoption. Having previously determined what obstacles stakeholders face within and after blockchain adoption, helps to provide more effective and efficient solutions. In the case of the Georgian government, one of the respondents admits that after the completion of the pilot project of the land titling "blockchainisation", NAPR sees the need for conducting research about the legislative framework of Georgia for supporting the further development of this blockchain project.

AS-IS Model of the Land Title Blockchain System: Based on the data collected from the public agency's records, documents and the interviews combined, to better understand the existing administration system of the land-titling of Georgia, we develop a corresponding business-process model. This blockchain-induced process comprises the following steps:

- Initially, seller and buyer physically pay a visit to the NAPR's local office for allowing the NAPR agent to visually verify the identities of both parties and submit a joint application for the registration of transfer.
- A PDF (land title doc) extract is generated at the registrar's desktop client application.
- This PDF is sent to the NAPR's database where the servers are maintained by the agency itself for signing the document digitally so that the offline PDF document is secured from data tampering.
- A digital signature-integration service via software for digitally signing PDF documents and placing a time stamp on them, requires new PDF documents from databases. Consequently, a file is ready for signing: In case there are specific factors restraining either seller, or buyer to execute a purchase then the document is ejected from further processing and at this point, the land

tilting process is over. Therefore, no document is sent to the blockchain. In case the transaction is bona fide then the processing continues.

- The digital signature-integration service sends the document for signing to the digital-signature Service.
- Via the digital-signature service, it is possible to sign the document. This task requires several sub processes to be complete such as:
  The hash of a PDF file signature is generated.
  The signature is added to the PDF file that is signed digitally with the private key held by NAPR only.
  Third-party timestamp is applied to the document.
- The signed PDF file is sent to a Blob storage and saved permanently. Blob is a server owned by NAPR and files preserved at this storage are immutable, i.e., they can not be deleted or edited.
- Upon entering the document into the Blob-storage blockchain, a gateway executes a transaction to the bitcoin blockchain where a transaction is hashed and validated by bitcoin blockchain miners. This phase consists of several sub processes such as:
  The gateway reads the newly signed files from the Blob storage and generates hash code of every single file.
  The gateway creates a Merkle's Tree of hashes.
  A new bitcoin-transaction object is created that contains the Merkle's Tree root hash.
  The transaction is sent to the bitcoin network for validation.
  Bitcoin miners verify the transaction, which involves producing a hash-based (SHA-256) Proof-of-Work (PoW).
- Once the transaction is validated, it is equally published on NAPR's publicly available webpage[6].

Figure 1 below is a graphical representation of the current land-title blockchain system of Georgia. The full version of the AS-IS model is represented in Appendix 6 of the original research paper [7] that we can not include here due to page limitations:

Figures 2 and 3 represent the sub processes of the following phases: "Digital signature service signs the document" and "Blockchain gateway makes transaction to Bitcoin blockchain", respectively.

Having the business process graphically displayed is important to analyze the possible drawbacks of the existing system. The given blockchain solution is applied to the land-titling existing system in a shallow sociotechnical way, i.e., the business model of the system is not modified, but the existing digital solution is improved by adding the additional blockchain layer to the land-titling process. This contradicts the extensively discussed [7] state of the art for blockchain technology in terms of decentralization, distribution and disintermediation. Thus, in Georgia the goal remains to centrally control the citizens' data under the authority's sub-ordinance and consequently, the blockchain gateway undertakes

---

[6] http://www.napr.gov.ge.

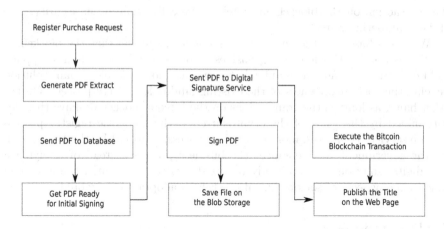

Fig. 1. Land-title business process.

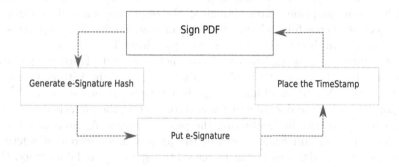

Fig. 2. Sub-processes of the phase "Digital signature service signs the document".

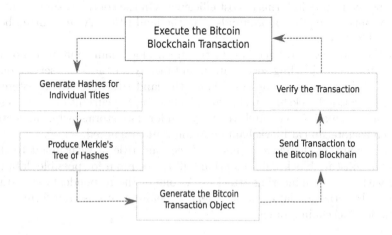

Fig. 3. Sub-processes of the phase "Blockchain gateway makes transaction to Bitcoin blockchain".

the transaction on the blockchain merely technically while other security risks of data tampering remain.

We stress based on the currently existing AS-IS model that the blockchain solution is applied to the existing business process merely as a shallow applied "add-on" service. Thus, it is difficult to estimate how this blockchain solution benefits the cost-effectiveness of the existing land-title registry process. On the other hand, as long as the transactions on the bitcoin blockchain have their fee determined by the value of the cryptocurrency, the land-title registry process as an e-service, is an even more expensive process. It would be the best option for the government to re-engineer the business process instead of applying a new digital solution to the already digitized services. Currently, the cost- and time-saving aspects of sociotechnical blockchain adoption are ignored.

5 Discussions

Based on the analysis of the data attained from the respondents, we postulate the following assumptions. Even though all the respondents in unison agree that the project is successful and praise Georgian government for supporting this project, there are drawbacks of the existing project. This project carries high risks of failure and it is unclear what outcomes to expect. Thus, the success of the project heavily relies on the blockchain expertise of the Bitfury Group and the expertise of NAPR in administering the electronic public services.

Upon reviewing the documentation and conducting the interviews, we do not detect specific metrics for evaluating the project results. As pinpointed within this research, the main achievement of the project is an increased safety and security of citizens' data, as well as increased transparency and data traceability. As to the quantitative metrics, or cost-effectiveness analysis, this aspect remains vague, as per the respondents' feedback. Thus, the blockchain solution does not yield tangible results in terms of cost efficiency. On the contrary, supporting this "add-on" service requires more funds than the land title service incurred before adding a blockchain layer.

Another project drawback is that the given blockchain solution is not integrated into the land-titling service itself and merely an "add-on" service on the existing land title registry process. Thus, the land titles are still registered as before integrating blockchain technology. Therefore, the current blockchain solution is merely an advanced "archive" platform for data storage while advantages of a deep sociotechnical blockchain adoption remain ignored.

After reviewing the current model of the land title, a weak point to stress is that the existing blockchain adoption still leaves room for possible data tampering with social engineering attacks[7]. As one of the respondents also stated, theoretically, citizens' data can be amended before a title is transferred to the immutable blockchain storage.

---

[7] https://resources.infosecinstitute.com/common-social-engineering-attacks/gref.

6   Limitations

Limitations also apply to the research, based on the state of art of casestudy designs, as such deployed methodology is useful for the casual and explanatory inquiries [20]. Generalizability capacity of case studies are limited and can also be a drawback as due to a highly context-specific nature they might be limited to only the study-object context. Intensive use of the empirical pieces of evidence attained within the casestudy research may also lead to overly complex theory [21]. Casestudies are limited to generating the hypotheses and in light of evidence from the study [22], underline they struggle "to summarize and develop general propositions and theories based on specific case studies" [22]. With respect to the limitations of casestudy research methodologies, most relevant to the current research are the following:

- Due to the limited scope of the research topic findings of the single casestudy might not be applicable to the other state services neither within Georgia nor in other countries.
- Opinions of the respondents employed at the NAPR as well as at the Bitfury Group could be biased and therefore, might not reflect the objective reality. Therefore, there exists a possibility that some aspects around the study object are unleashed, or vague as a limitation of the paper.
- Sparse data about other blockchain adopters can be deemed as a minor limitation as well. Even though paper provides an overview of several countries besides Georgia that are also integrating blockchain-based land registries, more nourished comparisons to the study object could be drawn with more thorough examination of the other adopters.

7   Conclusion

This research examines a land-title project of Georgia by analyzing primary and secondary data sources such as semi-structured interviews with stakeholders of the aforementioned project and the project-related documentations respectively. For this blockchain-supported land-title process that we also graphically represent, the main benefits and drawbacks of the status quo are determined. Additionally, cases of other early blockchain adopter countries are reviewed for specifying final conclusions that facilitate the adoption of blockchain technology in the public sector.

Assuming the application of blockchain technology increases the overall government efficiency and improves the quality of service-delivery processes, it is important to determine additional incentives for government to adopt blockchains in public administration processes. Besides the aspiration for Gerogia to portray a high e-governance development standard, reducing project risk for the government by initiating public-private cooperation is identified as a major incentive. Additionally, in the Georgian case, costs of the project along with the technology maintenance expenditures are covered by the private blockchain service-provider company.

In the course of this research, specific quantitative metrics for evaluating the efficiency of the project we can not identify while main metrics for characterizing the technology application within the land registry state service are the increased security for possessing sensitive data of citizens and boosted transparency of government activities. Blockchain technology has the potential of reducing data tampering risks, increasing security and safety of the state records, along with providing decentralized governance that Georgia intends to exploit in the future of the land-title project. Currently, the land-title service does not transform the business-process models and is merely added as an additional service layer.

We identify as future work the need for guiding the land-title project towards a deep adoption of blockchain technology that triggers sociotechnical changes such as a considerable optimization of the currently existing business processes. In an optimum case, such deep adoption results in a complete automation of land-titling for taking maximum advantage of the cost-cutting and time-saving potential of blockchain technology. We understand the implications as the consequence of full automation is a near complete redundancy of the current employees coupled with the need of stakeholders to employ state-of-the-art paperless technology for land-title management.

References

1. Rannenberg, K., Royer, D., Deuker, A.: The Future of Identity in the Information Society, Challenges and Opportunities. Springer, Heidelberg (2009). https://doi.org/10.1007/978-3-642-01820-6
2. Porter, M.E., Millar, V.E., et al.: How information gives you competitive advantage (1985)
3. Mehr, H., Ash, H., Fellow, D.: Artificial intelligence for citizen services and government. Ash Cent. Democr. Gov. Innov. Harvard Kennedy Sch. no. August 1–12 (2017)
4. Ølnes, S., Ubacht, J., Janssen, M.: Blockchain in government: benefits and implications of distributed ledger technology for information sharing (2017)
5. Snellen, I.T.M., van de Donk, W.B.H.J.: Public Administration in an Information Age: A Handbook, vol. 6. IOS Press (1998)
6. Kirkman, G., Cornelius, P., Sachs, J., Schwab, K.: The Global Information Technology Report 2001–2002. New York: Oxford, vol. 4 (2002)
7. Lazuashvili, N.: Integration of the blockchain technology into the land registration system. A case study of georgia. Master's thesis, Tallinn University of Technology, Ehitajate tee 5, 19086 Tallinn (2019). https://doi.org/10.13140/RG.2.2.35689.13920/1
8. Alketbi, A., Nasir, Q., Talib, M.A.: Blockchain for government services—use cases, security benefits and challenges. In: 2018 15th Learning and Technology Conference (L&T), pp. 112–119. IEEE (2018)
9. Ølnes, S., Jansen, A.: Blockchain technology as s support infrastructure in e-government. In: Janssen, M., et al. (eds.) EGOV 2017. LNCS, vol. 10428, pp. 215–227. Springer, Cham (2017). https://doi.org/10.1007/978-3-319-64677-0_18
10. Carter, L., Ubacht, J.: Blockchain applications in government. In: Proceedings of the 19th Annual International Conference on Digital Government Research: Governance in the Data Age, p. 126. ACM (2018)

11. Lyons, T., Courcelas, L., Timsit, K.: Blockchain for government and public services. Technical report, European Commission. European Union Blockchain Observatory & Forum, December 2918

12. Ølnes, S.: Beyond bitcoin-public sector innovation using the bitcoin blockchain technology. In: International Conference on Electronic Government and the Information Systems Perspective, pp. 253–264. Springer (2015)

13. Zheng, Z., Xie, S., Dai, H.-N., Chen, X., Wang, H.: Blockchain challenges and opportunities: a survey. Int. J. Web Grid Serv. **14**(4), 352–375 (2018)

14. Sekhari, A., Chatterjee, R., Dwivedi, R., Negi, R., Shukla, S.K.: Entangled blockchains in land registry management

15. Kothari, C.R.: Research Methodology: Methods and Techniques. New Age International (2004)

16. Runeson, P., Höst, M., Rainer, A., Regnell, B.: Case study research in software engineering. In: Guidelines and Examples. Wiley Online Library (2012)

17. Yin, R.K.: Case Study Research and Applications: Design and Methods. Sage Publications, Thousand Oaks (2017)

18. Jarratt, D.G.: A comparison of two alternative interviewing techniques used within an integrated research design: a case study in outshopping using semi-structured and non-directed interviewing techniques. Mark. Intell. Plann. **14**(6), 6–15 (1996)

19. Bowen, G.A.: Document analysis as a qualitative research method. Qual. Res. J. **9**(2), 27–40 (2009)

20. Krusenvik, L.: Using case studies as a scientific method: advantages and disadvantages (2016)

21. Eisenhardt, K.M.: Building theories from case study research. Acad. Manag. Rev. **14**(4), 532–550 (1989)

22. Flyvbjerg, B.: Five misunderstandings about case-study research. Qual. Inq. **12**(2), 219–245 (2006)

A Conceptual Blueprint for Enterprise Architecture Model-Driven Business Process Optimization

Dóra Őri and Zoltán Szabó[(⊠)]

Department of Information Systems, Corvinus University of Budapest,
Fővám tér 8, Budapest 1093, Hungary
{dora.ori,zoltan.szabo}@uni-corvinus.hu

Abstract. Business process management (BPM) is a traditional approach to achieve process excellence, and a key success factor of digitization initiatives. It facilitates strategic alignment by streamlining business processes, and harmonizing business and IT domains. The main goal of this research is to map BPM and enterprise architecture management (EAM), to provide a systematic review of EAM-supported process optimization methods. BPM is focusing on the business architecture layer of EAM frameworks, so EAM can be a major facilitator of BPM lifecycle activities, especially the optimization phase. Our proposed analytical framework can contribute to the evaluation of process architecture, considering the context and dependencies of the process-related models to the components of an information architecture.

Keywords: Business process management ·
Enterprise architecture management · Modelling · Optimization

1 Introduction

Success in digitalization, implementation of disruptive innovations, integrating digital technologies (social media, mobile applications, business analytics and cloud-based services), and effective and fast integration of emerging new business models require a solid base in technology governance and business process management too. Maturity in business process management (BPM) is a key success factor to implement digital strategies and transform the business.

Business process management is a traditional approach that focuses on business operations, seeking for process excellence. BPM integrates several methods and techniques for modelling, analysing, reorganizing, operating and monitoring the processes of an organization. It is an efficient management method that facilitates strategic alignment by streamlining business processes, and harmonizing business and IT domains. BPM ensures flexibility and dynamic fit between external and internal domains. It is a key enabler of harmonization focusing on product/market, strategy, administrative structures, business processes and IT [1]. Although BPM is recognized as a strategic instrument of business revitalization, it is still interpreted simply as modelling business activities and implementing workflows.

C. Di Ciccio et al. (Eds.): BPM 2019 Blockchain and CEE Forum, LNBIP 361, pp. 234–248, 2019.
https://doi.org/10.1007/978-3-030-30429-4_16

As a result of growing complexity in technology and organizational configurations, process innovation is a real challenge; the harmonization of processes, organizational structure and underpinning technology needs considering several factors in a dynamic environment. Enterprise architecture management (EAM) enables technology-related planning, management of implementation, but also maintains a comprehensive model of the organization. This EA model of the organization provides a solid base for the management of complexity and integrates technology and business domain-related details. The goal of this paper is to prepare a conceptual framework that facilitates process improvement and optimization through enterprise architecture model-based analytical opportunities and methods.

The rest of the study is organised as follows: Section 2 describes the most relevant aspects of business process management, focusing on optimization and innovation. Section 3 provides an overview of enterprise architecture management, maps BPM concepts with EAM, and finally presents an EA-based analysis method that can be utilized in business process optimization.

2 Business Process Management Overview

Business process management is a key factor of surviving in the turbulent economic environment. Since the seminal work of Hammer [2, 3], business process reengineering (BPR) has become one of the most popular and successful business movements. As it is widely accepted, reengineering is a radical, IT-driven approach to improve business efficiency. Reengineering has two main approaches: Business Process Redesign is concentrating on streamlining individual processes, while Business Reengineering has a wider focus, its purpose is to rethink and redesign the business as a whole. A less radical, incremental approach is Continual Process Improvement.

Business Process Redesign is considered as "the analysis and design of workflows and processes within and between organisations" [4]. The main features of reengineering are [5]: the creation of customer orientation, the examination of existing value-adding processes (process- and cross-functional orientation), the questioning of outdated organisational principles, the elimination of unnecessary activities, the minimisation of delays between process stages, the reduction of effort-duplications, the improvement in internal communication, the empowerment of the staff, benchmarking, outsourcing and the use of IT as an enabler. Based on a holistic view, Rosemann and Brocke [6] suggest six core elements of BPM: strategic alignment, governance, methods, information technology, people, and culture.

2.1 BPM Life Cycle

Business Process Excellence is the traditional and generally accepted major goal of process management [7]. Key dimensions of a process – time, cost and quality – are always on the focal point of business initiatives; matured process management can be a strategic asset for the organization. BPM is also an appropriate tool to efficiently support the day-to-day operations in an organization, as regulations, roles and responsibilities are clearly defined in process models, that can be interpreted in an easy-to-use form for the relevant staff. Process-oriented measurement – monitoring of process performance and reporting of process KPIs – is a common practice that enables the smooth operation of many huge organizations. BPM is a complex and comprehensive approach, its scope covers strategy, organizational structure, supporting technology, skills and knowledge. The lifecycle of BPM has several phases [8], covering all aspects of process-related tasks necessary for achieving process excellence [7]:

- Business process strategy, that defines the strategic goals and prepare a process portfolio
- Process documentation, that prepares the process models and collect relevant information
- Process analysis and design, that investigates process-related problems (cycle time, cost, quality, etc.), and optimises the process, defining an integrated system of the process, organization and technology
- Implementation and change management, that ensure the realization of plans, IT projects and organizational changes
- Process operation, that maintains an appropriate organizational environment for the utilization of processes
- Process controlling/monitoring, that collects process-related KPIs and provides a feedback mechanism for further development.

BPM is a radical change program, integrating radical top-down initiatives with a set of continuous efforts towards process excellence. Within the overall framework of BPM lifecycle model, process analysis and design is the most challenging phase, that should aim at optimizing processes according to business needs and strategy.

2.2 Knowledge and Semantic Aspects of BPM

Maddern et al. [9] discusses the importance of a holistic approach, the end-to-end process management, and presents BPM-related symptoms of fragmentation in modelling, optimization. They reported that the ongoing maintenance of a process infrastructure is a very challenging task for organizations. End-to-end process management raises the question of complexity, especially in the case of inter-organizational processes.

The necessity of the fusion between knowledge and process management is a recognized issue and challenge in the literature [10]. Semantic Business Process Management (SBPM) is a new approach that can increases the level of automation in the translation between business and IT domains [11]. A major challenge in BPM is the management of the knowledge, related to the process portfolio. The distributed nature of knowledge represented in numerous information systems makes integration even more challenging. Lin and Krogstie [12] presents a framework for semantic annotation of processes to avoid the problem of the heterogeneity of distributed process models to facilitate the management of process knowledge.

BPM is a well-established method and technology for many companies, but the extension of modelling towards automated application generation, extended functionality, and integration with other technologies (interoperability) are still major trends in R&D. Recently, the focus of BPM activities is on the implementation phase: process modelling is a tool that has to support (semi-) automatic IT development [13]. The extension towards performance measurement, knowledge-based applications, and compliance check [14, 15], etc. are also promising directions.

Semantic technologies have been integrated to BPM in the last decades to facilitate automated utilization of process models for the development of applications. Semantic description (machine processable representation) of processes can bridge the gap between the business logic and the IT perspective [11]. Semantic annotation of the models also enhances the services built on process models. SBPM integrates BPM methodologies and tools with Semantic Web Services frameworks and ontology representation [16]. Management of the knowledge dimension of business processes is a recognized problem, many initiatives purpose ontology-based semantics, even fuzzy ontology to manage organizational knowledge [17].

2.3   Optimization in BPM

In Business Process Management, we consider optimization as the fundamental rethinking of business processes to achieve substantial improvements, which are then reflected in the critical performance variables of time (speed), costs, quality, service/customer satisfaction. Business process optimization initiatives reduce lead (cycle) time, decrease cost, improve quality of products/services, and enhance customer satisfaction, to sustain the competitive advantage of the company. Optimization of processes in the above-presented dimensions is based on several methods. Some of them are based on experiences and management techniques, like brainstorming, others use formal methods, like simulation. In this context we have to distinguish between business-oriented optimization (in the sense of innovation) and formal (mathematical) optimization.

There are several process modelling techniques that capture and address different aspects of a business process, emphasizing that only a limited number of these process modelling approaches allow extensive quantitative analysis, and only a few are appropriate for more complex, structured process improvements [18].

Traditionally, process improvement is based on relatively simple techniques, like observation, workshops and high-level KPI-based evaluation methods (performance analysis) to identify nonvalue-added activities, redundancy, rework, and bottlenecks. To eliminate these problems, the typical approaches are the simplification or combination of activities, and the parallel/concurrent execution of synchronized tasks. Process models and process controlling-based data are major facilitator of the optimization, but it is still a trial and error-based approach. There are opinions that the analysis and improvement of the process is not transparent, there is no formal underpinning methodology to ensure the logical consistency [18].

Grant [19] investigates the available business analysis techniques (problem analysis, root cause analysis, duration analysis, activity-based costing, outcome analysis, technology analysis, business process analysis and activity elimination), and concluded that complexity of process innovation requires a variation of multiple techniques to diagnose problems. Tsakalidis and Vergidis [20] argue that Evolutionary Computing (EC) techniques can effectively support multi-criteria optimization (optimization based on multiple evaluation criteria). Multi-criteria optimization is necessary to avoid discrepancies between the key dimensions and requires holistic frameworks, and potentially evolutionary approaches.

There are new, more formal emerging methods, that concentrate on the performance (behaviour) of the processes. Process mining is an analytical approach to discover, monitor, and improve processes. It is based on data mining techniques (classification, clustering, regression, association rule learning, etc.) using event data [21]. Process mining can also be used for the automatic discovery of process-related information [22]. Process simulation facilitates process diagnosis and optimization too. Simulation is an effective approach when scenarios of proposed changes should be evaluated to determine the optimal set of changes, using sensitivity analysis of modifications in process activities, resource usage, schedules, etc., to achieve performance improvements in throughput, costs, cycle times, and resource utilization [23].

3   Enterprise Architecture Management and BPM

3.1   Overview of EAM

Architecture is regarded as the fundamental structure of a system, including its components and their relationships. It is a formal description which also shows the main architectural principles and guidelines that facilitate the construction and operation of the system. In this respect, enterprise architecture (EA) is the construction of an enterprise, described by its entities and their relationships. EA is an organising logic for business processes and IT infrastructure in order to review, maintain and control the whole operation of an enterprise. This organising logic acts as an integrating force between business planning, business operations and enabling technological infrastructure. Enterprise architecture integrates information systems and business processes into a coherent map. Enterprise architecture supports IT strategy, IT governance and business-IT alignment [24]. It also helps to capture a vision of the entire system in all its dimensions and complexity [25]. Enterprise architecture is a structure which helps, (1) coordinate the many facets that make up the fundamental essence of an enterprise and (2) provide a structure for business processes and supportive information systems [25].

Enterprise architecture management provides instruments to build and maintain enterprise architectures. The management of enterprise architecture results in increased transparency, documented architecture vision and clear architecture principles and guidelines. These factors contribute to efficient resource allocation, the creation of synergies, better alignment, and reduced complexity. In the end, better business performance can be achieved by using the EAM concept. EAM promotes the vertical integration between strategic directions and tactical concepts, design decisions, and operations. Additionally, it provides horizontal alignment between business change and technology. In addition, EAM improves the capability of an enterprise for perceiving, analysing and responding to organisational changes. It helps (1) to align the organisation with strategic goals, (2) to coordinate interdependencies in business and IT, (3) to prepare an organisation for an agile reaction. EAM plays a role in strategy formulation as well. Strategic EAM helps (1) to analyse the current situation, (2) assess strategic options, (3) formulate strategic initiatives, (4) develop an architectural vision, (5) roadmap migration activities, (6) assess and prioritise project portfolio and (7) monitor architecture evolution [26, 27].

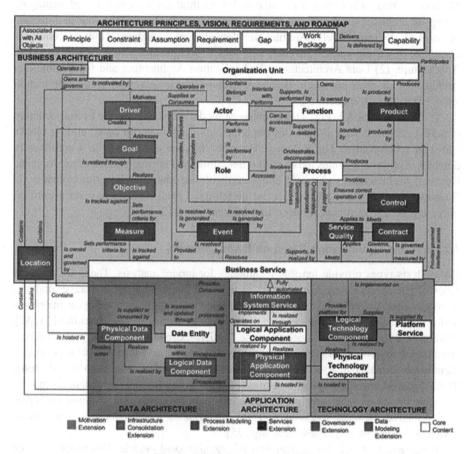

Fig. 1. TOGAF metamodel [23]

In order to cope with architecture complexity, different frameworks, methods, and tools have been developed. An enterprise architecture framework is a collection of descriptions and methods to create and manage enterprise architecture. The most recognised frameworks are the Zachman Framework [24], for rather theoretical purposes, and the TOGAF framework [25], for rather practical usage. While the Zachman Framework is defined as a taxonomy for organising architectural elements, TOGAF is a process-oriented EA framework which breaks an EA into different EA layers.

TOGAF (The Open Group Architecture Framework) is a commonly used architecture framework. It is a holistic approach which describes a metamodel for enterprise architecture and proposes different methods for building and maintaining enterprise architectures. The framework has four main components, (1) Architecture Capability

Framework, (2) Architecture Development Method (ADM), (3) Architecture Domains and (4) Enterprise Continuum. The latter consists of different reference models (e.g. Technical Reference Model, Standards Information Base, The Building Blocks Information Base). The core of the TOGAF approach is the Architecture Development Method (ADM), which proposes an iterative method for developing and managing enterprise architecture. It consists of 10 phases. Phase B-D cover the four architecture domains (1–4), respectively. Architecture domains are considered different conceptualisations of an enterprise. TOGAF provides 4 architecture domains: (1) Business Architecture, (2) Data Architecture, (3) Application Architecture and (4) Technology Architecture. In their approach, Business Architecture is served by Data, Application and Technology Architectures.

TOGAF metamodel (Fig. 1) is a reference model which sets up the formal structure of an EA model as well as provides implementation guidance on core building blocks and their relationships. The metamodel depicts the core entities of the 4 architecture domains. Entities are connected to each other within and between architecture domains. Business Architecture is primarily connected with the other 3 architecture domains via Business Service. Business Service is, therefore, a bridge between several entities, refracting the direct routes between the different items [25].

3.2 Process Optimization Based on EAM Concepts

EA analysis types provide feasible techniques for model analysis. There are different types of EA analyses, e.g. dependency analysis, network analysis, coverage analysis, interface analysis, complexity analysis, heterogeneity analysis, enterprise interoperability assessment, enterprise coherence assessment, inconsistency checking [28–30]. Frameworks for EA analysis include some TOGAF-based techniques, e.g. architecture compliance review, architecture governance assessment, architecture maturity assessment or performance analysis [25, 27]. Sources for EA analysis may also include some TOGAF-based approaches, e.g. consolidated gaps, solutions and dependencies matrix, EA state evolution table, business interaction matrix, information systems interoperability matrix, business footprint diagram, governance log, architecture compliance review log and maturity assessment log [25].

EA assessment includes an overview of organisational models. This process can be approached in two influential ways. On the one hand, architecture domains can be reviewed using, e.g. the architecture landscape technique or other architecture overview methods. On the other hand, alignment of business and technology domains can be reviewed on an EA basis.

The approach of architecture domain overview includes (1) perspectives of the architecture landscapes (e.g. views, viewpoints and different reference models, TOGAF artefact-based overview, artefact chains, in-layer and between-layer artefact groups, architecture domain building blocks), (2) different architecture overview methods (e.g. portfolio analysis, domain analysis, change impact analysis, landscape management, blueprint management) [26, 27, 31–33] and (3) supportive concepts for architecture overview (e.g. EA model entity relationships, EA measurement items, architecture principles or architecture patterns) [27, 34, 35].

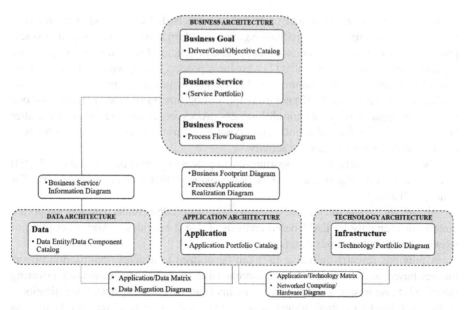

Fig. 2. A collection of EA models for inter-domain architecture comparison

A feasible approach for an EA-based process optimization overview is to connect the process management concepts with TOGAF artefacts [25]. In this approach, TOGAF artefacts are attached to corresponding BPM domains. In the proposed framework this kind of EA-based description of BPM domain will be used. Figure 2 presents specific artefacts feasible for detecting process-related issues in enterprise architecture context.

To translate the above introduced methodology into a BPM-based approach, we need the following concepts:

- BPM optimization dimension: this list contains the corresponding optimization categories for opportunity detection.
- Process-related problem catalog: this list comprises the perceived/potential process-related issues, under-utilized opportunities or actual errors.
- Artifact catalog: this list encompasses the possible containing EA models for process related problems.
- EA analysis catalog: This list includes the possible EA analysis types to recommend for opportunity detection.
- Presence in the artefact: This concept describes the sign of the process-related issue in the EA models.
- Occurrence on model entity level: This concept defines how the process-related issue is manifested on model entity level.
- Occurrence in XML model export: This item describes how the process-related issue is manifested in the XML export of the EA model.

Process-related problems and optimization aspects that can be explored in enterprise architecture environment include e.g. undefined organisational goals and business process goals in business process models, lack of relation between process goals and organisational goals, the signs that (1) a business process is supported by more than the minimum number of applications, (2) business activities are supported by multiple applications - unnecessarily, (3) not each application functionality supports at least one business process activity, (4) not all business processes activity create, update and/or delete at least one information entity, or (5) not all information entity attributes are read by at least one business process activity.

The list of potential issues/opportunities in process optimization (based on [7, 36]) is mapped to EA-related components and situations that can be described by EA concepts (Table 1):

All of the above-mentioned optimization aspects/potentials can be supported directly or indirectly by EAM-based analysis. Table 2 provides a short description of relevant analytical methods (artefacts).

A previous research initiative [37] can be utilized to analyse optimization opportunities based on EA models. The comprehensive model of an organization covering information and business architecture domains is an ideal base to detect organizational problems related to organizational design. The analysis method transforms process management-related concepts into formalized rules that are appropriate for testing on relevant EA models. Process-related issues, problems and opportunities are translated (mapped) to combination of EA artefacts, which potentially contain the symptoms of the non-optimized situation. The test assessment technique is suitable for detecting these symptoms by analysing EA models, discovering existing or missing relationships, linkages between the process-related objects of the EA models. The formal implementation of the analysis method is based on rule construction and testing techniques and assesses the XML export of the EA models with XML validation techniques, using the Schematron assertion query language [38].

As the above-mentioned examples illustrated, process-related issues can be detected within EA scope, as process optimization areas encompass and overarch the TOGAF architecture domains. Optimization potentials can be explored by EA artefacts and EAM-based analysis types, and the presented rule-based research initiative can be applied to business process-related issues as well (Table 3).

The analytical potential of enterprise architecture concept forms a feasible and comprehensive basis for assisting business process optimization. The mapping of potential process issues/opportunities and related EA components and situations can be extended, as well as further EA-based business process optimization areas can be translated into executable rules.

Table 1. Optimization opportunities and EAM-related components

Optimization aspects/opportunity	Related EAM models/opportunities
Optimization potential in the organisation: - Clear organizational structures - Competence & transparency - Expertise & responsibility - Integrated perception of tasks - Optimized use of resources - Decentralization vs. centralization	Analysis of business architecture components to discover: - Undefined organizational strategy and organizational goals - Undefined business process goals - Lack of relation between process goals and organizational goals - Multiple hierarchy or lines of reporting
Optimization potential in data - High data quality - Up-to-datedness & uniformity - Completeness & accuracy - No data redundancy - Integration of data records for everyone involved in process - Up to date/fast availability of information - Reduction of documents to be kept manually	Analysis of dependencies between business architecture and data architecture components to discover: - Lack of data ownership - Undefined security requirements over the information entities - Lack of data quality controls
Optimization potential in activities - Analysis of critical tasks - Analysis of standardization of tasks - Increase in IT support - Reduction of functions that create no value - Reduction of response costs	Analysis of business architecture components to discover: - Standardization problems - Non-value adding activities - Lack of IT support in process activities
Optimization potential in IT - Unification, modernization, and standardization of applications and PC tools - Integration of operational applications - Uniform user interface - Comprehensive linking of transactions - Comprehensive transfer of data due to common database - Plausibility checks for complete processing of all necessary activities - Determination of statistical key performance indicators for processes (wait times/processing times) - Improved know-how transfer to operational departments involved	Analysis of dependencies between business architecture and application architecture components to discover: - Undefined security requirements over the information entities - Users managed differently in different applications - Undefined capacity and performance requirements - Lack of application interfaces - Multiple applications managing the same information
Optimization potential in products and services - Critical product analysis - Comparison of product portfolio with core competences - Analysis of range of services - Outsourcing	Analysis of business architecture components to discover: - Potential synergies between products

(continued)

Table 1. (*continued*)

Optimization aspects/opportunity	Related EAM models/opportunities
Optimization potential in processes - Elimination of organizational interfaces - Elimination of media interfaces - Reduction of throughput times - Short control loops - Shorter decision-making paths - Forward shift in responsibilities - Increase in process quality - Automatic control functions - Automatic information forwarding/processing	Analysis of business architecture components combined with external data (e.g. process mining results) to discover: - Non value-adding activities - Control loops - Quality problems - Manual activities

Table 2. Review of relevant EAM artefacts

Artefact	Brief content
Driver/Goal/Objective catalogue	A breakdown of drivers, goals, and objectives to provide a cross-organisational reference of driver fulfilment
Process flow diagram	A model to show sequential flow of tasks within a business process
Data entity/Data component catalogue	A list of all the data used across the enterprise, incl. data entities & components
Application portfolio catalogue	A catalogue to identify and maintain all the applications in the organisation
Technology portfolio catalogue	A catalogue to identify and maintain all the technology across the organisation
Business footprint diagram	A mapping of business goals, organisational units, business functions, business services, and delivering technical components
Process/Application realisation diagram	A diagram to depict the sequence of events when multiple applications are involved in executing a business process
Data migration diagram	A diagram that displays the flow of data from the source to the target applications
Application/Technology matrix	A mapping of applications to technology platform
Business service/Information diagram	Shows the information needed to support one or more business services
Data dissemination diagram	Shows the relationship between data entity, business service, and application components
Application/Data matrix	Depicts the relationship between applications (i.e., application components) and the data entities that are accessed and updated by them
Networked computing/Hardware diagram	Documents the mapping between logical applications and the technology components (e.g., server) that support the application both in the development and production environments

Table 3. Detection of a process management problem in the EA scope

Aspect	Process management related problem
Symptom Definition	*Not all data entities attributes are read at least by one process*
Suitable EA Analysis to detect the process management problem	- Dependency analysis - Coverage analysis
Occurance, Presence in EA Model	By scanning data usage in business process models, there are data entities that are not used by any business process task
Containing EA Model	- Process Flow Diagram - Data Entity/Data Component Catalogue - Data Entity/Business Function Matrix
Occurance on Model Entity Level	There are data entities from the data entity catalogue that are not present on any business process model
Occurance in XML-based EA Model Export	Comparison of business process models and data entity catalogue in terms of data entities
Occurance on Model Entity Level in XML Export	Comparison of elements between Node type: data entity in the business process model and Node type: data entity in the data entity catalogue
XML-based Query	For every node where node type = data entity: • Compare the attribute names with the data entity attribute names from process flow diagram • Alert data entity nodes if they are not present in the process flow
Query in Schematron Language	<pattern name="Not all data entities attributes are read at least by one process"> <rule context="Object Definition [@Node Type='*{data entity}*']"> <assert test="Attribute Definition [@AttributeDefinition.Type= '*{attribute name}*']//PlainText[@TextValue=document ('process flow diagram.xml')//Object Definition[@Node Type='*{data entity}*']//Attribute Definition [@AttributeDefinition.Type='*{attribute name}*']//PlainText//@TextValue]"> Alert: </assert> </rule> </pattern>

4 Conclusion

The outlined approach described in this paper provides the opportunity to make use of formal EAM-based analytical methods for discovering optimization opportunities in business architecture, analysing dependencies and relationships within process architecture models, and also between business architecture and information architecture components (existing information systems, data, and technology). EAM models cover the core aspects (dimensions) of an organization, providing solid base for comprehensive, multi-dimensional analysis. Business processes are immanent components of an EA, and the integrity, coherence, and consistency of business architecture with the other elements of the enterprise architecture is critical. A rule-based analysis approach can be a formal diagnostic tool to discover subjects for improvement. EAM contains a formal and comprehensive representation of organizational resources, and all components should fit to the overall architecture. The proposed approach offers a formal way of checking and controlling the discrepancies in a complex enterprise architecture model base. The major limitation of the approach rooted in the quality and the coverage of the available models – in many companies there are several, domain specific, isolated models. This issue can be sorted out: the rule-based testing approach provides great flexibility by integrating heterogeneous model environments in the analysis.

There are many open questions in the application of the EAM-based analytical methods. As part of future work translation of process related problems into testable rules, integration of the approach to the other formal methods of BPM are in the focus, and the framework needs further adjustments in terms of automation and analytic potential.

Acknowledgement. The publication was prepared within the Széchenyi 2020 program framework (EFOP-3.6.1-16-2016-00013) under the European Union project titled: "Institutional developments for intelligent specialization at the Székesfehérvár Campus of Corvinus University of Budapest".

References

1. Henderson, J.C., Venkatraman, N.: Strategic alignment: leveraging information technology for transforming organisations. IBM Syst. J. **32**(1), 4–16 (1993)
2. Hammer, M., Champy, J.: Reengineering the Corporation: A Manifesto for Business Revolution. HarperBusiness, New York (1993)
3. Hammer, M.: Reengineering work: don't automate, obliterate. Harv. Bus. Rev. **68**(4), 104–112 (1990)
4. Davenport, T.H., Short, J.E.: The new industrial engineering: information technology and business process redesign. Sloan Manag. Rev. **31**, 11–27 (1990)
5. Talvar, R.: Business re-engineering – a strategy-driven approach. Long Range Plan. **26**(6), 22–40 (1993)
6. Rosemann, M., vom Brocke, J.: The six core elements of business process management. In: vom Brocke, J., Rosemann, M. (eds.) Handbook on Business Process Management 1. IHIS, pp. 105–122. Springer, Heidelberg (2015). https://doi.org/10.1007/978-3-642-45100-3_5
7. Scheer, A.-W., Abolhassan, F., Jost, W., Kirchmer, M.: Business Process Excellence - ARIS in Practice. Springer, Heidelberg (2002). https://doi.org/10.1007/978-3-540-24705-0
8. Dumas, M., La Rosa, M., Mendling, J., Reijers, H.A.: Fundamentals of Business Process Management, vol. 1, p. 2. Springer, Heidelberg (2013)
9. Maddern, H., Smart, P.A., Maull, R.S., Childe, S.: End-to-end process management: implications for theory and practice. Prod. Plann. Control Manag. Oper. **25**(16), 1303–1321 (2014). https://doi.org/10.1080/09537287.2013.832821
10. Records, L.R.: The fusion of process and knowledge management. BPTrends (2005). (http://www.bptrends.com/publicationfiles/09-05%20WP%20Fusion%20Process%20KM%20-%20Records.pdf). Accessed July 2015

11. Hepp, M., Leymann, F., Domingue, J., Wahler, A., Fensel, D.: Semantic business process management: a vision towards using semantic web services for business process management. In: IEEE International Conference on e-Business Engineering, ICEBE 2005, pp. 535–540, 12–18 October 2005 (2005). https://doi.org/10.1109/icebe.2005.110
12. Lin, Y., Krogstie, J.: Semantic annotation of process models for facilitating process knowledge management. Int. J. Inf. Syst. Model. Des. 1(3), 45–67 (2010). https://doi.org/10.4018/jismd.2010070103
13. Ternai, K., Török, M.: Semantic modeling for automated workflow software generation – an open model. In: 5th International Conference on Software, Knowledge Information, Industrial Management and Applications (SKIMA 2011), Benevento, Italy, 8–11 September (2011)
14. Namiri, K., Stojanovic., N.: A formal approach for internal controls compliance in business processes. In: 8th Workshop on Business Process Modeling, Development, and Support (BPMDS07), Trondheim, Norway (2007)
15. Ternai, K., Szabó, I., Varga, K.: Ontology-based compliance checking on higher education processes. In: Kő, A., Leitner, C., Leitold, H., Prosser, A. (eds.) EGOVIS/EDEM 2013. LNCS, vol. 8061, pp. 58–71. Springer, Heidelberg (2013). https://doi.org/10.1007/978-3-642-40160-2_6
16. Karastoyanova, D., et al.: A reference architecture for semantic business process management systems. In: Multi konferenz Wirtschaftsinformatik GITO-Verlag, Berlin (2008)
17. Alexopoulos, P., Gómez-Pérez, J.M.: Dealing with vagueness in semantic business process management through fuzzy ontologies. In: Proceedings of the 7th International Workshop on Semantic Business Process Management, Heraclion, Greece, 27–31 May 2012 (2012). (http://sbpm2012.fzi.de/images/SBPMp4.pdf)
18. Vergidis, K., Tiwari, A., Majeed, B.: Business process analysis and optimization: beyond reengineering. IEEE Trans. Syst. Man Cybern. Part C (Appl. Rev.) 38(1), 69–82 (2008)
19. Grant, D.: Business analysis techniques in business reengineering. Bus. Process Manag. J. 22 (1), 75–88 (2016)
20. Tsakalidis, G., Vergidis, K.: Towards a comprehensive business process optimization framework. In: 2017 IEEE 19th Conference on Business Informatics (CBI), Thessaloniki, 2017, pp. 129–134 (2017). http://ieeexplore.ieee.org/stamp/stamp.jsp?tp=&arnumber=8010714&isnumber=8010609
21. Aalst, W.M.: Process mining: overview and opportunities. ACM Trans. Manag. Inf. Syst. 3, 7:1–7:17 (2012)
22. Alves de Medeiros, A.K., van der Aalst, W.M.P.: Process mining towards semantics. In: Dillon, T.S., Chang, E., Meersman, R., Sycara, K. (eds.) Advances in Web Semantics I. LNCS, vol. 4891, pp. 35–80. Springer, Heidelberg (2008). https://doi.org/10.1007/978-3-540-89784-2_3
23. Fu, M.C., Glover, F.W., April, J.: Simulation optimization: a review, new developments, and applications. In: Proceedings of the Winter Simulation Conference 2005, Orlando, FL, p. 13 (2005)
24. Zachman, J.A.: A framework for information systems architecture. IBM Syst. J. 26(3), 276–292 (1987). https://doi.org/10.1147/sj.263.0276
25. TOG: The Open Group: TOGAF Version 9. The Open Group Architecture Framework (TOGAF) (2015). http://theopengroup.org/. Accessed 21 Jan 2015
26. Ahlemann, F., Stettiner, E., Messerschmidt, M., Legner, C.: Strategic Enterprise Architecture Management: Challenges, Best Practices, and Future Developments. Springer, Heidelberg (2012). https://doi.org/10.1007/978-3-642-24223-6

27. Lankhorst, M.: Enterprise Architecture at Work. Modelling, Communication and Analysis. Springer, Heidelberg (2013). https://doi.org/10.1007/978-3-642-29651-2
28. Buckl, S., Matthes, F., Schweda, C.M.: Classifying enterprise architecture analysis approaches. In: Poler, R., van Sinderen, M., Sanchis, R. (eds.) IWEI 2009. LNBIP, vol. 38, pp. 66–79. Springer, Heidelberg (2009). https://doi.org/10.1007/978-3-642-04750-3_6
29. Niemann, K.D.: From Enterprise Architecture to IT Governance. Elements of Effective IT Management. Friedr. Vieweg & Sohn Verlag, Wiesbaden (2006)
30. Wagter, R., Proper, H.A.(Erik), Witte, D.: A practice-based framework for enterprise coherence. In: Proper, E., Gaaloul, K., Harmsen, F., Wrycza, S. (eds.) PRET 2012. LNBIP, vol. 120, pp. 77–95. Springer, Heidelberg (2012). https://doi.org/10.1007/978-3-642-31134-5_4
31. Sunkle, S., Kholkar, D., Kulkarni, V.: Solving semantic disparity and explanation problems in regulatory compliance- a research-in-progress report with design science research perspective. In: Gaaloul, K., Schmidt, R., Nurcan, S., Guerreiro, S., Ma, Q. (eds.) CAISE 2015. LNBIP, vol. 214, pp. 326–341. Springer, Cham (2015). https://doi.org/10.1007/978-3-319-19237-6_21
32. van der Linden, D.J.T., Hoppenbrouwers, S.J.B.A., Lartseva, A., Proper, H.A.(Erik): Towards an investigation of the conceptual landscape of enterprise architecture. In: Halpin, T., et al. (eds.) BPMDS/EMMSAD -2011. LNBIP, vol. 81, pp. 526–535. Springer, Heidelberg (2011). https://doi.org/10.1007/978-3-642-21759-3_38
33. Simon, D., Fischbach, K.: IT landscape management using network analysis. In: Poels, G. (ed.) CONFENIS 2012. LNBIP, vol. 139, pp. 18–34. Springer, Heidelberg (2013). https://doi.org/10.1007/978-3-642-36611-6_2
34. Aier, S., Winter, R.: Virtual decoupling for IT/Business alignment – conceptual foundations, architecture design and implementation example. Bus. Inf. Syst. Eng. **2009**(2), 150–163 (2009). https://doi.org/10.1007/s12599-008-0010-7
35. Hoogervorst, J.A.: Enterprise Governance and Enterprise Engineering. Springer, Heidelberg (2009). https://doi.org/10.1007/978-3-540-92671-9
36. Dumas, M., La Rosa, M., Mendling, J., Reijers, H.A.: Process redesign. In: Dumas, M., La Rosa, M., Mendling, J., Reijers, H.A. (eds.) Fundamentals of Business Process Management, pp. 297–339. Springer, Heidelberg (2018). https://doi.org/10.1007/978-3-662-56509-4_8
37. Őri, D.: On exposing strategic and structural mismatches between business and information systems: misalignment symptom detection based on enterprise architecture model analysis. Ph.D. thesis. Corvinus University of Budapest, May 2017
38. Őri, D., Szabó, Z.: Pattern-based analysis of business-IT mismatches in EA models: insights from a case study. In: Hallé, S., Dijkman, R., Lapalme, J. (eds.) Proceedings of the 2017 IEEE 21st International Enterprise Distributed Object Computing Conference Workshops and Demonstrations (EDOCW 2017), pp. 92–99 (2017)

Individual Process Orientation as a Two-Dimensional Construct: Conceptualization and Measurement Scale Development

Monika Klun[1(✉)] and Michael Leyer[2,3]

[1] University of Ljubljana, Ljubljana, Slovenia
monika.klun@ef.uni-lj.si
[2] University of Rostock, Rostock, Germany
michael.leyer@uni-rostock.de
[3] Queensland University of Technology, Brisbane, Australia

Abstract. Organizations continuously aim for improved business performance through a process-oriented transformation. Such a transformation, however, is not limited only to the organizational level, but permeates the individual level as well. Research so far has not investigated the role of employees' behavior and thinking, as individual process-orientation remains under-researched. A first step in this regard, is the clarification of the main construct of interest. Hence, the goal of this paper is to provide deeper insights into the construct of process orientation at the individual level. The paper proposes a two-dimensional conceptualization of individual process orientation that distinguishes between process-oriented thinking and process-oriented behavior. Drawing on this conceptualization, the paper provides a four-stage approach to developing a scale for measuring individual process orientation.

Keywords: Individual process orientation · Measurement scale · Process-oriented thinking · Process-oriented behavior

1 Introduction

Several papers have discussed how the advantages of process-oriented organizations in terms of market competition and business performance aid them in outperforming function-oriented ones [1–3]. They are proposedly more equipped to change during market shifts, focus more on customer needs and deliver high-quality output faster [1, 4, 5]. However, such benefits are only achievable when process-oriented thinking and behavior are established among employees [6]. Nevertheless, literature on process orientation at the individual level remains remarkably scarce [7].

In a first attempt, Leyer, Hirzel and Moormann [7] discuss individual process orientation (IPO) of employees as the way of thinking and behavior of individual employees regarding their daily work activities within the organization. Their literature review has found the concept of process orientation at the individual level strongly under-researched [7] and lacking operationalization. Some exceptions to that are a

© Springer Nature Switzerland AG 2019
C. Di Ciccio et al. (Eds.): BPM 2019 Blockchain and CEE Forum, LNBIP 361, pp. 249–263, 2019.
https://doi.org/10.1007/978-3-030-30429-4_17

limited stream of research that measured process-oriented thinking for the purpose of identifying adequate learning modes. Among these papers, Leyer and Wollersheim [8] and Wollersheim, Leyer and Spörrle [9] describe a measurement based on activities, roles and goals in a process while Leyer, Moormann and Wang [10] extend this view by including the understanding of individuals regarding process orientation on an organizational level.

Another stream of research focusses on researching individual process-oriented behavior [1, 7, 11, 12], which is focused on exploring the aspect of IPO that is observable to companies. These papers incorporate facets such as knowledge, coordination and awareness, contributing to a multifaceted conceptualization of process-oriented behavior. However, some overlap with facets of process-oriented thinking, indication an established link between process-oriented thinking and behavior on an individual level. What remains missing are a theoretical foundation, subsequent conceptualization and a refined measurement scale, to distinguishing between measuring process-oriented behavior and process-oriented thinking.

Several managerial approaches, such as Business Process Management (BPM), discuss the importance of individuals in changing business processes and organizations becoming process-oriented. People are regarded as a core element of BPM [13] and [2] addresses the importance of employees' focus on business processes, however none of these aspects include the individual's perspective, rather they denote them as a group of stakeholders as seen from an organizational level. Similarly, culture also refers to a plurality of individuals, making up a distinct group (e.g. organization, department), indicating a person can hold numerous cultural identities simultaneously [14, 15]. On the other hand, exploring process orientation from the perspective of an individual differs immensely from looking at how an organization thinks and behaves in terms of process-orientation.

Based on this background, we raise the following research questions: (1) How is IPO conceptualized and (2) how can a measurement instrument be operationalized. In answering the research question, we adopt an individual's perspective and propose the two-dimensionality of the process orientation construct, which can be based theoretically in cognitive psychology theory [16–21]. Individuals form a mental model regarding the idea of process orientation (representation of process-oriented thinking) which can then lead to the decision to act in a process-oriented way (process-oriented behavior). Hence, this paper describes the underlying theory and explores existing conceptualizations for IPO. Based on this foundation, we describe IPO as a two-dimensional construct. Finally, we develop the measurement scale to provide empirical evidence for the theoretical underpinnings.

The paper is structured as follows. Section 2 describes the theoretical foundation of our research focus. Section 3 introduces the literature review and resulting conceptualization while Sect. 4 presents the methodology section with the scale measurement operationalization stages. Section 5 provides a description of the results. In Sect. 6 we provide the conclusion and future research possibilities.

2 Theoretical Background

2.1 Process Orientation on the Individual Level

Described as a multidimensional construct, process orientation contains both tangible and intangible elements [22, 23]. According to Leyer, Hirzel and Moormann [7] organizational structure, task description, and goal setting represent the tangible elements, while customer focus, process improvement, and personal responsibility represent the intangible elements. Identifying these elements allows for an identification of process orientation on both the organizational and the individual level [12].

On an organizational level, process orientation requires employees to be organized along processes, the placement of process owners, and minimal interfaces between employees and customers [24–26]. Employees should have an understanding of their role in a process they are working in from beginning to end [12, 27]. It is important that employees coordinate with all who are involved in their processes, and that they are allowed a certain degree of freedom in process execution [26]. Organizational goals should be clearly aligned with the processes along with being linked to personal goals [28, 29]. As suggested by Kohlbacher and Gruenwald [30] an important dimension in achieving process orientation is the formation of a "corporate culture in line with the process approach". However, such broad claims can lead to generic statements like the importance of "proper organizational culture" which leads to "I do not know what the question is but I know that top management support and organizational culture is the answer." type of conclusions [31]. Thus, we need a more precise investigation of IPO.

On an individual level, Leyer, Hirzel and Moormann [7] IPO represents an individual's "execution of the daily working routine". Existing studies that have discussed IPO, focus predominantly on a more general notion of IPO [7, 11, 12] and the process-oriented behavior of individuals. Because of the limited research on process orientation at the individual level, there is an important conceptual limitation associated with the extant literature. Additionally, there are no established scales for measuring IPO, apart from Leyer, Hirzel and Moormann [7], measuring the change of process-oriented behavior of employees.

2.2 Cognitive Psychological Theory

The underlying theory of our IPO conceptualization is within the field of cognitive psychological theory which focusses on the mental processes that affect behavior [17]. A major concept of cognition is the mental representation of an individual's environment termed as mental model. The relationship between a mental model/mental representation and observable behavior is a result of subsequent decisions [21, 32–34]. A mental model describes a subjectively perceived representation of the cause-and-effect relation of several factors [35]. It is one's subjective view on an observed system of relations and it can be used by a person being involved in such a system to take actions [21].

In the context of IPO, the mental model relates to the way of an individual's thinking. Process-oriented thinking means that individual employees have an understanding that activities should be designed and executed from the perspective of processes rather than functions. It means linking the different activities mentally in a broader picture to a mental model in which an individual connects the activities and employees from a process perspective.

This way of thinking influences the observed behavior, i.e., how one decides individually to behave when executing activities. The underlying mechanism is supported by sense-making as a cognitive process, i.e., whether one is seeing a sense in translating process-oriented thinking in process-oriented behavior. The sense-making perspective as our relevant theory within cognitive psychology specifies that their answer determines how they will engage in that situation [34]. In order for individuals to be able to function in the world in a rational manner, they draw a meaning or a sense from a situation [36]. Sense-making can thus be considered a "primary generator of individual action" [37]. One can find different interpretations of "individuals' meanings"; labeled by some as frames [38], cognitive maps [39], schemata [40] or enactments [41]. Regardless of the terminology, the commonalities include three steps; an individual developing his internal map of events, actions and consequences that are guided by a subjective cause-and-effect interpretation; placing himself within this map; and taking distinct steps (action), based on this map as guideline for the unfolding of events [37]. As such process-oriented thinking translates into process-oriented behavior (Fig. 1) in the sense that individuals interpret their reasoning or sense-making into determined and intended behavior.

Fig. 1. Two-dimensionality of IPO from a cognitive psychological perspective

3 Conceptualization of IPO

3.1 Procedure of Literature Identification

The starting point of our analysis was an extensive search for the topic keyword combinations in SCOPUS and Web of Science (WOS). The correspondence of keywords was prepared by the authors and additionally assessed (and complemented) by an external researcher to provide objectivity and validity. The keyword combinations include: "indivi*"/"worker*"/"employ*" together with "process orientation"/"process-orien*". In the next step, abstracts of the resulting hits from the two databases were scanned to ensure the relevance of the papers. After excluding unrelated papers, we were left with a total number of seven papers from both databases discussing IPO with this chosen keyword combination.

However, since the goal of the literature review was to identify relevant work on the topic of process orientation at the individual level, we expanded the search and included all the referenced papers featured in the resulting seven papers. Along with the definitions of IPO explicitly defined at the individual level, we also found process orientation defined as an individual-characteristic or activity. For the purpose of the literature review, we explored the various definitions of process orientation that inherently refer to personal or individual abilities or characteristics. Namely, even relatively early mentions of process orientation, e.g. by McCormack and Johnson [42] or Peppard and Fitzgerald [43], denote process orientation as a specific "view" or "thinking" in an organization, therefore denoting an intrinsically individual characteristic. Table 1 features the found descriptions and definitions of process orientation that are explicitly or indirectly referring to process orientation at the individual level.

Table 1. Exemplary description of process-oriented thinking and behavior.

	Description	Paper author(s)
Process-oriented thinking	Achieving process orientation among employee's states as the goal establishing process-oriented behavior, however first they must adopt process-oriented thinking	Leyer, Hirzel and Moormann [7]
	Process orientation by staff is the ability to think in terms of processes and includes knowing one's position in the process value chain, identifying (internal and external) customers and adding to customer value	van Assen [44]
	Process orientation means working and thinking in a cross-functional and customer-oriented way	McCormack [2]
	Without this [process-oriented] mindset, employees cannot visualize the impact of their work	Reijers [45]
Process-oriented behavior	IPO can be deduced from the organizational level and describes the ideas and behaviors of individual employees regarding their daily work activities within such an organizational design	Kettenbohrer, Beimborn and Leyer [12]
	IPO is expressed in the execution of the daily working routine of the employees	Kettenbohrer, Beimborn and Eckhardt [11]
	Process orientation means working and thinking in a cross-functional and customer-oriented way	McCormack [2]
	The individual's process orientation is expressed in the execution of each employee's day-to-day work routine within the process	Leyer, Hirzel and Moormann [7]

3.2 Two-Dimensional Conceptualization of IPO

The results of the literature review showcase a number of individual-level attributes used to describe the notion of process orientation. The manner-based keywords (behave, act) relate to the process-oriented behavior of individuals, which was introduced by [7]. Organizations have long since been aware of the importance of employees in determining the successfulness of any organizational change and have thus paid greater attention to how individuals act at work. Hence, process-oriented behavior is characterized as a "critical success factor" in implementing process orientation at the organizational level [46]. An individual's process-oriented behavior is defined as the behavior of an individual, within the framework of the organization, that emphasizes process and describes their process-focused manner of executing their everyday work tasks [7].

However, observing behavior alone is not enough to understand the orientation of individuals and even change-compliant behavior of employees can be reversed, if the underlying feelings and beliefs of individuals remain unexplored. As Nonaka [47] puts it sustainable behavior change is very difficult to achieve. In order to categorize the definitions of process orientation on the level of individuals, we follow the aspect duality approach by Feldman and Pentland [48] (adapted from Latour [49]) of two mutually constitutive aspects – the ostensive and performative. While Latour [49] and Feldman and Pentland [48] use the terms to describe power and routines respectively, the concepts can also be applied for IPO. The ostensive concept denotes the understandings of individuals that can be embodied as cognitive states and can vary throughout the organization [50]. Moreover, we also identified the term "process-oriented attitude" in the literature review. However, the intended meaning was the same cognitive feature as denoted with the keywords "view" or "thinking" and not what attitude inherently implies, i.e. the favorable or unfavorable opinion of an individual regarding the attitude object. The performative aspect is represented by specific people, at specific times, in specific place [50]. Feldman [51] describes this aspect as "existence in practice", characterizing the realization or execution of an actual performance by individuals. Building on these findings from literature and in line with the cognitive psychological lens, we define IPO as a compilation of two mutually constitutive aspects – the "dispositional" or "innate" process-oriented thinking which leads to the "realized" process-oriented behavior of individuals.

While often mentioned in the literature as the process-oriented mindset, view or thinking of individuals, the attributes denoting an individual's way of thinking about process orientation remain little addressed and at a very general level. Addressing this lack of operationalization of the concept of IPO, we develop a measurement scale in the following to operationalize and validate IPO as a two-dimensional construct.

4   Development of the Measurement Scale

In order to develop a measurement scale, we investigate, operationalize, and validate IPO in four stages. In doing so, we follow the approach of Karpen, Bove, Lukas and Zyphur [52] who describe a profound procedure how to develop an adequate measurement scale.

Preparing an adequate measurement model rests on an underlying theory and subsequent conceptualization. Based on the examination of prior literature, the concept of IPO consists of several components, representing the two different dimensions of the overall construct. Table 2 gives an overview on the steps and empirical sources.

Table 2. Stages of measurement scale development

Measurement scale development stages	Study details
Stage 1: Item selection	Preparing initial pool from qualitative items regarding process orientation Pool of 60 indicators reduced to 49
Stage 2: Item evaluation	Item sorting (16 academics) 2 dimensions and 10 items
Stage 3: Item purification	Item formulation testing Study: 66 participants (employees)
Stage 4: Item validation	Confirmatory factor analysis, discriminant and convergent analyses Study: 368 participants (employees) Control study: 100 participants (employees working in companies with more than 10 employees)

4.1 Stage 1: Item Selection

Existing literature provides several examples of process orientation constructs or dimensions, such as Kohlbacher and Gruenwald [30], Kohlbacher [24], Willaert, Van den Bergh, Willems and Deschoolmeester [23], Reijers [45] and Hammer [53] to name a few. However, since our paper deals with the perspective of individuals not all researched indicators are relevant. The focus of IPO are items representing thinking and behavior in a process-oriented manner, thus all items or indicators reflecting an organization's perspective were excluded from item selection. Additionally, any specific individual-based items depicting a specific role (e.g. process owner existence) or management level (e.g. top management support) were excluded, as there are unsuitable for portraying the perspectives, abilities and actions of individuals across the organization. From the seven process orientation dimensions identified by Kohlbacher and Gruenwald [30] and earlier Kohlbacher [24] only two contained individual-level items; among these were items such as customer-focused attitude of employees, worker's knowledge about process execution and employees' accountability for firm results to name a few. The indicator *customer-focus of employees* captured whether employees are aware of the customers' needs and their role in fulfilling them. The item was adapted from other models by Willaert, Van den Bergh, Willems and Deschool-meester [23], Reijers [45] and Hammer [53], also discussing possible process orientation components. The indicator *worker's knowledge* about process execution, discussed by Kohlbacher and Gruenwald [30] as originating from the model by Hammer [53] as whether an employee can describe the design of the business process he is part of and consequently how it affects other employees and customers within the process and the process performance itself. Contrarily, [2] in his definition of business process orientation discusses three dimensions, where the items although discussing employees (e.g. "The average employee views the business as a series of linked processes") do not really reflect the individual employees' perspectives, but rather an assessment of the cumulative outlook and general behavior of employees as seen by one or a few selected individuals within the organization (usually CEO, CIO, process owners, etc.). All of the above items and other were found (in similar form) in the empirical data, gathered by Leyer, Stumpf-Wollersheim and Kronsbein [54] so the authors chose to base their initial pool on the 60 items, which reflect the personal perspective of "employees, affected by process-orientation in the day-to-day business", exactly the perspective determined for IPO.

This original data was categorized into advantages or disadvantages of process orientation, according to individual perception. For the purpose of evaluating item appropriation across the proposed dimensions, the item pool required some amendments - the next step involved excluding any duplicated content and unifying definitions in order to portray the individual perspective. Additionally, we deleted four items that appeared as opposite aspects (antonyms), since the emphasis was on allocating perception of IPO into categories of thinking or behavior, irrespective of the connotation (e.g. flexibility and inflexibility, we took only flexibility). Furthermore, we adjusted the existing items to improve their readability, clarity and comprehension. In order to receive evaluation of the appropriateness of our items we proceeded with the item evaluation.

4.2 Stage 2: Item Evaluation

The resulting measurement items were submitted for evaluation and ranking into the most appropriate dimension, i.e. process-oriented thinking or behavior, or proposed to be excluded, if considered not relevant. The items were given to a set of 16 academics, chosen for their research expertise in the domain of process orientation. The experts were targeted via an online questionnaire, in which they evaluated the perceived suitability and importance of each item. The key item retention criterion was a 70% consensus for each item, confirming their individual relevance and dimension suitability. This resulted in a set of the following ten items: holistic thinking, goal orientation, customer orientation and organizational width were categorized under the process-oriented thinking dimension, while productivity, effectiveness, knowledge transfer, cooperation, speed and deviations were sorted into the process-oriented behavior dimension.

4.3 Stage 3: Item Purification

In the third stage we examined the formulation of the indicators and the dimensions captured by performing a first confirmatory factor analysis (CFA). We gathered 66 employees using clickworker, a platform for micro tasks and paying participation adequately according to the recommendation of the platform. Participants should refer to their workplace regarding their perceived process orientation. We applied common settings for CFA with principal axis factoring in combination with a varimax rotation. The resulting value of Bartlett's test of sphericity proved significant and the Kaiser-Mayer-Olkin test was appropriate as well, i.e. greater than .50. The results revealed that the items were not loading adequately to the two factors but provided a mixed assignment. The reason could be identified in ambiguous wording. Consequently, we reformulated the items to provide unambiguous texts.

4.4   Stage 4: Item Validation

In the fourth stage, we gathered another sample of employees again on clickworker (excluding prior participants), that resulted in 558 viable questionnaires (42 were deleted as the participants did not pass attention tests). The condition was that employees work at least part-time in an organization. We then used again a CFA to evaluate the remaining items and perform comparative model fit analyses to assess our tentative model. These results regarding item validation are presented in the results section.

Additionally, we collected a control sample of 108 respondents that was referring to employees working in organizations with more than 10 employees. The number of 10 ensures that there the work environment is large enough to be out of personal control of employees. The reasoning for this control sample is drawn from Spector and Brannick [55], that it should enable researchers to remove predictor-criterion contamination by including confounding variables in their analyses. We included attitude (i.e., whether employees "like" each of the items) regarding the items of both thinking and behavior. In addition, we included the control aspect of behavior (i.e., whether employees had the aspects of behavior within their control) as the behavior of individuals can be considered to some degree prescribed Swann [56] due to adherence to rules and procedures in an organizational environment.

5   Results

We started the analysis with a CFA with principal axis factoring in combination with a varimax rotation that was fulfilling the criteria regarding Bartlett's test of sphericity and the Kaiser-Mayer-Olkin test. According to the standard procedures of CFA, we kept all the items with satisfactory weights and modification indices and factor loadings that were above .60 [57]. This resulted in deleting the item regarding deviation as the value was only .386, hence taking nine items into account further on. The final set of items can be found in Table 3.

The second step was testing the reliability of our variables (Table 4), in which case the composite reliability scores are used to indicate whether all values are above the threshold of 0.7, which our results confirm. Also, we can see that the indicator reliability is fulfilled, because all values for average variance extracted were above the threshold of 0.5.

For the third step, we tested discriminant validity applying the heterotrait–monotrait (HTMT) ratio of correlation [58]. By using this criterion, the results provide greater accuracy in terms of detecting discriminant validity when compared to using the Fornell-Larcker criteria. The value of 0.670 was well below the threshold of 0.9.

Fourth, for the purpose of analysing our research model, we conducted a linear regression analysis for which the criteria were fulfilled by our dataset. The results reveal a beta coefficient of .562 and an explained variance of .314 (Adjusted R^2). Thus, our two-dimensional construct including the influence of thinking on behaviour is supported.

Table 3. Final assignment of items.

Items:	Process-oriented thinking	Process-oriented behavior
Holistic thinking: I understand how my tasks within the processes they are part of contribute to the overall company success	X	
Goal-orientation: I understand how I contribute to achieve the goals of the processes my tasks are part of	X	
Customer-orientation: I understand how I contribute to fulfil customer needs within the processes my tasks are part of	X	
Organizational width: I understand how my tasks are connected with other employees' tasks within the same process	X	
Knowledge transfer: I share knowledge of my process execution with other employees with whom I work together in processes		X
Effectiveness: I execute my tasks in a way that the effectiveness of the processes my tasks are part of is increased		X
Productivity: I execute my tasks in a way that the productivity of the processes my tasks are part of is increased		X
Cooperation: I execute my tasks in cooperation with other employees with whom I work together in processes to reach the goals of this processes		X
Speed: I execute my tasks in a way that the speed of orders in the processes my tasks are part of is increased		X

Table 4. Reliability values of the variables.

	Composite reliability	Average variance extracted
Process-oriented thinking	0.871	0.575
Process-oriented behavior	0.910	0.716

Fifth, we determined the power of our analysis by conducting a post hoc statistical power test for multiple regressions [59]. The test shows an observed statistical power of .99999868 for a probability level of 99%, which is well above the recommended threshold of .8 and indicates strong statistical power of our results [60].

Finally, given the value of .314 as explained variance, the results indicated that there are other factors influencing the gap between thinking and behavior. Hence, we included the personal attitude regarding thinking and behavior as well as individual control regarding behavior. This can be attributed to the fact that most employees' behavior in the workplace is prescribed and constrained to a certain degree [56, 61].

Again, we performed the described steps to evaluate the results using SmartPLS for this more complicated model. The first result of these tests revealed that the attitude regarding process-oriented behavior has a HTMT-value of 1.046 which indicates that both constructs are too similar. This is supported by a significant correlation of .798. Hence, the variable attitude regarding process-oriented behavior is removed. Figure 2 provides an overview.

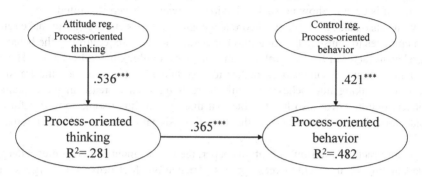

Fig. 2. Controls regarding IPO

6 Conclusion and Future Work

Our paper provides a deeper understanding of the concept of IPO, theoretically, conceptually and empirically. The two dimensions are conceptualized through an extensive literature review and confirmed in the empirical part.

Based on our results, the theoretical implications are as follows. First, we provide a theoretical analysis that describes the causal relationship between thinking and behavior. This theoretical underpinning explains why and how process-oriented thinking leads to process-oriented behavior, thus, revealing the underlying mechanism between the two constructs.

Second, by providing a clear, more in-depth understanding of IPO, we introduce the two dimensions of process-oriented thinking and process-oriented behavior, underpinned by the review and analysis of existing literature. Hierarchical or multidimensional constructs, such as our proposed two-dimensional IPO construct, are claimed to have many theoretical as well as empirical contributions [62–64]. Proponents argue that they reduce model complexity and allow for more theoretical parsimony [62, 63]. These conceptual benefits are complemented by empirical issues such as the reliability and validity of the measures of the multidimensional construct [62]. In terms of higher-order constructs the degree of criterion-related validity is proposedly higher, especially when they are considered predictors [65].

Third, we provide a validated instrument for empirical measurement of the two-dimensional IPO. The results provide confirmation of our developed measurement scale, introducing it as a reliable, valid and stable measurement instrument for IPO. We also include relevant direct control variables to ensure that the relationship is not hampered by individual attitudes as well as not being able to control process-oriented behavior.

Fourth, our results regarding the control study show that the attitude regarding behavior is almost similar to showing such behavior while this does not hold true for thinking. This means that the way of process-oriented thinking is partly determined by the attitude of an individual towards process orientation highlighting the more cognitive aspects of this variable. The attitude is not quite strong in still thinking that process orientation is useful. Showing such behavior is however driven by attitude which is in line with sensemaking within our theoretical cognitive perspective. It has to make sense for employees to translate thinking into behavior. Furthermore, control of the behavior is a relevant factor in further exploring the gap between thinking and behavior. Hence, the organizational circumstances matter to a certain extent and reduce the transformation of thinking into behavior. While there is quite an increase in the explained variance, one however also has to note that there is still quite some room for further explanatory factors. Nevertheless, the two-dimensionality of the construct remains stable.

As for practical contributions of this paper, the management can be offered a deeper understanding of their employees' process orientation. McCormack [2] argues that process-oriented employees have a clear view and understanding of the organization's processes and can more easily facilitate innovative process improvement. Arguably such individuals would also fair better in difficult and pressing work situations. Understanding their role in the business process could increase their sense of importance and contribution to the customer, since process-oriented employees thus considers it their work to satisfy the needs of customers [30]. Additionally, we provide a viable tool for practice to assess their employees' current state of IPO across the organization. Organizations, prone to understanding process orientation on a company level thus gain insight into the workings and understanding of their employees and can explore their current process-oriented thinking and process-oriented behavior levels. Such employee status information can prove crucial, when deciding whether to embark on a BPM project.

As with any research, there are limitations. First, our quantitative data in steps 3 and 4 stems from clickworker as an unsupervised online platform on which participants are paid for participating in a survey. We followed the recommendations of Goodman et al. [66] with having a short survey and including attention checks. However, in order to overcome the bias of a certain group of employees joining clickworker, the study should be extended to question employees in cooperation with companies. Second, we have not tested antecedents and outcomes of IPO which might have an influence on the reflection of participants regarding their perceived process orientation. Future studies should link the constructs to antecedents such as group cohesion and psychological ownership or outcomes such as work engagement and innovation behavior. Third, we did not measure organizational process orientation although we had an additional study including the perceived possibilities due to the organizational environment. Future case studies should be conducted to include organizational process orientation as an individual's view is limited to the directly perceived work environment. Fourth, we develop a measurement scale for IPO as a construct not considering antecedents and outcomes such as performance. Results using the scale should be gathered in future work and compared with other studies providing evidence regarding the antecedents and effects of IPO.

References

1. Leyer, M., Hirzel, A.-K., Moormann, J.: Achieving sustainable behavioral changes of daily work practices: the effect of role plays on learning process-oriented behavior. Bus. Process Manag. J. **24**, 1050–1068 (2018)
2. McCormack, K.: Business process orientation: do you have it? Qual. Prog. **34**, 51 (2001)
3. Škrinjar, R., Bosilj-Vukšic, V., Indihar Štemberger, M.: The impact of business process orientation on financial and non-financial performance. Bus. Process Manag. J. **14**, 738–754 (2008)
4. Braganza, A., Bytheway, A.: Process orientation. A key to managing an unpredictable future. Effective organizations. Looking to the future, pp. 29–32. Cassell, London (1997)
5. Hammer, M., Champy, J.: Reengineering the Corporation. HaperCollins, New York (1993)
6. Riege, A., Zulpo, M.: Knowledge transfer process cycle: between factory floor and middle management. Aust. J. Manag. **32**, 293–314 (2007)
7. Leyer, M., Hirzel, A.-K., Moormann, J.: Effectiveness of role plays on process-oriented behaviour in daily work practices: an analysis in the financial services sector. In: Proceedings of the European Conference on Information Systems, p. 26 (2015)
8. Leyer, M., Wollersheim, J.: How to learn process-oriented thinking: an experimental investigation of the effectiveness of different learning modes. Schmalenbachs Bus. Rev. **65**, 454–473 (2013)
9. Wollersheim, J., Leyer, M., Spörrle, M.: When more is not better: the effect of the number of learning interventions on the acquisition of process-oriented thinking. Manag. Learn. **47**, 137–157 (2016)
10. Leyer, M., Moormann, J., Wang, M.: How should we teach the logic of BPM? Comparing e-learning and face-to-face setting in situated learning. In: Australasian Conference on Information Systems, ACIS 2014 (2014)
11. Kettenbohrer, J., Beimborn, D., Eckhardt, A.: Examining the influence of perceived job characteristics on employees' process orientation (2016)
12. Kettenbohrer, J., Beimborn, D., Leyer, M.: Examining the impact of business process management system use on employees' process orientation (2016)
13. Rosemann, M., vom Brocke, J.: The six core elements of business process management. In: vom Brocke, J., Rosemann, M. (eds.) Handbook on Business Process Management 1. IHIS, pp. 105–122. Springer, Heidelberg (2015). https://doi.org/10.1007/978-3-642-45100-3_5
14. Huntington, S.P.: Clash of Civilizations and the Remaking of World Order Touchstone. Touchstone, New York (1997)
15. Tajfel, H., Turner, J.: The social identity theory of intergroup behavior. In: Jost, J.T., Sidanius, J. (eds.) Key Readings in Social Psychology. Psychology Press, New York (2004)
16. Braisby, N., Gellatly, A.: Cognitive Psychology. Oxford University Press, Oxford (2012)
17. Neisser, U.: Cognitive Psychology, Classic edn. Psychology Press, New York (2014)
18. Anderson, J.R.: Cognitive Psychology and Its Implications. Macmillan, London (2005)
19. MacLin, M.K., Solso, R.L.: Cognitive psychology. Pearson Education Limited, Harlow (2007)
20. Eysenck, M.W., Keane, M.T.: Cognitive Psychology: A Student's Handbook. Psychology Press, New York (2013)

21. Gary, M.S., Wood, R.E.: Mental models, decision rules and performance heterogeneity. Strat. Manag. J. **32**, 569–594 (2011)
22. Kohlbacher, M., Reijers, H.A.: The effects of process-oriented organizational design on firm performance. Bus. Process Manag. J. **19**, 245–262 (2013)
23. Willaert, P., Van den Bergh, J., Willems, J., Deschoolmeester, D.: The process-oriented organisation: a holistic view developing a framework for business process orientation maturity. In: Alonso, G., Dadam, P., Rosemann, M. (eds.) BPM 2007. LNCS, vol. 4714, pp. 1–15. Springer, Heidelberg (2007). https://doi.org/10.1007/978-3-540-75183-0_1
24. Kohlbacher, M.: The effects of process orientation: a literature review. Bus. Process Manag. J. **16**, 135–152 (2010)
25. Škrinjar, R., Trkman, P.: Increasing process orientation with business process management: critical practices. Int. J. Inf. Manag. **33**, 48–60 (2013)
26. Zarei, B., Chaghouee, Y., Ghapanchi, A.H.: Investigating the relationship between business process orientation and social capital. Knowl. Process Manag. **21**, 67–77 (2014)
27. Kohlbacher, M.: The impact of dynamic capabilities through continuous improvement on innovation: the role of business process orientation. Knowl. Process Manag. **20**, 71–76 (2013)
28. Forsberg, T., Nilsson, L., Antoni, M.: Process orientation: the Swedish experience. Total Qual. Manag. **10**, 540–547 (1999)
29. Nilsson, L., Johnson, M.D., Gustafsson, A.: The impact of quality practices on customer satisfaction and business results: product versus service organizations. J. Qual. Manag. **6**, 5–27 (2001)
30. Kohlbacher, M., Gruenwald, S.: Process orientation: conceptualization and measurement. Bus. Process Manag. J. **17**, 267–283 (2011)
31. Trkman, P., de Oliveira, M.P.V., McCormack, K.: Value-oriented supply chain risk management: you get what you expect. Ind. Manag. Data Syst. **116**, 1061–1083 (2016)
32. Schaffernicht, M., Groesser, S.N.: A comprehensive method for comparing mental models of dynamic systems. Eur. J. Oper. Res. **210**, 57–67 (2011)
33. Kelton, A.S., Pennington, R.R., Tuttle, B.M.: The effects of information presentation format on judgment and decision making: a review of the information systems research. J. Inf. Syst. **24**, 79–105 (2010)
34. Gonzalez, C., Lerch, J.F., Lebiere, C.: Instance-based learning in dynamic decision making. Cogn. Sci. **27**, 591–635 (2003)
35. Schaffernicht, M.F.G., Groesser, S.N.: The SEXTANT software: a tool for automating the comparative analysis of mental models of dynamic systems. Eur. J. Oper. Res. **238**, 566–578 (2014)
36. Duffy, M.: Sensemaking in classroom conversations. In: Openness in Research: The Tension Between Self and Other, pp. 119–132 (1995)
37. Drazin, R., Glynn, M.A., Kazanjian, R.K.: Multilevel theorizing about creativity in organizations: a sensemaking perspective. Acad. Manag. Rev. **24**, 286–307 (1999)
38. Bateson, G.: Steps to an Ecology of Mind. Ballantine Books, New York (1972)
39. Porac, J.F., Thomas, H., Baden-Fuller, C.: Competitive groups as cognitive communities: the case of Scottish knitwear manufacturers. J. Manag. Stud. **26**, 397–416 (1989)
40. Poole, P.P., Gioia, D.A., Gray, B.: Influence modes, schema change, and organizational transformation. J. Appl. Behav. Sci. **25**, 271–289 (1989)
41. Weick, K.E.: The Social Psychology of Organizing Addison-Wesley. Addison, Reading (1979)
42. McCormack, K., Johnson, W.C.: Business Process Orientation: Gaining the E-Business Competitive Advantage. St. Lucie Press, Florida (2001)

43. Peppard, J., Fitzgerald, D.: The transfer of culturally-grounded management techniques: the case of business reengineering in Germany. Eur. Manag. J. **15**, 446–460 (1997)
44. van Assen, M.: Process orientation and the impact on operational performance and customer-focused performance. Bus. Process Manag. J. **24**, 446–458 (2018)
45. Reijers, H.A.: Implementing BPM systems: the role of process orientation. Bus. Process Manag. J. **12**, 389–409 (2006)
46. Chen, H., Tian, Y., Daugherty, P.J.: Measuring process orientation. Int. J. Logist. Manag. **20**, 213–227 (2009)
47. Nonaka, I.: A dynamic theory of organizational knowledge creation. Organ. Sci. **5**, 14–37 (1994)
48. Feldman, M.S., Pentland, B.T.: Reconceptualizing organizational routines as a source of flexibility and change. Adm. Sci. Q. **48**, 94–118 (2003)
49. Latour, B.: The powers of association. Sociol. Rev. **32**, 264–280 (1984)
50. Pentland, B.T., Feldman, M.S.: Designing routines: on the folly of designing artifacts, while hoping for patterns of action. Inf. Organ. **18**, 235–250 (2008)
51. Feldman, M.S.: Organizational routines as a source of continuous change. Organ. Sci. **11**, 611–629 (2000)
52. Karpen, I.O., Bove, L.L., Lukas, B.A., Zyphur, M.J.: Service-dominant orientation: measurement and impact on performance outcomes. J. Retail. **91**, 89–108 (2015)
53. Hammer, M.: The process audit. Harv. Bus. Rev. **85**, 111–123 (2007)
54. Leyer, M., Stumpf-Wollersheim, J., Kronsbein, D.: Stains on the bright side of process-oriented organizational designs: an empirical investigation of advantages and disadvantages. Schmalenbach Bus. Rev. **18**, 29–47 (2017)
55. Spector, P.E., Brannick, M.T.: Methodological urban legends: the misuse of statistical control variables. Organ. Res. Methods **14**, 287–305 (2011)
56. Swann, A.: The Human Workplace: People-centred Organizational Development. Kogan Page, London (2017)
57. Hulland, J.: Use of partial least squares (PLS) in strategic management research: a review of four recent studies. Strat. Manag. J. **20**, 195–204 (1999)
58. Henseler, J., Ringle, C.M., Sarstedt, M.: A new criterion for assessing discriminant validity in variance-based structural equation modeling. J. Acad. Mark. Sci. **43**, 115–135 (2015)
59. Soper, D.: Post-hoc statistical power calculator for multiple regression [Software] (2018)
60. Cohen, J., Cohen, P., West, S.G., Aiken, L.S.: Applied Multiple Regression/Correlation Analysis for the Behavioral Sciences. Lawrence Erlbaum Associates, Mahwah (2003)
61. Katz, D.: The motivational basis of organizational behavior. Behav. Sci. **9**, 131–146 (1964)
62. Edwards, J.R.: Multidimensional constructs in organizational behavior research: an integrative analytical framework. Organ. Res. Methods **4**, 144–192 (2001)
63. MacKenzie, S.B., Podsakoff, P.M., Jarvis, C.B.: The problem of measurement model misspecification in behavioral and organizational research and some recommended solutions. J. Appl. Psychol. **90**, 710 (2005)
64. Petter, S., Straub, D., Rai, A.: Specifying formative constructs in information systems research. MIS Q. **31**, 623–656 (2007)
65. Wetzels, M., Odekerken-Schröder, G., Van Oppen, C.: Using PLS path modeling for assessing hierarchical construct models: Guidelines and empirical illustration. MIS Q. **33**, 177–195 (2009)
66. Goodman, J.K., Cryder, C.E., Cheema, A.: Data collection in a flat world: the strengths and weaknesses of Mechanical Turk samples. J. Behav. Decis. Mak. **26**, 213–224 (2012)

Performance Effects of Dynamic Capabilities: The Interaction Effect of Process Management Capabilities

Jasna Prester[1] , Tomislav Hernaus[1(✉)] , Ana Aleksić[1] ,
and Peter Trkman[2]

[1] Faculty of Economics and Business,
Department of Organization and Management, University of Zagreb,
J. F. Kennedy sq. 6, 10000 Zagreb, Croatia
thernaus@efzg.hr
[2] School of Economics and Business,
Academic Unit for Business Informatics and Logistics, University of Ljubljana,
Kardeljeva ploscad 17, 1000 Ljubljana, Slovenia

Abstract. Process management is a performance-relevant capability that integrates exploitation of existing processes and exploration of new processes. Although important, it has been neglected and not well addressed organizational-level practice within the dynamic capabilities view (DCV). Therefore, this two-study survey research examines whether process management (i.e., process exploration and process exploitation) capabilities represent potential mediating/moderating mechanisms between dynamic capabilities (i.e., learning and coordinating) and business performance. Specifically, a dual-stage moderated mediation model has been developed and tested on the cross-industry sample of 104 Croatian companies (Study 1) and international sample of 529 manufacturing companies (Study 2). Conditional process analyses using PROCESS macro for SPSS revealed that: (1) the coordinating capability has a supplementary effect on learning capabilities in pursuing process exploration; (2) high process exploration and low process exploitation capabilities result in highest levels of business performance; and (3) the multi-capability mix should be used to explain business performance results. Our findings give support to the capability view of business process management.

Keywords: Dynamic capabilities · Process management capabilities ·
Process exploration · Process exploitation · Conditional process analysis

1 Introduction

Process management is a performance-relevant organizational-level capability that suits well within the dynamic capabilities view (DCV). A firm's capacity to deploy resources using organizational processes [4] is essential for achieving superior performance and assuring long-term survival. Although the rationale is well addressed [16, 57], yet inconsistent empirical results exist in strategic management literature on dynamic capability operationalizations. Both direct and indirect (via ordinary capabilities) effects

© Springer Nature Switzerland AG 2019
C. Di Ciccio et al. (Eds.): BPM 2019 Blockchain and CEE Forum, LNBIP 361, pp. 264–279, 2019.
https://doi.org/10.1007/978-3-030-30429-4_18

of dynamic capabilities on organizational performance have been reported throughout the last two decades, thus leading scholars [46] to argue that the theory of capabilities or even a coherent framework of capability is still not existent.

In addition, though being informative, we also lack rigorous empirical insights about the interplay between (dynamic and ordinary) capabilities and firm performance [33]. Specifically, no agreement has been reached how certain dynamic capabilities affect specific ordinary capabilities [3, 15, 23, 27]. This is even more true when questioning the role of process exploration and process exploitation, topics mainly addressed within the operations management field. Often approached as the opposites, both process exploration (e.g., cross-functional activities related to new product launch or new technology adoption) and process exploitation (i.e., cross-functional activities intended to formalize, stabilize and/or rationalize organizational routines) might represent potential mediating and/or moderating mechanisms between dynamic capabilities and firm performance. Such conceptualization of process management follows the rationale that dynamic capabilities are anchored in a firm's ability to both exploit and explore [35, 40]. Yet, it also calls into question a traditional and still widespread view of process management as an operational initiative focused on incremental and exploitative innovation [8].

Therefore, the aim of the paper is to explore the interplay between different dynamic and ordinary capabilities, i.e. to determine whether and how process management capabilities (as a specific type of ordinary capabilities) play a part in the relationship between dynamic (learning and coordinating) capabilities and business performance. We conducted a two-study survey research on a cross-industry sample of 104 Croatian companies (Study 1) and on the international sample of 529 manufacturing companies (Study 2) to test our dual-stage moderated mediation model (see Fig. 1). Conditional process analyses using PROCESS macro for SPSS revealed that: (1) the coordinating capability has a supplementary effect on learning capabilities in pursuing process exploration; (2) high process exploration and low process exploitation capabilities result in highest levels of business performance; and (3) the multi-capability mix should be used to explain business performance results.

Our intended contribution is threefold. First, we moved beyond the dominant stream of research exploring dynamic capabilities by pointing out "details" of how process management capabilities are used is what creates better business performance results. Thus, we followed the advice from Helfat and Winter [27] who argued that the impact of dynamic capabilities can be seen in their influence on routines and practices, in our case on process exploration and process exploitation activities. Second, to best of our knowledge, this paper is among first empirical attempts to examine interaction effects between a specific set of dynamic and ordinary capabilities using a complex dual-stage moderated mediation model. Not only we showed that significant interaction (both moderation, mediation and moderated mediation) effects exist among focal constructs, but we also managed to validate these findings across two different organizational-level samples. Finally, we intend to reinforce the bridge between strategic management and operations management literatures in studying performance effects of dynamic and ordinary capabilities. Specifically, by placing an emphasis on the importance of process management capabilities, we hope to give additional support to the capability view of business process management [42, 63].

2 Theory and Hypotheses

2.1 Organizational Capabilities and Business Performance

Organizational capability refers to ability of an organization to coordinate and use resources, in order to carry out competitively sustainable tasks, activities and achieve desired goals [4, 20, 24, 36]. Hesselbein and Goldsmith [28] consider capabilities as something that organization is doing well to gain value, while Dosi et al. [12] suggest capabilities can be understood as organizational "know-how" that enables managers and employees to perform and upgrade their existing activities.

We can distinguish between two types of capabilities, dynamic and ordinary ones. Flynn et al. [18] report that ordinary capabilities represent specific group of skills, procedures and routines closely related to problem solving and operational activities at the organizational unit level. As opposed to ordinary, dynamic capabilities emphasize the key role of strategic management in appropriately adapting, integrating, and reconfiguring organizational skills and resources, including ordinary capabilities within a changing environment [57, 60]. They consist of information-retrieving and knowledge-assimilation activities intended to unveil the need for change, variation of the existing firm's resource configuration, selection of the appropriate configurations, and their retention through implementation [58]. As such, dynamic capabilities do not only represent an organizational capability to sense and seize opportunities for accessing new external resources, but also consist of learning and coordinating as important internal elements that facilitate internal resource reconfiguration. The latter is no less important than the former for achieving organizational success. According to Helfat and Peteraf [25], the sensing, seizing, and reconfiguring capacities are connected to each other following a certain order and logic. While some interrelatedness among dynamic capabilities has been already addressed [34], we still lack insights about the dynamics of learning and coordinating capabilities.

Learning as a dynamic capability can be conceived of as a principal mean of attaining strategic renewal. Renewal requires that organizations explore and learn new ways while at the same time exploit what they have already learned [35]. Teece et al. [57] argue that learning is a very important process, which leads to better, and quicker resolution of specific problems through experimentation and repetition, and at the same time learning capability enables firms to identify new production opportunities [49].

On the other hand, coordination as dynamic capability describes the firm's ability to assess the value of existing ordinary capabilities and integrate them to shape new ones [4]. Implementation of new configurations of ordinary capabilities emerges from the effective coordination of a variety of tasks and resources, as well as through synchronization of different activities [11, 25]. Moreover, the coordinating capabilities enhance the exchange and integration of tacit and codified knowledge, thus allowing firms to deliver their products more cost effectively and acquire additional information about customers' needs [26].

Previous research has shown that there is significant connection among organizational resources, capabilities and performance [6, 10, 51]. We thus know that organizational capabilities are related to competitive advantage [45]. However, relationships among different types of capabilities and firm performance are still unclear. Some of the pioneering work in the field [57] assumed there is a direct link between dynamic and ordinary capabilities, and indirect link between dynamic capabilities and firm performance via ordinary capabilities. However, numerous theoretical [3, 15, 16, 29, 60] and few empirical papers [49] that followed, approached to dynamic capabilities as antecedents of ordinary capabilities, which in turn has a significant effect on firm performance [29]. Thus, we know that chain of causality designates an indirect (mediating) link between dynamic capabilities and firm performance, although the underlying mechanisms are still not well understood [14, 17].

2.2   Organizational Capabilities and Business Performance

Process management has been traditionally defined as concerted efforts to map, improve, and adhere to organizational processes [8]. More recently, it started to be perceived as an important organizational capability [5, 30, 44] that enables managers to attain speed, flexibility, and cost economy [39]. Falling into a pool of ordinary capabilities, process management stands for a meta-process in which the embedded dynamic capability is manifested [7].

Process exploitation and process exploration are two defining aspects of process management that ultimately lead to performance [40]. Much more interest has been given to exploitation-oriented dimension of process management. Process exploitation is primarily focused on assuring process control, enabling process formalization and pursuing standardization goals. It stabilizes and rationalizes organizational routines while establishing a focus on easily available efficiency and customer satisfaction measures [8]. Process exploitation is also likely to spur innovation [61].

On the other hand, exploration-oriented dimension of process management is more oriented towards change and adaptability of existing or introduction of new business operations. Process exploration is a type of innovation that has received limited academic attention despite its growing importance [9]. Among a few, McElheran [38] argued that market leaders will enjoy economies of scale in pursuing business process innovation goals. Both process improvement (i.e., incremental change) and process redesign (i.e., radical change) are very much needed explorative activities for meeting growth and development targets. In addition, these change-oriented efforts might and often do help to reduce organizational complexity and thus result in notable performance increases. As process management can help to make innovation a lasting capability in an organization [31], we assume that process exploration capability should be approached as a desired first-order outcome of dynamic capabilities. In other words, interaction between learning and coordinating capabilities should enable exchange of experience and expertise within an organization, that will in turn build up the process exploration capability.

Hypothesis 1: Coordinating capability moderates the relationship between learning capability and process exploration capability, making it more positive when learning capability is high.

As process exploitation and process exploration co-exist and represent legitimate organizational goals, particularly interesting is to examine how their relationship shapes the bottom-line performance. Although both types of activities are important for organizational survival, exploration and exploitation are dominantly perceived as contradictory organizational processes [57]. For instance, the seminal work of March [35] warn that trade-off exists between exploitation and exploration. Furthermore, Benner and Tushman [8] added that process exploitation tends to drive out experimentation. By pursuing consistency and efficiency through process exploitation, organizations will strengthen their 'deep structure' [62], and thus will increase rigidity and destroy employees' adaptive processes.

However, Ng et al. [40] contend that process management should be defined more completely as an integrated organizational capability that manifests itself through a set of mutually supportive routines and practices in order to exploit existing processes and explore new processes. They strike out a potential complementarity effect, building on an argument that newly explored processes trigger the need for exploitation through fine-tuning and streamlining [53]. Thus, their perspective suggests exploitation and exploration not only coexist but are interdependent and mutually supportive [40].

Previous findings have shown that financial performance is positively affected by process management capability [39]. According to Benner and Tushman [8], through process exploration, an organization becomes increasingly skilled at producing outputs that leverage existing knowledge. They continue by arguing that new (process) innovations that further utilize exploitation capabilities will benefit from these efficiencies and lend themselves to even more measurable successes.

As these opposing theoretical perspectives should be also empirically examined, we decided to follow a larger stream of research and hypothesize about trade-off relationship between process exploration and process exploitation.

Hypothesis 2: The positive relationship between process exploration capability and business performance is stronger when process exploitation capability is low.

The literature on the resource-based view (RBV) has echoed the idea of performance being attributable to a duality of capabilities. An interplay between different organizational capabilities (both dynamic and ordinary) might create such configurations of abilities which might be not only idiosyncratic and impossible to imitate, but would result in performance increase. Interestingly, existing research do highlight that differences in performance are a result of how well the combined resources create distinct capabilities that can support an organisation's strategic goals [52]. More specifically, study conducted by Wong et al. [63] showed that different types of process management capabilities (i.e., both managerial and technical) have a positive impact on performance. Therefore, we might assume that complex (moderation, mediation, and moderated mediation) interaction effects exist between dynamic and ordinary capabilities that shape performance results of an organization.

Hypothesis 3: Coordinating and process exploitation capabilities moderate the indirect effect of learning capability on business performance through process exploration capability, so that the indirect effects are realized when coordinating capability is high and process exploitation capability is low.

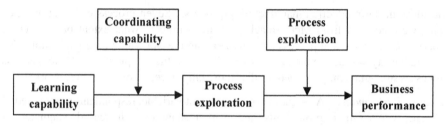

Fig. 1. Research framework

3 Study 1: Method and Results

3.1 Sample

Two empirical research studies were done to address the proposed research framework and related hypotheses. In our first study the conditional process research model has been tested on a cross-industry sample of medium-sized and large-sized organizations in Croatia. A self-reported anonymous questionnaire was sent to executive directors of medium- and large-sized organizations in Croatia, i.e. companies with more than a hundred employees listed in an on-line database of the Croatian Chamber of Economy. While the entire population of organizations meeting this size criteria has been approached, a cross-sectional survey data were collected from 113 organizations. Few responses had to be discarded due to invalid or incomplete data entries, leading to the final sample of 104 organizations (the overall response rate is 9.0%) covering different industry sectors (31.1% processing industry, 12.6% construction, and 10.7% wholesale and retail trade). In terms of the ownership structure, a 1:2 ratio was reported in favor of privately-owned companies.

3.2 Measures

We decided to ask managers how well their firm performs particular tasks or how good their firm's ability in given tasks is, thus following a predominant mean of conducting capabilities research [33]. The research instrument has been developed using validated measurement scales from prior studies. All questionnaire items were measured on a five-point Likert-type frequency scale with anchors 1 (never) and 5 (always).

Dynamic Capabilities. Learning capability as an independent variable was measured by using an adapted 3-item version of the scale developed by Pavlou and El Sawy [43] that showed an adequate level of reliability ($\alpha = .806$). The sample item is "We are effective in transforming existing information into new knowledge". Coordinating capability scale consisting of five statements has been adopted from the same source ($\alpha = .836$), with a sample item "We ensure that there is compatibility between group members expertise and work processes".

Process Management Capabilities. Process exploration scale was derived on grounds of work of Acar and Zehir [1]. We adapted four items from their production capability scale ($\alpha = .848$) with a sample item "Organization is capable of adopting new methods and ideas in the production/manufacturing process." Seven process exploitation scale items were adopted from McCormack [37], measuring to what extent process view, process management and process measurement are present within an organization. The scale reliability was above the cut-off (α = .879), and the sample item is "The business processes are sufficiently defined so that most employees know how they work".

Business Performance. As regard to our dependent variable, respondents were asked to estimate whether their profitability and market share have increased, stagnated or decreased compared to previous year's results.

As control variables we used *organizational size, ownership structure* and *industry sector type.*

In addition to Cronbach alpha statistics, a confirmatory factor analysis (CFA) with maximum likelihood estimation procedures using AMOS version 21 has been conducted to determine the underlying structure among the set of items and further validate the chosen measurement instrument. The expected four-factor solution (learning capability, coordinating capability, process exploration capability, process exploitation capability) displayed an adequate fit with the data (Chi-square [140] = 1.795, CFI = .909, RMSEA = .088). We tested alternative nested models to examine whether a more parsimonious model achieved an equivalent fit, but the Chi-square difference tests indicated that the proposed four-factor model achieved a significantly better fit.

3.3 Procedure

To test our research model, we used the PROCESS macro version 2.16.3 for SPSS [21]. Hypotheses testing was conducted by examining nested (1) the first-stage moderated mediation, i.e. the role of coordinating capability, (2) the second-stage moderated mediation, i.e. the role of process exploitation capability; and (3) the dual-stage moderated mediation, i.e. moderated mediation model with the Preacher, Rucker, and Hayes [48] bootstrapping procedure with confidence intervals that provide evidence of significant indirect effects when they exclude zero [56]. The index of partial moderated mediation was initially used to provide a formal test indicating if the moderated mediation for one moderator was significant when the other moderator was held constant [22]. Likewise, the index of moderated mediation was used to provide a formal test for the full model (a dual-stage moderated mediation).

3.4 Results

Hypothesis 1 stated that dynamic capabilities (i.e., learning and coordinating capabilities) would interact to predict process exploration representing an ordinary capability of the firm. As shown in the results for the first stage of the conditional process (mediator variable) model, the regression coefficient for the interaction term between learning and coordinating capabilities was positive and marginally significant (a_3 = .183; p = .076; 95% CI = $-.0195$ to .385). A simple slope analysis (see Fig. 2) shows that organizations reported the highest level of process exploration capability when having both high level of learning capability and high level of coordinating capability, providing support to our first hypothesis.

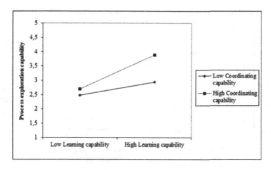

Fig. 2. Interaction plot of the first stage moderation (Study 1)

Hypothesis 2 stated that process exploration and process exploitation would interact to predict business performance. Specifically, we expect to boost positive performance effects of process exploration while having low level of process exploitation capability. Similar to Hypothesis 1, it was tested by examining the second stage of the conditional process (dependent variable) model. The interaction between process management capabilities was negative and therefore a significant predictor of business performance ($b_3 = -.186$; $p = .035$; 95% CI = $-.359$ to $-.013$). The interaction plot shown in Fig. 3 suggests that organizations with developed process exploration capabilities achieve higher business performance results when not having process exploitation capability well developed. However, with an increase in process exploitation, performance results deteriorate, thus confirming the hypothesized relationship.

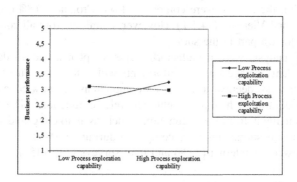

Fig. 3. Interaction plot of the second stage moderation (Study 1)

For testing our final hypothesis, we conducted analyses of the conditional indirect effects of learning capability on the business performance as a dependent variable using the PROCESS macro. The indirect effects were significant only in situation when process exploitation was low, while coordinating capability was either at the mid- (indirect effect = .119; $p = .002$; 95% CI = .019 to .289) or high-level (indirect effect = .162; $p = .002$; 95% CI = .033 to .336). Overall, these findings are aligned with our Hypothesis 3. Conditional indirect effects are depicted in Fig. 4.

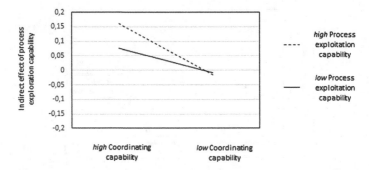

Fig. 4. Conditional indirect effects of a dual-stage moderated mediation model (Study 1)

4   Study 2: Method and Results

4.1   Sample

The large and unique dataset from the Global Manufacturing Research Group (GMRG) has been used for the purpose of conducting our Study 2. The original database has been created as a result of the Round V GMRG survey data collection effort and includes responses from 1008 companies across 16 countries. Mid-sized companies (50 to 250 employees) dominate throughout the research sample (41.4%), although small-sized (up to 50 employees) and large-sized companies (over 250 employees) are also well represented by 31.5% an 27.1% respectively. However, due to some missing values, our total international sample counted 975 manufacturing organizations. Mostly represented within the sample were companies from Croatia (20.8%), USA (15.7%), Poland (15.1%), and Vietnam (14.7%). However, countries from all continents except South America took a part in the survey.

The unit of analysis were manufacturing sites or plants, and all data have been collected from plant managers as key informants within that site. These managers are targeted since they are deemed to possess a comprehensive knowledge of the plant's operations, in addition to having insight into related functions. The managers are advised to solicit input from other functions, such as marketing and finance, when appropriate. Most questionnaires were completed during an on-site visit (43%) by the researcher, followed by Internet (29%) and mail surveys (23%) [55].

4.2   Measures

The standardised survey instrument has been initially developed in English and refined at GMRG annual meetings open to all members [59]. For each language/country of research, a rigorous translation-back translation procedure has been followed using language and subject matter experts [13, 32].

Dynamic Capabilities. Measurement items for learning and coordinating capabilities were obtained from the work of Pavlou and El Sawy [43], Protegerou et al. [50], Wu et al. [64], and Wang et al. [58]. The learning capability scale consisted of four internally consistent items ($\alpha = .879$). The sample item is "Employees in this plant are experts in their particular jobs and functions." Likewise, the measure of coordinating capability was also reliable ($\alpha = .841$), and consisted of three items (e.g., "Employees from different departments feel comfortable calling each other when need arises").

Process Management Capabilities. Both measurement scales for process exploration and process exploitation capabilities were adapted from the work of Wu et al. [64], Protogerou et al. [50], Saunila [54] and Pisano [46]. The level of process exploration capability was evaluated by using six Likert-type agreement statements ranging from 1 – not at all, to 7 – to a great extent. The scale was reliable ($\alpha = .852$), and the sample item is "Your plant has unique manufacturing process capabilities." On the other hand, process exploitation capability was measured with four agreement statements such as "Processes in our plant are well defined". This measure was also internally consistent ($\alpha = .889$).

Business Performance. We adopted Protogerou et al.'s [50] compound measurement scale of sales growth, profitability growth and market share growth. The respondents had to assess the Total sales, Profitability and Market share increase or decrease within the last two years by using objective performance data received from their accounting and finance departments. Seven response categories were provided, ranging from 1- reduced more than 25% to 7 – increased by more than 25%.

4.3   Procedure

We decided to split the total sample to be able to pre-test the validity of our measurement instrument. The reliability analysis was conducted on the subsample of 446 organizations that were excluded from the subsequent analyses. For each of our measurement scales within the pre-test sample, Cronbach's alpha scores were above the cut-off value of .70 [41], ranging from .751 (coordinating capability) to .912 (business performance), and thus the internal consistency of the measure has been confirmed.

Confirmatory factor analysis with maximum likelihood estimation procedures was then performed on the main study data (n = 529) to establish the hypothesized factor membership. The expected five-factor solution (learning capability, coordinating capability, process exploration capability, process exploitation capability, business performance) displayed an adequate fit with the data (Chi-square [314] = 3.671, CFI = .886, RMSEA = .007), and composite reliability (CR) statistics indicates strong construct reliability in each case; all values are well above .7 [19].

Independent samples t-test for equality of means showed no difference in focal variables between two subsamples, except for the process exploration capability [t (973) = -3.218, p < .05]. As Cohen's d was .021, this small effect size should not make a significant difference in our research model results across subsamples.

To test our research model, the same procedure to run process conditional analysis has been followed as in Study 1.

4.4   Results

Following the same procedure pattern as in Study 1, we initially checked results for the mediator variable model. The regression coefficient for the interaction term between dynamic capabilities was positive and significant (a_3 = .069; p = .027; 95% CI = .008 to .129). A simple slope analysis (see Fig. 5) shows the same supplementary effect between learning and coordinating capabilities on process exploration capability as reported in Study 1, that is, organizations with a well developed set of dynamic capabilities report to practice a high level of process exploration. Thus, we provided additional support to our first hypothesis.

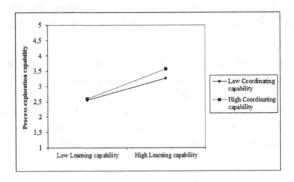

Fig. 5. Interaction plot of the first stage moderation (Study 2)

Next, we proceeded with the second hypothesis testing. While the interaction effect between process exploration (independent variable) and process exploitation (moderator variable) was again negative and significant (b_3 = −.100; p = .035; 95% CI = −.174 to −.026), the simple slope analysis (see Fig. 6) suggested a somewhat different conclusion. Specifically, we found the existence of a supplementary effect between process management capabilities within sampled manufacturing companies. In other words, Study 2 results show that high levels of process exploitation might not be detrimental to business performance as hypothesized.

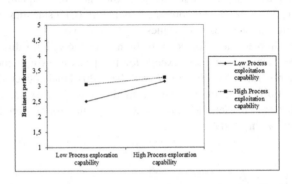

Fig. 6. Interaction plot of the second stage moderation (Study 2)

For testing our third hypothesis, we ran conditional process analysis which revealed that indirect effects of process exploration capability on the relationship between learning capability and business performance were not significant only when a high level of process exploitation was present. In situations with a low process exploitation capability, indirect effects were significant irrespectively of the level of coordinating capability (indirect effect = .117; p = .000; 95% CI = .066 to .187 for low-coordinating capability; indirect effect = .142; p = .000; 95% CI = .086 to .218 for mid-coordinating capability; indirect effect = .167; p = .000; 95% CI = .099 to .253 for high-coordinating capability). Similar findings across coordinating capability' levels are valid for organizations which have a medium level of process exploitation capability (indirect effect = .076; p = .000; 95% CI = .040 to .123 for low-coordinating capability; indirect effect = .142; p = .000; 95% CI = .086 to .218 for mid-coordinating capability; indirect effect = .109; p = .000; 95% CI = .058 to .168 for high-coordinating capability). Overall, these findings (see Fig. 7) confirm our Hypothesis 3.

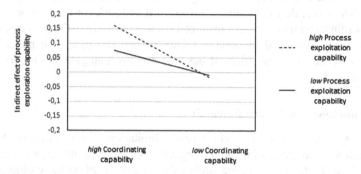

Fig. 7. Conditional indirect effects of a dual-stage moderated mediation model (Study 2)

5 Discussion and Conclusion

5.1 Theoretical Implications

The embeddedness of dynamic capabilities in a firm's processes and routines provides a potential source of competitive advantage [2, 47]. Still, a more coherent framework of organizational capabilities and clear understanding of interaction effects between dynamic and ordinary capabilities is needed. In order to fill this gap, the present study investigated the role of process management capabilities, as ordinary capabilities, in the relationship between dynamic capabilities and business performance. We made a clear distinction between learning and coordinating, as well as process exploration and process exploitation capabilities and thus responded to Helfat and Winter's call [27] to uncover the performance-driven relationship between dynamic and ordinary capabilities.

By using and replicating a complex dual-stage moderated mediation model our research indicates that dynamic and ordinary capabilities affect performance, with both learning and coordinating capabilities having indirect effects on performance through their effect on process management capabilities. In other words, results indicate that highest levels of performance can be expected when organizations have developed routines and practices for their daily activities but at the same time learn and change according to market demands.

Second, we give additional support to the capability view of business process management. A traditional and still widespread view of process management as an operational initiative focused on incremental and exploitative innovation [8]. Our research stressed the importance of inclusion of explorative capability as an integral part of process management, as process exploitation drives business performance, thus helping organizations to successfully respond to internal and external requirements.

5.2 Practical Implications

This study implies organizations should bear in mind that a multi-capability mix approach is essential for long-term business performance. Managers should not only invest in routines and standardized practices that exploit their current resources, as they may overlook the importance of scanning external environment and changing market demands. Therefore, they constantly need to learn and seek for new opportunities, as well as coordinate human resources to embed knowledge into existing processes. At the same time, they also need to achieve a balance between process exploitation and exploration, so that synergic effect of business process management on performance can be achieved.

5.3 Limitations and Future Research

Study findings need to be seen in light of certain limitations. Our research was based on self-evaluations and perception of an organization representative, and therefore a subject to bias. In that sense, future studies should aim to collect more objective data from various sources instead of just relying on widely used individual perceptions obtained from a single source.

While we present results of two studies and upgrade existing research in the field trying to holistically relate important concepts, additional research is needed to further uncover causal mechanisms among different organizational (dynamic and ordinary) capabilities, and performance. We addressed the role of internal dynamic capabilities in capabilities performance relation, so future research should additionally include analysis of external dynamic capabilities, as well as to take into consideration the dynamics of industries. As environmental complexity can have a significant influence on evolution of dynamic capabilities, it would be interesting and useful to further examine the link between capabilities (ordinary and dynamic) on performance in highly dynamic environments.

References

1. Acar, A.Z., Zehir, C.: Development and validation of resource based business capabilities measurement instrument. J. Trans. Manag. **14**(3), 215–240 (2009)
2. Ambrosini, V., Bowman, C.: What are dynamic capabilities and are they a useful construct in strategic management? Int. J. Manag. Rev. **11**, 29–49 (2009)
3. Ambrosini, V., Bowman, C., Collier, N.: Dynamic capabilities: an exploration of how firms renew their resource base. Br. J. Manag. **20**(S1), S9–S24 (2009)
4. Amit, R., Schoemaker, P.J.H.: Strategic assets and organizational rent. Strat. Manag. J. **14**, 33–46 (1993)
5. Anand, G., Ward, P.T., Tatikonda, M.V., Schilling, D.A.: Dynamic capabilities through continuous improvement infrastructure. J. Oper. Manag. **27**(6), 444–461 (2009)
6. Auw, E.: Human capital, capabilities & competitive advantage. Int. Rev. Bus. Res. Pap. **5**, 25–36 (2009)
7. Benner, M.J.: Dynamic or static capabilities? Process management practices and response to technological change. J. Prod. Innov. Manag. **26**, 473–486 (2009)
8. Benner, M.J., Tushman, M.: Exploitation, exploration, and process management: the productivity dilemma revisited. Acad. Manag. Rev. **28**(2), 238–256 (2003)
9. Brynjolfsson, E., Saunders, A.: Wired for Innovation: How Information Technology is Reshaping the Economy. The MIT Press, Cambridge (2010)
10. Carmeli, A., Tishler, A.: Resources, capabilities, and the performance of industrial firms: a multivariate analysis. Manag. Decis. Econ. **25**, 299–315 (2004)
11. Collis, D.J.: Research note: how valuable are organizational capabilities? Strat. Manag. J. **15**, 143–152 (1994)
12. Dosi, G., Nelson, R.R., Winter, S.G.: Nature and Dynamics of Organizational Capabilities. Oxford University Press, New York (2001)
13. Douglas, S.P., Craig, C.S.: International Marketing Research. Prentice-Hall, Englewood Cliffs (1983)
14. Easterby-Smith, M., Lyles, M.A., Peteraf, M.A.: Dynamic capabilities: current debates and future directions. Br. J. Manag. **20**(S1), S1–S8 (2009)
15. Easterby-Smith, M., Prieto, I.M.: Dynamic capabilities and knowledge management: an integrative role for learning? Br. J. Manag. **19**, 235–249 (2008)
16. Eisenhardt, K.M., Martin, J.A.: Dynamic capabilities: what are they? Strat. Manag. J. **21**, 1105–1121 (2000)
17. Fainshmidt, S., Pezeshkan, A., Frazier, M.L., Nair, A., Markowski, E.: Dynamic capabilities and organizational performance: a meta-analytic evaluation and extension. J. Manag. Stud. **53**(8), 1348–1380 (2016)
18. Flynn, B.B., Wu, S.J., Melnyk, S.: Operational capabilities: hidden in plain view. Bus. Horiz. **53**, 247–256 (2010)
19. Fornell, C., Larcker, D.F.: Evaluating structural equation models with unobservable variables and measurement error? J. Mark. Res. **18**(1), 39–50 (1981)
20. Grant, R.M.: The resource-based theory of competitive advantage: implications for strategy formulation. Calif. Manag. Rev. **33**, 114–135 (1991)
21. Hayes, A.F.: Introduction to Mediation, Moderation, and Conditional Process Analysis: A Regression-Based Approach. Guilford Press, New York (2013)
22. Hayes, A.F.: An index and test of linear moderated mediation. Multivar. Behav. Res. **50**, 1–22 (2015)
23. Helfat, C.E., et al.: Dynamic Capabilities: Understanding Strategic Change in Organizations. Blackwell, Malden (2007)

24. Helfat, C.E., Peteraf, M.A.: The dynamic resource-based view: capability lifecycles. Strat. Manag. J. **24**, 997–1010 (2003)
25. Helfat, C.E., Peteraf, M.A.: Understanding dynamic capabilities: progress along a developmental path. Strat. Organ. **7**(1), 91–102 (2009)
26. Helfat, C.E., Raubitschek, R.S.: Product sequencing: co-evolution of knowledge, capabilities and products. Strat. Manag. J. **21**(10–11), 961–979 (2000)
27. Helfat, C.E., Winter, S.G.: Untangling dynamic and operational capabilities: strategy for the (N)ever-changing world. Strat. Manag. J. **32**, 1243–1250 (2011)
28. Hesselbein, F., Goldsmith, M.: The Organization of the Future 2: Visions, Strategies, and Insights on Managing in a New Era. Jossey-Bass, San Francisco (2009)
29. Jurksiene, L., Pundziene, A.: The relationship between dynamic capabilities and firm competitive advantage: the mediating role of organizational ambidexterity. Eur. Bus. Rev. **28**, 431–448 (2016)
30. Kim, D.Y., Kumar, V., Kumar, U.: Relationship between quality management practices and innovation. J. Oper. Manag. **30**(4), 295–315 (2012)
31. Kirchmer, M.: Enabling Innovation Through Business Process Management. Accenture, London (2011). White Paper
32. Kull, T., Wacker, J.: Quality management effectiveness in Asia: the influence of culture. J. Oper. Manag. **28**(3), 223–239 (2010)
33. Laaksonen, O., Peltoniemi, M.: The essence of dynamic capabilities and their measurement. Int. J. Manag. Rev. **20**, 184–205 (2018)
34. Maijanen, P., Jantunen, A.: Dynamics of dynamic capabilities: the case of public broadcasting. Int. J. Bus. Excell. **9**(2), 135–155 (2016)
35. March, J.G.: Exploration and exploitation in organizational learning. Organ. Sci. **2**, 71–87 (1991)
36. Maritan, C.A.: Capital investment as investing in organizational capabilities: an empirically grounded process model. Acad. Manag. J. **44**, 513–531 (2001)
37. McCormack, K.: Business process orientation: do you have it? Qual. Prog. **34**, 51–58 (2001)
38. McElheran, K.: Do market leaders lead in business process innovation? The case(s) of E-business adoption. Manag. Sci. **61**(6), 1197–1216 (2015)
39. Mithas, S., Ramasubbu, N., Sambamurthy, V.: How information management capability influences firm performance. MIS Q. **35**(1), 237–256 (2011)
40. Ng, S.C.H., Rungtusanatham, J.M., Zhao, X., Lee, T.S.: Examining process management via the lens of exploitation and exploration: reconceptualization and scale development. Int. J. Prod. Econ. **163**, 1–15 (2015)
41. Nunnally, J.C.: Psychometric Theory. McGraw-Hill, New York (1978)
42. Ohtonen, J.: Business Process Management Capabilities: A Scientific Edition. Turku School of Economics, Turku (2015)
43. Pavlou, P.A., El Sawy, O.A.: Understanding the elusive black box of dynamic capabilities. Decis. Sci. **42**, 239–273 (2011)
44. Peng, D.X., Schroeder, R.G., Shah, R.: Linking routines to operations capabilities: a new perspective. J. Oper. Manag. **26**(6), 730–748 (2008)
45. Phong Tuan, N., Yoshi, T.: Organizational capabilities, competitive advantage and performance in supporting industries in Vietnam. Asian Acad. Manag. J. **15**, 1–21 (2011)
46. Pisano, G.P.: A normative theory of dynamic capabilities: connecting strategy, know-how, and competition. Harvard Business School. Working Paper, No. 16-036 (2015)
47. Power, D., Schoenherr, T., Samson, D.: The cultural characteristic of individualism/collectivism: a comparative study of implications for investment in operations between emerging Asian and industrialized Western countries. J. Oper. Manag. **28**, 206–222 (2010)

48. Preacher, K.J., Rucker, D.D., Hayes, A.F.: Addressing moderated mediation hypotheses: theory, methods, and prescriptions. Multivar. Behav. Res. **42**(1), 185–227 (2007)
49. Protogerou, A., Caloghirou, Y., Lioukas, S.: Dynamic capabilities and their indirect impact on firm performance. In: 25th Celebration Conference on Entrepreneurship and Innovation - Organizations, Institutions, Systems and Regions, Copenhagen (2008)
50. Protogerou, A., Caloghirou, Y., Lioukas, S.: Dynamic capabilities and their indirect impact on firm performance. Ind. Corp. Change **21**, 615–647 (2011)
51. Raduan, C.R., Jegak, U., Haslinda, A., Alimin, I.I.: A conceptual framework of the relationship between organizational resources, capabilities, systems, competitive advantage and performance. Res. J. Int. Stud. **12**, 45–58 (2009)
52. Ray, G., Barney, J.B., Muhanna, W.A.: Capabilities, business processes, and competitive advantage: choosing the dependent variable in empirical tests of the resource-based view. Strat. Manag. J. **25**(1), 23–37 (2004)
53. Rohleder, T.R., Silver, E.A.: A tutorial on business process improvement. J. Oper. Manag. **15**, 139–154 (1997)
54. Saunila, M.: Innovation capability for SME success: perspectives of financial and operational performance. J. Adv. Manag. Res. **11**(2), 163–175 (2014)
55. Schoenherr, T., Narasimhan, R.: The fit between capabilities and priorities and its impact on performance improvement: revisiting and extending the theory of production competence. Int. J. Prod. Res. **50**(14), 3755–3775 (2012)
56. Shrout, P.E., Bolger, N.: Mediation in experimental and nonexperimental studies: new procedures and recommendations. Psychol. Methods **7**(4), 422–445 (2002)
57. Teece, D.J., Pisano, G., Shuen, A.: Dynamic capabilities and strategic management. Strat. Manag. J. **18**, 509–533 (1997)
58. Wang, C.L., Senaratne, C., Rafiq, M.: Success traps, dynamic capabilities and firm performance. Br. J. Manag. **26**, 26–44 (2015)
59. Wiengarten, F., Pagell, M., Fynes, B.: Supply chain environmental investments in dynamic industries: comparing investment and performance differences with static industries. Int. J. Prod. Econ. **135**(2), 541–551 (2012)
60. Winter, S.G.: Understanding dynamic capabilities. Strat. Manag. J. **24**, 991–995 (2003)
61. Winter, S.G.: Organizing for continuous improvement: evolutionary theory meets the quality revolution. In: Baum, J., Singh, J. (eds.) Evolutionary Dynamics of Organizations, pp. 90–108. Oxford University Press, New York (1994)
62. Wollin, A.: Punctuated equilibrium: reconciling theory of revolutionary and incremental change. Behav. Sci. **16**(4), 359–367 (1999)
63. Wong, W.P., Tseng, M.L., Tan, K.H.: A business process management capabilities perspective on organisation performance. Total Qual. Manag. Bus. Excell. **25**(5–6), 602–617 (2014)
64. Wu, S.J., Melnyk, S.A., Flynn, B.B.: Operational capabilities: the secret ingredient. Decis. Sci. **41**(4), 721–754 (2010)

Robotic Process Automation: Systematic Literature Review

Lucija Ivančić$^{(\boxtimes)}$, Dalia Suša Vugec ,
and Vesna Bosilj Vukšić

Faculty of Economics and Business, University of Zagreb, Zagreb, Croatia
{lucija.ivancic,dalia.susa,vesna.bosilj}@efzg.hr

Abstract. Robotic process automation (RPA) emerges as a new technology which is focused on automation of repetitive, routine, rule-based human tasks, aiming to bring benefits to the organizations that decide to implement such software solution. Since RPA is a relatively new technology available on the market, the scientific literature on the topic is still scarce. Therefore, this paper aims to investigate how academic community defines RPA and to which extent has it been investigated in the literature in terms of the state, trends, and application of RPA. Moreover, the difference between RPA and business process management is also addressed. In order to do so, the systematic literature review (SLR) based on Web of Science and Scopus databases has been conducted. The paper provides the results of the conducted SLR on RPA providing an overview of the RPA definitions and practical usage as well as benefits of its implementation in different industries.

Keywords: Robotic process automation · Literature review · Business process management

1 Introduction

Changes in the global economy driven by the development of new technologies require businesses to become more agile and to quickly respond to the needs, wishes, and demands from their customers. Moreover, competitive and financial pressures force organizations to be more efficient, thus constantly seeking for new technologies and methodologies that would help them become more productive, save costs and add value to their business.

One of the solutions which is emerging as a new technology is robotic process automation (RPA) which can replace employees on repetitive tasks and automate them, and therefore, enable employees to be involved in more complicated tasks which can bring organization more value. According to the reports of consulting companies RPA is recognized as an emerging and disruptive technology that is already delivering value (e.g. [10, 15]).

Although there is a number of authors reporting various benefits of implementing RPA within an organization (e.g. [7, 8, 16, 29, 39]), according to authors' best knowledge, RPA is, at the moment, more often implemented in practice than it is investigated by the researches. Thus, it very important to discuss differences, similarities, and

© Springer Nature Switzerland AG 2019
C. Di Ciccio et al. (Eds.): BPM 2019 Blockchain and CEE Forum, LNBIP 361, pp. 280–295, 2019.
https://doi.org/10.1007/978-3-030-30429-4_19

complementarities between RPA and similar technologies and approaches, one of which is business process management (BPM). For example, there is a recommendation for investigating the integration of BPMS and RPA [33]. Moreover, investigating the state of the BPM market, Harmon [20] indicated that 30% of the surveyed practitioners would like to add some kind of RPA capabilities to their process modeling suite.

Therefore, aiming to properly understand RPA, to assess its relevance within the research community and to investigate its link to BPM, a systematic literature review (SLR) has been conducted. In that sense, this paper reports on three research questions related to the state and progress of the RPA research, its definition and practical usage, which are addressed in more detail later in this paper. Moreover, the paper aims to provide an understanding of the differences between RPA and BPMS.

With the purpose of meeting the paper's goal and to answer the research questions, the paper is structured as follows. After this introduction, a brief background on RPA is given in the second part of the paper, explaining RPA in theory and practice and its relation to BPM. The third part of the paper refers to the employed research methodology, in terms of identification of research questions as well as the SLR protocol. Next, research results regarding three research questions are presented in the fourth part of the paper, while in fifth, they are discussed. Last, the sixth part of the paper brings the conclusion.

2 Background on Robotic Process Automation

2.1 Robotic Process Automation in Theory and Practice

According to the findings of preliminary literature overview, RPA is defined as the application of specific technology and methodologies which is based on software and algorithms aiming to automate repetitive human tasks [16, 21, 33, 39]. It is mostly driven by simple rules and business logic while interacts with multiple information systems through existing graphic user interfaces [17]. Its functionalities comprise the automation of repeatable and rule-based activities by the use of non-invasive software robot, called "bot" [27, 29, 38].

Recently, RPA definition is extended towards its conjunction with artificial intelligence (AI), cognitive computing, process mining, and data analytics. The introduction of advanced digital technologies allows RPA to be reallocated from performing repetitive and error-prone routines in business processes towards more complex knowledge-intensive and value-adding tasks [3, 17, 45].

To assess the state of the RPA market Forrester [15] identified 12 RPA vendors offering enterprise-level, full-corporate solutions that can support the requirements of a "shared service" or enterprise-wide RPA utility. Though some RPA vendors offer industry-specific solutions, Schmitz et al. [42] see "the general concept of RPA as industry agnostic". On the other hand, the RPA vendors' partnership with the leading artificial intelligence providers enabled the extension of traditional RPA functionalities with the new, emerging technologies such as self-learning from the process discovery, training robots, AI-screen recognition, natural language generation and automated processes documentation generation [3].

A majority of 400 companies surveyed by Deloitte [10] have started on their RPA journey and almost a quarter more plan to do so in the next two years. They also report that payback periods are averaging around a year and their expectations of cost reduction, accuracy, timeliness, flexibility, and improved compliance are met or exceeded [10]. Forrester [15] estimates that by 2021, there will be over 4 million robots automating repeatable tasks, but the focus will be moved toward integrations with AI and improvements of RPA analytics. Similarly, Everest Group [12] points out that though a majority of buyers are highly satisfied with RPA solutions, they require the enhancement of analytics and cognitive capabilities.

Despite the high benefits from RPA, only 5% of companies involved in Deloitte research [10] have implemented more than 50 robots in their operations. Organizational capability and the understanding of business goals of RPA implementation are crucial for the success of RPA projects. A lack of understanding of what RPA means and where it can be applied, a lack of management support and a fear of job loss by employees are identified key challenges for automating processes [43]. A change management strategy, a change of organizational culture and a shift in mindset could help to bridge the gap between RPA being an IT tool and the business side of it [10, 28, 43]. On the other side, Everest Group study [13] participants rated good customer support, training and educational materials, RPA maintenance services and good RPA vendor ecosystem for complementary technologies as very important drivers of RPA adoption. Besides, the introduction of new technologies brings up questions about the management of robots, its' central control, and governance [15].

2.2   Robotic Process Automation and Business Process Management

As already indicated, it is important to investigate similarities and differences, as well as complementarities between RPA and like technologies. In that sense, since RPA and BPM are neighboring disciplines having complementary goals, Mendling et al. [33] call for the BPM research community to investigate business process management systems (BPMSs) and RPA integration.

BPM is a multidimensional approach aiming to achieve better business performance through continuous process improvement, optimization and digital transformation. BPMS as a holistic software platform that encompasses a wide range of functionalities such as process design, analytics, and monitoring is very often one of the BPM initiative inevitable perspectives [6]. On the other side, RPA deals with discreet, repetitive tasks and execute processes as a human would. According to Cewe et al. [8] "BPMS is used to orchestrate end-to-end process, and to manage human, robots and system interactions, RPA is responsible for repetitive sequences of tasks that can be fully delegated to software robots".

Though these technologies are very often used separately, the authors from business practice [14, 36] strongly suggest combining both to gain even more business value. In a case of the lack of resources and/or time to completely implement BPMS, RPA can be a valuable and relatively inexpensive tool to solve or complement some of the unfulfilled goals.

3 Research Methodology

3.1 Identification of Research Questions

The results of the brief literature overview (as presented in Sect. 2) revealed the significance of RPA for business practitioners and researchers, and the lack of SLR in the RPA domain. The preliminary findings showed the gaps in research contexts, the lack of theoretical frameworks and discrepancies in the definition of RPA and its content. Besides, the ad-hoc portrait of recent RPA literature showed that RPA is recognized in business practice as a leverage for performance improvement. Though many benefits and challenges of RPA implementation were addressed, the need to systematize experiences from business practice referring to the usage of RPA was noticed. Finally, the discussion regarding RPA as a newly emerged area of BPM was evidenced in both professional and academic literature.

Following the previous annotations about scientific and professional papers that focus their attention on RPA, the research questions are determined. They are defined from more general to more specific, as follows:

RQ1 What is the state and progress of research on RPA?; **RQ2** How is RPA defined (**RQ2-1**) and what is a difference between RPA and BPMSs according to the researchers (**RQ2-2**)?; **RQ3** How is RPA used in business practice, as mentioned in the scientific literature?

While RQ1 is related to the results of bibliometric analysis, the answers on RQ2 and RQ3 are grounded on the qualitative outcomes from the detailed content analysis of the sampled articles.

3.2 Systematic Literature Research Protocol

In order to fulfill the objectives of this paper and to answer the research questions, a SLR approach was adopted. SLR methodology has been originated in medicine researches, but during the last two decades, this approach became popular in management and information systems field researches because it systematizes knowledge from a prior body of research and ensures the fidelity, completeness, and quality of findings [32, 35, 44, 48]. According to a typical SLR guideline [5, 24], our literature retrieval was conducted through a three-step approach: (1) SLR protocol definition and literature search and selection; (2) quality appraisal and extraction of relevant articles; and (3) qualitative analysis and synthesis of the accepted articles.

For the first step of SLR, a research protocol was designed and presented (Table 1). Next, the articles were browsed in two collections: Scopus and Web of Science Core Collection (WoS). These digital databases were chosen in order to comprise articles from two fields related to RPA: social sciences and information systems. According to our inclusion criteria, the search string was composed of the keywords "robotic process automation" while the search was not restricted, neither to a specific time limit nor to a specific field or index. This search strategy was employed to comprise all useful findings from various fields giving an insight into the evolution of RPA researches until the end of March 2019, which is when our research was conducted.

As a result of our search 46 articles were found (12 in WoS and 34 in Scopus). After excluding the duplicate articles, 36 articles remained (8 in both WoS and Scopus, 2 only in WoS, 18 only in Scopus).

Table 1. RPA research protocol

SLR Protocol element	Translation in RPA research
Digital sources	Scopus and Web of Science Core Collection (WoS)
Searched term	Robotic process automation
Search strategy	No publication date limit; no topic limit; search term contained anywhere in the articles; articles and conference papers only (no editorial, review, conference review)
Inclusion criteria	Search string "robotic process automation"
Exclusion criteria	Articles without full access; extended abstracts (without full text); book chapters; professional papers; articles citing the term "robotic process automation" with a different meaning

For step 2 several exclusion criteria were applied. As we sought to analyze peer-reviewed journal articles and scientific conference papers, the articles without full access (2), extended abstracts only (2) and the articles mistakenly classified as peer-review articles (1 book chapter and 1 professional paper) were excluded. Consequently, a total of 30 potentially appropriate articles remained for further analysis. Besides, the abstracts of all the 30 articles were analyzed to determine its' relevance to the goals of this research. As a result of abstract analysis, 3 articles with a different meaning of "robotic process automation" than the one understood in the context of our research (as presented in Sect. 2.2), were found. Finally, 27 articles were extracted as revealing significance for the objective of this SLR. Appendix outlines the articles resulting from the SLR.

Step 3 of our SLR protocol is where the selected research articles were further analyzed based on the full text reading and codded by using the programs MS Excel and NVivo. The quantitative results from MS Excel were used to answer RQ1, while the results of the qualitative analysis conducted in NVivo gave the answers to RQ2-RQ3.

4   Research Results

4.1   SLR Results: The State and Progress of Research on RPA

This section responds to **RQ1** presenting the basic bibliographic results obtained from the analysis of the coded fields: 'Year of publication', 'Publication outlet' (a journal or a conference proceeding), 'Study strategy' (a theoretically applied approach, an empirical research or a review) and 'Journal title'.

Figure 1 presents a publishing frequency (2016-2018) regarding publication outlet. A total of 20 out of 27 articles were published in 2018, among which 14 conference papers and 6 journal articles. Only 4 journal articles and 3 conference papers were published in 2016 and 2017.

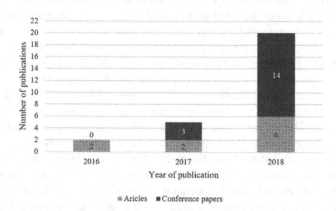

Fig. 1. Appearance of RPA articles by publication year (2016-2018) and the publication outlet

From the methodological point of view, the articles are grouped into 3 study strategies: empirical researches (a qualitative or a quantitative), a theoretical applied approach and literature review articles.

The majority of articles (18) used the empirical research strategy among which 16 qualitative (12 case studies and 4 reviews of a specific type of RPA technology) and 2 quantitative researches (questionnaire surveys) were found. A half (6) of the case study articles were published in peer-reviewed journals. A theoretical applied approach was employed in 4 articles (1 journal article and 3 conference proceeding articles) while the results of a literature review were presented in 5 articles (2 journal articles and 3 conference proceeding papers). Within the last category, only 1 was an SLR article. In total, 67% of the articles can be classified as empirical research, 18% as a literature review, and 15% as a theoretical research papers.

Two journals containing the highest number of RPA papers were Journal of Information Technology Teaching Cases (4) and MIS Quarterly Executive (2) while most of the conference proceedings papers came from ACM International Conference Proceeding Series (3) and Lecture Notes in Business Information Processing series (3).

Appendix outlines the articles resulting from the SLR and the bibliographic results used to respond RQ1.

4.2 SLR Results About RPA Definition and Understanding the Difference Between RPA and BPM

For RQ2-1, the results of the brief literature overview (as presented in Sect. 2.2) show that the definitions of RPA vary in the extant professional and academic literature. While some of the available articles incorporate a narrow view of using specific software and algorithms aiming to automate repetitive manual tasks, the others have built their definitions on the extension of the traditional RPA functions with the advanced digital technologies such as: AI (e.g. machine learning, image recognition), drones and remote sensing technologies. The content of the articles is analyzed in order to identify the definition of RPA, its characteristics and functionalities as addressed by the researchers.

Most of the definitions provided within the observed articles define traditional RPA as an emerging technology which automates repetitive human tasks, both digital and physical (e.g. [1, 7, 16, 18, 19, 30, 39]). Moreover, Geyer-Klingeberg et al. [17], as well as Leno et al. [29], stress out that those tasks are usually error prone and therefore are suitable for automation. Furthermore, Aguirre and Rodriguez [1], Anagnoste [3], Gupta et al. [18] as well as Tsaih and Hsu [45] view RPA as the usage of cognitive technology and refer to it as cognitive automation. Gejke [16], Mendling et al. [33] and Penttinen et al. [37] emphasize that RPA is a software solution configured to interact with existing applications and systems the way like a human would do.

According to Issac et al. [22], functionalities of the traditional RPA are: (i) front office (attended) automation and back office (unattended) automation; (ii) script based designer and visual process designer; (iii) the openness of the platform; (iv) macro recorders for process mapping; (v) control through coding; (vi) execution of automated test cases on remote machines; (vii) bot development and core functions; (viii) the control room, system management, reporting and resilience, and; (ix) RPA analytical potential.

The results of detailed content analysis of the sampled articles show that the integration of RPA with the emerging technologies is elaborated in Anagnoste [3], Kobayashi et al. [25], Kulbacki et al. [26], Lin et al. [31], Schmider et al. [41], Tsaih and Hsu [45]; and Van Belkum et al. [47]. All of these 7 articles were published in 2018. Table 2 summarizes the findings and contributes to the understanding of what impact these technologies will have on RPA future development and implementation (**RQ2-1**).

Table 2. Traditional RPA and advanced digital technologies integration

Technology		Field of deployment	Ref.
AI	Machine learning	Healthcare (product development and life-cycle management of healthcare products)	[47]
		Healthcare (processing of adverse event reports)	[41]
		Tourism (tourist behavior prediction)	[45]
	Machine vision/image, screen, voice, pattern recognition	Sales (vendors' documentation processing)	[3]
		Semiconductor manufacturing (controlling the equipment and using screen image recognition)	[31]
	Natural language processing	Consulting (chatbots applied in the HR department)	[3]
		Tourism (chatbots used to provide one-stop-shop for travel information)	[45]
Drones and associated technologies		Agriculture (usage of drones, sophisticated, cameras, and RPA for agriculture automation)	[26]
Internet of Things (IoT)		Distribution, delivery (parcel delivery service using IoT, QR code recognition and RPA)	[25]

To address the **RQ2-2** of what is a difference between RPA and BPMSs the content of the sampled articles is retrieved and analyzed. BPM is mentioned in a total of 10 out of 27 articles. However, only 6 articles [1, 8, 27, 37, 43, 50] discuss the characteristics that distinguish RPA from BPMS, specify the steps of RPA deployment and explain how RPA complements BPMS.

While BPMS interacts with business applications through APIs, RPA connects the process with the applications by interacting with the user interface [9, 46]. According to Cewe et al. [8] "RPA can be taken for a special kind of BPMS that relies on the graphic user interface (GUI) automation adaptors instead of regular interfaces (i.e. application programming interfaces – APIs) for intersystem communication". In a case of BPMS development advanced programming skills are usually necessary for hard coding and integration with the existing systems via APIs [1, 8]. On the other side, the development of RPA is considerably less time and cost consuming, the knowledge of programming is mostly not needed. The most important conclusions of these articles are in line with the RPA/BPMS preliminary overview presented in Sect. 2.2.

4.3   SLR Results: RPA in Business Practice

To respond to **RQ3** about the usage of RPA in business practice content of 12 case studies is further investigated looking at the organization's industry type, a type or name of process chosen for automation and a country the organization comes from (Table 3).

The results show that two-thirds of RPA implementation projects as mentioned by the researchers come from two industries - services (7) and telecommunications (3) while the other implementations are related to finance and insurance (2), healthcare management (1), sales (1) and oil & gas (1) industry. Though human resource management, finance and accounting, and administrative back-office processes are detected as the best candidates for automation, the organizations conducted RPA initiatives in outsourcing services, sales and purchasing processes. As presented in Table 3 RPA initiatives are mostly conducted by organizations having its headquarters in the developed countries, such as Finland, UK, and the USA and by global companies.

These results can lead towards the assumption that digital competitiveness of a country and the high level of organization's ICT maturity positively influence RPA implementation. Moreover, the usage of RPA in business practice has been investigated from a benefits point of view, analyzing the content of 12 case studies. The results reveal the following benefits of the RPA implementation in business practice: (i) increased efficiency [1, 39]; (ii) reducing human labor, i.e. reducing workforce [39]; (iii) employees can concentrate on value creation [39]; (iv) costs savings [1, 17, 19, 37, 39]; (v) ease of use [2, 19, 37]; (vi) increased volume of performed tasks [17, 39], and; (vii) increased quality of work, i.e. tasks are performed accurately, correctly and consistently [1, 17, 39].

Table 3. Implementation of RPA by industry type, process type and country

Industry type	Process type	Country	Ref.
Services	Recruitment (HRM services)	India	[18]
	Payroll process (outsourcing services)	Finland	[19]
	Financial process automation	Finland	[4]
	Payment receipt (outsourcing services)	Colombia	[1]
	Process of promotion in HRM (outsourcing services)	n/a	[2]
	HRM, IT management, Public relations, Knowledge management (consulting services)	n/a, global company	[3]
	HRM (audit, tax, and consulting services)	n/a, global company	[50]
Telecommunications	Purchasing	n/a, global company	[17]
	Sales (capacity check for bid processing) Subscription-based online service	Finland	[37]
	Back-office processes	UK	[27]
Financial and Insurance	Healthcare claims adjudication process	USA	[11]
	Administrative back-office process; Premiums processing; E-policies offshore process	n/a, global company	[50]
Healthcare management	Administrative, back-office processes	Finland	[39]
Sales	Vendor information processing	n/a, global company	[3]
Oil and Gas	Finance and accounting: the process of reconciliation the bank with the cash from the stations in the previous day	n/a	[2]

5 Discussion

The aim of this section is to analyze and discuss the previously raised research questions. To address the **RQ1** the bibliometric analysis of a sample of articles was conducted showing that the research on RPA was almost tripled in 2018 in comparison to period 2016–2017. This can lead to the conclusion that the number of RPA researches will continue the growth in the future. Having in mind that RPA is a rather new and emerging field, the results identifying the appearance of 17 conference papers against 10 journal articles imply that the full research potential on RPA topic hasn't been achieved yet. Hence, it can be concluded that the studies on RPA have only begun to emerge and it is expected they will achieve its proliferation in the next few years, including appearance in peer-reviewed journals.

A total of 18 out of 27 articles fell into the "empirical research" category indicating the scarcity of RPA theoretical researches and conceptual frameworks. Only 1 structured literature study (e.g. SLR article) investigating RPA case studies proved our assumption about the lack of SLR approach in the field. The top 2 conferences publishing RPA studies are information-systems related (Lecture Notes in Business

Information Processing Series), and IT and computing-related (ACM International Conference Proceeding Series). Similarly, half of the journal articles about RPA were published in journals covering the management of information systems issues (MIS Quarterly Executive) and case studies on contemporary information and communications technology themes (Journal of Information Technology Teaching Cases). Only 3 authors (Lacity, Willcocks, and Anagnoste) contributed with more than one paper.

The goal of **RQ2-1** is two-fold, first to define the aim and scope of RPA form a traditional point of view; and second, to examine how RPA extends towards the emerging technologies. Responding **the first goal of RQ2-1**, the analysis on the definitions of RPA indicates that a common agreement is achieved among the researchers defining RPA as a "relatively new technology for process automation based on software and algorithms aiming to emulate a human work and to perform manual activities by interacting with information systems through existing user interfaces" [16, 33, 39]. From a business perspective, RPA is mainly used to "capture and interpret existing applications for processing a transaction, manipulating data, triggering responses and communicating with other digital systems" [47]. Thus, it is considered "suitable for high volume, repetitive, monotonous, well-structured and standardized tasks, where there is no need for subjective judgment, creativity or interpretation skills" [1]. RPA solutions are minimally invasive, easy to use, inexpensive and quite simple to implement since RPA sits on the top of existing information systems, does not store any transactional data and does not require a database [1, 19, 33, 50].

The results of the analysis about the RPA and advanced technologies integration indicate what is coming next to RPA, so giving the answer on **the second goal of RQ2-1**. According to Anagnoste [3], RPA solutions are moving toward AI technologies, such as: "IOCR, chat-bots, machine learning, cognitive platforms, anomaly detection, pattern analysis, voice recognition, data classification and many more". Besides, the implementation of the "advanced RPA" within different fields is evidenced (e.g. healthcare, tourism, agriculture, distribution, and sales), thus proving the wide range of integrated RPA and advanced technologies applicability.

A discussion point we want to explore in relation to **RQ2-2** is whether the RPA research field is in conjunction with the concept of BPM and how it can be integrated with BPMSs. The researchers agree that despite the differences BPMS and RPA complement each other [1, 8, 46]. Thus, deployed together BPMS and RPA can help the digital transformation and business performance improvement.

For **RQ3**, the findings refer to the benefits of RPA implementation in different industries (e.g. banking and insurance services, healthcare and pharmaceuticals, telecommunications) and business processes [4, 27]. Several business functions are recognized by business practitioners as good candidates for RPA implementation, among which the most often mentioned are sales, finance and accounting, and human resources management [43]. A majority of early RPA adopters automated their back-office tasks and internal support processes, like accounting, billing, travel expenses, master data management, keeping employee records and claims processing [1, 43, 49], but recently several researchers documented a number of RPA applications aiming to automate core business processes and shared service operations [40, 42]. According to Willcocks et al. [50], the significant expansion of RPA initiatives not only in back office processes automation but also amongst business process outsourcing (BPO) service providers started in 2016.

The results of the comprehensive analysis reveal that the perceived value of RPA is mainly related to organizational performance enhancement and costs reduction by reducing human labor in routine business processes, and also by increasing the quality of the work [23]. However, the outcomes that cannot be directly measured financially are also comprised, such as competence, market position, innovation, knowledge discovery, research and development [34, 39]. Since the costs of RPA development and maintenance can exceed the obtained savings, business processes must be carefully analyzed in order to evaluate their suitability for RPA [7, 17].

6   Conclusion

This paper presented the results of SLR on RPA based on the search results from WoS and Scopus databases. According to the authors' best knowledge, this paper represents the first SLR paper focused on all RPA related publications from the named two databases, which is one of its contributions. The results of the SLR conducted for the purpose of this paper revealed the existence of another RPA related SLR; however, it dealt only with case studies and not all available publications [51]. Moreover, named SLR has been focused on publications available on the public Web and Google Scholar.

Besides the named contribution, this paper focused on opinions and writings of the academics regarding the RPA, elaborated through three research questions presented in the methodology section of the paper. In that sense, the paper gives an overview of definitions, usage, and benefits of RPA in practice, as well as the explanation of the difference between RPA and BPMS. Moreover, the results of the conducted SLR revealed lack of theoretical studies on RPA, indicating that the area is still relatively new and that no theoretical frameworks have been formed.

The limitations of this paper include lack of access to two papers which have been found through the search process and therefore their exclusion from the presented analysis. Based on the results of the conducted SLR, research gap in terms of the lack of both theoretical as well as empirical research has been noticed. Therefore, future research of this topic suggests researches towards filling this gap. One of the possible directions for future research is the investigation of both direct and indirect effects of RPA on organizational performance.

Appendix

Articles resulting from the SLR

Ref	Year	Title of the paper	Col.		SS
			W	S	
[7]	2018	Towards a Process Analysis Approach to Adopt Robotic Process Automation		+	EA
[26]	2018	Survey of Drones for Agriculture Automation from Planting to Harvest		+	LR
[18]	2018	Automation in recruitment: a new frontier		+	EA
[31]	2018	Apply RPA (Robotic Process Automation) in Semiconductor Smart Manufacturing		+	EA
[39]	2018	Robotic process automation - Creating value by digitalizing work in the private healthcare?		+	EA
[47]	2018	Artificial intelligence in clinical development and regulatory affairs – Preparing for the future		+	LR
[33]	2018	How do machine learning, robotic process automation, and blockchains affect the human factor in business process management?		+	LR
[16]	2018	A new season in the risk landscape: Connecting the advancement in technology with changes in customer behaviour to enhance the way risk is measured and managed		+	TA
[17]	2018	Process mining and Robotic process automation: A perfect match		+	EA
[37]	2018	How to choose between robotic process automation and back-end system automation?		+	EA
[29]	2018	Multi-Perspective process model discovery for robotic process automation		+	LR
[30]	2018	Identifying candidate tasks for robotic process automation in textual process descriptions		+	TA
[41]	2018	Innovation in Pharmacovigilance: Use of Artificial Intelligence in Adverse Event Case Processing		+	EA
[45]	2018	Artificial intelligence in smart tourism: A conceptual framework		+	TA
[25]	2018	SNS Door Phone as Robotic Process Automation	+	+	EA
[22]	2018	Delineated Analysis of Robotic Process Automation Tools	+	+	EA
[51]	2018	The key factors affecting RPA-business alignment	+	+	LR
[8]	2018	Minimal effort requirements engineering for robotic process automation with test driven development and screen recording	+	+	TA

(continued)

(continued)

Ref	Year	Title of the paper	Col.		SS
			W	S	
[19]	2018	How OpusCapita used internal RPA capabilities to offer services to clients	+	+	EA
[3]	2018	Robotic Automation Process - The operating system for the digital enterprise	+		EA
[50]	2017	Robotic process automation: Strategic transformation lever for global business services?		+	EA
[11]	2017	Resolving tussles in service automation deployments: Service automation at Blue Cross Blue Shield North Carolina (BCBSNC)		+	EA
[1]	2017	Automation of a business process using robotic process automation (RPA): A case study	+	+	EA
[43]	2017	Software bots -The next frontier for shared services and functional excellence		+	EA
[2]	2017	Robotic Automation Process - The next major revolution in terms of back office operations improvement	+		EA
[4]	2016	Turning robotic process automation into commercial success - Case OpusCapita		+	EA
[27]	2016	Robotic process automation at telefónica O2	+	+	EA

Note: Col. – Collection; W – WoS; S – Scopus; SS – Study strategy; EA – Empirical approach; TA – Theoretical approach; LR – Literature review

References

1. Aguirre, S., Rodriguez, A.: Automation of a business process using robotic process automation (RPA): a case study. In: Figueroa-García, J.C., López-Santana, E.R., Villa-Ramírez, J.L., Ferro-Escobar, R. (eds.) WEA 2017. CCIS, vol. 742, pp. 65–71. Springer, Cham (2017). https://doi.org/10.1007/978-3-319-66963-2_7
2. Anagnoste, S.: Robotic automation process-the next major revolution in terms of back office operations improvement. In: Proceedings of the International Conference on Business Excellence, vol. 11, no. 1, pp. 676–686, De Gruyter Open (2017)
3. Anagnoste, S.: Robotic automation process – the operating system for the digital enterprise. In: Proceedings of the International Conference on Business Excellence, vol. 12, no. 1, pp. 54–69, De Gruyter, Poland (2018)
4. Asatiani, A., Penttinen, E.: Turning robotic process automation into commercial success – case OpusCapita. J. Inf. Technol. Teach. Cases **6**, 67–74 (2016)
5. Boell, S.K., Cecez-Kecmanovic, D.: On being 'systematic' in literature reviews in IS. J. Inf. Technol. **30**(2), 161–173 (2015)
6. Bosilj Vukšić, V., Brkić, Lj., Tomičić-Pupek, K.: Understanding the success factors in adopting business process management software: case studies. Interdisc. Description Complex Syst. **16**(2), 194–215 (2018)
7. Bourgouin, A., Leshob, A., Renard, L.: Towards a process analysis approach to adopt robotic process automation. In: ICEBE 2018 - 15th International Conference on e-Business Engineering, pp. 46–53. IEEE (2018)

8. Cewe, C., Koch, D., Mertens, R.: Minimal effort requirements engineering for robotic process automation with test driven development and screen recording. In: Teniente, E., Weidlich, M. (eds.) BPM 2017. LNBIP, vol. 308, pp. 642–648. Springer, Cham (2018). https://doi.org/10.1007/978-3-319-74030-0_51

9. Chappell, D.: Introducing blue prism: automating business processes with presentation integration (2010). http://www.davidchappell.com/writing/white_papers/Introducing_Blue_Prism_v1.0-Chappell.pdf. Accessed 5 Mar 2019

10. Deloitte: The robots are ready. Are you? Untapped advantage in your digital workforce (2017). https://www2.deloitte.com/content/dam/Deloitte/tr/Documents/technology/deloitte-robots-are-ready.pdf. Accessed 5 Mar 2019

11. Dunlap, R., Lacity, M.: Resolving tussles in service automation deployments: service automation at Blue Cross Blue Shield North Carolina (BCBSNC). J. Inf. Technol. Teach. Cases **7**(1), 29–34 (2017)

12. Everest Group: Robotic process automation annual report 2018-creating business value in a digital-first word (2018). https://www2.everestgrp.com/reports/EGR-2018-38-R-2691. Accessed 5 Mar 2019

13. Everest Group: Defining Enterprise RPA (2018). https://www.uipath.com/company/rpa-analyst-reports/defining-enterprise-rpa-everest-research-report. Accessed 5 Mar 2019

14. Forrester: Building a center of expertise to support robotic automation: preparing for the life cycle of business change (2014). http://neoops.com/wp-content/uploads/2014/03/Forrester-RA-COE.pdf. Accessed 5 Mar 2019

15. Forrester: The Forrester Wave™: Robotic Process Automation, Q1 2017 - The 12 Providers That Matter Most and How They Stack Up, Forrester Research, Inc. (2017). https://www.forrester.com/report/The+Forrester+Wave+Robotic+Process+Automation+Q1+2017/-/E-RES131182. Accessed 5 Mar 2019

16. Gejke, C.: A new season in the risk landscape: connecting the advancement in technology with changes in customer behaviour to enhance the way risk is measured and managed. J. Risk Manag. Finan. Inst. **11**(2), 148–155 (2018)

17. Greyer-Klingeberg, J., Nakladal, J., Baldauf, F.: Process mining and robotic process automation: a perfect match. In: 16th International Conference on Business Process Management, Sydney, Australia (2018)

18. Gupta, P., Fernandes, S.F., Jain, M.: Automation in recruitment: a new frontier. J. Inf. Technol. Teach. Cases **8**(2), 118–125 (2018)

19. Hallikainen, P., Bekkhus, R., Pan, S.L.: How OpusCapita used internal RPA capabilities to offer services to clients. MIS Q. Exec. **17**(1), 41–52 (2018)

20. Harmon, P.: The State of the BPM market – 2018 (2018). https://www.redhat.com/cms/managed-files/mi-bptrends-state-of-bpm-2018-survey-analyst-paper-201803-en.pdf. Accessed 5 Mar 2019

21. Institute for Robotic Process Automation: Introduction to Robotic Process Automation (2015). https://irpaai.com/wp-content/uploads/2015/05/Robotic-Process-Automation-June2015.pdf. Accessed 5 Mar 2019

22. Issac, R., Muni, R., Desai, K.: Delineated analysis of robotic process automation tools. In: ICAECC 2018 - Second International Conference on Advances in Electronics, Computers and Communications, pp. 1–5. IEEE (2018)

23. Kirchmer, M.: Robotic process automation - pragmatic solution or dangerous illusion?. Business Transformation & Operational Excellence World Summit (BTOES) (2017)

24. Kitchenham, B., Charters, S.: Guidelines for performing systematic literature reviews in software engineering. EBSE Technical report EBSE-2007-01 (2007)

25. Kobayashi, T., Nakashima, R., Uchida, R., Arai, K.: SNS door phone as robotic process automation. In: Proceedings of the 2018 ACM International Conference on Interactive Surfaces and Spaces, pp. 457–460. ACM (2018)

26. Kulbacki, M., et al.: Survey of drones for agriculture automation from planting to harvest. In: INES 2018 22nd International Conference on Intelligent Engineering Systems, pp. 353–358. IEEE (2018)

27. Lacity, M., Willcocks, L.P.: Robotic process automation at telefónica O2. MIS Q. Exec. **15**, 21–35 (2016)

28. Lacity, M., Willcocks, L.P.: Robotic process automation: the next transformation lever for shared services. In: The Outsourcing Unit Working Research Paper Series, Paper 16/01 (2016). http://www.umsl.edu/~lacitym/OUWP1601.pdf. Accessed 5 Mar 2019

29. Leno, V., Dumas, M., Maggi, F.M., La Rosa, M.: Multi-perspective process model discovery for robotic process automation. In: CEUR Workshop Proceedings, vol. 2114, pp. 37–45 (2018)

30. Leopold, H., van der Aa, H., Reijers, H.A.: Identifying candidate tasks for robotic process automation in textual process descriptions. In: Gulden, J., Reinhartz-Berger, I., Schmidt, R., Guerreiro, S., Guédria, W., Bera, P. (eds.) BPMDS/EMMSAD -2018. LNBIP, vol. 318, pp. 67–81. Springer, Cham (2018). https://doi.org/10.1007/978-3-319-91704-7_5

31. Lin, S.C., Shih, L.H., Yang, D., Lin, J., Kung, J.F.: Apply RPA (Robotic Process Automation) in Semiconductor Smart Manufacturing. In: 2018 e-Manufacturing and Design Collaboration Symposium (eMDC), pp. 1–3. IEEE (2018)

32. McLean, R., Antony, J.: Why continuous improvement initiatives fail in manufacturing environments? a systematic review of the evidence. Int. J. Prod. Perform. Manag. **63**(3), 370–376 (2014)

33. Mendling, J., Decker, G., Hull, R., Reijers, H.A., Weber, I.: How do machine learning, robotic process automation, and blockchains affect the human factor in business process management? Commun. Assoc. Inf. Syst. **43**, 297–320 (2018)

34. Ojala, A., Helander, N.: Value creation and evolution of a value network: a longitudinal case study on a platform-as-a-service provider. In: 47th Hawaii International Conference on System Sciences (HICSS). IEEE (2014)

35. Okoli, C.: A guide to conducting a standalone systematic literature review. Commun. Assoc. Inf. Syst. **37**(43), 879–910 (2015)

36. Ovum: Robotic Process Automation: Adding to the Process Transformation Toolkit - The role that RPA can play within service providers and enterprises (2015). http://research. globalriskcommunity.com/content76913. Accessed 5 Mar 2019

37. Penttinen, E., Kasslin, H., Asatiani, A.: How to choose between robotic process automation and back-end system automation?. In: 26th European Conference on Information Systems (2018)

38. Rajesh, K.V.N., Ramesh, K.V.N.: Robotic process automation: a death knell to dead-end jobs? CSI Commun. Knowl. Dig. IT Commun. **42**(3), 10–14 (2018)

39. Ratia, M., Myllärniemi, J., Helander, N.: Robotic process automation - creating value by digitalizing work in the private healthcare. In: ACM International Conference Proceeding Series, International Academic Mindtrek Conference (2018)

40. Scheer, A.W.: Performancesteigerung durch Automatisierung von Geschäftsprozessen, AWS Institut fur digitale Produkte und Prozesse gGmbH (AWSi) (2017). https://www.aws-institut.de/wp-content/uploads/2017/11/031117_GPPerformance_44seiten_final_300dpi_2Aufl_einzel.pdf. Accessed 5 Mar 2019

41. Schmider, J., Kumar, K., LaForest, C., Swankoski, B., Naim, K., Caubel, P.M.: Innovation in pharmacovigilance: use of artificial intelligence in adverse event case processing. Clin. Pharmacol. Ther. **105**(4), 954–961 (2019)

42. Schmitz, M., Dietze, C., Czarnecki, C.: Enabling digital transformation through robotic process automation at Deutsche Telekom. In: Urbach, N., Röglinger, M. (eds.) Digitalization Cases. MP, pp. 15–33. Springer, Cham (2019). https://doi.org/10.1007/978-3-319-95273-4_2

43. Suri, V.K., Elia, M., van Hillegersberg, J.: Software bots - the next frontier for shared services and functional excellence. In: Oshri, I., Kotlarsky, J., Willcocks, Leslie P. (eds.) Global Sourcing 2017. LNBIP, vol. 306, pp. 81–94. Springer, Cham (2017). https://doi.org/10.1007/978-3-319-70305-3_5

44. Tranfield, D., Denyer, D., Smart, P.: Towards a methodology for developing evidence informed management knowledge by means of systematic review. Br. J. Manag. **14**(3), 207–222 (2003)

45. Tsaih, R., Hsu, C. C.: Artificial intelligence in smart tourism: a conceptual framework. In: Proceedings of The 18th International Conference on Electronic Business, ICEB, Guilin, China, 2–6 December, pp. 124–133 (2018)

46. Valdes-Faura, M.: RPA and BPM, it's all about the process! (2018). https://www.bonitasoft.com/news/rpa_bpm_all_about_process. Accessed 5 Mar 2019

47. Van Belkum, S., Brun, N., Cleve, S., McGovern, P., Lumpkin, M., Schaeffer, P.E., Pauli, T., Trethowan, J., Netzer, T.: Artificial intelligence in clinical development and regulatory affairs – preparing for the future. Regul. Rapp. **15**(10), 17–21 (2018)

48. Webster, J., Watson, R.T.: Analyzing the past to prepare for the future: writing a literature review. MIS Q. **26**(2), 13–23 (2002)

49. Wilcock, L., Lacity, M., Craig, A.: The IT function and robotic process automation. In: LSE Research Online Documents on Economics from London School of Economics and Political Science, LSE Library (2015). http://eprints.lse.ac.uk/64519/ Accessed 5 Mar 2019

50. Wilcocks, L., Lacity, M., Craig, A.: Robotic process automation: strategic transformation lever for global business services? J. Inf. Technol. Teach. Cases **7**(1), 17–28 (2017)

51. Zhang, N., Liu, B.: The key factors affecting RPA-business alignment. In: Proceedings of the 3rd International Conference on Crowd Science and Engineering, p. 10. ACM (2018)

An Empirical Investigation of the Cultural Impacts on the Business Process Concepts' Representations

Gregor Polančič[1(⊠)], Pavlo Brin[2], Saša Kuhar[1], Gregor Jošt[1], and Jernej Huber[1]

[1] Faculty of Electrical Engineering and Computer Science, University of Maribor, Koroška cesta 46, 2000 Maribor, Slovenia
{gregor.polancic,sasa.kuhar,gregor.jost, jernej.huber}@um.si
[2] National Technical University, Kharkiv Polytechnic Institute, 21 Frunze str., Kharkiv 61002, Ukraine
pavel.brin@ukr.net

Abstract. Business Process Diagrams serve several purposes, including process analysis, process-related communication, and process automation. Considering communication, modelers must ensure that all participants understand a process diagram and the corresponding notation in the same way. With globalization, this might get challenging, since different cultural environments may imply implicitly different meanings to specified symbols, whereas the same concepts may be associated with different representations. Thus, our efforts are directed towards investigating the intuitiveness of common Business Process Concepts' representations. In this manner, we performed empirical research on a sample of novice modelers in two cultural environments, who were instructed to design graphical representations for the defined concepts. Our findings show which Business Process Concepts' representations are intuitive to novice modelers and how the cultural background impacts it.

Keywords: Business Process Concepts · Visual vocabulary · Cultural impacts

1 Introduction

To perform effective 'diagrammatic communication', it must be ensured that Business Process Diagrams (hereinafter referred to as BPD) are 'readable', which means that a process analyst is able to understand the vocabulary of the language, as well as the grammatical rules which constitute the modeling notation. This might become challenging since different cultural environments may add different meanings to specified symbols, and the same concepts may be associated with different representations. Moreover, the graphical representation of BPDs has an equal, or even greater, influence on the cognitive effectiveness (i.e. the speed, ease and accuracy with which a representation can be processed by the human mind) of their content [1–3]. Thus, the focal objective of our efforts was to investigate the intuitiveness of the representations of common Business Process Concepts in a way that subjects were asked to visualize

© Springer Nature Switzerland AG 2019
C. Di Ciccio et al. (Eds.): BPM 2019 Blockchain and CEE Forum, LNBIP 361, pp. 296–311, 2019.
https://doi.org/10.1007/978-3-030-30429-4_20

stated process modeling concepts. In this light, we defined the following research questions, which could be tested empirically:

- *RQ1: How would a 'novice user' visualize a common process model concept?*
- *RQ2: How does the subjects' (cultural) context impact the visualizations?*

By considering the above stated objective and questions, we organized the research and this article as follows. The next chapter presents the theoretical foundations and related work of the subject matter briefly, namely, visual languages, semiotics, semantic transparency and cultural impacts. In respect to cultural impacts, we assumed that different cultural environments are associated with academic institutions from different regions. The third chapter summarizes the method and the operation of the empirical research which was performed to attain the main objective of the paper. The fourth chapter presents the results of the performed research and the article ends with a Discussion chapter.

2   Research Background and Related Work

The foundations of the conceptual representations may be found in semiotics, which specifies a sign as a combination of a signifier (i.e. any material thing that is signified, be it an object, words on a page, or an image) and signified (i.e. the concept which the signifier refers to) (Fig. 1, left). Based on the relation between the signifier and signified, semiotics defines three types of signs: (1) An icon, where a signifier resembles the signified physically (i.e. the letter and person sign in Fig. 1); (2) A symbol, where the signifier presents the signified with an arbitrary or conventional relation (i.e. the circle shape on Fig. 1); and (3) index, where the signifier is related to the signified by an associative relation (i.e. the dashed line in Fig. 1).

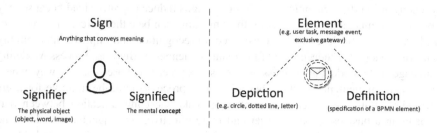

Fig. 1. Main terms in semiotics (left) and OMG's namespace (right)

In the process languages' space (Fig. 1, right), a sign is commonly referred to as an element, whereas the signifier is commonly referred to as a depiction of an element [4]. The definition of a process element has an equal meaning as a 'signified' in semiotics, meaning the specification of a language concept.

A quick review of the latest process related standards like BPMN, CMMN and DMN, reveals that modeling languages tend to use the semiotic terms rather inconsistently. The term 'sign' is used for external conventional symbols only, e.g. plus sign (+). The term 'icon' is used in BPMN specification as defined in semiotics (e.g. a message icon). The term 'symbol' is used for representing some language concepts (e.g. conversation symbol) and their constituent parts (e.g. multi-instance symbol). The term 'shape' is used mainly to depict a basic language concept (e.g. a service task object shares the same shape as a task).

Since the focus of our investigation is on process languages, we will use the terms according to the process languages` namespace, i.e. a *'process element consists of its definition and depiction'*.

In respect to intuition, it may be specified as *"an immediate apprehension of an object by the mind without the intervention of any reasoning process"* [5]. So, if something is intuitive, we can understand it immediately without any prior knowledge or training. While intuitiveness has a subjective notion, it is commonly formalized with the concept of semantic transparency. Caire et al. [6] stated that *"The key to designing visual notations that are understandable to naïve users is a property called semantic transparency"*, which means that the meaning (semantics) of a sign is clear (i.e. intuitive, transparent) from its appearance alone (as in the case of onomatopoeia in spoken languages). Therefore, addressing semantic transparency is recognized as one of the most powerful approaches for improving the understandability, especially for novice users [6].

Semantic transparency of a sign is a continuous function with two endpoints. On the positive side, a sign may be semantically transparent, which means that a novice reader could deduce the meaning of a sign accurately from its appearance (e.g., a drawn tree representing a tree). Semantically transparent signs tend to be defined either by similarity or an associative relationship (index). In contrast, semantic perversity means that a novice reader would likely deduct an incorrect meaning from the sign's appearance (e.g., an arrow directed in an opposite way to an actual flow). On the midpoint, a sign may be defined as semantically opaque, which means that it is defined by a convention [6]. Semantically transparent signs reduce cognitive load because they have built-in mnemonics: As a result, their meaning can be either perceived directly or easily learnt [7]. Such representations speed up recognition and improve intelligibility to naïve users [8, 9]. Indeed, one of the main challenges of Business Process Modeling Languages is to model the business processes in a precise and user-friendly way, where each graphical element that describes a business process should be intuitive for users [10]. The intuitive graphical representations make the communication between participants in a business process easier and more effective, consequentially making the acceptance of the modeling technique wider in a non-academic environment [11].

With respect to the cultural aspects of visual languages, the authors in [12] have stressed that their subjects, regardless of their home country, were not able to generate consistent ad-hoc grouping of 30 visual business formats. The authors suspect that this could be due to lack of prior knowledge of business visualization formats, and because no application context was provided.

The results of the article [13] show that the usage of secondary notation elements, such as a specific color scheme, impacted the understanding efficiency and perceived difficulty of BPMN notation positively, when such color scheme was applied to the diagrams which were interpreted by Chinese subjects. On the other hand, the German population has not been affected from such usage of secondary notation.

The authors in [14] found that when designing interactive environments for cross-cultural collaboration, different visual design patterns in the form of illustrations must be used in order to ensure successful collaboration, even when many aspects of cultural orientation are similar (e.g. among the Asian cultures).

3 Empirical Research

By considering the stated research objective and research questions, the measures of the research model were specified in line with the 'Goodman's theory of symbols [15], which relates to the encoding part of the 'concept – graphical symbol' mapping (Fig. 1). In respect to 'symbol deficit', we specified M1 as '*the number of unspecified representations*', with lower values preferred. 'Symbol redundancy' was operationalized with '*the number of alternative representations*' (M2, lower values preferred), as well as with '*the average distance of the most representative depiction in respect to the alternative ones*' (M3). Average Distance (AD) was specified as follows:

$$AD = \frac{\sum_{k=1}^{|S|} |S_k - P|}{|S|},$$ (1)

where 'P' represents the most representative depiction and 'S' represents the remaining set of depictions of the stated concept. We normalized $AD_\%$ additionally with respect to the total number of depictions, which may vary across stated concepts (e.g. a subject may propose zero, one or several depictions of a concept). We recognized (normalized) Average Distance ($AD_\%$) to be a valid indicator for the 'consistency of the representation' of a stated process modeling concept, with higher values preferred.

To obtain values to the specified measures an empirical research was performed, in which a name and a definition of a process model concept were provided to subjects, where their task was to draw a depiction for the stated process model concept. The sample of subjects consisted of two groups of students (i.e. sample clusters), which came from two distinct research institutions. The first group consisted of IT, as well as Media Communication students from the University of Maribor, Slovenia (hereinafter referred to as Cultural Group 1 – CG1), whereas the second group consisted of Economy and Business students, coming from the National Technical University, KPI, Ukraine (hereinafter referred to as Cultural Group 2 – CG2). Neither of the groups were subjected to any formal training in process modeling notations or professional experiences in this manner, and so represented proxies for novice users of two different cultural settings. Overall, the sample was defined as a nonprobability convenience sample.

The focal research instrument was a paper-based questionnaire, consisting of process-related concepts' definitions, with blank areas specified for drawing the corresponding representations. We focused mainly on the concepts that may be represented based on similarity (i.e. icon) or association (i.e. index), whereas the concepts which are represented with conventional symbols (e.g., a task, which is represented with a rectangle shape) were mainly omitted. This was reasonable, since convention-based signs must be learned. In line with the specified subjects' groups CG1 and CG2, the questionnaire was created in the Slovenian (Latin alphabet) and Ukrainian languages (Cyrillic alphabet). The actual research was performed in January 2018 for CG1 (87 subjects) and March 2019 for CG2 (23 subjects).

The Qualitative Data Analysis (QDA), was performed as follows: A macro was defined in the Photoshop application, which selected individual regions of each scanned questionnaire (a region contained a single drawn sign) and stored it as a separate image (Fig. 2). Afterwards, each image was annotated automatically with the unique ID of the participant.

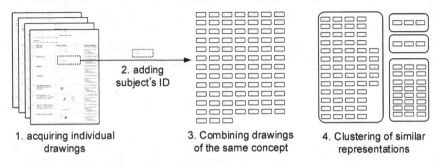

1. acquiring individual   3. Combining drawings   4. Clustering of similar
   drawings   of the same concept   representations

Fig. 2. Parsing of individual signs from the questionnaire and clustering

Finally, all images were imported into MS Visio, where we were able to perform clustering of the signs based on visual similarity (convergence of visually similar signs and divergence of visually distinct signs). In the case that at least two signs of the same concept indicated a visual similarity, a cluster was established (Fig. 3). The cardinality of the cluster 'X' (|X|) was defined as a measure of the 'number of the elements' in the cluster, and was applied to specified measures M1–M3.

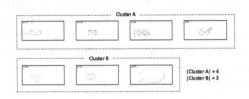

Fig. 3. Two clusters of message signs

4   Results

Since prior knowledge of the business process notations may impact subjects' responses, we initially asked subjects about their expertise in Business Process Modeling notations. The following figure (Fig. 4) represents the percentage of subjects who analyzed or modeled at least one diagram in a specific notation.

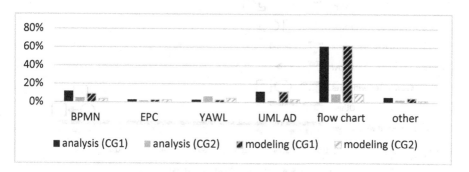

Fig. 4. Subjects' prior expertise in process modeling notations

As is evident from Fig. 4, there is a large discrepancy between CG1's and CG2's participants regarding the prior knowledge of using flow charts. More concretely, over 60% of CG1's and less than 10% of CG2's participants have either analyzed or modeled at least 1 flow chart diagram. CG1's participants were also slightly more experienced in modeling and analyzing BPMN and EPC diagrams. The only exception was in the case of the YAWL notation, where CG2's subjects reported more occurrences of analyzing or modeling at least one YAWL diagram.

4.1   Qualitative Data Analysis Results

By following the Qualitative Data Analysis process as specified in Sect. 3, the following clusters of representations were specified for individual process modeling concepts. In this manner, the following graphs provide detailed answers to the questionnaire's statement *"Draw a sign which best suits the stated concept"*. Note that the number of total responses might exceed the number of subjects, since some of the subjects have provided several alternative depictions. The cluster entitled 'Phrase' was used where the concept was represented with a word phrase or textual description. The cardinality of clusters was normalized, since individual subjects may specify several depictions for an individual concept, and there was also a significant difference between the sizes of CG1 and CG2. The results are as follows.

Process. Subjects responded consistently when drawing a 'process' concept, as the majority (65%) drew 'shapes connected with an arrows' symbol. As is evident in Fig. 5, other representations were 'shapes connected with lines' (6%), 'arrow' and 'line with markers' (both 4%), 'shapes' and 'stairs' (both 3%), and 'checklist' (2%). Also, while responses from CG1 and CG2 are similar, differences can be spotted in drawings of 'shapes connected with arrows' (17% fewer answers from CG2), 'arrow' and 'shapes' (no answers from CG2) and in 'stairs', as well as 'checklist', (no answers from CG1) symbols.

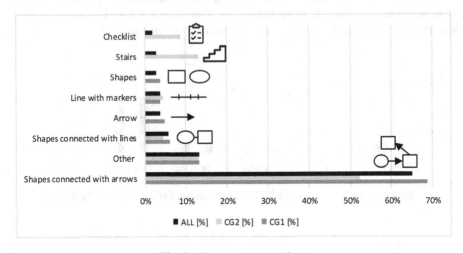

Fig. 5. Process representations

Message. In respect to the 'message' concept, all 110 subjects proposed at least one message sign, where the answers were classified into five clusters representing the signs shown in Fig. 6. Again, the subjects responded consistently, proposing four different representations for the message concept, where only one participant drew a shape that did not fit the defined clusters. 63% of the responses were associated with an 'envelope' symbol, followed by the 'callout' symbol (29%), 'postcard' symbol (5%) and a symbol representing 'two persons communicating' (2%). Some differences can be observed in responses from CG1 and CG2, i.e. participants from CG1 drew the symbol 'envelope' more frequently (19% more) than participants from CG2, whereas participants from CG2 drew more 'postcard' symbols (10% more).

Time and Date. Figure 7 demonstrates that the subjects also responded consistently in the case of the 'time and date' concept. 57% of subjects decided to represent the stated concept with an 'analog clock' symbol and 28% with a 'calendar' symbol. The number of responses exceeds the number of subjects, since 25 subjects drew both symbols (separately for time and date). Twelve subjects (9%) decided to draw 'date fields' and six (4%) to use the phrase 'HH: MM' or 'DD: MM: YY'. No major differences can be spotted between CG1 and CG2 responses; the maximum difference (6%) is in the drawings of date fields in favor of CG1 participants.

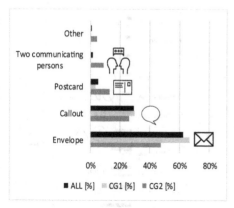

Fig. 6. Message representations

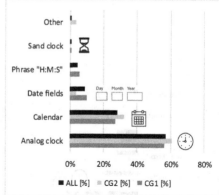

Fig. 7. Time and date representations

Error. As is evident from Fig. 8, the subjects provided several alternative depictions for the 'error' concept, including the phrase 'Error' which was provided nine times. In general, subjects drew two main symbols: An exclamation mark and letter 'X', both in two variants: As a standalone symbol, and as a bordered symbol (similar to the corresponding 'traffic sign' for representing a danger on the road). Together, the letter 'X' was provided 57 times (48%), whereas the exclamation mark was provided 41 times (35%). Subjects from CG2 additionally drew both, 'question mark' and 'sad smiley', twice. Furthermore, while CG2 subjects drew an 'exclamation mark' only twice (33% less than subjects from CG1), but chose the letter 'X' more often (8% more than subjects from CG1).

Cancel/Interruption. Figure 9 shows various alternative depictions for the 'Cancel/Interruption' concept. Interestingly, some of the drawings were the same as drawings for Error representations (the letter 'X' and the 'exclamation mark'). Again, letter 'X' was drawn most often (32%), whereas many answers could not be clustered at all (14% for CG1 and 17% for CG2), which indicates an inconsistent understanding of the concept among participants. Furthermore, many differences between CG1 and CG2 can be noticed. Subjects from CG2 drew the letter 'X' only once, while there was no depiction of the 'exclamation mark'. However, subjects from CG2 did illustrate the concept as a 'gap-in-line' (39%), as 'line drawn in half of the space' (13%), and as 'persons with an arrow' (13%). Those were the most frequent answers in CG2, however, none of those were found among CG1 drawings.

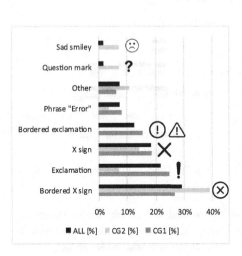

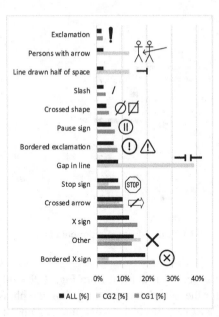

Fig. 8. Error representations   **Fig. 9.** Cancel/interruption representations

User Task. Respondents were able to provide consistent results in the case of 'user task' (Fig. 10). 60% of subjects decided to represent a 'user task' with a 'personal computer' symbol, an additional 16 subjects added a 'person' symbol to the 'computer' symbol, and four CG1 subjects added a 'checkmark' to the 'computer' symbol. Answers from participants in CG1 were distributed in eight clusters, while participants from CG2 achieved a higher degree of coherence, as their answers were clustered in only three groups (none of the CG2 participants drew a 'computer mouse', a 'person', a 'magnifier' or a 'document').

Manual Task. In the case of the 'manual task' concept, the responses were less consistent (Fig. 11), which was again indicated by a high number of clusters. Mainly, two symbols were proposed: A 'palm' symbol (32% of all subjects) and a variation of a manual 'hand tools' for home improvement, which present 19% of all answers (only in the case of CG1 participants). Further cultural differences are visible in 'crossed computer' and 'person' symbols, which were drawn only by subjects from CG1, whereas 'pen and page', 'person with hand tool', and 'crossed computer with human' symbols were drawn only by subjects from CG2.

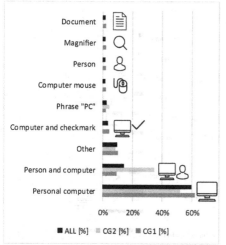

Fig. 10. User task representations

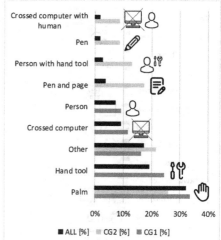

Fig. 11. Manual task representations

Automated Service. Figure 12 indicates that users' responses diverged in the case of representing an automated service. The majority, 33% of responses, could not be clustered, meaning 35 different kinds of representations were provided in a single instance. Additionally, 14 responses were left out, which may indicate that subjects had difficulties understanding or visualizing the concept. The biggest clusters consist of 'globe' and 'computer' symbols (both 9%), followed by phrases 'www' and 'online' (6%) and phrase 'auto' (5%). The 'globe', internet-related phrases (e.g. 'www' and 'online'), 'Chrome icon', and 'network of computers' may be related to the association of the term 'online' service. Again, cultural differences are present, as CG2 subjects did not respond with any of the following symbols: 'globe', phrase 'auto', 'arrows in a circle', 'wheel', 'application window', 'shopping cart', and 'Chrome icon'. On the other hand, subjects from CG2 did draw 'network of computers' and 'person and computer', symbols not illustrated by subjects from CG1.

Program or Script. In the case of the 'program or script' concept, again, subjects responded less consistently; 10 clusters are shown in Fig. 13. 37% of all subjects drew a 'document with a programming code', which complies with the BPMN Script task. Some of the following clusters were similarly related to visualizing 'programming code', either as a 'display with code' (9%) or as a part of the code, e.g. 'tag symbol' (5%) and 'binary code' (3%). The textual answers were related to 'execution' or 'programming language' (both 5%). Again, many responses were given only once (13%). Subjects from CG1 provided more answers related to programming ('document with code', 'tag symbol', all of the phrases and 'application window' (none of which were given by subjects from CG2), while subjects from CG2 gave more visual answers, 'square' and 'flowchart' (those answers were not presented by subjects from CG1).

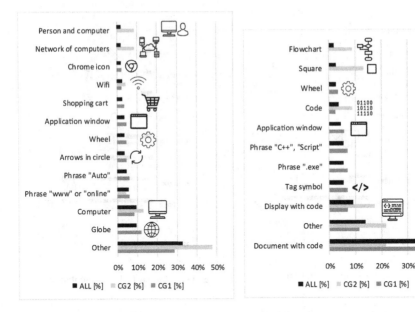

Fig. 12. Automated service representations   **Fig. 13.** Program or script representations

4.2 Measurement Results

Table 1 represents measurements which resulted from the clusters' cardinalities, analyzed as specified in Sect. 3. Note again that the number of depictions may vary, due to the fact that some subjects have proposed several depictions of a stated Process Modeling Concept.

By considering Table 1, we may conclude the following. In respect to M1, which measures the number of unspecified depictions of a stated concept (lower values were preferred), the 'process', 'time/date', 'message' and 'error' concepts were depicted with at least one symbol by each subject, whereas, in total, seven subjects (13%) were not able to provide a depiction for the 'program/script' concept.

In respect to M2, where again, lower values were preferred, the fewer clusters were generated in total (CG1/CG2, since both groups of subjects may have specified the same clusters) by message (4 clusters) and time/date concept (4 clusters), where higher values were associated with cancel/interruption (12 clusters) and automated service concepts (12 clusters). Besides, 'message' and 'time/date' concepts have three out of four clusters in common.

In respect to M3%, which represents the normalized Average Distance between the clusters of depictions of a concept (with higher values preferred), the higher values, when considering both groups of subjects, are associated with the process concept (61%), followed by user task (56%) and message (51%). The lowest M3% was measured at depiction of 'automated service' concept (6%).

Table 1. Measurements of the depictions of specified concepts

		Process	Message	Time/Date	Error	Cancel/Interruption	User task	Manual task	Automated service	Program/Script
Number of depictions	CG1	83	90	107	97	87	87	86	84	87
	CG2	23	23	28	23	23	23	23	23	23
	CG1 + CG2	106	113	135	120	110	110	109	107	110
M1: Number of unspecified depictions	CG1	0	0	0	0	2	2	2	0	5
	CG1 [%]	0%	0%	0%	0%	2%	2%	2%	0%	6%
	CG2	0	0	0	0	0	0	1	3	2
	CG2 [%]	0%	0%	0%	0%	0%	0%	4%	13%	9%
	CG1 + CG2	0	0	0	0	2	2	3	3	7
	CG1 + CG2 [%]	0%	0%	0%	0%	2%	2%	3%	3%	6%
M2: Number of alternative representations (i.e. clusters)	CG1	5	4	4	5	8	8	4	10	8
	CG2	3	4	4	5	4	2	5	3	4
	CG1 ∪ CG2	7	4	4	7	12	8	8	12	10
	CG1 ∩ CG2	1	3	3	4	3	2	1	2	3
M3: Average distance	CG1	53,3	45	44,7	10	15,2	50,9	20	6	31
	CG1 [%]	64%	50%	42%	10%	17%	59%	23%	7%	36%
	CG2	9,3	8	8	7	6,3	4	3	1	2
	CG2 [%]	40%	35%	29%	30%	27%	17%	13%	4%	9%
	CG1 + CG2	65	57,3	58,3	22	15	62	28	6	36
	CG1 + CG2 [%]	61%	51%	43%	18%	14%	56%	26%	6%	33%

5 Discussion

In respect to the stated research questions, the following answers are provided.

RQ1: How would a 'novice user' visualize a common process model concept?

Table 2 summarizes how a novice user would visualize the stated process model concepts. In the case of the 'service' concept, the proposal is unknown (n/a), since no consensus for the representation could be found out of the reported data.

Table 2. Standardized and proposed representations of process-related concepts

Process related concept	Process	Message	Time or date	Error	Cancel	User task	Manual task	Service	Program or script
BPMN representation	-	✉	🕐	N	(×)	👤	☞	⚙	📜
Research results	[process icon]	✉	🕐	(×)	(×)	🖥	☞	N/A	📜
Related work [16]	-	✉	🕐	!	-	-	☞	👥	-

As is evident from Table 2, the depictions of five out of nine investigated concepts coincide with the standardized BPMN depictions. In respect to the process concept, which does not have a visual representation in BPMN, our results show that subjects preferred to depict it with a combination of "flow" symbols. Our research validated empirically (see metric M3 in Table 1) claims stated in [16], i.e. 'time and date', 'message' and 'manual' symbols were identified as semantically immediate by both studies. In addition, our study confirms that the 'program or script' symbol (as defined in the BPMN specification) can also be regarded as such.

On the other hand, we identified the symbols for 'error' and 'service' concepts as being non-intuitive, or even semantically perverse. The evidence in our study also shows that subjects drew non-standardized representations for the concepts 'user task', 'service' and 'error', which is aligned with the related work [16]. Additionally, the 'exclamation' mark, proposed in the related work [16] for the 'error' concept, was the second most preferred symbol (25%) in our research as well (Fig. 8). Since none of the participants proposed a similar symbol for the 'error' concept as defined in the BPMN specification, and considering that the 'exclamation' mark symbol is present in both our and related studies, we can foresee the possibility for improving the existing symbol.

Finally, none of the 110 participants from both cultural groups drew the same symbol for 'service' as it was proposed by Genon et al. [16], which the authors acknowledged as being more semantically transparent. Based on this and all the observed metrics (M1–M3), we can conclude that the 'service' concept appears to be the most difficult concept to depict.

RQ2: How does the subjects' (cultural) context impact the visualization?

In accordance with RQ1, the symbols that were deemed semantically transparent had a higher consensus between different cultural groups in the case of most of the proposed symbols. Specifically, in the case of 'manual task' representation, the 'palm' symbol was drawn more consistently between the cultural groups, as opposed to 'cancel/interruption' representations. Similar can be concluded for other semantically transparent symbols as well, e.g., 'message', 'time and date', as well as 'user task' representations. However, alternative representations for the aforementioned concepts were not so aligned between the two cultural groups. For example, in the case of the 'message' concept, 'postcard' was proposed by 13% of CG2 participants and only 3% of the CG1 counterparts. In some examples, such as 'cancel/interruption', none of the CG2 participants proposed a letter 'X', as opposed to 16% of the CG1 participants. On the other hand, with respect to the 'manual task' concept, 'pen and page' was not proposed by any of the CG1 participants, which contrasts with the 17% of CG2 responses.

Considering RQ2, our study complements the related work in the following ways. The results are in accordance with the existing empirical research (e.g. [17]) which suggests that replacing abstract shapes with well-established symbols aids comprehension of process diagrams in the case of novice users. Non-expert users participated in this study, and, based on the results, it is evident that they proposed symbols rather than abstract shapes. However, basic shapes were proposed in the case of abstract concepts such as 'process'. With respect to different cultural groups, the findings complement the existing body of literature as follows. While it was proven that a color scheme impacts the understanding efficiency and perceived difficulty of BPMN notation in different cultural groups [18], based on the results represented in this paper, we can conclude the same for some shapes and symbols (e.g., 'cancel/interruption' and 'manual task' concepts). Moreover, in accordance with another related study [19], the consistency of providing graphical symbols varied for different concepts. This research also opens an exploration into investigating the cultural differences and how they affect the cognitive fit theory, which was highlighted by Moody et al. [20].

5.1 Implications

We foresee several implications of our investigation. First, experts involved in developing and evolving process languages may consider our research results, as well as the approach on how to define the visual vocabulary. Second, researchers who investigate visual languages and corresponding diagrams may consider our research to identify the reasons why some languages and approaches are more effective than others. Our research may also be of use for researchers who investigate and propose simplifications of complex process languages, as well as for the ones who extend existing visual languages.

5.2 Research Limitations and Future Work

The results of this research should be considered with the following internal and external limitations in mind. With respect to the external validity, there is a certain degree of risk of generalizing results above the research sample. While students reported and demonstrated as not being skilled in process languages, another group of subjects could provide different results (e.g. subjects from another environment could be impacted by other signs in their everyday life). Second, to keep the research instrument within reasonable limits, only a subset of common process concepts was investigated. A complementary study with the remaining concepts could be performed in the future.

With respect to internal validity, there was a certain degree of freedom when performing Qualitative Data Analysis (i.e. clustering of drawn symbols), which could be addressed by replicating the data analysis. Another threat to the internal validity is also the analysis of the results, since both the Ukrainian and Slovenian clustering was performed separately by different researchers. However, the Ukrainian researchers had the Slovenian results already available, so they were able to mimic the approach. Furthermore, it is important to acknowledge that a recent body of literature in the field of Linguistics and Anthropology [17] suggests, that it remains unclear to what extent the culture and language may interact. Meaningful research in this area is particularly difficult, because of the interdisciplinary nature of the topic. Thus, the fundamental questions, such as 'How to define culture?', 'Is culture even a useful concept?', 'Is it possible to distinguish culture from language?' etc., remain unanswered. This was considered when translating the questionnaire from Slovenian to the Ukrainian language, hence, the guidelines proposed by Peña [21] were used. In this light, a native language speaker performed the translation of the questionnaire to the Ukrainian language, following well defined clustering instructions. Furthermore, for each question there was also English text available. In this light, we ensured the linguistic equivalence of both the Slovenian and Ukrainian questionnaire. Still, as Peña [21] stressed, there are threats that are inherent to translation methods in cross-cultural studies.

Besides minimizing validity threats, we also plan to extend the analysis of obtained data. First, we plan to investigate the potential differences between the investigated groups of subjects (e.g. previous knowledge). Second, we plan to extend the research by investigating additional concepts (e.g. how a 'rule' concept is depicted, which process language has the most intuitive common elements, etc.), which were excluded from this paper due to scope limitations. Third, for each answer, subjects also provided some qualitative insights about what impacted their decision for a sign. This could provide us some insights on how subjects decide to draw the concepts. Fourth, besides the "drawing" part, subjects also performed in the opposite way, i.e. comprehension of stated process-related symbols, where potential "drawing – comprehension" correlations might be investigated.

Acknowledgments. The authors acknowledge the financial support from the Slovenian Research Agency (Research Core Funding No. P2-0057).

References

1. Larkin, J.H., Simon, H.A.: Why a diagram is (sometimes) worth ten thousand words. Cogn. Sci. **11**(1), 65–100 (1987)
2. Siau, K.: Informational and computational equivalence in comparing information modeling methods. JDM **15**(1), 73–86 (2004)
3. Zhang, J., Norman, D.: Representations in distributed cognitive tasks. Cogn. Sci. **18**, 87–122 (1994)
4. OMG: Business Process Model and Notation version 2.0, 03 January 2011. http://www.omg. org/spec/BPMN/2.0/. Accessed 15 Mar 2011
5. Fowler, H.W.: A Dictionary of Modern English Usage: The Classic First Edition. Oxford University Press (2010)
6. Caire, P., Genon, N., Heymans, P., Moody, D.L.: Visual notation design 2.0: towards user comprehensible requirements engineering notations. In: 2013 21st IEEE International Requirements Engineering Conference (RE), pp. 115–124 (2013)
7. Petre, M.: Why looking isn't always seeing: readership skills and graphical programming. Commun. ACM **38**(6), 33–44 (1995)
8. Britton, C., Jones, S.: The untrained eye: how languages for software specification support understanding in untrained users. Hum. Comput. Interact. **14**(1–2), 191–244 (1999)
9. Britton, C., Jones, S., Kutar, M., Loomes, M., Robinson, B.: Evaluating the intelligibility of diagrammatic languages used in the specification of software. In: Anderson, M., Cheng, P., Haarslev, V. (eds.) Diagrams 2000. LNCS (LNAI), vol. 1889, pp. 376–391. Springer, Heidelberg (2000). https://doi.org/10.1007/3-540-44590-0_32
10. Hruby, P.: Structuring Specification of Business Systems with UML (with an Emphasis on Workflow Management Systems). In: Patel, D., Sutherland, J., Miller, J. (eds.) Business Object Design and Implementation II, pp. 77–89. Springer, London (1998). https://doi.org/ 10.1007/978-1-4471-1286-0_9
11. Neiger, D., Churilov, L., Flitman, A.: Business process modelling with EPCs. In: Value-Focused Business Process Engineering : a Systems Approach, vol. 19, pp. 1–31, Springer, Boston (2009). https://doi.org/10.1007/978-0-387-09521-9_5

12. Eppler, M.J., Ge, J.: Communicating with diagrams: how intuitive and cross-cultural are business graphics?, Università della Svizzera italiana (2007)
13. Kummer, T.-F., Recker, J., Mendling, J.: Enhancing understandability of process models through cultural-dependent color adjustments. Decis. Support Syst. **87**, 1–12 (2016)
14. Schadewitz, N.: Design patterns for cross-cultural collaboration. Int. J. Des. **3**(3), 37–53 (2009). http://www.ijdesign.org/index.php/IJDesign/article/view/276/273. Accessed 30 May 2019
15. Goodman, N.: Languages of Art: An Approach to a Theory of Symbols. Oxford University Press, Oxford (1968)
16. Genon, N., Heymans, P., Amyot, D.: Analysing the Cognitive Effectiveness of the BPMN 2.0 Visual Notation. In: Malloy, B., Staab, S., van den Brand, M. (eds.) SLE 2010. LNCS, vol. 6563, pp. 377–396. Springer, Heidelberg (2011). https://doi.org/10.1007/978-3-642-19440-5_25
17. vom Brocke, J., Rosemann, M. (eds.): Handbook on Business Process Management 1. IHIS. Springer, Heidelberg (2015). https://doi.org/10.1007/978-3-642-45100-3
18. Masri, K., Parker, D., Gemino, A.: Using iconic graphics in entity-relationship diagrams: the impact on understanding. J. Database Manag. (JDM) **19**(3), 22–41 (2008)
19. Irani, P., Tingley, M., Ware, C.: Using perceptual syntax to enhance semantic content in diagrams. IEEE Comput. Graph. Appl. **21**(5), 76–85 (2001)
20. Moody, D.L., Heymans, P., Matulevičius, R.: Visual syntax does matter: improving the cognitive effectiveness of the i* visual notation. Requirements Eng. **15**(2), 141–175 (2010)
21. Peña, E.D.: Lost in translation: methodological considerations in cross-cultural research. Child Dev. **78**(4), 1255–1264 (2007)

Central and Eastern Europe Forum Posters

Using Enterprise Models for Change Analysis in Inter-organizational Business Processes

Martin Henkel[(✉)], Georgios Koutsopoulos, Ilia Bider, and Erik Perjons

Department of Computer and Systems Sciences, Stockholm University, Stockholm, Sweden
{martinh,georgios,ilia,perjons}@dsv.su.se

Abstract. Organizations increasingly participate in and rely on inter-organizational processes to carry out work. However, inter-organizational processes may be complex, especially when there is a need to introduce and decide upon changes that affect the process. In this paper we examine the problems that may arise when changing inter-organizational processes. As the foundation for our examination, we use a case study performed at a healthcare region in Sweden. In the case, a number of potential changes to an inter-organizational process have been identified. Based on the analysis of the case, we identify the basic constituents that enterprise models need to contain in order to be useful tools for representing changes to inter-organizational processes.

Keywords: Modeling · Business process · Inter-organizational · Decision-making

1 Introduction

Even though modern economies, being based on knowledge, favor the formulation of inter-organizational cooperation, the phenomenon of organizations that cooperate within networks is not new [1]. Compared to internal organizational processes, the complexity is significantly increased for inter-organizational processes, and this may hinder the management and change of the process [2]. Several tools and methods may be applied in order to support the change of inter-organizational processes. One particular support that we examine in this paper is enterprise models.

The research reported in this paper is based on a practical example of inter-organizational process owned by a healthcare region in Sweden, a public organization which is responsible for healthcare in the region. The process concerns providing healthcare guidance by phone to the region's residents and visitors. The guidance is given by professional nurses specially trained for this job and supported by various information sources incorporated in the software they use.

To help the region in assessing areas that require attention when a new proposal on change in the process is received, a special research project has been started. The goal of the project was to try other types of modeling techniques than the ones that the region already had as a tool for analyzing incoming proposals. The goal of this paper is

© Springer Nature Switzerland AG 2019
C. Di Ciccio et al. (Eds.): BPM 2019 Blockchain and CEE Forum, LNBIP 361, pp. 315–318, 2019.
https://doi.org/10.1007/978-3-030-30429-4_21

to examine the case and identify the support needed by enterprise models in order to support the change of inter-organizational processes.

Inter-organizational processes, and models thereof, are defined by the fact that the process is jointly executed by autonomous units. Creating models describing inter-organizational processes include for example describing external organizations, and what part of the process should be public [3].

As pointed out by [4] the ability to *change* is an important factor for managing inter-organizational work. As pointed out by Huerta Melchor [5] a part of management of change is to identify and deal with both intended and unintended consequences. Effort has been put into creating methods for performing changes, such as Kurt Lewin's [6] unfreeze-change-freeze approach, or Fernandez's eight guidelines for change [7]. In contrast to these approaches, we focus on the examination of what needs to be changed, rather than how to perform the changes. We do this by examining a case study, and based on that we elaborate on the utility of enterprise model to aid the analysis.

2   The Health Guidance Case

The region's guidance process is complex. An obvious part of the complexity comes with the wide range of health care issues that the service need to cater to – ranging from trivial issues and even prank calls, to life threatening issues. A part of the complexity is also due to the fact that health guidance is an entry point to the regional health care – thus there is a need not only for the regional resident to know about the service – but the health guidance operators also need to know about the region's health care providers in order to advice the patients towards the right provision of care.

To carry out the work, the guidance process uses a number of resources. Most notably, a set of expert nurses that are trained to guide the patient are needed. Moreover, there are a number of IT systems supporting the process such as a telephony system and journal systems. There is also a specific guidance system that the nurses use as a way of guiding the conversation with the callers. Furthermore, a provider catalogue system works as a resource that allows finding care providers.

The region's guidance process is in constant change. Whenever a change is proposed, it needs to be analyzed to determine the effect on the service. We have selected two recent change requests – (a) a proposed change in the guidance support that allows the nurses to guide the callers directly to a care provider based on their symptoms and (b) the desire for the health guidance service to book times at local emergency clinics. In subsequent sections we describe the two change cases, and how enterprise models may help in the analysis of the change needed.

2.1   Case A – Guidance Support Improvements

A proposed improvement of the Guidance support system is to have a better support for recommending health care providers in the region. The proposed benefit with this change is improved service for the patient, since they will be guided to a provider. Furthermore, a benefit is that the patient can be guided to the providers with the best expertise. As the research project reported in this paper was active, the implementation of the change had started with forming an expert group of physicians that mapped the providers to symptoms. The work of the expert group would then result in both a web system than can be used directly, and a XML export file that may be used in other systems.

Analysis of the Change: When the change has been performed, the use of resources will have changed. There will be a new development process that maintains the new provider-symptom mapping data and associated web system. This development process will need to utilize expert physicians to map the symptoms to the providers. Furthermore, the development will produce data successively fed into the development of the provider catalogue.

Impact on the Use of EM: The change will introduce both new (sub-) processes and new combinations of resources. New sub-processes are straightforward to express in traditional process modeling languages, such as BPMN. However, the exchange of resources, and the ownership of resources may not be straightforward to represent in a model. Most notably, the new development process is producing resources in the form of the XML file that are used by another organization. This can be made clear during analysis if indicating the ownership of the resources is possible. Modeling languages that clearly indicate the ownership of resources, such as i-star and value models [8], may be useful for this. Moreover, during analysis, there is a need to clearly identify existing contracts on the use of resources, and to identify the need to create a new contract if imposed by the change.

2.2   Case B – Time Booking at Emergency Clinics

Another proposed change is to extend the capabilities of the region's guidance process to also include the ability to book time slots at local care providers. An example of local care providers are the local emergency clinics. The purpose of doing this is firstly to provide better service to the patients. Beside the convenience of having a booked time, it also makes the patient feel more secure. Secondly, the ability to book times also makes it possible to have control of the flow of patients, enabling the booking of timeslots at clinics that are having the shortest queue at the moment.

Analysis of the Change: The change entails adding the support infrastructure to enable the expert nurses to use an IT system to book times. The maintenance of this needs to be based on an API provided by the local clinics' journal system provider. Another option was a manual routine that allows the clinics to indicate which time slots are bookable. For both the use of an API and for the manual routines there is a need of a contract that regulates what kind of symptoms the clinics should be capable of handling and also the use of the journal system API.

Impact on the Use of EM: In this case there is a need to identify contact points that are used to communicate between organizations, be it manual or automated via APIs. If an enterprise model would be used for this, there needs to be a way to identify both IT systems and their service APIs. This may be performed by, for example, using value and goal models [8]. Not all collaborations need explicit contracts thought. Thus, there is also a need to specify what kind of relationship there is between organizations. For example, Lee and Kim [9] have identified two main styles of relationship in this kind of collaboration – the transactional, relying on formal contracts while the relational style is more information. Different types of relationships, such as transactional and relational, are commonly not part of enterprise models.

3 Conclusion

In this paper we have briefly examined how the analysis of changes of inter-organizational business processes requires support from enterprise models. Our examination is based on the need of a Swedish healthcare organization to describe and assess change proposals that would affect their business. An initial idea is that enterprise models, being the "blueprint" of an organization, could assessing the impact of the proposed changes. As a future research, we plan to examine how specific types of models may support the analysis.

References

1. Mäkipää, M.: Inter-organizational information systems in cooperative inter-organizational relationships: study of the factors influencing to success. In: Suomi, R., Cabral, R., Hampe, J. F., Heikkilä, A., Järveläinen, J., Koskivaara, E. (eds.) I3E 2006. IIFIP, vol. 226, pp. 68–81. Springer, Boston, MA (2006). https://doi.org/10.1007/978-0-387-39229-5_7
2. Breu, R., et al.: Towards living inter-organizational processes. In: 2013 IEEE 15th Conference on Business Informatics, pp. 363–366. IEEE, Vienna, Austria (2013)
3. Ziemann, J., Matheis, T., Freiheit, J.: Modelling of cross-organizational business processes - current methods and standards. Enterp. Model. Inf. Syst. Architect. **2**, 23–31 (2015)
4. Diirr, B., Cappelli, C.: A systematic literature review to understand cross-organizational relationship management and collaboration. In: The Hawaii International Conference on System Sciences (2018)
5. Melchor, O.H.: Managing Change in OECD Governments: An Introductory Framework. OECD Publishing, Paris (2008)
6. Burnes, B.: Kurt Lewin and the planned approach to change: a re-appraisal. J. Manag. Stud. **41**, 977–1002 (2004)
7. Fernandez, S., Rainey, H.G.: Managing successful organizational change in the public sector. Public Adm. Rev. **66**, 168–176 (2006)
8. Henkel, M., Johannesson, P., Perjons, E.: An approach for e-service design using enterprise models. Int. J. Inf. Syst. Model. Des. (IJISMD) **2**(1), 1–23 (2011)
9. Lee, J.-N., Kim, Y.-G.: Effect of partnership quality on IS outsourcing success: conceptual framework and empirical validation. J. Manag. Inf. Syst. **15**, 29–61 (1999)

Business Process Management vs Modeling of the Process of Knowledge Management in Contemporary Enterprises

Agnieszka Bitkowska[(✉)] [iD]

Faculty of Management, Warsaw University of Technology, Warsaw, Poland
Agnieszka.Bikowska@pw.edu.pl

Abstract. Business Process Management is considered to be an up-to-date approach to an organization's operation, while process structures offer a sense of order. Knowledge resources are treated as inseparable elements of operation of processes. Moreover Knowledge Management may not be separate from Business Process Management. Modeling of the process of Knowledge Management is intended to systematize these informal rules and relations existing in process-based organizations. The main aim of this paper is to identify the modeling of the process of Knowledge Management in enterprises, which implemented Business Process Management. The article presents selected research results carried out in Poland on 122 process-oriented enterprises.

Keywords: Business Process Management ·
Process of Knowledge Management

1 Introduction

Under the circumstances surrounding the highly volatile economy of the 21st century, the business environment is unpredictable. In order to preserve a competitive market position, it is necessary to continuously improve an organization. One of the concepts here is Business Process Management (BPM) [2, 5, 8, 15] which focuses on organizations improve the effectiveness of existing systems, processes, products, using the available philosophies, principles, tools and management methods. Business Process Management in an organization should take into account the knowledge resources that the organization possesses in order to ensure that employees have access to knowledge regarding specific tasks which are part of particular business processes. It is oriented towards cognitive processes used to create and modify knowledge and requires a combination of creative, analytical and practical abilities/skills with respect to employees [16]. Thus, in the Business Process Management, visible elements of Knowledge Management (KM) appear. In addition, according to the principles of Knowledge Management, previous experience in Business Process Management should be used in future processes and in new situations, thus creating a learning organization [16].

Therefore, the processes occurring in an enterprise should be increased based on individual, team, and organizational knowledge and, consequently, become more and

© Springer Nature Switzerland AG 2019
C. Di Ciccio et al. (Eds.): BPM 2019 Blockchain and CEE Forum, LNBIP 361, pp. 319–323, 2019.
https://doi.org/10.1007/978-3-030-30429-4_22

more flexible as well as adjusted to the changing environmental conditions [14]. Process modeling is concerned with the transformation of knowledge about the functioning of a selected (business) area in an organization and the processes that take place within it into the corresponding models.

The main objective of this paper is to identify the modeling of the process of Knowledge Management in enterprises, which implemented Business Process Management. Prior to conducting analysis, the following hypothesis have been put forward: Business Process Management has a positive influence on modeling of the process of Knowledge Management in enterprises.

2 Theoretical Background

Focusing on Business Process Management, organizations improve the effectiveness of existing systems, processes, products, using the available philosophies, principles, tools and management methods. One of the stage of BPM lifecycle is business process modeling which allows understanding the functioning of the organization through defining, structuring, designing, integrating and improving the processes. The result of business process modeling is a process model - a graphic illustration of the links and mutual interactions within the process. Process modeling usually takes place based on two approaches: the top-down approach and bottom-up [5, 7, 13, 15]. A process model is a formalized representation of an actual process (recorded with a specific notation system f. e. BPMN), which allows to demonstrate its structure and the interrelations between its elements (i.e. the tasks, data, resources, and other). Enterprises use star-standard solutions in the form of good practices, reference models, industry models, and use models of maturity, which allow to indicate further directions of development in the field of Business Process Management. One of the basic standards is BPM CBoK (Business Process Management Common Body of Knowledge) [4], which requires the use of specific models, methodologies, standards and guidelines in the form of specific standards that contain elements of knowledge and a project approach. (It contains Process Modeling). Moreover, organizations use a multi-dimensional approach that includes IT, social or organizational dimension [5, 15–17].

Knowledge is a key element of any process, and in companies where knowledge and processes are treated separately, they quickly become obsolete and will not be competitive with other companies that allow teams a synergistic approach to knowledge management and process management [18]. On the other hand, a large contribution to the development of the process model of Knowledge Management has been provided by Davenport and Prusak, Probst, Romhardt and Raub [3, 11, 14]. In line with the process model, Knowledge Management is all the processes allowing to create, disseminate, and use knowledge in order to fulfill the purposes of an organization. There are three main phases of knowledge management: acquisition (creation) of knowledge, sharing knowledge, and transforming knowledge into decisions. Process model used mainly by large organizations is based on methods proven in practice. There is also the so-called Japanese model [10]. Knowledge Management based on the principle of a spiral is a repeating cycle of four processes of knowledge conversion: internalization, socialization, externalization, combination.

To use the synergies of Knowledge Management and Business Process Management, it is necessary to enable the use of knowledge not only during the design and then analysis of the processes performed, but above all during their implementation. According to U. Remus, knowledge-oriented knowledge management is necessary, while at the same time conscious shaping of business processes so that they use and support Knowledge Management [9]. Modeling of the process of Knowledge Management it applies to the same rules and standards as for other business processes.

The process of Knowledge Management is an element of the concept of Integrated Business Process Management (IBPM), which was placed in the process architecture, in the support processes category [1]. Enterprises can use for this purpose a PFC solution in practice, prepared by APQC, for the standardizations where individual Knowledge Management processes have been defined [12]. If appropriate organizational conditions are created as well as awareness of the management and the staff is awoken, it allows to diffuse knowledge which contributes to the development of innovative ideas and solutions [6, 9, 11, 17]. Successful promotion of new ideas, effective acquisition and sharing of good practices, and integration of various areas of specialist knowledge altogether create conditions for the development and growth of a company as well as creation of innovation [17].

3 Research Methodology and Selected Results

Empirical research has been carried out on a sample of 122 companies operating on the territory of Poland in 2019. A selection of enterprises for the study was performed by the method of target screening, taking into account only organizations that have implemented and adopt Business Process Management. So far there has been no research on modeling of the process of Knowledge Management in the process oriented organizations. An important criterion for the division of the companies under examination was the number of employees. The companies under analysis were classified into the following groups: small enterprises – 10–49 people (24.6%) medium-sized enterprises – 50–249 people (24.6%), and large ones – 250 and more people (50.8%). The survey questionnaire was filled in by the management staff, the executives, owners, process managers, experts in process management, representatives for quality management, members of process offices, business analysts, and project managers.

Process modeling is carried out by 41.8% of the surveyed enterprises. The intensively developing market of BPMS tools requires additional skills from users, modernization of tools adapted to new technologies. The surveyed enterprises use the following solutions: cloud computing (19.7%) in the field of automation and robotics (14.8%) of artificial intelligence (4.1%). IT tools for modeling Knowledge Management processes are the same as for other core and support processes. The use of Knowledge Management in the surveyed process-oriented enterprises amounted to 26.9%, while 22.1% use the knowledge portal on Business Process Management. In the case of 22.1% of enterprises, the Knowledge Management process is modeled (the Knowledge Management model was built and implemented). Companies have noticed that implementation of the model of Knowledge Management brings some benefits. First and foremost, it was possible to use the collected knowledge more extensively as well as assess document, and gathered it (20.1%), moreover, knowledge was shared among employees who learned and developed their competences (18.1%).

In order to test the correlations between the Business Process Management and the model of the process of Knowledge Management has been used the Yule's, Pearson's, and Bykowski's coefficients. Inferences concerning the main hypothesis point to the fact that Business Process Management has a positive influence over the modeling of Knowledge Management processes (the Yule's coefficient 0.95, Pearson's coefficient 0.81 and Bykowski's coefficient 0.79).

4 Conclusions

Business Process Management is considered to be an up-to-date approach to an organization's operation. It is easier for organizations using Business Process Management to create the model of Knowledge Management processes; because knowledge is collected in databases of processes in repositories. There are knowledge resources and they are used, modified, shaped, and perpetuated. The modeling of process of Knowledge Management is intended to systematize these informal rules and relations existing in process-based organizations and make them objective. In natural way combines Business Process Management and Knowledge Management. Coping with this sphere and its operationalization by means of specific strategic, structural, technological, and personal solutions by specific KPI constitute a challenge for each and every process-based organization.

References

1. Bitkowska, A.: Od klasycznego do zintegrowanego zarzadzania procesowego [From Classic to Integrated Business Process Management]. C.H. Beck, Warszawa (2019)
2. Burlton, R.: Business Process Management: Profiting From Process. SAMS. Pearson Education, London (2001)
3. Davenport, T., Prusak, L.: Working Knowledge: How Organizations Manage What They Know. Harvard Business School Press, Boston (1997)
4. Guide to the Business Process Management Common Body of Knowledge
5. Harmon, P.: Business Process Change, 2nd edn. Morgan Kaufmann Publishers, Burlington (2007)
6. Hislop, D.: Knowledge Management in Organizations: A Critical Introduction. Oxford University Press, Oxford (2013)
7. Indulska, M., Green, P., Recker, J.C., Rosemann, M.: Business process modelling: perceived benefits. In: 28th International Conference on Conceptual Modelling, 9–12 November 2009, Gramado, Brazil (2009)
8. Jeston, J., Nelis, J.: Business Process Management: Practical Guidelines to Successful Implementations. Routledge, London and New York (2014)
9. Maier, R., Remus, U.: Defining process-oriented knowledge management strategies. Knowl. Process Manag. 7(4), 103 (2002)
10. Nonaka, I., Takeuchi, H.: The Knowledge Creating Company: How Japanese Companies Create the Dynamics of Innovation, p. 284. Oxford University Press, New York (1995)

11. Probst, G., Raub, S., Romhardt, K.: Managing Knowledge. Wiley, London (2000)
12. Process Classification Framework PCF APQC, Cross Industry. https://www.apqc.org. Accessed 12 June 2019
13. Recker, J., Rosemann, M., Indulska, M., Green, P.: Business process modelling: a comparative analysis. J. Assoc. Inf. Syst. **10**, 333–363 (2009)
14. Richter-von Hagen, C., Ratz, D., Povalej, R.: A genetic algorithm approach to self-organizing knowledge intensive processes. In: Proceedings of I-KNOW 2005, Graz, Austria (2005)
15. Smith, H., Fingar, P.: Business Process Management: The Third Wave. Meghan-Kiffer Press, Tampa (2003)
16. Trocki, M.: Inteligencja procesowa, czyli inteligentne zarządzanie procesowe [Process intelligence, Intelligent Business Process Management]. Studia i Prace Kolegium Zarządzania i Finansów Szkoły Głównej Handlowej, Zeszyt Naukowy, nr 149, Warszawa (2016)
17. Vaccaro, A., Parente, R., Veloso, F.M.: Knowledge management tools, inter-organizational relationships, innovation and firm performance. Technol. Forecast. Soc. Change **77**(7), 1076–1089 (2010)
18. Zhu, P.: Knowledge Management (KM) vs. Business Process Management (BPM) (2015). http://futureofcio.blogspot.de/2013/10/knowledge-management-km-vs-business.html. Accessed 12 June 2019

BPM Adoption in Serbian Companies

Dragana Stojanović[✉], Ivona Jovanović, Dragoslav Slović,
Ivan Tomašević, and Barbara Simeunović

University of Belgrade Faculty of Organizational Sciences, Belgrade, Serbia
{dragana.stojanovic,ivona.jovanovic,dragoslav.slovic,
ivan.tomasevic,barbara.simeunovic}@fon.bg.ac.rs

Abstract. This paper analysis BPM adoption in context of companies operating in Serbia. The goals were to determine level of BPM adoption in companies in Serbia and identify what factors contributing the most to the success in BPM adoption. Questionnaire was used for data collection. BPM adoption was measured through Process Performance Index (PPI). Parametric statistical tests were used on survey data to identify factors that contribute the most to successful BPM adoption. Results in this research shows several factors that significantly contribute to success of BPM adoption measured through PPI. First, companies who have formally trained their employees in process analysis/ redesign experienced more significant success in BPM adoption. Second factor is strategic orientation, expressed through criteria such as enterprise-wide business process architecture design and change efforts, increased market share and revenue, reduction of business risk, etc. This shows that strategic focus can even make up for the lack of operational knowledge, and increase chances for success of BPM adoption.

Keywords: BPM adoption · Process Performance Index · BPM practice

1 Introduction

Business Process Management (BPM) plays an important role for maintaining efficiency and effectiveness of the operations of companies and organizations [6]. Empirical research suggests positive correlation between BPM and business success [8], and have shown that organization can benefit from BPM through better financial and nonfinancial performance which can drive to competitive advantage [12].

Considering the influence BPM implementation might have on gaining competitive advantage, BPM stands out as a viable solution for improving company performance in transition economies [12]. Recent investigations [4] confirmed the impact of business process orientation on organizational performance in Slovenia and Croatia. Therefore, it is interesting to analyze current level of BPM adoption in Serbia, as transitional economy, which is the main purpose of this paper. Bandara et al. [2] define BPM success as "the resulting status of when the intended goals of the BPM initiative are met to a satisfactory level". Although BPM is often used for improving organization's operational competitiveness, research has shown that many BPM projects have been unsuccessful in practice [1, 13], which is why it is important to consider key success factors for BPM adoption. Relevant literature suggests several ways of measuring the

© Springer Nature Switzerland AG 2019
C. Di Ciccio et al. (Eds.): BPM 2019 Blockchain and CEE Forum, LNBIP 361, pp. 324–327, 2019.
https://doi.org/10.1007/978-3-030-30429-4_23

success of BPM adoption [5, 10, 11]. Process Performance Index (PPI), created by Rummler-Brache Group [10] is empirically validated, quantitative, and publicly available [5], making it suitable as BPM adoption measuring instrument. PPI consists of 10 criteria: Alignment with strategy, Holistic approach, Process awareness by management and employees, Portfolio of process management initiatives, Business process improvement (BPI) methodology, Process metrics, Customer focus, Process management, Information systems, and Change management. It offers good balance between overall measure of BPM adoption and more detailed analysis of criteria that define the success of BPM adoption, which is why it has been chosen as a primary metric for this research.

2   Research Methodology

The purpose of this study is to determine level of BPM adoption in companies in Serbia measured through PPI, to see what factors contribute the most to high level of PPI and drivers and challenges encountered in BPM practice in Serbia. Survey research was conducted, with questions adapted from BPTrends survey [3], Process Excellence Network survey [9], and Marshall [7]. The questions required single or multiple choices, while some of them included an open form. For each company, total PPI score is calculated, as a sum of ratings by criteria. The data were gathered during March and April of 2019. Questionnaires were sent to 600 companies in Serbia. Total of 61 responses was received, representing 10.16% response rate. All of the responses were included in the results presented in this paper.

3   Results

Most companies described the scope of BPI initiatives as enterprise wide (44.3%). The need to improve productivity/efficiency (49 companies), The need to save money (40), The need to improve business coordination and control (30), and The need to improve customer satisfaction (27) are identified as most significant drivers, while Increase in market share and revenue (11) and One time event (4) are least significant. Business process modeling/documenting (46), Business process management (44) are widely implemented, while initiatives that companies plan to implement are related to Core process redesign (23) and Process analysis/redesign training (24). Companies usually face challenges regarding Lack of interest within top management (22) and Absence of skills (18) and Obstacles in new technology implementation (17).

The PPI values range from 10 to 50 for each company. PPI value can be considered moderate (mostly between 30 and 38), meaning success of BPM adoption in companies is moderate. PPI criteria with highest average scores are Holistic approach (3.97) and Process metrics (3.67), while criteria with lowest average scores are Customer focus (3.44), BPI methodology (3.38), and Portfolio of process management initiatives (3.25). Holistic approach, Process management, and Alignment with strategy have relatively low standard deviation, while Process awareness by management and employees, Customer focus, and BPI methodology have relatively high standard deviation.

Participants were divided into four groups based on the scope of their BPI initiative (1: The managers are trained, but there are no formal programs; 2: Small-scale pilot projects; 3: One or more business units, 4: Enterprise wide). Scores for four groups were statistically different at level p < .05. Post-hoc comparisons revealed that companies without formal BPI initiative have smaller PPI than companies with programs in one or more business units or preferably on enterprise level.

Results of t-test show that companies oriented more towards market share and revenue have higher PPI ($t(59) = -2.157$, $p = 0.035$). The magnitude of differences in means ($MD = -5.196$ 95% CI: -10.017 to -0.376) is moderate ($\eta^2 = .07$). Companies oriented more towards reducing business risk have higher PPI ($t(59) = -1.975$, $p = 0.05$), with the effect that can be considered moderate ($MD = -4.274$ 95% CI: -8.603 to 0.055, $\eta^2 = .06$). Companies that worked on business process architecture development initiatives have higher PPI ($t(59) = -2.780$, $p = 0.007$) with the effect closed to large ($MD = -5.030$ 95% CI: -8.650 to -1.410, $\eta^2 = .12$). Companies that worked on Process change on enterprise level have also higher PPI ($t(59) = -2.662$, $p = 0.01$), with moderate magnitude of differences in means ($MD = -4.919$ 95% CI: -8.617 to -1.221, $\eta^2 = .10$).

Mann-Whitney U test revealed that companies with trained employees in Process analysis/redesign have succeeded in identifying and eliminating problems and disagreement ($Md = 4.00$, $N = 15$), $U = 195.000$, $z = -2,699$, $p = 0.00$, $r = 0.35$) more than companies without trained employees ($Md = 3.00$, $N = 46$).

4   Discussion and Conclusion

There are certain discrepancies between main drivers behind process change and business process initiatives implemented in companies. While drivers are oriented more towards improving operational performance, initiatives are mainly focused on high-level transformation of the company. This points to misalignment of goals and tools used to achieve those goals. Misalignment is also evident with drivers behind process change initiatives and the effects of these initiatives as measured by PPI criteria. For example, customer satisfaction is recognized as one of the main drivers behind process change initiatives, while customer focus is one of the PPI criteria with the lowest score. Lack of knowledge regarding process initiatives might be the cause of this, calling for more systematic education regarding options managers have at hand. The results back this claim up, as companies that undertook more serious process analysis/redesign training had more success in identifying and eliminating problems and inconsistencies. PPI criteria such as alignment with strategy and holistic approach to BPM show high level of agreement among respondents, meaning that strategic orientation of BPM is recognized among companies in Serbia. However, the results show lack of systematic approach to business process initiatives. For example, criteria such as Portfolio of process management initiatives or the existence of formal BPI methodology show more dispersion in the answers. These results are in line with comments expressed earlier, confirming misalignment between goals and ways to operationalize those goals, which means that both education and the development of formal approach to BPM are needed. The results show that strategic orientation towards BPM significantly contributes to success of BPM adoption measured through PPI. This is in line with results showing that companies who have formally trained their employees in process analysis/redesign experienced more significant success in BPM adoption. This is expressed through drivers such as increased market share and revenue, and reduction of business risk, and by decision to perform enterprise wide BPI initiatives such as business process architecture development and enterprise level process change management. This shows the importance of process management efforts on an enterprise level, rather than through isolated process improvement initiatives. In addition, it shows that strategic focus can even make up for the lack of operational knowledge, and increase chances for success of BPM adoption.

References

1. Bai, C., Sarkis, J.: A grey-based DEMATEL model for evaluating business process management critical success factors. Int. J. Prod. Econ. **146**(1), 281–292 (2014)
2. Bandara, W., Guillemain, A., Coogans, P.: Prioritizing process improvement: an example from the Australian financial services sector. In: vom Brocke, J., Rosemann, M. (eds.) Handbook on Business Process Management 2. IHIS, pp. 289–307. Springer, Heidelberg (2015). https://doi.org/10.1007/978-3-642-45103-4_12
3. BPTrends HomePage. http://www.bptrends.com/bpt/wp-content/surveys/2012-_BPT%20SUR VEY-3-12-12-CW-PH.pdf. Accessed 26 Dec 2018
4. Hernaus, T., Pejić Bach, M., Bosilj Vukšić, V.: Influence of strategic approach to BPM on financial and non-financial performance. Baltic J. Manag. **7**(4), 376–396 (2012)
5. Hribar, B., Medling, J.: The correlation of organizational culture and BPM adoption success. In: Twenty Second European Conference on Information Systems, Recanati Business School Tel Aviv University, Tel Aviv, pp. 1– 16 (2014)
6. Indihar Štemberger, M., Buh, B., Milanović Glavan, L., Mendling, J.: Propositions on the interaction of organizational culture with other factors in the context of BPM adoption. Bus. Proc. Manag. J. **24**(2), 425–445 (2018)
7. Marshall, D.A.: Lean Transformation: Overcoming the Challenges, Managing Performance, and Sustaining Success. University of Kentucky, Lexington (2014)
8. McCormack, K., Johnson, W.: Business Process Orientation: Gaining the E-Business Competitive Advantage. St. Lucie Press, Florida (2001)
9. Process Excellence Network HomePage. http://www.processexcellencenetwork.com/lean-six-sigma-business-transformation/white-papers/trends-and-success-factors-in-business-process. Accessed 26 Dec 2014
10. Rummler-Brache Group. https://www.rummlerbrache.com/process-performance-index. Accessed 27 Nov 2018
11. Škrinjar, R., Trkman, P.: Increasing process orientation with business process management: critical practices. Int. J. Inf. Manag. **33**(1), 48–60 (2013)
12. Stojanović, D., Tomašević, I., Slović, D., Gošnik, D., Suklan, J., Kavčič, K.: BPM in transition economies: joint empirical experience of Slovenia and Serbia. Econ. Res.-Ekonomska Istraživanja **30**(1), 1237–1256 (2017)
13. Trkman, P.: The critical success factors of business process management. Int. J. Inf. Manag. **30**(2), 125–134 (2010)

Conceptualizing the Convergence Model of Business Process Management and Customer Experience Management

Dino Pavlić[(⊠)] and Maja Ćukušić

Faculty of Economics, Business and Tourism, University of Split, Split, Croatia
{dpavlic,mcukusic}@efst.hr

Abstract. Although business process management (BPM) and customer experience management (CXM) as strategic approaches aim to fulfill organizational prerequisites for achieving customer satisfaction, and the customer focus has been in the definitions of BPM from its very beginning, related efforts are often not aligned in practice. We posit that the analysis, and consequently, the results would be more successful if a structured, BPM-CXM convergent approach is followed. The paper proposes a convergence model for BPM-CXM and the findings of its initial validation are briefly reported along with considerations for its implementation and the expected benefits.

Keywords: Business process management ·
Customer experience management · Process analysis · Customer journey ·
Focus group

1 Introduction

Organizations are normally focused on their internal processes – their analysis and optimization, and often neglect the needs of their customers [1, 2]. Recent research studies stress out the importance of involving customers in internal business process analysis and optimization, as well as in business transformation programs [e.g. 3]. Authors point out the need for further research in the field of business process management (BPM) and customer experience management (CXM), and refer to a lack of a clearly formulated model or a structure for integrated modeling and analyzing of internal business processes and customer experiences external to the organization [4–8]. Although these strategic approaches aim to enable organizational prerequisites for achieving customer satisfaction, their efforts are often not aligned [4] – and further investigation in BPM and CXM convergence is a must [4, 6, 8–10].

More specifically, identification, discovery, analysis, redesign, and control of processes should be performed in convergence with identification, discovery, analysis, redesign, and control of customer experience, and should not be addressed independently [2]. To achieve a really great customer experience an excellent business process is a requirement – we postulate that the analysis leading to both would be more successful if a structured BPM-CXM convergence approach is followed. In an effort to design and operationalize a convergence model for BPM and CXM, a study was

© Springer Nature Switzerland AG 2019
C. Di Ciccio et al. (Eds.): BPM 2019 Blockchain and CEE Forum, LNBIP 361, pp. 328–332, 2019.
https://doi.org/10.1007/978-3-030-30429-4_24

conducted and is presented hereinafter. The second section of the paper presents the concept of the BPM-CXM convergence and the third one outlines the feedback from a focus group study with the view to demonstrate the feasibility of the concept with experts from the EMEA region. The fourth section of the paper provides plans for further work and concludes the paper.

2   The Concept of BPM-CXM Convergence

Several authors suggest the need for further research on the convergence of BPM and CXM. Gloppen et al. [9] imply the need of investigation in the field of strategic use of customer journeys for innovation and business transformation, but also the need for convergence of knowledge of employees, business process designers, and analysts, as well as customers. Also, Kumar et al. [11] emphasize that BPM as a key factor in achieving customer satisfaction. Johnston and Kong [12] point out the importance of involving the customers in business transformation programs, and not just as information providers, but also through the active involvement in forums, panels and also as internal teams. Richardson [13] suggests that the "traditional" end-to-end approach to business transformation would end, and forecasts a specific type of targeted modelling of customer touchpoints with the organization, and their analysis and optimization in the context of internal organization. He also recognizes customer journey mapping as a new "outside-in" approach to BPM. Still, there is no standardized approach for BPM-CXM convergence and the lack of engagement of a customer is a frequent and major issue observed in business settings by the authors of the paper. Consequently, the conceptualization and the formulation of a BPM-CXM convergence approach was our main goal as we postulate that by analyzing the effects of the convergent approach multiple benefits could be expected compared to traditional BPM approaches. The expected effects would include the following: reduction of emphasis on internal business process mapping or "modelling because of modelling" within the BPM initiatives, reduction of functional silos effect and better alignment between the organizational departments, improved coordination between the organizational departments in defining the key performance indicators, increase of innovation level in organizations, design of business processes which take the interactions with the customer into the account and enable customer expectations fulfilment, development of products and services that are really needed by the customers, rational usage of organizational resources and more.

In order to formulate and systematically validate the convergence concept and its expected effects, a two-part study is envisaged and is in progress. All the specifics of the proposed approach are not presented here but are planned to be systematically described in future publications. Conceptually, the customer experience is designed and analyzed by using customer journey mapping, which is used as an input for BPM initiatives – from strategic identification of processes for initiating BPM initiatives, to analysis and optimization of processes [2, 14–18]. BPM-CXM convergence approach should reflect the way customer experience can be perceived and analyzed through the whole BPM lifecycle [19]. That is why the proposed concept lays precisely on those foundations and is based on standard BPM lifecycle [20].

3   Evaluation of BPM-CXM Convergence Model with Experts

An integral part of the design process, a focus group was conducted in March 2019 with 6 experts in BPM and CXM fields. All the experts have over 10 years of experience in both BPM and CXM projects. As all the experts have worked on projects in the EMEA region (primarily in Croatia, Serbia, Bosnia and Herzegovina, and Montenegro), the results of the study reflect their understanding and experience that cannot be easily generalized to other regions. Consolidated views of the group are only outlined here. Experts agree that at the moment BPM initiatives do not put enough focus on CX. They are missing information about the actual CX and CX KPIs. There is no proper way of getting the real data about the CX and pairing them with the internal process models. BPM experts are too focused on internal business processes, while communication with CX departments and customers is something that is missing within BPM initiatives. Internal processes are only considered in the context of CXM if a customer is complaining – this is too late since the negative experience already occurred. Overall, there is a consensus that BPM initiatives are not set up as enablers of an amazing CX.

Experts found that the proposed BPM-CXM model structured around BPM lifecycle and operationalized in a way that was presented to them is well structured to support the BPM and CXM convergence. With the experts, specific calculations were formulated for the overall customer experience of a customer journey and other elements, attributes and color coding of a customer journey landscape were discussed as well as all other detailed artefacts that enable efficient implementation of the convergence model. Their suggestions were collected and embedded in the subsequent iteration of the convergence model. One potential shortcoming was identified in the proposed approach – the experts emphasized that the ownership roles are not clear enough. This could lead to inadequate governance of BPM-CXM convergent approach.

To provide a functioning and structured convergent approach that could be used in practice, a number of artifacts were then developed mapped to ARIS Value Engineering methodology and ARIS platform [21] due to the popularity of the tool in the region.

4   Conclusions and Planned Work

This paper introduced an effort to structure a BPM-CXM convergence approach. At the moment, after further validation and operationalization of the model, there are specific plans for its implementation in a real-life setting in order to further demonstrate the feasibility and value of the proposed convergence approach. The follow-up evaluation would be realized through in-depth interviews with international experts in BPM and CXM fields that participate in the project. The findings would be used to adjust the proposed work if necessary, detect issues and measure the effects of BPM-CXM convergence approach on the internal organization, alignment of business processes of an internal organization with the needs of the customer, and the customer experience itself.

Acknowledgment. This work is supported by the Croatian Science Foundation [grant number HRZZ-UIP-2017-05-7625].

References

1. Temkin, B.D.: Mapping the customer journey. Forrester Res. **3**, 1–19 (2010)
2. Davis, R.: It's the customer journey that counts. BPTrends Column, pp. 1–5 (2011). https://www.bptrends.com/processes-in-practice-its-the-customer-journey-that-counts/
3. Van Den Bergh, J., Thijs, S., Viaene, S.: Transforming through processes leading voices on BPM People and Technology. Springer, London (2014). https://doi.org/10.1007/978-3-319-03937-4
4. Straßer, J.: Aligning Customer Journey Management with Business Process Management. Masters Thesis, University of Amsterdam (2016)
5. Surbakti, F.P.S.: Customer process management: a systematic literature review. Eng. Manag. Res. **4**, 1–8 (2015). https://doi.org/10.5539/emr.v4n2p1
6. Følstad, A., Kvale, K., Halvorsrud, R.: Customer journeys: involving customers and internal resources in the design and management of services. In: ServdesOrg, pp. 412–417 (2014)
7. Van Den Bergh, J., Thijs, S., Isik, Ö., Viaene, S.: The world is not enough: customer centricity and processes. Bus Process Trends, pp. 1–7 (2012). https://www.bptrends.com/the-world-is-not-enough/
8. Hewing, M.: Business process blueprinting: A Method For Customer-Oriented Business Process Modeling. Springer, Berlin (2014). https://doi.org/10.1007/978-3-658-03729-1
9. Gloppen, J., Lindquister, B., Daae, H.-P.: The customer journey as a tool for business innovation and transformation. In: DeFillippi, R., Rieple, A., Wikström, P. (eds.) International Perspectives on Business Innovation and Disruption in Design, pp. 118–138. Edward Elgar Publishing, Cheltenham (2016)
10. Rosenbaum, M.S., Otalora, M.L., Contreras Ramírez, G.: How to create a realistic customer journey map. Bus. Horiz. **60**(1), 143–150 (2017). https://doi.org/10.1016/j.bushor.2016.09.010
11. Kumar, V., Smart, P.A., Maddern, H., Maull, R.S.: Alternative perspectives on service quality and customer satisfaction: the role of BPM. Int. J. Serv. Ind. Manag. **19**(2), 176–187 (2008). https://doi.org/10.1108/09564230810869720
12. Johnston, R., Kong, X.: The customer experience: a road map for improvement. Manag. Serv. Qual. Int. J. **21**(1), 5–24 (2011). https://doi.org/10.1108/09604521111100225
13. Schooff, P.: End of the road for end-to-end process transformation. Interview with Clay Richardson. In: BPM Today blog (2016). http://bpm.com/bpm-today/blogs/1136-end-of-the-road-for-end-to-end-process-transformation. Accessed 26 Apr 2019
14. Vanwersch, R.J.B., et al.: A critical evaluation and framework of business process improvement methods. Bus. Inf. Syst. Eng. **58**, 43–53 (2016). https://doi.org/10.1007/s12599-015-0417-x
15. Moormann, J., Palvolgyi, E.Z.: Customer-centric business modeling: setting a research agenda. In: 15th Conference on Business Informatics, pp. 173–179 (2013). https://doi.org/10.1109/cbi.2013.33
16. Flint, D.J., Larsson, E., Gammelgaard, B., Mentzer, J.T.: Logistics innovation: a customer value-oriented social process. J. Bus. Logist. **26**, 113–147 (2005). https://doi.org/10.1002/j.2158-1592.2005.tb00196.x

17. Chen, H., Daugherty, P.J., Landry, T.D.: Supply chain process integration: a theoretical framework. J. Bus. Logist. **30**, 27–46 (2009). https://doi.org/10.1002/j.2158-1592.2009.tb00110.x
18. Lee, C.-H., Huang, S.Y., Barnes, F.B., Kao, L.: Business performance and customer relationship management: the effect of IT, organisational contingency and business process on Taiwanese manufacturers. Total Qual. Manag. Bus. Excell. **21**, 43–65 (2010). https://doi.org/10.1080/14783360903492595
19. Ruland, Y.: Customer experience and its potential to extend business process management. Master thesis - UHasselt (2016). http://hdl.handle.net/1942/22258
20. Dumas, M., La Rosa, M., Mendling, J., Reijers, H.A.: Fundamentals of Business Process Management. Springer, Heidelberg (2018). https://doi.org/10.1007/978-3-662-56509-4
21. Software AG product website. https://www.softwareag.com/in/products/aris_alfabet/bpa/aris_architect/default.html. Accessed 26 Apr 2019

The Value of Customer Journey Mapping and Analysis in Design Thinking Projects

Péter Fehér and Krisztián Varga[✉]

Corvinus Business School, Budapest, Hungary
{peter.feher,krisztian.varga}@uni-corvinus.hu

Abstract. In Corvinus Business School we are organizing innovation projects with the methodology of Design Thinking from year to year with multiple partners representing more industries. In this paper, we use three industries as case studies to show our experiences of the added value of Customer Journey Mapping and Analysis in Design Thinking projects.

Keywords: Digital Transformation · Design Thinking · Customer Journey Analysis and Mapping

1 Introduction

In Corvinus Business School we are organizing innovation projects with the methodology of Design Thinking from year to year with multiple partners representing more industries like banking, FMCG, investment.

This paper examines our experiences of the added value of Customer Journey Mapping and Analysis in the above-mentioned Design Thinking projects – and in general as well.

1.1 Design Thinking and Our Applied Method: "Digital Sprint"

The need of a better-grounded design of products and services started by Herbert Simon [1], as defining the role of design as "the transformation of existing conditions into preferred ones [1]". Nonetheless of the evolvement of the design process, further thinking still refers back to Simon's framework [2]. The art of design, the systematic way of designing products and serviced is labelled as "Design Thinking" [3]. Because of the nature of a general Design Thinking approach, it is able to be a basis of digital innovations [4, 5].

In our projects we always have one working week or 1–1 day in five weeks for the research projects. We created the "Digital Sprint" (in some cases, we call it "One-Week-Sprint") format [6] that consists of the following steps and content:

- **Discovery:** get an overview with interviewing or inspecting the customers.
- **Interpretation:** transform experiences into meaningful insights.
- **Ideation:** generating many ideas.
- **Experimentation:** picking ideas and bringing them to life via rapid prototyping.
- **Evolution:** the development of the final concept of the chosen idea.

C. Di Ciccio et al. (Eds.): BPM 2019 Blockchain and CEE Forum, LNBIP 361, pp. 333–336, 2019.
https://doi.org/10.1007/978-3-030-30429-4_25

During the research projects, we make teams from international students of 4 or 5. Coordination of the teams and methodological assistance were provided by two leading researchers, in the role of Design Thinking coaches.

1.2 Customer Journey Mapping and Analysis

To know a company's customers, and the challenges they are facing, Design Thinking recommends using Customer Journey Mapping and Analysis with Personas.

Customer Journey Mapping is the process of tracking and describing all the experiences that customers have as they encounter a service, taking into account not only what happens to them, but also their responses to their experiences. Used well, it can reveal opportunities for improvement and unmet, real customer needs, acting as a strategic tool to ensure every interaction with the customer is as positive as it can be [7].

Based on the literature [8, 9], the general stages of the Customer Journey are: (1) Awareness; (2) Discovery; (3) Interest; (4) Consideration or Selection; (5) Purchase or Onboarding; (6) Use or Service; (7) Advocacy. (Some models combine Discovery and Interest to Research phase).

2   Investigating the Value of Customer Journey Mapping and Analysis in Different Design Thinking Projects

In this section we will evaluate four projects and conclude their takeaways. The first research project is in the industry of FMCG, then two use cases is in banking, finishing with investments.

2.1 Use Case 1: FMCG

Using our Digital Sprint and finding out Customer Journeys seemed like an easy research project in the field of and FMCG (fast moving consumer goods) store. Most people (if not all of them) had daily or at least weekly experiences with "shopping". All of the research teams felt that a physical journey itself did not add that much value to the project. Making interviews with the customers and asking their feelings and pain points during their journey indeed added value.

The Takeaways from the FMCG Project. It is important to understand, that the Customer Journey is not only the "route" itself. We always have to add the thoughts and feelings with the touchpoints of the company.

2.2 Use Case 2: Consumer Banking

Using Design Thinking does not mean that we must start with the identification of an unmet customer need without any focus area. The Consumer Bank named property loan and mortgages as the area they want to have better customer experience.

Based on all Customer Journeys to the Personas, we were able to identify, that the bank not only should be involved in financial issues, since the customers need help with other actions in their whole Customer Journey.

The Takeaways from the Consumer Bank Project. This project was the most ideal from all of ours. We were able to get enough information from the affected field and we had a lot of costumer data. In the Customer Journey, we were able to identify the sequence of actions with the feelings and thoughts of the customers. We identified possible new touchpoints between the customers and the bank.

2.3   Use Case 3: Corporate Banking

In another research project, our partner was the Corporate Bank. They had a looser focus: they wanted to know what kind of services they should implement to their SME bank accounts.

In Corporate Bank creating a Customer Journey was a harder task for student groups, since they knew less about companies' general banking activities. At the end, we came up with the idea, that the Customer Journey is the lifecycle of a company, since different lifecycle elements require different services from banks.

The Takeaways from the Corporate Bank Project. We were able to understand to importance of Discovery phase, where the goal is to gain better understanding of the industry and the field with the customers as well. In this project we were unable to use the most important part of Design Thinking; which is Empathy. Without empathy we cannot generate a meaningful Customer Journey, and the whole project will be unrealistic.

2.4   Use Case 4: Investment Products for the Non-investing

In this project, the target group were those who are not doing any investment activities; so they do not have any ongoing Customer Journey. The realization that the customer has no journey yet made the challenge even harder to the research teams. We used the general Customer Journey from Sect. 1.2 in order to find out where are the pain points, which stages are unreachable and why.

Our research showed, that most people cannot even reach the third phase (Interest), or the Customer Journey cannot even start: because the customer thinks that they do not have enough money for investment purposes.

The Takeaways from the Investment Project. It was interesting to see, that a general Customer Journey can be helpful to find where customers stuck in it. The earlier stage they stuck, the less data we can find out from their feelings and thoughts, but – on the other hand – we will find problems to solve easily.

3 Conclusions

We believe, and our research showed, that the Design Thinking approach can provide a deeper understanding of customer-centric challenges than traditional surveys or case studies through deeper involvement of observation. The Design Thinking approach also help to identify and evaluate as many challenges, as possible, and ideate as many solutions, as possible.

During our projects, we were able to realize that the Customer Journey is not only a route, but all the data what we know from our customers during their activities: feeling, thoughts, touchpoints. We were able to realize, that the Customer Journey helps us to see all possible touchpoints of the customers and the company, and this may give us innovative product or service ideas. We learned, that in some research areas extra time is needed to know and understand the affected processes. We saw, that that the usage of a general journey can be beneficial if we target non-customers, because we can find out where did they stop in their journey, or why didn't they start it.

Acknowledgment. The publication was prepared within the Széchenyi 2020 program framework (EFOP-3.6.1-16-2016-00013) under the European Union project titled: "Institutional developments for intelligent specialization at the Székesfehérvár Campus of Corvinus University of Budapest".

References

1. Simon, H.: The Sciences of the Artificial, 1st edn. MIT Press, Cambridge (1969)
2. Huppatz, D.: Revisiting Herbert Simon's "science of design". Des. Issues **31**(2), 29–40 (2015)
3. West, S., Di Nardo, S.: Creating product-service system opportunities for small and medium size firms using service design tools. Procedia CIRP **47**, 96–101 (2016)
4. Izukura, S., Hosono, S., Sakaki, H., Numata, E., Kimita, K., Shimomura, Y.: Bridging non-functional requirements and it service design. Procedia CIRP **30**, 24–29 (2015)
5. Hosono, S., Numata, E., Shimomura, Y.: Servitization methodology in ICT service system design. Procedia CIRP **47**, 18–23 (2016)
6. Fehér, P., Varga, K.: Using design thinking to identify banking digitization opportunities – snapshot of the Hungarian banking system. In: 30th Bled eConference: Digital Transformation (Conference Proceedings), pp. 151–168 (2017)
7. HM Government: Customer journey mapping - a guide for practitioners (2017). http://webarchive.nationalarchives.gov.uk/+/http://www.cabinetoffice.gov.uk/media/123970/journey_mapping1.pdf
8. SAP Hybrids: The customer journey - a handbook for meaningful (and profitable) engagement (2016). https://www.hybris.com/medias/sys_master/root/h7f/hee/8812826066974/saphybris-customer-journey.pdf
9. Oracle: The digital customer journey: how to build an online experience that drives sales and loyalty (2013). http://www.oracle.com/us/products/middleware/digital-customer-journey-wp-2028079.pdf

The Presence of Order-Effect Bias in Moscow Administration

Dmitry Romanov[1(⊠)], Nikolai Kazantsev[1,2], and Elina Edgeeva[1]

[1] National Research University "Higher School of Economics", Moscow, Russia
dromanov@hse.ru
[2] The University of Manchester, Manchester, UK

Abstract. This paper studies 'the order effect' in decision making based on classification results of 120 000 citizen claims to Moscow Government. We use machine learning methods and derive that with 60% probability the first out of two consequent claims is prioritized. We conclude that this impact must be considered whilst developing artificial intelligence units.

Keywords: Text classification · Order effect · Cognitive bias · Quantum probability theory · Machine learning · G2C

1 Introduction

Existing behavioral models do not encompass all impacts of intuition, emotional reactions and prior interactions on decision-making [1]. Order effects are one of the known variants of cognitive bias that describes that the sequence of the obtained information influences the human-made decisions [4–11], e.g. when sequence of questions influences survey answers [10, 11]. Currently, this effect is seen also in public administration bodies, where similar citizen claims might be resolved differently. Discovering why some documents are considered more important than the latter [2, 3] gave as motivation to write this paper. The goal of this work is to *investigate whether there is a dependence of document sequence on classification*. Table 1 describes the identified areas where order effect is manifested.

In this paper, we extend this research to the area of public administration, when employees classify documents [3] prior to decision-making, whilst the IT-enabled topic predictors are not used [12]. We analyze a data set of claims to public authority that has (a) unpredictable topic of incoming claims; (b) weakly-structured character of handling process; (c) employees' overload. Consequently, our research question is:

RQ: Does argument order in citizen claims affect its thematic classification?

2 Methods

We analyze 120 000 incoming claims from electronic services supporting Moscow Government[1] in 2014–2015. In this process 8–12 people classify messages using the universal range of thematic categories, such as "Municipal development", "Healthcare",

---

[1] Research was supported by РФФИ, grant № 17-07-01441.

C. Di Ciccio et al. (Eds.): BPM 2019 Blockchain and CEE Forum, LNBIP 361, pp. 337–341, 2019.
https://doi.org/10.1007/978-3-030-30429-4_26

Table 1. Areas and manifestations of order-effect.

Id	Area	Order effect	Manifestation	Source
1	Sociology	Survey answer decision-making	The sequence of questions influences indicated beliefs and survey answers	[10, 11]
2	Science	Journal ranking decision-making	Experts overestimate journals located higher in the list	[4]
3	Politics	Electoral decision-making	80% of cases of elections depend on the sequence of candidates' names in a voting bulletin	[5]
4	Medicine	Patients' treatment acceptance decision-making	If patients were informed about small risks after potential benefits, they were less likely to accept the treatment	[6]
5	Medicine	Diagnosis decision-making	The sequence of clinical information shown to the doctor influenced diagnosis	[7]
6	Tourism	Vacation decision-making	Early introduction of any travel feature increased the importance of it in the eyes of tourists	[8]
7	Finance	Investment decision-making	Not only quality and amount of disclosing financial statements influenced potential investors, but also the order how those statements were sorted	[9]

"Transport", "Education", "Housing and communal services". We knew which category was chosen by an employee. Thus, we reproduce the mode of human decision-making whilst processing of unstructured text. We consider a text message received by a government body not as a single phrase, but as a sequence of words. We use Latent Dirichlet Allocation and Naive Bayes Classifier methods to attach weights to text, depending on its significance and revealing topics which are most presented in it. Classical machine learning methods use simple model of "a bag of words", being limited only to the morphological analysis and not carrying out syntactic analysis and the semantic analysis of offers.

3   Findings

The 'order effect' was tested on arrays 'Dataset 1' and 'Dataset 2' (Table 2). Commonly, several topics exist in a message – more than in one third of all messages where parts were different from each other. However, in the first part subject X indicated, and in the another – subject Y, then in 60% of cases an employee decides to apply the category of the first part (X) to whole message. That characterizes all dataset of claims and gives a positive answer to RQ.

Table 2. Parameters and datasets.

Parameter name	Dataset 1	Dataset 2
Total number of addresses in selection	6116	33393
N_{AB} is the number of the messages having various categories at the 1st and 2nd part	828	12648
$N_{AB \to A}$ is the number of messages with the choice of total category for the 1st part	348	4900
$N_{AB \to B}$ is the number of messages with the choice of total category for the 2nd part	475	3403
$\Pr(AB \to A)$ – choice probability for all address of category of the first part, %	61,42	59,01

To check order effect dependence on the claim probabilities $\Pr(A_iB \to A_i)$ and $\Pr(BA_i \to A_i)$ were estimated, where A_i an exact category from the general list from 53 categories. At the same time the number of messages in which the category A_i occurred in the first and in the second part was separately considered. The received results are reflected in Fig. 1.

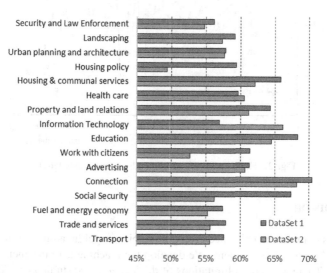

Fig. 1. Order effect for different categories, where blue color represents the choice of the first topic in classification (Color figure online)

In the 'Dataset 1' all categories show such 'order effect' with the higher probability of applying the first topic to the whole citizen's claim. The most categories "Dataset 2" are characterized by reduction of observed order effect by 1–2%. However, for some thematic categories the order effect is changed strongly: drastic reduction of order effect is observed with topics 'Housing Policy' and 'Social security' and drastic growth (attention to 15%) with the topic 'Information Technologies'.

Figure 2 reveals that the asymmetry exists in all texts which size exceeds $\sim$ 100–200 bytes (about one-two lines of the text). An Average value of an order effect -60%, but at the same time quasiperiodic fluctuations are observed – the effect of an order changes in quite wide limits from 50% to 80%, and at some values of length of the text even "changes the sign" (decrease in probability of the choice of the first part lower than 50% means that the choice of category of the second part of the message becomes more probable). The period of such fluctuations is $\sim$ 150–250 bytes. Also, the correlation between schedules for two data arrays with lengths of text from 300 to 1200 bytes attracts attention. Such messages make the majority in the studied datasets and the received values of probabilities are more exact.

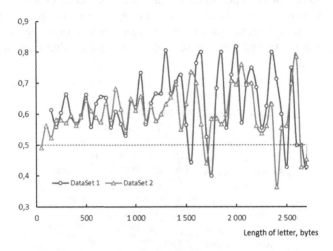

Fig. 2. How 'order effect' depends on messages length

4   Conclusion

Our findings confirm the existence of cognitive bias in public administration using the example of Moscow Government. We develop the machine learning method to reveal order effect. There are certain limitations of this paper as we studied only one weakly-structured process. Future research will analyse other processes where decisions are made based on the manual analysis of documents – appeals to technical support, coordination of documents and consideration of credit card in banking.

References

1. Tversky, A., Kahneman, D.: Judgment under uncertainty: heuristics and biases. Science **185** (4157), 1124–1131 (1974)
2. Tetlock, P.E.: Accountability and the perseverance of first impressions. Soc. Psychol. Q. **46** (4), 285–292 (1983)
3. Wang, B., Zhang, P., Li, J., Song, D., Hou, Y., Shang, Z.: Exploration of quantum interference in document relevance judgement discrepancy. Entropy **18**(4), 144 (2016)
4. Serenko, A., Bontis, N.: First in, best dressed: the presence of order-effect bias in journal ranking surveys. J. Informetrics **7**(1), 138–144 (2013)
5. Chen, E., Simonovits, G., Krosnick, J.A., Pasek, J.: The impact of candidate name order on election outcomes in North Dakota. Elect. Stud. **35**, 115–122 (2014)
6. Bergus, G.R., Levin, I.P., Elstein, A.S.: Presenting risks and benefits to patients: the effect of information order on decision making. J. Gen. Intern. Med. **17**(8), 612–617 (2002)
7. Bergus, G.R., Chapman, G.B., Levy, B.T., Ely, J.W., Oppliger, R.A.: Clinical diagnosis and the order of information. Med. Decis. Making **18**(4), 412–417 (1998)
8. Oppewal, H., Huybers, T., Crouch, G.I.: Tourist destination and experience choice: a choice experimental analysis of decision sequence effect. Tourism Manag. **48**, 467–476 (2015)
9. Theis, J.C., Yankova, K., Eulerich, M.: Information order effects in the context of management commentary—initial experimental evidence. J. Manag. Control **23**, 133–150 (2012)
10. Haugtvedt, C.P., Wegener, D.T.: Message order effects in persuasion: an attitude strength perspective. J. Consum. Res. **21**(1), 205–218 (1994)
11. McFarland, S.G.: Effects of question order on survey responses. Public Opin. Q. **45**(2), 208–215 (1981)
12. Romanov, D., Ponfilenok, M., Kazantsev, N.: Potential innovations (new ideas/trends) detection in information network. Int. J. Future Comput. Commun. **2**(1), 63–66 (2013)

Author Index

Aleksić, Ana 264
Alt, Rainer 43

Batoulis, Kimon 119
Bider, Ilia 315
Bitkowska, Agnieszka 319
Borkowski, Michael 3
Bosilj Vukšić, Vesna 280
Brin, Pavlo 296

Cappiello, Cinzia 166
Comuzzi, Marco 166
Ćukušić, Maja 328

Daniel, Florian 166
di Angelo, Monika 103
Draheim, Dirk 219

Eder, Johann 87
Edgeeva, Elina 337

Fehér, Péter 333
Fernando, Duneesha 136
Franceschetti, Marco 87
Frauenthaler, Philipp 3

Grechenig, Thomas 151

Haarmann, Stephan 119
Henkel, Martin 315
Hernaus, Tomislav 264
Huber, Jernej 296
Hunka, Frantisek 203

Iqbal, Mubashar 13
Ivančić, Lucija 280

Jošt, Gregor 296
Jovanović, Ivona 324

Kakarott, Julian 29
Kazantsev, Nikolai 337
Klinkmüller, Christopher 71

Klun, Monika 249
Köpke, Julius 87
Koutsopoulos, Georgios 315
Kuhar, Saša 296

Lamber, René 151
Lange, Maik 43
Lazuashvili, Nino 219
Leiter, Steven Chris 43
Leyer, Michael 249

Matulevičius, Raimundas 13
Meroni, Giovanni 55, 166

Nikaj, Adriatik 119
Norta, Alex 219

Őri, Dóra 234

Pavlić, Dino 328
Perjons, Erik 315
Pinter, Karl 151
Plebani, Pierluigi 55
Polančič, Gregor 296
Ponomarev, Alexander 71
Prester, Jasna 264

Ranasinghe, Nalin 136
Romanov, Dmitry 337

Salzer, Gernot 103
Schäffer, Markus 103
Schmelz, Dominik 151
Schulte, Stefan 3
Sigwart, Marten 3
Simeunović, Barbara 324
Skwarek, Volker 29
Sliż, Piotr 185
Slović, Dragoslav 324
Stojanović, Dragana 324
Strobl, Stefan 151
Suša Vugec, Dalia 280
Szabó, Zoltán 234

Tomašević, Ivan   324
Tran, An Binh   71
Trkman, Peter   264

van der Aalst, Wil   71
van Kervel, Steven   203
Varga, Krisztián   333

Vona, Francesco   55

Weber, Ingo   71
Weske, Mathias   119

Zeuch, Katharina   29

Printed in the United States
By Bookmasters